Emotion in ADULT DEVELOPMENT

Emotion in ADULT DEVELOPMENT

Edited by

Carol Zander MALATESTA
Carroll E. IZARD

SAGE PUBLICATIONS Beverly Hills London New Delhi

For information address:

SAGE Publications, Inc.
275 South Beverly Drive
Beverly Hills, California 90212

SAGE Publications India Pvt. Ltd.
C-236 Defence Colony
New Delhi 110 024, India

SAGE Publications Ltd
28 Banner Street
London EC1Y 8QE, England

Printed in the United States of America

Library of Congress Cataloging in Publication Data
Main entry under title:

Emotion in adult development.

1. Emotions. I. Malatesta, Carol Zander. II. Izard, Carroll E.
BF531.E485 1984 155.6 84-1937
ISBN 0-8039-2156-X

FIRST PRINTING

CONTENTS

PREFACE

This book is about adult development, emotion, and the interaction between emotion and other domains of human capability and experience. Historically speaking, it was a long time in the making.

Over the past few years there has been belated but growing recognition that emotion plays a central and dynamic role in all aspects of human ability — in cognition and learning, personality, and interpersonal behavior. Some theorists, moreover, consider emotion to be the primary motivational system in humans (Izard, 1971; Tomkins, 1962; Plutchik; 1965) and to be a driving, organizing force in human development (Izard & Malatesta, in press). However, it is a point of history that the role of emotion in human development had a hard time earning the recognition it deserves, even when considered from within the broader framework of motivation. For example, Bernice Neugarten's (1968) *Middle Age and Aging,* a popular set of readings formerly widely used in courses in adult development, contains only one paper devoted to the subject of motivation; furthermore, there is not one chapter specifically addressed to the emotions and their role in development. This was not a bias or oversight of the editor, but a reflection of the times. Part of the reason for the inattention to the construct of motivation in adult development — not to mention emotion — has to do with the fact that it is hard to study motivation apart from other psychological functions. There is motivation for learning, motivation for retaining certain memories, motivation for forgetting, motivation for problem solving, motivation for forming, keeping, or changing one's personality, motivation for developing defense mechanisms, and so on. However, there is no "pure" motivation. The developing field of emotions research has now made it possible to talk both more generally and more specifically about motivation. But it is still the case that the task of understanding emotion and motivation will be easier if examined in conjunction with the cognitive and motor skills with which it is bound. Thus, the present volume considers the ways in which the powerful motivational system of emotion informs and is informed by other domains of adult functioning.

Although this volume is first directed at academicians and clinicians involved in the fields of human development, personality and emotion, it is designed as well as a text for courses in adult development and aging. In fact, the original idea for this particular collection of readings was set into motion by reaction to frustration. It was two years ago that the first editor attempted to teach a graduate level course in adult development and discovered that there were no texts or sets of readings that would meet the multiple purposes of the course. Sets of readings were especially biased, focusing almost exclusively on cognitive functions — learning, memory, problem solving, or on social gerontology. An attempt to remedy the situation by assigning outside readings that would cover a wider territory was fraught with problems. Many of the readings were not easily accessible, and collecting them became a chore for both instructor and students alike. Eventually, we became convinced that there was a need for a collection of up-to-date reading that reflected the recent accumulation of research and thinking about emotions and their interface with other systems. Once the idea and motivation became more clearly focused, we began to put the volume together. We started out by identifying several areas within the adult developmental literature that had received the most attention over the past ten years, what might be considered as traditional foci — intellectual development, moral judgment, personality development, interpersonal relations, psychopathology, cross-cultural research. We then contacted a number of scholars in these areas and invited them to think about the role of emotion in their area of research and share their thoughts and findings with us and other professionals. The result is the present volume with 17 chapters divided up into a theoretical section and six other content areas. The selections should be of interest to anyone who has spent any time contemplating what makes people — adult people — grow and develop.

Theoretical Perspectives. The opening three chapters by Malatesta and Izard, Averill, and de Rivera, deal with the conceptual issues involved in thinking about and researching adult emotional development. Several models, such as the constructivist approach, structural theory, and differential emotions theory, are proposed as a means of organizing and directing future research in the field.

The remaining chapters treat six more "traditional" domains of lifespan research, but do so with consideration of the role of emotion in organizing, directing, filtering, or accompanying the various psychological processes.

Emotion and Psychological Wellbeing. Lawton, and Cohler and Boxer, treat the area of psychological wellbeing, one of the oldest areas of research in lifespan developmental pyschology and the area that is most immediately related to the emotions. Each chapter focuses on a slightly different aspect of the literature on wellbeing. Lawton addresses the multidimensional aspect of the construct; Cohler and Boxer examine the relationship between mental health, morale, and wellbeing, stressing the fact that the timing of life events is a critical feature of the emotional significance of an event and its impact on wellbeing.

Historical Influence on Emotion Development. A recurrent theme in lifespan psychology has been that sociohistorical changes influence individuals and affect their psychological development. Two chapters take this influence into account. Felton and Shaver examine the case for a cohort effect in people's reported level of happiness and wellbeing. Gelfond advances an interesting thesis about the changing incidence of agoraphobia in women within an explicitly dialectical developmental model, suggesting that additional perspective on adult psychiatric symptomatology may be gained by considering the broader socio-environmental context in which a clinical entity is manifest.

Emotion and Personality. Costa and McCrae's chapter serves as a bridge between the section on psychological wellbeing and personality, maintaining that personality is probably the strongest known predictor of wellbeing. In the McAdams chapter we are treated to the interesting proposition that identity — the most personal aspect of personality — undergoes formation and reformation during adulthood and that identity may be perceived of as a life story. Malatesta and Culver look at the interaction between personality traits, affects, and changing life roles in a longitudinal study of women. The chapter by Hansson, Hogan and Jones provides a bridge between the section on personality and that of interpersonal interaction. They note that specific emotional patterns evolve as they become adaptive in social context, that social contexts change as people age, and therefore that emotional patterns may be different in old age.

Emotion and Interpersonal Interaction. In this section Cornelius provides a rule model of adult emotional expression that is an extension and elaboration of Averill's theory, with empirical examples of social weeping and intimacy. Halberstadt shows how emotion styles found in adulthood are forged within the context of family and discusses how these expressive patterns might change with age. Finally, Malatesta and Izard examine formal changes in the communication of emotion over the adult years and relate these changes to other developments within the affective system.

Cognition and Emotion. In this section Stewart and Healy consider the development of emotion from the perspective of changing cognitive functions. The chapter by Roodin, Rybash, and Hoyer critiques the cognitive model of moral judgment and shows how consideration of the emotional context of real-life decisions informs moral judgments.

Keeping Culture in Perspective. Finally, the chapter by Sommers addresses the cross-culturally variable aspects of emotion expression and experience. It serves as a reminder that it is especially important to keep culture in perspective as we attempt to construct models of adult emotional development.

The above areas treated in the present volume do not exhaust the ways in which emotion is interwoven in the various facets of adult development. It is hoped, however, that this treatment will stimulate further attempts to conceptualize and research the role of affect in adult development and the development of affect in adults.

This volume was two years in the making from conception to production. As with most other involved endeavors, many individuals got into the act, and we would be remiss not to acknowledge their substantial contributions. First, we thank Jeannette Haviland, Eric Labouvie, and Lillian Troll for initiating the first editor into the joys and trials of the study of adult development and emotions research. Second, we thank NIMH for supporting the first editor on a National Public Health Research Award (1F32MH08773-01), which permitted her to take a one-year postdoctoral leave of absence from the Graduate Faculty of the New School for Social Research; it was during this year that the study reported in Chapter 14 was completed and the present volume was begun. We thank New School Chairs Arien Mack and Nathan Kogan for making it possible for her to take time off from teaching responsibilities to pursue the postdoctoral research. We also thank our families for their prior and continuing support, our graduate students for the impetus to keep developing our ideas, and Donna O'Brien and Claire Martin for their professionalism and abiding good humor while they typed and improved the original manuscript.

— Carol Zander Malatesta
Carroll E. Izard

References

Izard, C. E. (1971). *The face of emotion.* New York: Appleton-Century-Crofts.

Izard, C. E., & Malatesta C. Z. (in press). A developmental theory of the emotions. *Behavioral and Brain Sciences.*

Neugarten, B. (Ed.) (1968). *Middle age and aging.* Chicago: University of Chicago Press.

Plutchik, R. (1962). *The emotions: Facts, theories and a new model.* New York: Random House.

Tomkins, S. (1962). *Affect, imagery, conciousness: Vol. I, The positive affects.* New York: Springer.

I

THEORETICAL PERSPECTIVES

The three chapters in this section present models for thinking about and exploring emotional development in adults. The first chapter by Malatesta and Izard provides an historical overview of the field of emotions research and articulates the problems involved in conceptualizing adult emotional development. They conclude by proposing a broad theoretical framework to guide future research. This model encompasses the developmental principles of differentiation and integration coupled with the theoretical superstructure of differential emotions theory.

Averill's chapter also illustrates the conceptual problems involved in the analysis of adult emotional development and offers a social-constructivist model as one tool of analysis. In this admittedly cognitive scheme, emotions are defined as transitory social roles involving rules that are acquired and modified through learning, learning that is lifelong. Averill argues that the rules of emotion are both regulative (modulating) as well as constitutive (i.e., constructed or created by society). It is these constructed emotions that undergo change as people move from one sociocultural context to another during the life cycle.

Finally, de Rivera attempts to use the structural theory of emotion to clarify what role emotions may play in development and to suggest what emotional developments may be ideal. He argues that it is most adaptive and desirable to possess a wide emotional range, so that situationally adaptive responses may be made to the variety of circumstances that confront adults in life.

1

Introduction

Conceptualizing Emotional Development in Adults

CAROL ZANDER MALATESTA
CARROLL E. IZARD

In the disturbing Russian film *Solaris,* four scientists investigating a planet find themselves the victims of a terrifying experience. Shortly after their arrival, under the influence of inexplicable forces, each man is confronted with the appearance of a humanoid creature, which, it turns out, is a reification of some previously hidden and personally intolerable emotional feeling — guilt in the case of one man (personified in the form of the image of a deceased wife), jealousy (in the form of a shrill-voiced midget) in the case of another. The creatures then proceed to harass and eventually undo each of these men. What made this film so disturbing was not just the forced confrontation with unwanted feelings or even their bizarre reification but, perhaps most upsetting of all, the involuntary, public exposure of private, and in this case, privately dreaded, negative, emotional feelings — the naked exposure of raw feelings.

As participants in the social commerce of everyday life, most of us are invested in maintaining harmonious interpersonal relationships, avoiding agonistic encounters, and in maintaining our sense of self-esteem with respect to others. There is a certain predictable quality to "everyday" life that includes predictable sequences of interactions with others, and part of this predictability flows from collective conformance to shared social conventions concerning the expression (or, more commonly, inhibition) of the overt component of emotional feelings. To act against the grain in these conventions is to risk social censure and consequent threat to self-esteem. Many of the social conventions governing emotion expression, at least in Western cultures, are directed at augmenting the more social, sanguine emotional expressions (smiling, interest, empathy) and *inhibiting* or muting those with potential to escalate benign interaction into conflict encounters (anger, jealousy, contempt) or those with potential to disturb others through contagion (sadness, anxiety). Hence we find the involuntary exposure of intense and unacceptable feelings in the film *Solaris* to be unsettling.

By the time a person has become an adult he or she will have assimilated the culture's social conventions with respect to emotion expression and will for the most part display less intense emotion than he or she did as a child. However, this is *not* to say that the (partial) desomatization of emotion results in a corresponding diminution of feeling. As we shall see later, there are ways of preserving the feeling component of emotion. Indeed, feelings are what give us the sense of being alive. As Saul Bellow (1969) has observed, people *like to feel* and will go to great lengths to wallow in the "passion-waters." Infants seek out novelty and excitement; adults at times seek out situations that may be fraught with danger so as to experience the exhiliration of risk-taking. The psychoanalyst Marianne Eckardt (1977) suggests that the fundamental conflicts of life are between being dead or alive, and bored or dead. Affectless people are usually bored people and are themselves boring to be with. In extremity, affectlessness is considered pathognomic (as in depersonalization and catatonia). It is hard to imagine a healthy individual, let alone a whole culture of individuals, in which all emotional feeling as well as emotional behavior are denied.

Our position, as well as that of most if not all of the other authors in this volume, is that emotion is a pivotal domain of experience in adult life and in development throughout life. To the extent that adults can be seen as developing through life, one looks to emotion as a source of common meaning in understanding continuities in development as well as psychological change.

In light of the above it may be hard to understand why the study of emotion in adults has escaped attention until fairly recently. In this introductory chapter we discuss some of the reasons why the topic has been neglected for so long and why it is particularly ripe for consideration at this time.

A Short History of the Study of Emotion, Adulthood, and Emotional Development

There are several reasons why discussion of the development of emotion in adulthood has been so sorely neglected as a focus of research inquiry and theoretical exposition; they are related to (1) the "problem" of emotion itself, (2) the "problem" of adult *development*, and (3) the problem of conceptualizing emotion as developing during adulthood.

The "problem" of emotion. Emotion has been a problem to psychologists since the turn of the century. It has been a problem because even though the topic of emotion had always been intrinsically attractive and interesting, it appeared to be refractory to empirical study, especially to study by the "brass instrument" psychology of the first few decades of this century.

Historically, emotion experiences have been viewed by many behavioral scientists as mentalistic events, unknowable as objective data and approachable only through phenomenology. Thus the currency of research on emotion feelings in the realm of science at any given era resembles that of phenomenolgy and self-report measures. When phenomenolgy of consciousness and self-report measures became admissible in psychology, the study of emotion experience became more acceptable. However, for a long period of time in psychology's history, emotion experiences were not "reals" — they were not notable, noteworthy, or knowable events.

The acceptability of studies of emotion experience also owes a great debt to the development of sophisticated measurement technologies for the study of the behavioral signs of emotion — that is, systems for coding, classifying and quantifying emotion expressions through video- and audiotape recording apparatuses and associated computer software for data reduction and analysis. This formidable armamentarium of nouveau brass instrumentation has helped to legitimize the study of emotion, taking it from the arena of the unknowable to the sphere of the measurable and thereby reducing the objection of those who dislike dependence on phenomenological approaches.

A second reason for the long neglect of emotion is that psychologists, just like everyone else, are ambivalent about emotion. Emotions can be pleasant and exciting or they can be very troublesome, to ourselves and to others. Naturally, this leads to mixed feelings about feelings, so much so that at times we are given to defensive stances. Throughout the literature one finds statements by psychologists and philosophers, to the effect that "emotions are nothing more than

_________." For example, Duffy (1950), during the heyday of activation theory, maintained that emotions were nothing more than a point or range of points on a continuum of organismic arousal.

There were some curiosities about activation theories of emotion. It had been proposed that sleep and emotion were two ends of the arousal continuum. In retrospect, it seems difficult to understand how activation theorists could have seriously convinced themselves — much less talked other people into believing — that the difference between, say, passionate love and passionate hate was merely a matter of degree of how awake or sleepy one's nervous system happened to be. To be sure, this kind of physiological reductionism was short-lived. Nevertheless, it points to the ready tendency to dismiss emotion as an epiphenomenon or reduce it to some other trivial process. The astute clinician will note that this trivialization of emotion sounds very much like denial, a defense that is readily mobilized under exasperating circumstances. And the study of emotion does confound. It is not only difficult to measure, it is even difficult to describe. As Zajonc (1980) pointed out in his much discussed APA address, "Feeling and Thinking: Preferences Need No Inferences," affective reactions can be exceedingly difficult to verbalize. Even the most articulate of psychologists can feel tongue-tied and humbled when trying to put into words what are quite often very subtle and complex experiential phenomena. Emotion, therefore, is conceptually and linguistically difficult to articulate, not to mention measure. The progress that has been made in the field of emotions research in recent times is a testimony to the tenacity and creativity of today's psychologists as they continue to struggle with age-old questions concerning the emotions.

The "problem" of development. A second thorny question concerns the issue of development and, more specifically, the issue of adult development. The field of adult developmental pyschology began to evolve in the first few decades of the twentieth century, years *after* the establishment of the child development branch of psychology in the latter part of the nineteenth century. Prior to the pioneering work of American and German scholars (G. Stanley Hall and others in this country, Charlotte Bühler and her colleagues in Germany), adulthood was viewed as a stage of completed growth and permanent stasis. As the concept of development within the field of child psychology became more articulated, students of adulthood began to formulate the concept of changing adult life courses. And this was a theoretically appealing idea. However, questions concerning the directionality, magnitude, and quality of change became topics of considerable debate within the field.

As Skinner (1983) noted in his recent APA address, many notions about human growth embrace the "horticultural" model of development in which individuals grow up, grow old, decay, and die. However, there is increasing recognition, anticipated in an early article by Kantor (1933), that the life history of an individual actually is comprised of a *set* of life courses with the biological trajectory of growth and decay being only one form of change. Kantor maintained and subsequent empirical work has confirmed that psychological functions show a variety of courses and some functions continue to show expansion and improvement up until the end of life.

The issue of *development* versus *change* is even more conceptually challenging. Few would deny that there are changes in various psychological functions over the lifespan. However, we are uncertain as to the quantity and quality of changes that qualifies as development. Does the acquisition of an increasingly large vocabulary over the adult years qualify as development? Are the changes in capacity for sharing and intimacy that accompany the dissolution of a marriage and the negotiation of a new relationship to be considered an instance of development? How does one distinguish between changes involving accretion and drift, and "genuine" development? Psychologists are not at all unanimous in their definitions of growth and development. To many, but certainly not all, growth and development in adulthood imply progress or improvement, and bear resemblance to the Wernerian concepts of differentiation and hierarchic integration. But even if there were universal agreement with this definition, it is not at all evident that there would be consensus about how such notions should inform the individual domains of psychological functioning such as reasoning, memory, perception, emotion. Here we consider only the concept of emotional development in adulthood.

Adult emotional development. Before we can talk about emotional development we have to define what we mean by emotion. As generally conceived, there are three aspects or components of the emotion system: the physiological (about which we will have little to say in this chapter), behavioral or expressive (facial, vocal, and postural changes), and the experiential or subjective (the feeling component). In this chapter and elsewhere in the volume a major focus is on understanding the coordination of feeling states and expressive behavior in adult lives and on expressive behavior in the context of social interaction.

Theoretically, developmental change can take place in any or all of the above components and the changes may be formal or functional in nature. (For a more detailed discussion of these issues see Izard & Malatesta, in press, and Malatesta & Haviland, in press.) Much developmental change obviously takes place during infancy and early childhood. It is likely that further changes take place during later childhood and during adulthood, but the task of describing the developmental change becomes increasingly more difficult as our subjects become older and more complex.

Early in infancy, affective reactions are almost exclusively elicited by physical stimuli; only later do psychological stimuli become predominant. The physical parameters of stimuli that elicit affective reactions in young infants include contour and brightness of visual stimuli, the pitch and rise time of auditory stimuli, and so on. However, the band of elicitors gradually expands to include stimuli that are more psychological or abstract in nature. Eventually, one can be disgusted not only by the taste of spoiled food but by repellant ideas as well. One can experience pleasure from a breathtaking view of the sea as well as by virtue of hearing a compliment. In addition, as individuals move beyond infancy emotional behavior becomes increasingly suffused with self-consciousness. We become aware of our own emotional behavior as well as that of others. We become aware of the need to modify our expressive behavior so as to be socially appropriate and develop the ability to use our expressive behavior instrumentally.

While most of the changes in the emotion system discussed above start to take place during childhood and are most salient at that time because the changes occur so quickly and dramatically, this is not to say that further change and development cannot take place later in life. However, in discussing emotional development in adults, here as elsewhere one must be careful to distinguish between simple change (accretion and drift) and developmental progression. Earlier we indicated that developmental change carries with it the connotation of growth or improvement. The most widely accepted developmental constructs implying growth or improvement are those of *differentiation* and *hierarchic integration.* In the following we examine how these two constructs might be applied to a theoretical treatment of emotional development.

Principles of development and the emotion system. The terms *emotional maturity* and *emotional integrity* (as discussed by Frank, 1954) appear to come close to capturing the spirit of the principles of differentiation and hierarchic integration. Emotional maturation is said to consist of movement toward "progressive alteration both in the kind and intensity of emotional reactions and in their overt expression" so as to be in accord with "the changing capacity, opportunities, and changing relationships with the world and people" (Frank, 1954, pp. 27-28). Frank is explicit in distinguishing between becoming simultaneously *more logical and less emotional,* which is the everyman conception of emotional development and perhaps a Western ideal, and *developing more adaptive ways of existing* in one's environment under changing environmental demands. In the first case emotional maturation is achieved by becoming incapable of responding emotionally for it is accomplished by suppression or intellectualization. In the second instance we are talking about an individual who has been able to relinquish, but not repress, familiar patterns of responding to emotional stimuli in favor of learning new and more adaptive patterns.

The second principle proposed by Frank and noted by other authors as well (Giele, 1980; Pearlin, 1980) is that of emotional integrity. Emotional integration is said to consist of growth towards "flexible, nonrigid personalities capable of reacting emotionally, of experiencing anxiety, guilt, and hostility, *when these are appropriate and legitimate responses to life experiences*" (Frank, 1954, p.32).

The above suggests that psychological growth in the emotional realm consists of a reduction in the intensity of overt expression while maintaining or even enhancing the capacity for the feeling component and for interpersonally adaptive social sentiments such as altruism and empathy. It also is responsive to the scheduled as well as unscheduled flux in the course of lives. For this author as well as lifespan researchers such as Neugarten (1969) and Pearlin (1980), then, emotion expression is not simply the enactment of feelings and dispositions acquired from childhood experiences but a continuing process of adjustment and readjustment to external circumstances. It is worth noting that the above approach attends to both the feeling and expressive components of emotion, and places development within a social as well as an historical context. It thus engenders a dialectical developmental model of the emotions — one that is most consistent with the stances taken by the authors in this volume (see especially Averill; Felton & Shaver; Hansson, Hogan & Jones; Gelfond; and Roodin, Rybash, & Hoyer).

The distinction between feelings and expressions and their differential developmental course has also been a focus of differential emotions theory (Izard, 1977; Malatesta & Izard, 1983; Izard & Malatesta, in press). This theory contains several additional formulations that have a bearing on predictions about adult development.

Differential emotions theory maintains that the experiential component of the various fundamental emotions is largely governed by patterned feedback of the facial musculature and proposes that there is suppression of the overt display of emotion with increasing age as children learn to moderate their expressions in response to socialization pressures and in accordance with cultural norms. However, the theory does not indicate that there will be a corresponding decrement in emotion feelings with age. There are two ways out of this seeming paradox. In the first place, the overt expression of emotion is said to find symbolic form as the capacity for representational memory and imagery develops. One can visualize making a sad face and begin feeling depressed, or one can reevoke a past emotional experience just by thinking about it. Second, although the grosser aspects of overt expression may become quite curtailed, especially during highly public occasions, these expressions may be replaced by more fleeting and miniaturized versions. In this fashion, the face continues to supply the appropriate patterned feedback that is necessary for discrete emotion experience while dampening the overt publically observable and socially contagious aspects.

The foregoing view emphasizes that facial displays of emotion and other expressive behavior occurs in a social context — that emotion in adults is, to a certain extent, transactional. It is not that adults are not emotional or are less emotional than children, it is that they exercise their emotional expressivity under a set of constraints in response to tacit social and idiographic rules. In our study of the facial expressions of young, middle-aged, and older women (Chapter 14) under affect induction conditions in which these women were given explicit permission to reenact their feelings, we demonstrate that they are in fact *very* facially expressive.

Finally, differential emotions theory emphasizes that the emotion system — one of several interacting subsystems of personality — constitutes the primary motivational system in humans, and that it remains so throughout the lifespan. Anger at unjust treatment can initiate the filing of a lawsuit; anxiety about nuclear annihilation can motivate mass protest; romantic love (in the form of that particularly intoxicating blend of joy and excitement) can impel mature as well as rash and reckless behaviors in relationships with others; intolerable boredom and the hope for excitement can prompt changes in careers; and so on. Although the sources of anger, fear, love, and boredom may vary as we move though life's vicissitudes, this theory proposes that there is some invariance in feeling — that is, that there is some experiential identity in the felt aspect of emotion thoroughout life although emotion obviously becomes more and more suffused with thought as the cognitive system develops and evolves, much in the fashion that Stewart (see Stewart & Healy, this volume) has proposed.

The aspect of the emotion system that is most likely to undergo obvious change is the overt, expressive component. Adults learn to attenuate and transform their emotion signals to serve a variety of social and personal purposes including the avoidance of social contagion of affect, maintenance of privacy, regulation of arousal, and reduction of energy expenditure. To the extent that these needs vary over the life span, they predict change in behavior; and this change may be of a qualitative or quantitative nature.

In summary, differential emotions theory, as an approach to understanding emotional development in adults, stresses both biological and social forces in the modification and evolution of emotional responsiveness and experience as individuals move through life. Details about the quality and pattern of modification and development await creative empirical investigation.

References

Bellow, S. (1969) *Mr. Sammler's Planet.* New York: Viking.

Eckardt, M. (1977) *New challenges for adulthood in our times.* Paper presented at the American Academy Conference on Love and Work in Adulthood, Palo Alto, May 6-7.

Duffy, E. (1957) The psychological significance of the concept of "arousal" or "activation." *The Psychological Review, 64,* 265-275.

Zajonc, R. B. (1980) Feeling and thinking: Preferences need no inferences. *American Psychologist, 35,* 151-175.

Skinner, B. F. (1983) Intellectual self-management in old age. *American Psychologist, 39,* 239-244.

Kantor, J. R. (1933) *A Survey of the science of psychology.* Bloomington: Principia Press.

Malatesta, C. Z. & Haviland, J. M. (in press). Signals, symbols and socialization: The modification of emotional expression in human development. In M. Lewis & C. Saarni (Eds.), *The socialization of affect.* New York: Academic Press.

Izard, C. (1978) Emotions as motivations: An evolutionary-developmental perspective. In H. E. Howe, Jr. (Ed.), *Nebraska symposium on motivation, Vol. 26.* Lincoln: University of Nebraska Press.

Izard, C. & Malatesta, C. Z. (in press). A developmental theory of the emotions. *Behavioral and Brain Sciences.*

Frank, L. K. (1954) *Feelings and emotions.* New York: Doubleday.

Giele, J. Z. (1980) Adulthood as transcendence of age and sex. In N. J. Smelser & E. H. Erikson (Eds.), *Themes of work and love in adulthood.* Cambridge: Harvard University Press.

Pearlin, L. I. (1980) Life strains and psychological distress among adult. In N. J. Smelser & E. H. Erikson (Eds.), *Themes of work and love in adulthood.* Cambridge: Harvard University Press.

Neugarin, B. (1969) Continuities and discontinuities of psychological issues into adult life. *Human Development, 12,* 121-130.

2

The Acquisition of Emotions During Adulthood

JAMES R. AVERILL

The title of this volume, *Emotion in Adult Development,* could encompass three different issues: (1) the influence of emotion — and stress in general — on aging and development; (2) the way age-related changes in physiological and psychological functioning influence emotional reactivity; and (3) the acquisition of new, or the relinquishment of old emotional experiences during adulthood. There is a growing literature on the first two of these issues although few definitive statements can be made. The third issue, which is the topic of this chapter, has been relatively ignored.

Let me begin with a few illustrations of what I mean by the acquisition and relinquishment of emotions during adulthood:

(1) Amok is an aggressive frenzy observed in several Southeast Asian societies. It involves indiscriminate killing while in a trance-like state

AUTHOR'S NOTE: Thanks are due Bram Fridhandler and Ervin Staub for helpful comments on an earlier draft of this manuscript.

until the person running amok is himself killed. In its "classical" form, amok did not involve psychopathology (e.g., a schizophrenic breakdown or neurological disorder) but was a ritualized response to certain socially defined situations (e.g., involving a loss of honor — see Murphy, 1973, for a historical review of amok). Van Wulfften Palthe (1936) reports that occasional Europeans living in Southeast Asia have run amok; however, he could cite no case of a Southeast Asian running amok while living in a European country.

(2) Lucas (1969) has described the experiences of six miners trapped by a cave-in. After three days, parched with thirst, they took the first tentative steps toward drinking their own urine. The initial attempts resulted in gagging and vomiting. A resocialization of the emotions had to occur. Lucas draws on the literature of religious conversions to explicate the underlying processes. Although a bit overdrawn, the comparison is enlightening. The men had to create and internalize a new set of social norms that made the drinking of urine not only intellectually permissible but emotionally acceptable. By the time they were rescued, the men were drinking urine, if not with gusto, at least without disgust.

(3) A common theme in feminist writings is the transformation of more passive emotional experiences, such as depression and lethargy, into more active states. Anger especially is viewed as a "tool for growth." Glennon (1979) quotes the following account by an anonymous participant in an informal feminist workshop:

> One woman becomes angry and pounds the floor and then suddenly another hears her and recognizes it and then all the women are angry. From an inarticulate moaning and pounding comes an angry fury as they rise together chanting "No! No! No!-No more shame." (p.83)

(4) The life of Mahatma Gandhi represents the epitome of courage. Yet, in his autobiography, Gandhi (1958) describes himself as a child in the following way:

> I was a coward. I used to be haunted by the fear of thieves, ghosts, and serpents. I did not dare to stir out of doors at night. Darkness was a terror to me. It was almost impossible for me to sleep in the dark. (quoted by Gergen, 1982, p. 150)

Numerous other examples of emotional change during adulthood could be offered from ethnographic sources, autobiographical accounts, and clinical case histories. Such examples tend to be too complex and lacking in detail to be demonstrative of any particular theoretical position. Nevertheless, they illustrate the type of phenomena that must be explained.

In this chapter I will analyze adult emotional development from a social-constructivist point of view. This is not the only nor even the most common view of emotion. My purpose, however, is not to provide a full account of all aspects of emotional development; that would be far too ambitious a goal. I hope merely to highlight some of the problems related to the study of adult emotional development and to adumbrate a few notions — particularly with respect to the rules of emotion — in order to facilitate further inquiry.

Theoretical Orientations

Before we can speak meaningfully of emotional development, whether in adults or in children, we must have some conception of what we mean by emotion and by development.

A Social Constructivist View of Emotion

I will only sketch in barest outline what I mean by a social-constructivist view of emotion, ignoring the qualifications and other accouterments typical of scholarly expositions. For details, the reader is referred elsewhere (Averill, 1974, 1976, 1980a, 1980b, 1982).

In cognitive terms, emotions may be conceived of as belief systems or schemas that guide the appraisal of situations, the organization of responses, and the self-monitoring (interpretation) of behavior. When conceived of in this way, the question arises: What is the source of emotional schemas? The more traditional answer to this question is that emotional schemas became hardwired into the nervous system during the course of evolution — that they represent innate affect programs (Izard, 1977; Tomkin, 1981). By contrast, a constructivist view assumes that emotional schemas are the internal representation of social norms or rules.[1]

In more behavioral terms, emotions may be defined as socially constituted syndromes. By a syndrome, I mean a set of interrelated response elements (pysiological changes, expressive reactions, instrumental responses, subjective experiences). Some of these component responses may be biologically based (e.g., certain expressive reactions). However, the way the components are organized into coherent syndromes is determined primarily by social and not biological evolution. Another way of stating this same idea is to say that emotions are transitory social roles — that is, institutionalized ways of interpreting and responding to particular classes of situations.

The social rules that help constitute emotional syndromes tend to be open-ended, allowing a great deal of improvization. Among other things, this means that emotional syndromes are polythetic. A polythetic syndrome is one in which no single component or subset of components is essential to the whole. The rules of anger, for example, can be instantiated in an indefinite variety of ways depending upon the individual and the circumstances. No single kind of response represents a necessary or sufficient condition for anger or for any other emotion. The importance of the polythetic nature of emotional syndromes for the issues of development will become apparent below.

Perspectives on Development

Any theory of ontogenetic development presupposes a theory of phylogenetic development, and any theory of adult development presupposes a theory of childhood development.

Phylogenetic development. A social-constructivist view of emotion does not envision a completely plastic organism, the proverbial blank slate on which experience can write unhindered. *Homo sapiens* is a biological species, and millions of years of hominid evolution make some patterns of response easy to acquire and others difficult or almost impossible. But this being granted, it must also be recognized that the biological constraints on human behavior are rather loose. Behavioral systems that have survived the course of human evolution (e.g., systems related to attachment, aggression, reproduction, etc.) are loosely organized, genetically speaking, and can be transformed and combined in an almost indefinite variety of ways.

Indeterminancy of behavior is itself a biological adaptation, perhaps the most important of our species. But indeterminacy cannot last. The world in which humans evolved was — and in many repsects still is — a dangerous place. Protection is provided by the group with its customs and practices, which themselves have evolved (socially, not biologically) through a slow process of trial and error (Campbell, 1975). The young child must be capable of acquiring these practices rapidly, or the child — and the group — will not survive long.

It follows from the above considerations that humans are by nature rule-generating and rule-following animals. Language acquisition offers a particularly salient example of this characteristic. When learning a language, an person does not simply acquire specific responses — phonemes, words, and whatever. Rather, the person learns the rules that make possible the prodution of an indefinite variety of meaningful utterances. Language is, of course, a specialized form of behavior; but the capacity for language did not evolve in isolation. The ability to generate and to follow rules underlies a wide range of human activity — including the emotions, as I will argue below.

One other feature of human evolution deserves brief mention — namely, neoteny. This refers to the retention in adulthood of traits that are characteristic of earlier (infantile, juvenile) stages of development. Neoteny, like the indeterminacy described above, is more pronounced in humans than in any other species (Gould, 1977; Montagu, 1981). Of particular relevance to our present concerns is the fact that humans retain into adulthood some of the openness and potential for change characteristic of childhood.

Infant and childhood development. In analogy with *phylogenesis*, which refers to the origins of characteristics during earlier stages of biological evolution, we may speak of *paedogenesis* when referring to the origins of behavior during infancy and childhood.[2] Ample evidence attests to the fact that intense stimulation or severe deprivation during the first few years of life can have profound — albeit highly variable — effects on later emotionality. Indeed, because the young child does not have the cognitive or behavioral skills to cope effectively with potentially threatening events, even seemingly innocuous occurrences (from an adult point of view) may have a major developmental impact. But beyond these widely accepted facts there is little agreement about the precise role and relative importance of paedogenesis for adult emotional behavior. Let us examine the issue a little more closely.

Recently a minor paradigm shift has occurred in the study of infant emotional development. The nature and significance of this shift are difficult to convey in a few words. It involves, on the one hand, a change in the conception of the infant from a reactive to an active organism; and it involves, on the other hand, a change in the unit of analysis from the infant per se to the mother-infant dyad (Trevarthen, 1979). The latter aspect is the more important for our present concerns. Although the infant can be conceived of a quasi-intentional agent that controls the conditions of its own development, the extent of its control is necessarily limited. This is not simply due to the undeveloped state of its behavioral and cognitive capabilities. It is also due to the nature of the developmental task. The infant is entering a world in which the meaning of an act has already been established. Therefore, it is up to the mother (or other caretaker) to interpret and complete the actions initiated by the infant and to put those actions into a meaningful framework.

Kaye (1982) likens the above process to an apprenticeship. An apprentice cobbler, for example, may stamp out the soles of shoes, but the overall plan for making a shoe is provided by the master. Likewise, the infant may engage in certain behaviors, but the overall plan of the interaction is provided by the caretaker. The analogy may be extended further. The master cobbler may be expert in making shoes, but the cobbler's trade is only one aspect of a larger system of clothing manufacture and design; and the latter is, in turn, only a part of a still larger sociocultural matrix. The master cobbler need not understand the larger social and economic forces that make his occupation meaningful in order to ply his trade. Similarly, the caretaker need not understand all the factors that enter into the socialization process in order to engage the infant in meaningful interaction.

At first, the metaphor of an apprenticeship might seem stretched when applied to infant emotional development. It is important to remember, however, that the infant is not simply a passive respondent to stimuli, whether internal or external; rather, the infant is an active participant in an ever-widening circle of relationships.

An informative illustration of emotional development — or apprenticeship — among older children has been provided by Bateson (1975). The focus of his analysis is the socialization for trance (an emotion-like experience) among the Balinese. Bateson begins by breaking the socialization process into components. These components, he emphasizes, do not exist in isolation but are always a part of an ongoing process. They are, in a sense, analogous to the segments of an earthworm. "Segmentation is itself not a quantity; it is a component or premise of the morphology of the worm" (p. 52).

With this rather graphic if somewhat opaque reminder, Bateson goes on to analyze the way Balinese children acquire the ability for trance. One of the components of socialization involves the phenomenon of clonus (i.e., the recurrent series of patellar reflexes that occurs endogenously when the leg is held in certain positions). Such automatic reactions, when placed in an appropriate social context, are used to reinforce the more general belief among the Balinese that the body can act in a semiautonomous or ego-alien fashion. Thus, although clonus is not a component of trance itself, it does enter into the socialization for trance. Other components of socialization include a wide variety of symbols, rituals, and "paradigm experiences" that help make the trance seem a natural and self-explanatory state. As Bateson observes, "the business of explanation and the business of socialization [for trance] turn out to be the same" (pp. 62-63).

Bateson's analysis of the *components of socialization* needs to be supplemented by an analysis of the *socialization of components.* As explained earlier, emotional syndromes can be broken down into component responses (expressive reactions, physiological changes, instrumental acts, subjective experiences). These components may undergo socialization independent of one another. For example, a person may learn to respond or to make certain kinds of judgments in a nonemotional context, and only later incorporate these components into an emotional syndrome. In this respect, the development of emotion does not differ from the development of many other complex patterns of behavior in which a great deal of transfer of training may be involved.

In some instances, of course, the socialization of a component may also be a component of socialization (in Bateson's sense). This occurs when a component response is so closely tied to a specific emotional syndrome that socialization of the part must necessarily involve some socialization of the whole. Perhaps the best example of such components are verbal responses. As children learn the proper use of such terms as "anger," "fear," "love," and so on they are also learning to make the discriminations, both with respect to situations and to their own behavior, that those terms imply. Stated somewhat differently, the acquisition of emotional concepts requires knowledge of many of the same rules that help constitute emotional syndromes. I will have much more to say about these rules shortly.

Adult development. At one time, it was common to speak of primary versus secondary socialization. Primary socialization presumably occurs during childhood and is more encompassing and enduring than secondary socialization. The problem with this formulation is that it is too global. Before one can speak meaningfully of differences between primary and secondary socialization, the specific behaviors being socialized as well as the conditions under which socialization occurs must be stipulated. In this regard, the only behavior that has received detailed attention is language.

There is evidence, both physiological and psychological (Lenneberg, 1967), to suggest that there are differences between children and adults in the readiness and ability to learn language. There is also reason to believe, however, that these differences have been exaggerated and that their theoretical significance has been overinterpreted (see, for example, Ervin-Tripp, 1978; Neufeld, 1979). Consider the following facts:

(1) The course of development differs depending upon the aspect of language involved. Phonology (sounds and their structure) tends to be acquired relatively early (during the first five to eight years); most older children and adults, especially, find it difficult to acquire a second language free of accent. The acquisition of syntax (the way words are combined to form sentences) is a more extended process, continuing into adolescence and beyond. Finally, the development of semantics (the meaning of words and sentences) continues throughout life.

(2) There are large individual differences in the ability to learn a second language. Some adults can acquire even the correct phonology of a

new language with relative ease. Does this mean that first and second language learning involves similar processes for some individuals but different processes for others?

(3) The conditions under which first and second language learning occurs are usually quite different. The child is immersed in a total environment, completely dependent on communication with adults. The most intensive instruction in a second language cannot match these conditions. Even living in another linguistic group is not comparable, for a person's first language allows a degree of independence in thought and action that is not possible for the child. To an unknown extent, some of the differences in first and second language learning may actually be due to situational factors such as these.

(4) As a person grows older, numerous physiological and psychological changes occur that influence the ease with which many kinds of behavior are acquired. Some, at least, of the differences in first- and second-language learning may be a function of more general changes in problem-solving ability, changes that have little to do with the acquisition of language per se.[3]

The above observations could be made *mutatis mutandis* with respect to emotional development. On the basis of much sparser evidence than we have in the study of language, it is often assumed that childhood emotional development is much different than adult emotional development. For such an assertion to have much theoretical significance, we would first have to distinguish which aspect of emotion is under consideration. For example, facial expression may undergo a different course of development than the appraisal of emotional situations. We would also have to take into account individual and situational differences, as well as more general physiological and psychological changes that might influence problem-solving in general.

To summarize briefly, I do not deny the importance of either phylogenesis or paedogenesis for an understanding of adult emotional behavior. I do, however, question the almost exclusive emphasis that has often been placed on these developmental stages. Emotional syndromes are not innate, nor are they predetermined by events occurring during childhood. Quite the contrary: The most reasonable assumption to make — on both biological and psychological grounds, as well as for the sake of parsimony — is that emotional development continues throughout the life span and that the underlying processes are basically similar (although not necessarily identical) in all age groups.

And what, precisely, is acquired during emotional development? As described earlier, emotional syndromes can be broken down into more elementary components (expressive reactions, physiological changes,

TABLE 2.1 Cross-Classification of the Rules of Emotion

	Scope of Rule			
Type of Rule	*Appraisal*	*Behavior*	*Prognosis*	*Attribution*
Constitutive				
Regulative				
Heuristic				

etc.). Some of these are biologically based; others are acquired in much the same way as any skill (such as dancing or riding a bicycle) might be learned. From a social-constructivist point of view, however, the most important feature of emotional development involves the acquisition of the social norms and rules that provide the component responses with their meaning and coordination.

Rules of Emotion

This brings us to the core of the present analysis, namely, the rules of emotion. No attempt will be made to enumerate specific rules for any given emotion (such as anger or fear). Rather, I will delimit broad classes of rules that apply to emotions in general. The rules of emotion can be distinguished both according to type and according to scope (i.e., the aspect of emotion to which they are primarily applicable). In neither case are the distinctions absolute; psychological reality seldom fits comfortably into the neat pigeonholes that we devise for analytical purposes. With this caveat in mind, Table 2.1 presents a cross-classification of the rules of emotion according to type and scope.

In order to illustrate the three types of rules — constitutive, regulative, and heuristic — represented in Table 2.1, let us begin with a nonemotional example. Consider a game, such as chess. Some rules (e.g., pertaining to the layout of the chessboard, the nature of the pieces, and the moves that are permissable) help constitute a game as a game of chess (as opposed, say, to backgammon). If there were no king, if pawns could move backward, and if rooks could be checkmated, then the game would no longer be chess. (Although in the case of children, one might say they were playing *at* chess.) Other rules are primarily regulative. For example, in a chess tournament, it might be stipulated that a certain number of moves be made within a given time limit. Regulative rules do not determine the kind of game that is being played, but they do influence the way the game is played. The third type of rule presented in Table 2.1, heuristic rules, determine the strategy of play. It is not possible to specify exhaustively or succinctly the heuristic rules for a game like chess. Such rules are the stuff of books and magazine articles (e.g., instructing players how to recognize situations in which one move might be more appropriate than another). Good chess players can be distinguished from poor ones by their (often intuitive) grasp of the heuristic rules of the game.

Constitutive, regulative, and heuristic rules also apply to the emotions. For example, a person cannot be proud of the stars. This is not because of some biological incapacity; rather, to be proud of something, the existence of which is not connected with the self even remotely or by association, violates one of the constitutive rules of this emotion. No matter how glowingly one feels on a starry night, the responses cannot count as pride. There are also rules that regulate how pride should be experienced and expressed. To violate a regulative rule does not invalidate the emotion as an instance of pride, but it may make the pride "sinful." The biblical story of Satan illustrates this point. But while pride may lead to great falls, it is also the necessary foundation for great accomplishments. The trick, if one wants to call it that, is to be proud without being boastful, arrogant, pompous, or conceited; but also without donning a false mask of humility. There are heuristics for pride; and from every indication, they are as difficult to master as the heuristics for chess.[4]

I will have much more to say about constitutive, regulative, and heuristic rules shortly. But first, let me explicate briefly the other set of distinctions depicted in Table 2.1. Rules of emotion may be distinguished depending upon whether they pertain to the evaluation of emotional objects (rules of appraisal), the organization of responses (rules of behavior), the time course and consequences of the emotion (rules of prognosis), and the connection between the instigation, the responses, and one's self (rules of attribution). Elsewhere (Averill, 1982) I have illustrated these four classes of rules as they apply to anger. Here, I can only indicate their general nature.

Rules of appraisal pertain to the way a situation is perceived and evaluated. Each emotion is characterized by its own set of appraisals. The appraisals determine what is sometimes called the intentional object of the emotion. For many emotions, the intentional object consists of three aspects: the instigation, the target, and the manifest aim or objective of the response. Thus, the object of anger is revenge for wrongdoing; the object of fear is escape from danger; the object of love is union with the loved one; and so forth. The intentional object, it must be emphasized, is part of an emotional syndrome, not a cause of any particular episode. It is a meaning imposed on events, for whatever reason.

Rules of behavior refer to the way an emotion is organized and expressed. As far as overt behavior is concerned, this class of rules is rather obvious. Perhaps the only thing that needs to be added is that "behavior" includes physiological responses and subjective experience. This is perhaps easiest to illustrate by example. During the Victorian period, it was expected of young ladies that they faint when confronted with certain situations — provided they could do so safely and with decorum. In other words, there were (implicit) rules for fainting, even though this is presumably an involuntary, largely physiological response.

Rules of prognosis concern the time course and progression of an emotional episode. Some emotions may last only a few moments (e.g., being startled) while others may last for months or even years and progress through various stages (e.g., grief). If the appropriate time course for an emotion is violated, then the authenticity of the emotion may be questioned or hidden motives sought. Rules of prognosis may sometimes even extend beyond the limits of a single emotional episode. Thus, a person who asks, "Am I really in love?" may be wondering not so much about butterflies in the stomach as about the long-term commitments he or she is willing to make.

Rules of attribution pertain to the way an emotion is explained or legitimized. These rules tie together the appraised object, the behavior, and the prognosis into a meaningful whole, and relate the entirety to the self. Stated somewhat differently, it is not sufficient to appraise a situation in a certain way or to make relevant responses; the entire syndrome must be interpreted and given meaning. When a response is interpreted as emotional, it cannot be judged by the same rules that govern rational, deliberate behavior. But although emotions may be "blind" (i.e., they do not follow standard rules of logic), they do have a logic of their own. (It is always possible to ask of an emotional response, "Is it reasonable?") Also, a person cannot be held fully responsible for emotional responses because emotions are supposedly beyond personal control. We are "gripped," "seized," and "torn" by emotion. Colloquialisms such as these do not describe intrinsic features of emotional responses. Rather, they are rule-governed interpretations of behavior, reflections of our naive and implicit theories of emotion.

Referring back to Table 2.1, 12 cells are created by crossing the three-fold distinction among constitutive, regulative, and heuristic rules with the four-fold distinction among rules of appraisal, behavior, prognosis, and attribution. Space does not allow a discussion of each of these cells. The reader will have to "fill in the blanks," so to speak. One proviso should be mentioned, however. Depending upon the emotion, some of the cells in Table 2.1 may be empty. For example, while rules of prognosis are prominent in emotions such as grief, they are much less important for emotions such as joy; similarly, some emotions (e.g., envy) are more subject to regulation than others; some require greater use of heuristics (e.g., love); and so forth.

Now let us explore some of the implications of the various kinds of rules represented in Table 2.1 for an understanding of adult emotional development. Much adult emotional development involves the acquisition and refinement of heuristic rules. That is, the person learns to make finer distinctions when appraising situations; responses become more skilled; expectancies are more realistic and clearly established; and attributions to the self and others become more sophisticated. In short, the person becomes more adept emotionally without necessarily adding new emotions to his or her repertoire.

In spite of their importance, relatively little research has been devoted to a systematic analysis of emotional heuristics. Perhaps the most notable exception to this generalization is work done by cognitive-behavioral therapists on "skills training" (e.g., Goldfried, 1980; Meichenbaum, 1977). As the name implies, skills training refers to the development of appropriate strategies for appraising situations and responding effectively.

The relative neglect of emotional heuristics stands in sharp contrast to the study of cognitive heuristics (e.g., by theorists interested in artificial intelligence). The reasons for this differential interest deserves brief comment. It is relatively easy to program a computer for the constitutive rules of a game (chess, say). Regulative rules can also be added if they are of any interest. The main problem in artificial intelligence is to program the computer to actually play the game in a manner that would compete with, or simulate the moves of, an accomplished human player. For this, the heuristic rules must be specified.

There have been few attempts to simulate human emotions (see Colby, 1981), and that is perhaps one reason why little attention has been devoted to an analysis of emotional heuristics. There is a second and more important reason, however. In comparison with heuristic rules, the constitutive and regulative rules of a game like chess are of relatively little psychological interest. In the case of the emotions, the situation is quite different. Here, the "rules of the game" (constitutive and regulative) are of primary interest. Until they are better understood, research on heuristic rules cannot proceed in a very systematic fashion.

Recently, a considerable amount of attention has been devoted to the rules that help regulate emotions and especially to the regulative rules of behavior. (For example, the display rules for facial expressions discussed by Ekman and Friesen, 1975, fall in this category.) *Less attention has been devoted to the regulative rules of appraisal, prognosis, and attribution; and still less to constitutive rules of all kinds.* In fact, not all theorists would even agree that "authentic" emotions are constituted (and not simply regulated) by rules. Yet from a developmental point of view constitutive rules are of prime importance, for only their acquisition makes possible truly new and different kinds of emotional experiences.

Emotional development — whether in childhood or adulthood — involves the internalization of the appropriate rules of emotion. When such internalization is inadequate or incomplete, characteristic disabilities may ensue. In the case of constitutive rules, inadequate socialization results in emotional syndromes that might best be described as *neurotic*. That is, the individual responds in a manner so unusual or bizarre that one does not know quite how to classify it. Examples would be the person who becomes "fearful" of harmless objects (thus violating a constitutive rule of appraisal); whose "love" is manifested in sadistic cruelty (violating a constitutive rule of behavior); whose "grief" is over in a day or prolonged for many years (violating a constitutive rule of prognosis); or whose "anger" is the product of paranoid delusions (violating a constitutive rule of attribution).

The person who cannot conform to regulative rules may to be considered *delinquent* rather than neurotic. An example would be the members of street gangs described by Toch (1969). These men often displayed anger that was well constituted (according to general cultural prescriptions) but inappropriately expressed. Lest there be misunderstanding, "delinquent" does not necessarily refer to behaviors that break the law. Rules of etiquette, civility, and good taste are also regulative. Thus, persons who weep too copiously, who become envious at the well-deserved success of a friend, who remain angry too long, or who respond with too much cunning and forethought are all emotionally delinquent in the sense that I am using the term.

Finally, the person who has failed to acquire an adequate set of heuristic rules is neither neurotic nor delinquent in the senses described above but simply *inept*. Illustrations of this state of affairs have been given in the preceding discussion.

Rather than further discussing the rules of emotion in the abstract, it might be more fruitful at this point to examine how a social-constructivist approach can help clarify some perennial issues realted to emotional development. Although these issues are multifaceted, in one way or another each involves a failure to take into account the rules of emotion and especially the distinction between constitutive and regulative rules.

Four Variations on a Common Theme

A common theme in psychological theory involves the notion that some core aspect of emotion exists (e.g., some pattern of neurological activity, or a peculiar feeling), and that this core aspect remains invariant through time despite many variations in eliciting conditions and transformations in modes of expression. The four variations on this theme that I will consider are the following: (1) the identity of childhood and adult emotions; (2) the significance of events in childhood for adult emotional experience; (3) civilizing the emotions; and (4) getting in touch with one's own true feelings.

The Identity of Childhood and Adult Emotions

To what extent are adult emotional experiences similar to those of young children? For example, is the anger of an adult primarily an extension and elaboration of the anger of a child, or is the adult emotion fundamentally different? Most contemporary theories of emotion assume an essential continuity between the emotional life of children and adults. By contrast, a social-constructivist view assumes that emotional syndromes can be acquired at any age; and that even when there is continuity (as between the anger of the child and that of the adult), the transformation may be so great that one can speak of the "same" emotion in only a limited sense.

The problem of identity through time has always been puzzling. The Greeks posed the problem in an allegory about the ship of Theseus. This ship had its boards replaced gradually, one at a time, until not a single plank of the original ship remained. Was the ship still the same ship of Theseus? This is not an especially problematic case. But consider the following extension of the story. Suppose that as each board was removed, it was carefully saved. After all the planks had been replaced, a new ship was constructed from the original boards. Are there now two ships of Theseus? If there were a dispute about the ships, which one has claim to being the "real" ship of Theseus — that which showed the greatest continuity in time (with gradual replacement of planks) or that closest to the original in material content (being rebuilt from the original planks)? It is easy to imagine even further variations on this story. Suppose that as the old planks were removed, they were destroyed so that a second ship like the original one could not be rebuilt from them. But also suppose that as the planks were being replaced, the ship was also being redesigned — its hull enlarged, the interior quarters rearranged, an extra deck added, and so forth. Eventually, the ship not only has completely new parts, but also a new configuration. Is it still the same ship of Theseus? And if not, at what point did the original ship cease to be and a new ship come into being?

Emotional development presents a puzzle not unlike the ship of Theseus. If we compare anger in the adult with the temper tantrum of an infant, there seems to be little in common. Yet, there is continuity, and it is not possible to say at any given point in time that now the infantile emotion has ended and the adult emotion has come into being. Because of this, we are tempted to conclude that there must be something, like a thread through time, that lends unity to the entire sequence. What might that something be? The "true" or "authentic" emotion perhaps?

According to our earlier definition of emotions as socially constituted syndromes of which no particular component is essential to the whole, there is no need to postulate an emotional *Ding an Sich* that somehow remains invariant through time. One can reasonably admit that an emotional syndrome (anger, say) is the "same" in adulthood and childhood and yet deny that the adult and childhood emotions share any important features in common. Moreover, as any "new" emotion must necessarily develop out of elements already present, there is a sense in which it is impossible to acquire as an adult an emotion that is completely different from anything that preceded it. But this says more about the way we use such concepts as "new," "different," and "same" than it does about any invariance in underlying states.

The Significance of Events in Childhood for Adult Emotional Experiences

Earlier, I introduced the term *paedogenesis* to refer to the origins of behavior in childhood. With respect to emotional behavior, paedogenesis has been elevated almost to the level of dogma. That is, nearly all discussions of emotional development start — *and stop* — with childhood. The present volume is unique in its focus on emotional development in adulthood. There is a sense, of course, in which all adult behavior has its roots in childhood experiences. The child is the father of the man. But discussions of emotional development often go beyond this truism and imply that adult emotions, if not innate, are constituted during infancy and early childhood. Psychoanalytic theory, for example, assumes that adult emotional reactions are basically determined by events occurring within the first six years of life. Other theories may not be as explicit on this issue, but the tenor of analysis is generally similar.

Without questioning the importance of paedogenesis as a general principle, one can well ask why such theoretical emphasis has been placed on childhood experiences as determinants of adult emotions. The dogma — as opposed to the principle — of paedogenesis is based, in part, on the notion discussed above — namely, that adult emotions are only elaborate and transformed versions of their childhood counterparts. But it is also based on a particular view of causality.

Individuals have a bias toward seeking causes that resemble their effects in terms of salient features. Major effects should have major causes, and emotionally relevant effects should have emotionally relevant causes (Nisbett & Ross, 1980). To take a specific (but nonemotional) example, Taylor (1982) found that cancer victims often search their past for some significant event to which they can attribute their disease. It is difficult to accept the fact that a disease so serious as cancer can be the result of numerous small and — of themselves — innoucuous insults to the body. Similarly, there is a tendency (not limited to laymen) to search for the causes of adult emotions — particularly if those emotions are unusual or dramatic — in specific and perhaps traumatic events that occurred during infancy or early childhood. The presumed events need not be actual, but may depend on the imaginings of the child; nevertheless, repressed or seemingly forgotten, they continue to exert their influence on adult behavior.

From a social-constructivist view, emotional development — whether in childhood or as an adult — typically follows a more subtle and nonspecific course. Like the development of most other complex forms of behavior, emotional development tends to be slow, piecemeal, and cumulative; indeed, for the most part, emotional development is not even particularly emotional. Consider the case of anger. In the adult, anger is typically based on complex judgments regarding intentionality and justification (i.e., with respect to the behavior of the instigator). The rules that guide such judgments are not peculiar to anger and they are not learned in all-or-none fashion as a consequence of some specific event. The same is true with respect to the expression of anger. The words spoken and responses made during anger are not necessarily different than the words and responses made in many other contexts. What makes them a manifestation of anger is the way they are organized and interpreted (experienced). In short, the development of anger — or of any other emotion — involves the acquisition of many components and the rules (of appraisal, behavior, prognosis, and attribution) that govern their organization and interpretation.

Civilizing the Emotions

The sociologist, Elias (1939/1979), has argued that much of the progress of Western civilization involved a taming of the affects. He cites many examples from medieval sources to illustrate attitudes and behaviors (e.g., regarding aggression, sexuality, and alimentary functions) that today would be considered extremely crude and even inhuman. Elias also argues that children undergo similar progression from the uninhibited expression of raw affect to the more refined and civilized emotional life of the adult.

Although most psychologists would probably agree that Elias has overstated his thesis, the view that socialization is primarily regulative is quite common. Consider the following observation by Tomkins (1979):

> Because the free expression of innate affect is extremely contagious and because these are very high-powered phenomena, all societies, in varying degrees, exercise substantial control over the unfettered expression of affect, and particularly over the free expression of the cry of affect. (p. 208)

Consider again the distinction between contitutive and regulative rules. The view adumbrated by Elias, Tomkins, and many others as well, assumes that the rules of emotion are almost exclusively regulative, at least as far as fundamental emotions are concerned. However, if we admit that some of the rules of emotion are also constitutive, then the role of society becomes constructive as well as regulative. (Needless to say, in this context I am not using "constructive" in its evaluative sense.) Indeed, much of the data reported by Elias could just as well be interpreted in this way. For example, the ferocity and bloodthirstiness extolled by the medieval knight are just as much social constructions as are the more benign emotions advocated by the most dedicated pacifist of today.

At this point, the question might be raised. If emotions are social constructions, why does every society exercise substantial control over their unfettered expression? The paradox implied by this question is more apparent than real. Many, if not most, social products are subject to regulation — weapons, drugs, automobiles, financial and professional institutions, and so forth. Once a person starts, it becomes difficult to think of a social product or institutionalized form of behavior that is *not* regulated in one fashion or another. The emotions are certainly no exception to this rule.

Getting in Touch with One's True Feelings

In popular psychology, we often read or hear about people who are "out of touch" with their feelings. To remedy the situation, groups devoted to "consciousness raising" abound. If people need to get in contact with their feelings, at some point they must have lost contact (or perhaps never have made contact to begin with). But at what point? When do people normally establish contact with their feelings? At six months of age? At ten years? Or is this a matter of adult emotional development? The question is certainly an odd one, but let us speculate nevertheless.

People often "discover" that they have lost contact with their feelings as they move from one sociocultural context to another. The move may involve physical relocation (e.g., immigration); it may be economic (e.g., getting promoted or losing a job); or it may be ideological (e.g., a religious or political conversion). Consider also the situation of women as they move from the home into the workplace; of men as they assume greater domestic responsibilities; of teenagers moving from high school and a family environment to a large and diverse university; of a gang member placed in a correctional agency; of the housewife after the last child has left home; of a person who retires after forty years on the job. All such transitions involve some emotional readjustment; sometimes they also require fundamental changes in values and beliefs. It is precisely when old values must be abandoned and new standards acquired that a person may face the need to get in contact with his or her "true" feelings.

The process of getting in touch with one's feelings is perhaps best exemplified during a religious or political conversion. How does the convert know when he or she has "arrived"? In part, by experiencing the emotions considered authentic by the new reference group. But there is a catch here. If the emotions are recognized as social constructions, they would lose some of their air of authenticity. Why should one emotion be considered more authentic than another if both are socially constituted? The way out of this dilemma is to postulate that the new emotions reflect one's true feelings. They were there all along but had been submerged, repressed, or otherwise denied awareness.

Of course, most social transitions do not involve such fundamental changes in values and beliefs (constitutive rules) that radically different emotions are evoked. For the most part, customary emotions may be adapted to fit new circumstances (e.g., instead of becoming depressed, the person may now become angry; or where anger was before, benign indifference may now prevail). Still, the underlying principles are similar. Getting in contact with one's feelings is not so much a process of discovery as it is an act of creation.

Concluding Observations

The acquisition of new emotions during adulthood, and the relinquishment of previously established emotions, is commonplace. Yet, such phenomena have been the subject of relatively little systematic investigation. The reasons for this neglect are more conceptual than empirical. Most theories view emotions as biologically primitive (innate) responses, or at least as behaviors that become well established in early childhood. From these perspectives, adult development is largely an issue of regulation (i.e., the inhibition or release of previously established tendencies). A neglect of adult emotional development is also fostered by the fact that most changes in affect (beyond childhood) are slow and continuous. Few of us experience saltatory leaps in our emotional lives. Even falling in love — perhaps the best example of the acquisition of a new emotion experienced by most adults — has ample precedent in earlier developmental stages. When continuity in development exists, the problem of identity becomes problematic, and debates about what is truly "new" or "different" may obfuscate rather than clarify underlying processes. To complicate matters even further, most emotional syndromes are quite complex. Some aspects (e.g., cognitive components) are more subject to change than are other aspects (e.g., certain expressive reactions). This makes it easy to defend almost any thesis with respect to continuity and change, depending on the aspect of emotion taken as fundamental.

The present chapter has focused on the cognitive aspects of emotions; or, more accurately, on the social norms and rules that, when internalized, help to form the cognitive schemas on which the experience and expression of emotion depend. Much has been left unsaid, or has been said only cursorily — for example, about the process of socialization itself and about the biological *anlage* or systems of behavior without which the social construction of emotion could not proceed. Other chapters in this volume will help to rectify these deficiencies. If I have been able to illustrate some of the conceptual problems involved in the analysis of adult emotional development, then the primary goals of this chapter have been realized. If, in addition, I have encouraged the reader to explore further the advantages (and limitations) of a social-constructivist view of emotion, then my goals have been more than achieved.

Notes

1. To a certain extent, the contrast I am drawing here between biologically and socially oriented theories is a matter of definition. What I am calling emotions, for example, Izard (1977) refers to as affective-cognitive structures. Izard limits the concept of emotion to a much narrower range of phenomena than do I; namely, to the innate neurochemical processes, expressive reactions, feelings and action tendencies associated with a few fundamental states. But lest the differences in orientation be dismissed as merely a matter of definition, two points should be noted. First, the way basic concepts are defined is of central importance to any scientific theory; it helps determine the kinds of phenomena that need to be explained, and hence the focus of research. Second, a social-constructivist view rejects the notion that there are a few fundamental emotions, however defined, that can be identified with innate biological processes.

2. The term paedogenesis (from the Greek *paedo*, child, and *genesis*, origin) was introduced in 1866 by the German embryologist, Karl von Baer, to designate the condition in which larval and even embryonic forms (e.g., of insects, newts, salamanders) attain reproductive capacity while the remainder of the body is still in an immature state (Montagu, 1981). The term is still sometimes used that way today. The meaning given to "paedogenesis" in this chapter — the origin of adult behavior in childhood experiences — is more in keeping with the original Greek roots.

3. In this discussion of the development of linguistic competencies, I am ignoring an important distinction, namely, between first versus second language learning on the one hand, and the acquisition of language during childhood versus adulthood on the other. Many children learn a second language at an early age; conversely, under conditions of extreme deprivation, it is conceivable that the acquisition of a first language might be delayed until adulthood. For our present purposes, however, consideration of this distinction is not critical.

4. As is usual when concepts derived from one domain are applied to another, the extension of the concept of rules to the domain of emotion is to a certain extent metaphorical. The metaphor is perhaps most limited in the case of heuristic rules. I may be able to simulate a skilled performance by specifying a set of heuristic rules, but this does not mean that a person is following those rules when responding. It is important to recognize the limitation of the rule metaphor, not only in the case of emotion but also as applied to language and other psychological phenomena (see Shotter, 1976, for a detailed critique). However, the issue is not whether emotions are governed by rules in *every* sense of the word; the issue is, rather, whether there are *any* senses in which it is profitable to apply the notion of rules to an analysis of emotional phenomena.

References

Averill, J. R. (1974). An analysis of psychophysiological symbolism and its influence on theories of emotion. *Journal for the Theory of Social Behavior, 4,* 147-190.

Averill, J. R. (1976). Emotion and anxiety: Sociocultural, biological, and psychological determinants. In M. Zuckerman & C. D. Spielberger (Eds.), *Emotion and anxiety: New concepts, methods, and applications.* New York: John Wiley.

Averill, J. R. (1980a). A constructivist view of emotion. In R. Plutchik & H. Kellerman (Eds.), *Theories of emotion.* New York: Academic Press.

Averill, J. R. (1980b). On the paucity of positive emotions. In K. R. Blankstein, R. Pliner, & J. Polivy (Eds.), *Assessment and modification of emotional behavior.* New York: Plenum.

Averill, J. R. (1982). *Anger and aggression: An essay on emotion.* New York: Springer-Verlag.

Bateson, G. (1976). Some components of socialization for trance. In T. Schwartz (Ed.), *Socialization as cultural communication.* Berkeley: University of California Press.

Campbell, D. T. (1975). On the conflicts between biological and social evolution and between psychology and moral traditions. *American Psychologist, 30,* 1103-1126

Colby, K. M. (1981). Modeling a paranoid mind [article with open peer review]. *Behavioral and Brain Sciences, 4,* 515-560.

Ekman, P., & Friesen, W. V. (1975). *Unmasking the face.* Englewood Cliffs, NJ: Prentice-Hall.

Elias, N. (1978). *The civilizing process: The development of manners* (E. Lephcott, Trans.). New York: Urizen Books. (Original work published 1939)

Ervin-Tripp, S. (1978) Is second language learning like the first? In E. M. Hatch (Ed.), *Second language acquisition.* Rowley, MA: Newburg House.

Gandhi, M. (1958). *All men are brothers.* New York: Columbia University Press.

Gergen, K. J. (1982). *Toward transformation in social knowledge.* New York: Springer-Verlag.

Glennon, L. M. (1979). *Women and dualism.* New York: Longman.

Goldfried, M. R. (1980). Psychotherapy as coping skills training. In M. J. Mahoney (Ed.), *Psychotherapy process.* New York: Plenum.

Gould, S. J. *Ontongeny and phylogeny.* Cambridge: Harvard University Press, 1977.

Izard, C. E. (1977). *Human emotions.* New York: Plenum.

Kay, K. (1982) Organism, apprentice, and person. In E. Z. Tronick (Ed.), *Social interchange in infancy: Affect, cognition, and communication.* Baltimore: University Park Press.

Lenneberg, E. H. (1967). *Biological foundations of language.* New York: John Wiley.

Lucas, R. A. (1969). *Men in crisis: A study of a mine disaster.* New York: Basic Books.

Meichenbaum, D. (1977). *Cognitive-behavior modification: An integrative approach.* New York: Plenum.

Montagu, A. (1981). *Growing young.* New York: McGraw-Hill.

Murphy, H. B. M. (1973). History and the evolution of syndromes: The striking case of *Latah* and *Amok*. *Psychopathology: Contributions from the social, behavioral, and biological sciences.* New York: John Wiley.

Neufeld, G. (1979). Towards a theory of language learning ability. *Language Learning, 29,* 227-241.

Nisbett, R. E., & Ross, L. (1980). *Human inference: Strategies and shortcomings of social judgment.* Englewood Cliffs, NJ: Prentice-Hall.

Shotter, J. (1976). Acquired powers: The transformation of natural into personal powers. In R. Harré (Ed.). *Personality.* Tutowa, NJ: Rowman and Littlefield.

Taylor, S. E. (1982). Social cognition and health. *Personality and Social Psychology Bulletin, 8,* 549-562.

Toch, H. (1969). *Violent men.* Chicago: Aldine.

Tomkins, S. S. (1979). Script theory: Differential magnification of affects. In H. E. Howe & R. A. Dienstbier (Eds.), *Nebraska symposium on motivation 1978* (Vol. 26). Lincoln: University of Nebraska Press.

Tomkins, S. S. (1981). The quest for primary motives: Biography and autobiography of an idea. *Journal of Personality and Social Psychology, 41,* 306-329.

Trevarthen, C. (1979) Communication and cooperation in early infants: A description of primary intersubjectivity. In M. Bullows (Ed.), *Before speech: The beginning of interpersonal communication.* Cambridge: Cambridge University Press.

van Wulfften Palthe, P. M. (1936). Psychiatry and neurology in the tropics. In C. D. deLanjen & A. Lichtenstein (Eds.), *A clinical textbook of tropical medicine.* Amsterdam: G. Kolff.

3

Development and the Full Range of Emotional Experience

JOSEPH DE RIVERA

How may we describe adult development? Either we may attempt to describe what happens to most persons as they grow older, or we may attempt to describe the progress of persons relative to some ideal, as when we say that some persons have achieved a higher degree of development than others (cf. Kaplan, 1983). For the most part, this chapter concentrates on the latter type of description.

While different cultures may have different ideals, our own society shares a certain consensus about ideal adult development. This consensus is reflected by our theorists: Both Werner (1940) and Lewin (1951) stress that development involves two separate processes — increased differentiation and increased integration or unity. Similarly, Angyal (1941) notes that two distinct developmental trends may be observed: On the one hand, as persons develop they become more autonomous (more separate and capable of independent action), on the other hand they become more homonomous (tending to join with others and be more capable of interdependence). In a related vein, Becker (1968) describes the ideally developed society as one that permits a maximum of individuality at the same time as it fosters a maximum of community.

Both Angyal and Becker also agree about one other important aspect of development — that there is an increased tendency to want one's life to be meaningful. However, it is not clear how this spiritual dimension is related to the first two aspects of development. Might a person's desire for meaning be satisfied by the development of autonomous activity or by becoming a part of a larger whole, or does this development require a complete transcendence of the self?

There also seems to be at least some agreement on the relative value of different emotional relationships. Certainly mutual love is valued more than "hostile integration" (Pearce and Newton, 1969); and probably most persons, at least in our culture, would agree that a fully developed adult would ideally have the capacity to be able to be alone yet also able to commit the self to a relationship with an other, to be responsive yet also assertive, to have ideals yet operate with realism, to creatively exercise abilities, to have attained enough spiritual development so that he or she has a genuine concern for others that outweighs egocentric biases. Most might even agree in principle with Ghandi's articulation of the relative merits of the different stances that an oppressed person may take towards an oppressor. That is, the most highly developed response would involve an assertion of one's freedom while at the same time loving and respecting the oppressor. Yet, aggressive action (taken with some sense of one's inherent dignity) would be preferable to passivity and a sense of worthlessness.

However, while there may be some agreement about the nature of ideal adult development and ideal emotional relationship, it is not at all clear what role emotions play in such development. Some theorists view emotions as disorganizing, primitive, and an inferior alternative to action; others see emotion as biologically functional or as having a cognitive component that is useful in revealing what is valuable; still others suggest that some emotions may aid and some hinder development. A case can be made for all of these positions, contradictory though they may seem. In this chapter, we shall attempt to use the structural theory of emotions (de Rivera, 1977) to integrate these different positions, to clarify what role emotions may play in development, and to suggest what emotional developments may be ideal. To orient the reader, we may anticipate our conclusions as follows:

According to the structural theory, persons are always in some emotional relationship with others. The "choice" of *which* particular relationship is critical. If the emotion that is chosen fits the person's actual circumstances then development will occur; if it does not then development will be retarded. As any particular emotion may be useful in certain circumstances, it follows that it is desirable for a person to have as wide an emotional range as possible.

The Structural Theory and the Definition of Emotional Range

The structural theory of the emotions asserts that each of the hundreds of emotions that are named in the various languages that humans have created has a unique set of very specific interdependent properties — a structure. Yet each of these many different ways of being affected may also be understood to be a "choice" about how the structure of personal relationship is to be transformed.

The Structure of an Emotion

In one sense, all emotions have the same structure. Each involves a set of three interrelated parts that give the emotion its unique properties and function together to transform the person's way of being. These aspects of any emotion involve the particular way in which the emotion transforms the person's perception of the situation, the specific way in which the body is changed, and the stance that the person is "instructed" to take (experienced as the "impulse" of the emotion).

The perceptual aspect of emotion is "transactional" in Ames's (1951) sense of the term. That is, it would be incorrect to say that a situation causes an emotion or that an emotion causes a perception of the situation. Rather the person's situation is always interpreted by some emotion (and conversely, some emotion always affects how the person perceives his or her situation). Thus, a person who is living the emotion of anger inevitably perceives the other to be challenging what the person asserts ought to exist. In actuality, the other may not be challenging the person's values but is mistakenly perceived as challenging. Conversely, an other may be challenging the person's values, yet the person will not become angry unless they perceive a challenge to what they assert ought to exist.

The "body" that is changed by emotion has been described by Merleau-Ponte (1962) as the "body subject." This is the body that behaves, the body to which we refer when we say that a skilled draftsman or pianist is "thinking with his or her fingers," the body that is more relaxed at home because "it" knows its way around. It is not the objectified body of physiology whose blood pressure goes up in some cases of anger and down in others (Ax, 1953) but the lived body that "bursts forth" when a person becomes angry (Stevick, 1971) and becomes "charged with energy" (as the term is used in acupuncture rather than thermodynamics) in response to a perceived challenge.

The emotion's "instruction" motivates the person towards a specific stance of action. Thus, anger's instruction — remove the challenge — impells the person toward some tone, gesture, or behavior that "expresses" the anger and attempts to remove the challenge. Of course, this expression may be resisted or masked. But this particular impulse is inevitably present in all cases of anger.

Note that the three aspects of an emotion are interwoven and functional. In the case of anger, the impulse to remove is made possible by the bursting body and is directed at the challenge that is perceived. The parts function together in an attempt to preserve what the person values — to remove the challenge to these values.

There are over two hundred distinguishable emotional states named in the English language, and many others are referred to in other languages. These are not arbitrary or unimportant distinctions. In every case we have examined, it has been possible to determine a unique set of properties — the threee parts of a structure with a unique function. For example, Lindsay-Hartz (1981) has shown that persons can reliably distinguish the aspects of emotions as closely related as gladness, elation, and joy. Thus, in the emotion we call gladness, the person perceives the situation as one in which a hope has been fulfilled, the body is changed so that the world appears brighter, and the person has an impulse to welcome the event that has occured. Whereas, in the emotion we call elation the person perceives that a wish has been fulfilled, the body is experienced as "up" and ungrounded (a "high"), and the person has an impulse to announce to others the wonderful thing that has happened. To comprehend the way in which these emotions function, one must understand the difference between hoping and wishing (cf. Marcel, 1967). The former is grounded in that the person believes the fulfillment of the hope is a real possibility. However, this fulfillment is dependent on something other than the self. Hence, there is always the possibility that the hope will not be fulfilled. The latter is ungrounded — in fact, it is in the realm of fantasy and is not really anticipated. The emotion of gladness leads a person to welcome an event that may be taken to be a fulfillment of the hope. It thereby functions to reinforce the possibility of the person's depending on something other than the self. The emotion of elation leads a person to publically announce what has happened, and thereby functions to help the person change a private fantasy into a public reality. Ecstasy, euphoria, exaltation, and so on, each have a specific set of properties with unique interpersonal functions.

Emotions as Transformations of an Interpersonal Structure

In spite of the unique specificity of the three aspects of each emotion, any emotion can be understood as one of the possible transformations of a single structure. This structure is a dyadic one. The dyad consists of the person who is living the emotion and an "other" who is either the explicit object of the emotion or an implicit subject. In the former case, the emotion appears to be directed at the other (e.g., tenderness, anger, fear, longing, and other "it" emotions that appear to focus on an object). In the latter case the self appears as the object of the emotion (e.g., serenity, depression, anxiety, confidence, and other "me" emotions). The transformation inherent in each emotion — the specific changes in perception, bodily state, and impulse — can all be derived from the transformation of the relationship between the person and the other in the dyad.

The dyadic relationship is constantly being transformed in an attempt to maximize what is valuable for the dyad as circumstances change. The transformations associated with "it" emotions occur when the person perceives the other to change value, and moves closer (in the case of positive value) or increases distance (in the case of negative value). The transformations associated with "me" emotions occur when the person perceives that the self has changed value and the (implicit) other moves toward or away from the self.

The transformations cf the relationship and "movement" of the emotion may be further specified by distinguishing other characteristics of value. Values may either be relative to a particular self or absolute. In the former case a person values what is good for the self and devalues what is bad for the self. In the latter case, goodness or badness is experienced as absolute — true for all selves. In Heider's (1958) terms, it is what a supraordinate other wants.

In the case of relative value, the person transforms the relationship to pull the valued other and the self together into a unit (as in emotions such as desire) or to pull the self back from the devalued other (as in fear). When the person experiences the self as valuable to the other there is an implicit convenant and an emotion such as confidence is experienced. When the self is devalued as bad for the other the implicit other pulls back and anxiety (or some related emotion) is experienced.

In the case of absolute value, the person transforms the relationship to extend the self to the other who is experienced as good in his or her own right (and an emotion such as love is experienced). If the other is "bad" — challenges what the person asserts *ought* to exist — the other is thrust away (as in emotions such as anger). Correspondingly, if the self

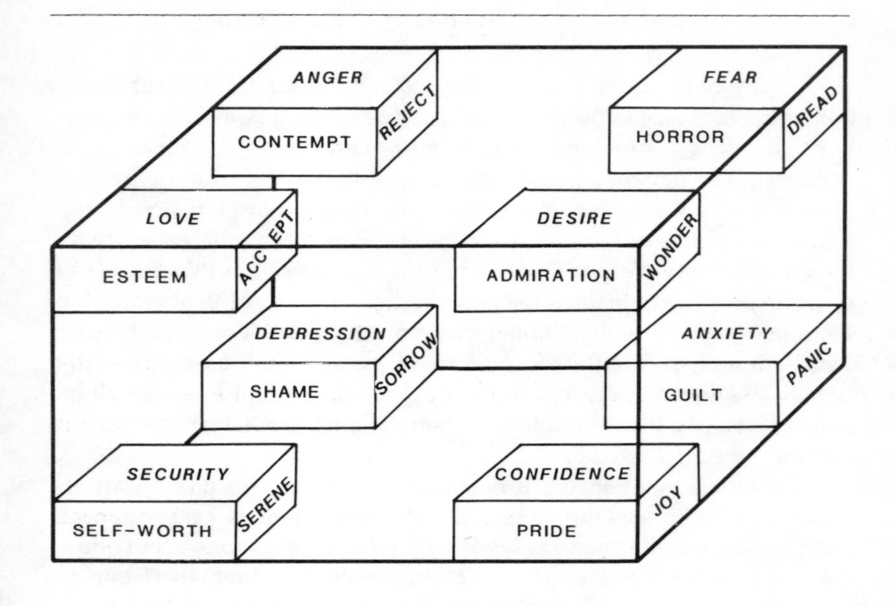

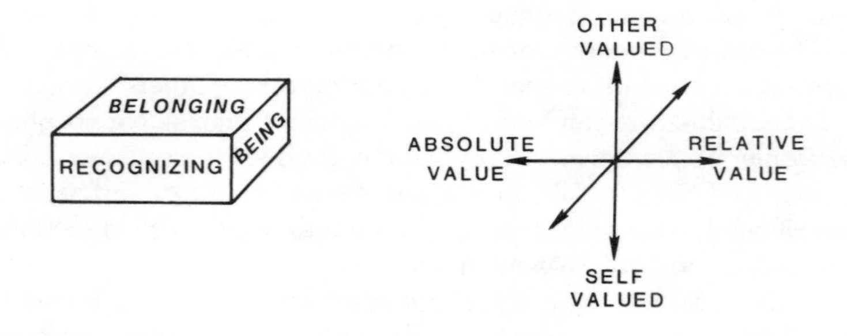

Figure 3.1 Matrix of Emotions

is experienced as absolutely good or bad in its own right, the implicit other moves toward the self or thrusts the self away and the person experiences emotions such as security or depression.

The transformations of the dyad may be further distinguished by articulating three different aspects of relationship: belonging, recognition, and being. A description of these aspects and other possible dimensions of relationship may be found in de Rivera (1977). It seems possible to describe all the different emotions in terms of the different possible transformations of the dyadic structure and to relate the function of each emotion to the enhancement of the values held by the person and the other who constitute the dyad. The different transformations described by the various dimensions of value constitute a matrix that describes 24 different emotions, as is shown in Figure 3.1

Figure 3.1 illustrates how a wide range of emotions may be understood to be the different transformations of value in the self-other dyad. It is interesting to observe that the 12 emotions on the bottom of the matrix may be regarded as mirror images of the 12 emotions directly above them. That is, we may regard security as a sort of mirror of love — the secure person feels loved by others. Likewise, the guilty person believes he or she has done something that is an object of horror. Depression occurs when the self is experienced as bad — as violating values and, hence, as the object of anger, and so on.

The Definition of Emotional Range

It seems clear that emotions are concerned with the perception of value and consequently, should be involved with cognitions about one's situation or action. In fact, Sommers (1981) has demonstrated that there is a positive relationship between the number of distinct emotion terms used by a person and the cognitive complexity of their social descriptions. She created the concept of "emotional range" and suggested that it might be an important personality variable. Person's with wider emotional ranges should have a more developed cognitive organization and a more structured value system.

Using the structural theory, we may offer a precise specification of emotional range. We are not limited to a consideration of only those emotions that invoke bodily disturbance or only those emotions that have clear facial expressions; nor do we have to include states such as hunger or sleep. Rather, we define emotion as any possible transformation of the self-other dyad. The range of emotional experience may then be defined by all the possible variations of the matrix that specify these transformations.

While the matrix presented in Figure 3.1 does not define all possible transformations, it specifies the major varieties; and it is possible to see how most other emotions can be related to positions on the matrix. Thus, ecstasy, elation, euphoria, and exaltation all seem related to each other and to the position that defines joy. Of course, the distinctions between the emotions involve important transmutations of the movement with the implicit other. Thus, while the person who experiences joy remains fully grounded as he or she experiences the presence of the other, the elated person is lifted and loses contact with the others, and the exalted person is elevated but remains in contact with the applauding audience. Still, the emotions can clearly be related to the matrix, as can many others.

Because it seemed possible to define emotional range by referring to the matrix, we made up a list of common emotion names and attempted to refer each of them to the matrix. We planned to use the list in interviews, both as a means of reminding persons of the full range of emotional life and as a way of inquiring into which emotions they felt comfortable in experiencing. However, in making up the list we came across a set of names that could easily be related to the first three variables of the matrix but not to any of the three aspects of relationship that had been articulated (belonging, recognition, and being). These terms did not easily fit next to any of the 24 emotion names in the matrix and were, therefore, included as a separate block of terms. Whether they can be regarded as transformations of a fourth aspect of relationship remains to be established.

The resulting list of 80 common emotion names is given in Table 3.1. The 40 names in the left column refer to "it" emotions, which are directed at transforming the relationship with the other; the 40 on the right refer to "me" emotions, which are directed at transforming the self. The top two rows of each of the eight blocks of words refer to 40 "negative" emotions concerned with increasing distance; the bottom two rows refer to 40 "positive" emotions concerned with descreasing distance. The top two blocks of names refer to the "belonging" emotions; the next two blocks to the "recognition" emotions (which influence social identity); the fifth and sixth blocks to the "being" emotions; and the bottom two blocks to the set of names that could be placed on the first three variables but were not obviously related to the three articulated aspects of relationships.

While the list is by no means exhaustive we can be sure that it defines the idea of emotional range in a systematic way, spreading a net that is wide enough to capture the main varieties of emotion.

Of course, emotion is only one aspect of emotional life. One thinks, for example, of a person's energy, strength, fortitude, determination, and courage, of sensitivity and the ability to empathize, of the capacity for loyalty and forgiveness, and the extent to which a person has curiosity and a sense of humor. However, all these emotional qualities depend on a person's ability to experience emotions. Thus, determination depends on the development of confidence that enables one to try; courage depends on the ability to face fear; sensitivity and empathy depend on the capacity to sympathize and the security necessary to explore the reality of others; loyalty and forgiveness depend on the extent of one's love and devotion; curiosity depends on wonder and fascination; and humor depends on amusement. Hence, Table 3.1

TABLE 3.1 The Range of Emotions

anger, irritation, rage	depression, helpless, discouraged, sad
fear, terror	anxiety, upset
desire, longing, liking	confidence, courage
love, affection, devotion, tenderness	secure
contempt, disgust	shame, embarrassed
horror, appalled	guilt, worthless
admiration	pride, satisfaction
esteem, respect, reverence	self-worth, goodness
rejection, dislike, hate, resentment	sorrow, hurt, lonely, despair
dread	panic
wonder, awe, fascination	joy, gladness, elation
acceptance, appreciation, gratitude	serenity, relief, hope
indifferent, uncaring	apathetic, bored
suspicious, jealous, envious	frustrated, disappointed, disinterest
trusting, faith	eager, excited, enthusiastic
sympathetic, compassion	content, cheerful, happy

provides us with a systematic way of assessing the critical elements, if not the critical compounds, of emotional life.

The Concept of Affective "Choice"

We have already alluded to the fact that every emotion invokes an interpretation of the person's situation. This implies that the emotion is not caused by external factors but involves a transaction between the person and the situation, the person actively makes sense of the situation. Then, too, the fact that we can organize the emotions in a matrix — that they are alternative transformations of a single relationship — suggests that one may "choose" one emotion or another. Finally, the possibility for a person to "own" an emotion — accept responsibility for the fact that he or she is experiencing a given emotion — implies that one chooses an emotion in the sense that one is interpreting the situation that is being lived and that this interpretation may or may not be justified or desirable. The structural theory postulates that a person is always in some emotional state and that there are inevitable consequences to this emotional "choice." To the extent that a person understands these consequences and develops the capacity to allow whatever emotion is required by his or her situation, the person extends his or her emotional range and becomes more fully developed as a person.

The "choices" that underlie emotions according to the structural theory, may be contrasted both with the view that emotions are "reactions" caused by physiological states (and/or environmental stimuli) and with the view that emotional behavior entails a "decision" to enact a social role. In regards to the former view, there are clear instances when emotion, or something very similar to emotion (such as the mood swings of a manic-depressive disorder), appear to be a nonadaptive reaction determined by some physiological or biochemical anomaly. In such cases, it may be important for a person to *not* accept responsibility for the emotion but, rather, to understand that his or her depression, euphoria, anger, and the like is an ego-alien imposition that is caused by external factors, an imposition that should be coped with in much the same manner as a broken arm or a case of measles. The extent to which these anomolies operate is unclear, as is the manner in which they mimic real emotions. We do know that once the person understands that his feelings are *caused* (by a drug, a brain abnormality, etc.) and, hence, that he or she is not responsible, the feelings no longer have the same emotional status and are much easier to cope with.

In regards to the view of emotional behavior as involving decisions to enact a social role, it is certainly true that one may decide to act *as though* one has an emotion and that one may encourage or discourage the presence of an emotion by behaving as though one has or does not have the emotion. Further, one may decide to place one's self in a situation where a given emotion is likely or unlikely to occur, or decide to avoid such a situation. And one may decide to express or mask the expression of an emotion that is already present. However, we are not referring to such conscious decisions when we speak of affective "choice." Rather, we are referring to a more primative and often non-conscious selection of one's stance toward the other. While this more primative selection can be influenced by the conscious decisions described above, the structural theory assumes that it is this underlying "choice" of how to relate to the other that determines a person's actual emotional state.

Allowing and Denying Emotion

Although a person cannot really *decide* which emotion to "choose" (this would be an act of will rather than being moved by emotion), he or she may develop the capacity to *allow* whatever emotion is required by the situation and to develop an acceptible way of expressing the emotion. The idea that a person may "allow" (or "deny") an emotion does not simply refer to whether the person feels the emotion but to whether he or she permits the particular "choice" to occur. That is, persons can structure their relationships and behavior in ways that will allow or discourage the occurance of particular emotions. For example, if a person does not want to experience anger he or she may simply avoid making assertions about what ought to be and adopt an accepting attitude. Or a person may assert what ought to be but create a "distance" between the self and any other who might appear to challenge the assertion. Thus, if the other is perceived as "only" a child, or a foreigner, or insane, the other does not have the status to have their behavior really be a challenge to what the person asserts ought to exist; hence, the person need not get angry. Either prejudice or separation creates a distance that obviates the need for anger. If circumstances prevent "distancing" (perhaps the person's family demands closeness), then the person can preserve closeness *and* his or her values by perceiving the self as responsible for the challenge to what ought to exist — thereby "choosing" to experience the emotion of depression.

A knowledge of the particular structure of a given emotion may help us to both comprehend its function and understand why and how it might be denied. Consider the example of elation. When a person suddenly apprehends that a wish has come true he or she cannot at first believe that this is so. There is a momentary questioning: "Did I really get the award?" "Is my lover really back?" "Is it really so?" The bodily component of elation lifts the person up into the realm of fantasy where wishing occurs (cf. Lewin, 1935). This "lifting" is not an idle metaphor. Thus, Wapner, Werner, and Krus (1957) have demonstrated that students who found they had received A's on an exam set a horizon line several inches higher than those with low marks. Once the person is up on the level of fantasy he or she believes the wish has come true (for in fantasy wishes can come true) and this releases the emotion's impulse to announce the wonderful news to everyone else. This begins to ground the event in social reality. The reaction of others confirms the fact that the person really did get the award, really does have their love, really is a successful playwright, and so on. Thus, the emotion has functioned to enable the person to *realize* a wish, to actually be in a different position than he or she was before.

Unfortunately, there is a shadow side to elation (and perhaps to all emotions). When the person is "up," he or she is also ungrounded and out of contact with others (cf. Jager, 1971). The person is unbalanced, there is a peculiar grin on the face and the person is so busy announcing the wonderful news that he or she does not want to listen to others. While some persons enjoy this "high" and welcome it as a restorative respite (or use it as an escape), others are afraid of the unbalance or feel guilty over the loss of contact with others and the irresponsibility inherent in the state. These latter do not allow themselves the emotion of elation. They prevent it by a very simple maneuver: They never make wishes! This successfully eliminates the emotion and its unwanted loss of grounding, but the solution is at the expense of the person's fantasy life. The emotional range has been slightly decreased.

Selection of the "Correct" Emotion

According to the structural theory persons are always in some emotional state — some relationship with the other. Because one aspect of every emotion is a particular perception of one's situation, whatever emotional state the person is in helps give meaning to whatever situation the person confronts. And as all emotions include bodily changes and "instructions" about how to behave, the emotion ideally functions to help the person create an adequate response to his or her situation. Unfortunately, because all emotion involves an interpretation of one's situation it is quite possible for a misinterpretation to occur. That is, the emotional state may or may not be called for by the actual situation that the person confronts; the person may or may not "choose" the correct emotion.

When a person's situation calls for the use of an emotion that the person does not allow, the person is unable to respond correctly and there are unfortunate consequences. This is true even when "negative" emotions are involved. A poignant literary example is portrayed in Brecht's one act play *The Jewish Wife* (1965). The heroine senses that her Aryan husband is beginning to lose his affection for her because of the antisemitism of the new Nazi regime. He refuses to let himself realize what is happening and she exclaims, "If only he could let himself feel the shame of letting someone else tell him whom he should marry." In the play the denial of this shame leads to the destruction of their relationship and the degeneration of the husband.

On the other hand, an emotion may be misused. For example, a high school senior, an only child who was dependent on her parents for emotional and financial support, was seen walking with a young man whom the parents disapproved. In actuality, the meeting between the young woman and man was unpremeditated but the parents were convinced that their daughter was cheating on them. When she protested her innocence they became terribly upset and withdrew, insisting that she was lying. The daughter met this situation by becoming guilty. That is, she accepted responsibility for the horrible thing that had occured, felt as if she were bad, and sought forgiveness (cf. Lindsay-Hartz, 1984). She used the emotion of guilt to defend against the anxiety of separating from her parents, or as an alternative to the anger necessary to confront them. The latter emotions, which would have been more in accord with the "reality" of the situation, evidently were not used because of the extent of her dependency and the absence of outside support.

There are a number of factors that work to distort emotional choice. First, most persons learn to deny certain emotions. If a child is rejected for exhibiting anger, affection, hate or any other emotion, the child learns to eliminate that emotion from his or her reportoire. Consequently, the person never learns how to handle the emotion by creating a socially acceptable expression and he or she continues to deny the emotion as an adult. Many adults never learn to feel at ease with emotions like anger and are reduced to tears from being upset; and a surprising number find it difficult to allow affection or even happiness (which may trigger guilt unless it is denied).

Second, most persons like to encourage and hold on to pleasant feelings. If an enjoyable situation changes and calls for action that would lead to a "negative" emotion, persons tend to want to hold on to the previous situation and, hence, resist the required restructuring. Thus, they lose contact with the reality of their situation and begin to live out a fantasy. When the fantasy is ruptured the person may be overwhelmed by the negative emotions that ensue, experiencing them as out of control and having little to do with the situation. Thus, if one's lover behaves in a way that reveals the possession of a different set of values than the person requires if intimacy is to continue, one may deny the problem rather than allow the anger and sorrow that the circumstances require. Ultimately, the person will be disillusioned, but then the person will have lost the chance to control the situation and may perceive the self as abandoned — experiencing the emotion of worthlessness. In fact, the reality of the new situation demands a separation and growth that requires the emotions of sorrow and faith.

Third, most persons like to avoid the unpleasantness that may accompany "negative" emotions and the vulnerability required by their acknowledgment and expression. Hence, they will often "choose" a less painful, less risky emotion, thereby misconstruing the nature of their situation. Thus, if a person feels more comfortable with anger than anxiety, he or she may substitute the emotion of anger (with its accompanying perception that someone else should take responsibility) for the emotion of anxiety (with its perception that the self must take responsibility) in spite of the fact that the person's actual situation may require the emotion of anxiety.

From the perspective of the structural theory there are no good or bad types of emotion. Both "positive" and "negative" can be misused or not used when they should be. In order to increase the probability of correct emotional choice it would seem desirable to increase a person's access to his or her emotions, so that the person may allow whatever emotion is called for by the circumstances. Theoretically, this should increase responsiveness and sensitivity and should decrease the chance of getting stuck in one emotion because of the unavailability of another emotion that is required by the situation. Such availability should be increased whenever a previously denied emotion is accepted by significant others and whenever a person is enabled to create socially acceptable expressions for an emotion. It may also be possible to facilitate correct emotional choice by practices, such as meditation, that cultivate a "letting go" as opposed to an "identification with" emotional states.

The Influence of Early Development and Culture

It seems possible that early emotional choices may establish the emotional underpinings for a person's general apprehension of life. Thus Macmurray (1957) has argued that when a child is weaned, he or she is faced with an apparent withdrawal of love. Under these circumstances, the child must choose to respond with either fear or love (perhaps "faith" would be a better term). To the extent that fear is chosen the child will perceive either that one must be out for oneself or that one must try to be "good" so that one will again be loveable. These attitudes later lead to certain social philosophies — the former to Hobb's view of the state, the latter to the idealism of Rouseau or Marx. To the extent that love is chosen, the child will perceive that one is worthwhile as one is and that one can safely care for others. This enables a social philosophy that stresses the give and take of community life.

While Macmurray describes the initial choice between love and fear as a response to the situation of weaning, he clearly views this choice as a recurrent one that all persons make repeatedly in their daily lives. However, it may be that some emotional states are experienced only by persons who have received certain types of early parenting. Thus, Nisenbaum (1984) has described the structure of an extreme type of loneliness that seems to be primarily experienced by persons with problematic early mothering.

Just as different persons may structure their lives in a way that encourages or discourages certain emotions, different peoples structure their cultures in specific ways that expand or constrict segments of the emotional range. The Utku Eskimos discourage anger by cultivating acceptance and by disassociating themselves from any expression of anger (cf. Briggs, 1970). If an Utku trip is blocked by an unexpected snowstorm the Eskimo does not become frustrated or experience a challenge to what ought to be. The Utku simply accepts the fact of the snowstorm and builds an igloo. However, occasionally an Utku male will go out and beat his dogs with no apparent cause and no acknowledgment of feelings of anger. (Observing such behavior, we would presume that something occured that could not be accepted and that the consequent challenge to what ought to be resulted in an anger that could not be acknowledged and thus had to be displaced.)

Our own culture discourages the emotion of "amae," an emotion that is cultivated in Japan (cf. Doi, 1973). This emotion involves a perception of the other as benevolent, a softening of the body, and an impulse to presume on the other's benevolence — a sort of "take-care-of-me" dependence that is ordinarily held in contempt by independence-minded Americans. The emotion is avoided by teaching children to do things for themselves, to think for themselves, to be able to be by themselves, and the like. However (as with the Utku's anger), the American's amae sometimes exists in disguised forms (one thinks of the unspoken demands spouses place on one another).

The Role of Emotion in Adult Development

In the course of living their lives, some persons appear to attain a higher degree of development than others. How may we account for these differences? Applying the structural theory we may suggests one answer.

We do not exist by ourselves but are always in relationship to some other. The various emotions are transformations of this relationship and the entire emotional system appears to be designed to promote the values of this dyad. Thus, whatever emotion is experienced informs the person about the location of value, instructs him or her how to act to maximize value (or minimize disvalue), and transforms the person's relationship so that these instructions may be accomplished. These outcomes will necessarily promote development *if* the emotion correctly fits the person's real situation, but will necessarily retard development if the emotion does not fit.

Consider the examples discussed in the preceeding section of this chapter. If Brecht's hero had allowed the shame that was called for by his situation, he would have been motivated to change and thus development rather than disintegration would have occured. If the high school student had allowed herself to become angry rather than guilty when she was falsely accused she would have developed rather than postponed the separation from her parents. If the structural theory is correct, development will always be facilitated when a person chooses an emotion that fits his or her circumstances and will be retarded whenever the "wrong" emotion is chosen.

To some extent this means that development is independent of one's life circumstances, for either fortune or adversity, stability or transition, call for specific emotions and provide opportunities for growth or decay. However, the probability of a correct emotional choice should be enhanced when a person has a fully developed emotional range and this capacity for choice should expand under certain favorable conditions. These include the opportunity to be loved and respected, to have meaningful work, to receive encouragement and assistance in developing emotional expression, and the skills needed to "let go" of emotions that are not functional.

Some Preliminary Research

In some preliminary research (de Rivera, in preparation), 13 men and 23 women were interviewed about the role that emotions played in their lives. The sample included 14 young (19-21 years), 13 midlife (30-60), and 9 older (over 70) adults. In the course of the interview, each person was given the list of emotion names shown in Table 4.1 and asked to place a check beside each emotion that had been experienced in the last year and a double check by those played the most important role. Using the list proved helpful in stimulating persons to think of a wide range of emotions rather than simply those that were commonplace or evoked by current mood; and the groupings within the list seemed to encourage an examination of each term's meaning.

The interviews clearly demonstrated that by the time persons reach adulthood almost all are aware of many different emotions and the choice between keeping feelings to oneself by controlling behavior or permitting feelings to be expressed in one's behavior. Many discriminated between a public everday "presented" self (that masked feelings such as depression in order not to bother others, or masked feelings such as anger, envy, or embarrasment in order not to be rejected by others) and a private "real" self whose feelings were shared with intimate others. Even when they were with intimate others, a number of persons reported difficulty in expressing particular emotions. As might be expected, anger was frequently mentioned in this regard; but individuals also reported restraining enthusiasm and excitement, and some had difficulty in spontaneously expressing affection.

Some persons clearly experienced a great deal more emotion than others. For example, the responses to the list of emotion names ranged from 11 checked and 0 double checked (a 19-year-old male student who said emotions did not play a large role in his life) to all 80 checked and 33 double checked (a 49-year-old woman who described herself as very emotional). Age had no clear systematic effect on the number of emotions checked. While some older persons felt that their 70s (or 80s) was a less emotional period, others reported feeling more emotion. As adults matured, some reported getting more in touch with their emotions, gaining more control over their expression and becoming less upset by events that would have been difficult in the past. Also, several persons in their late 70s and 80s reported having less of a need to present the self to others. One unfortunate development appears to occur when aging persons who are not used to expressing their emotions have to cope with the loss of cohorts. In these circumstances, persons may believe that their situation cannot be understood by others. Such persons begin to express even less emotion and this appears to lead to a lessening of emotional experience. In general, it seemed clear that a person's life circumstances were much more important than chronological age in influencing the extent to which emotions pervaded life.

Persons were asked which emotions helped them to achieve their ideal self and which hindered this attainment, whether there were some emotions which they got "stuck in," and whether they felt drawn to some emotions and avoided others. Certain "positive" emotions were most frequently mentioned as helpful: the "me" emotions of faith, confidence, pride, and cheerfulness, and the "it" emotions of compassion, trust, love, and respect. And certain "negative" emotions were most frequently mentioned as a hindrance: the "me" emotions of helplessness, upset, hurt, and frustration, and the "it" emotions of contempt, disgust, and anger. However, there were instances where persons felt their love or trust was harmful and their anger was helpful. As one reads over the interviews it seems clear that any particular emotion might be useful or detrimental in particular circumstances. What seemed important in the attainment of ideal development were the following:

(1) The cultivation of positive emotions which are helpful to a person's circumstances (such as cheerfulness and compassion in a home for the aged).
(2) The ability to "let go" of either "positive" or "negative" emotions that are harmful in given circumstances (such as inopportune love, feelings of hurt, upset or jealousy).
(3) The ability to create useful expressions for "negative" emotions (such as anger) that could be helpful in some circumstances.

(4) The ability to respect but not get stuck in negative emotions such as depression.
(5) Learning to recognize and create a socially appropriate expression for whatever emotion is being experienced.

In conclusion, it would seem that there are no *necessary* emotional developments that accompany aging. Rather, as we age we have the opportunity to acquire the emotional range and wisdom that should, theoretically, help us develop towards our ideals. We may, however, persist in a relatively undeveloped state. Of course, at present we lack empirical evidence for the proposition that the choice of the "correct" emotion is a critical factor in development. The testing of this proposition would seem to be an important direction for future research.

References

Ames, A., Jr. (1951). Visual perception and the rotating trapezoidal window. *Psychological Monographs, 65* (7).

Angyal, A. (1941). *Foundations for a science of personality.* Cambridge, MA: Harvard University Press.

Ax, A. F. (1953). The psychological differentiation between fear and anger in humans. *Psychosomatic Medicine, 15,* 433-442.

Becker, E. (1976). *The structure of evil.* New York: The Free Press.

Brecht, B. (1965). The Jewish wife. In *The Jewish wife and other short plays* (Eric Bentley, Trans.). New York: Grove Press.

Briggs, J. L. *Never in anger.* Cambridge, MA: Harvard University Press.

de Rivera, J. (1977). *A structural theory of the emotions.* New York: International Universities Press.

Doi, T. (1973). *The anatomy of dependence* (J. Bester, Trans.). Tokyo: Kodanska.

Heider, F. (1958). *The psychology of interpersonal relations.* New York: John Wiley.

Jager, B. (1973). Horizontality and verticality: A phenomenological explanation. In A. Giorgi, W. F. Fischer, & R. VonEckartsberg (Eds.), *Duquesne studies in phenomenological psychology, Vol. 1* (pp. 212-235). New York: Humanities Press.

Kaplan, B. (1983). A trio of trials. In R. M. Lerner (Ed.), *Developmental psychology: Historical and philosophical perspectives,* pp. (185-228). Hillsdale, NJ: Lawrence Erlbaum.

Lewin, K. *Dynamic theory of personality.* New York: McGraw-Hill, 1935.

Lewin, K. (1951). Regression, retrogression, and development. In K. Lewin (Ed.), *Field theory in social science,* New York: Harper & Row.

Lindsay-Hartz, J. (1961). Elation, gladness, and joy. In J. de Rivera (Ed.), *Conceptual encounter: A method for the study of human experience.* Washington, DC: University Press of America.

Lindsay-Hartz, J. (1984). Shame and guilt. *American Behavioral Scientist, 27,* 6.

Macmurray, J. (1957). *Persons in relation.* New York: Harper & Brothers.

Marcel, G. (1967). Desire and hope. In N. Lawrence & D. O'Connor (Eds.), *Readings in existential phenomenology* (pp. 277-285). Englewood Cliffs, NJ Prentice-Hall.

Merleau-Ponte, M. (1962). *The phenomenology of perception.* New York: Humanities Press.

Nisenbaum, S. (1984). Varieties of aloneness. *American Behavioral Scientist, 27,* 6.

Pearce, J., & Newton, S. (1969). *The conditions of human growth.* New York: Citadel.

Stevick, E. L. (1973). The experience of anger. In A. Giorgi, W. F. Fischer, & R. VonEckartsberg (Eds.), *Duquesne studies in phenomenological psychology, Vol. 1.* New York: Humanities Press.

Sommers, S. (1981) Emotionality reconsidered: The role of cognition in emotional responsiveness. *Journal of Personality and Social Psychology, 41,* 553-561.

Wapner, S., Werner, H., & Krus, D. M. (1957). The effect of success and failure on space localization. *Journal of Personality, 25,* 752-756.

Werner, H. (1940). *The comparative psychology of mental development.* New York: Harper & Row.

EMOTION AND PSYCHOLOGICAL WELLBEING

There are four chapters in this volume that deal with psychological wellbeing. The first two, which provide critical summaries of the diverse studies that constitute the wellbeing research literature, are presented in the current section (Lawton, and Cohler and Boxer). Another chapter, by Costa and McCrae, is reserved for the section on personality and affect inasmuch as it links wellbeing to personality and selfhood. A fourth chapter by Felton and Shaver examines the wellbeing literature for cohort effects and is therefore included in the section on historical influences.

The literature on wellbeing is now old enough to have generated a lively heterogeneity of opinion regarding its parameters, as manifest in the four chapters presented in this volume. All agree that the relationship between wellbeing and aging is complex! In the present section, the chapters by Lawton and by Cohler and Boxer provide reviews of the literature that order it in unique ways. Lawton provides a critical integration of the diverse wellbeing literatures (including studies of morale, life satisfaction, mental health, and happiness) by showing that there are two primary factors in the wellbeing construct — interior wellbeing and exterior wellbeing — and that they have different determinants. He demonstrates that negative affect is better predicted by intrapersonal indices (such as functional health) than by external environmental transactions (such as time use or interaction with friends), and that the opposite pattern obtains for the predictors of positive affect. The chapter by Cohler and Boxer focuses on morale, mental health, and the nature and timing of life events and subsequent adjustment and coping strategies. They stress that perception of the life course is tied up with notions of the appropriateness of the timing of most life events and show that the timeliness or lack thereof of life events (that is, whether or not they are "on time" or dysynchronous) plays a role in determining wellbeing.

4

The Varieties of Wellbeing

M. POWELL LAWTON

In contrast to many of the topics that are explored for the first time in other chapters of this book, psychological wellbeing is a construct that has been seen as relevant to geronotology from its beginning. The present chapter attempts to use the earlier research findings on such diverse constructs as morale, life satisfaction, and mental health while organizing them within a framework that includes aspects of wellbeing other than psychological. Conclusions resulting from this critical integration of the literature include an emphasis on affect, as originally construed by Bradburn (1969), as a construct that may be differentiated from the other facets of psychological wellbeing. It will be plain from the scarcity of references to the affective experiences of older people how

AUTHOR'S NOTE: This chapter was presented as the Distinguished Contribution Award address, Division 20, presented at the annual meeting of the American Psychological Association, August 26, 1982, Washington DC. Research supported by grant MH 30665 from the National Institute of Mental Health. With minor changes, this chapter was reprinted from *Experimental Aging Research* 1983, Vol. 9, pp. 65-72, with the permission of the author and the editors. Copyright Beech Hill Publishing Company, 1983.

most of the basic research on emotions has bypassed the latter end of the life span.

One of the most basic dialectics is expressed by the term "person and environment," now a scholarly subdiscipline on its own but an implicit or explicit source of conceptual tension in virtually every view of human growth. Beginning with my modification (1982a) of Lewin's (1935) basic ecological equation $B = f(P, E, PXE)$, I shall discuss person and environment and the outcomes of their transactions — that is, behavioral competence and psychological wellbeing. In the process, other dualistic constructs such as positive versus negative life events, extraversive versus introversive personality types, origin versus pawn behavioral causality, and positive versus negative affect (Bradburn's two-factor conception of psychological wellbeing, 1969) will be discussed. The broadest intent of the discussion will be to explore further the external and internal determinants of psychological wellbeing and to show that these determinants will vary depending on which facet of wellbeing is being considered.

I have suggested that each of four sectors of human existence stands on its own as a defensible intrinsic personal and social goal: behavioral competence, perceived quality of life, psychological wellbeing, and the objective/external environment (1983). Wellbeing in one sector does not need to be justified in terms of its dependence on another sector. On the other hand, the four sectors are members of a total interacting system. The purely intrapersonal sector, consisting of what is commonly called "personality" and "self," must be added to the four sectors of the good life to complete the specification of the entire behavioral system. Even while recognizing the totally interdependent nature of all members of the system, for convenience I shall speak of the ultimate outcome as being represented by psychological wellbeing. Also, because both psychological wellbeing and perceived quality of life are evaluations that refer to the quality of inner experience, they may together be designated as "subjective wellbeing." As both objective environment and the external aspects of behavioral competence can be observed and evaluated by others, they may be thought of together as "objective wellbeing"

Dimensions of Subjects Wellbeing: State of the Art

Perceived quality of life is the set of evaluations that a person makes about each major domain of his or her current life. While the number and identity of such domains have not been definitely established, the number is relatively small and there probably would be high consensus among researchers that domains such as family life, friends, standard of living, leisure activities, and residential environment are domains salient to most people. The best-known research in this area has been by Andrews and Withey (1976), and Campbell, Converse, and Rodgers (1976). Their work has shown that evaluations of the quality of one's life in such domains are substantially related to the psychological wellbeing sector, the behavioral competence sector, and the objective environmental sectors. The more enthusiastic devotees of the perceived quality of life approach see such evaluations as a preferred kind of social indicator — preferred because each individual is seen as best capable of judging for himself, on the basis of his idiosyncratic needs and standards, the extent to which the important domains of life are satisfying. While there are many limitations on the validity of such judgments, a view of the good life would be incomplete without knowledge of such assessments. Age-specific analyses of these two (Andrews & Withey, 1976; Campbell et al., 1976) and other similar data sets have shown a tendency toward a higher level of satisfaction among the aged (Herzog & Rodgers, 1981a) but a similar factor structure across a wide age range (Herzog & Rodgers, 1981b). Confirmatory factor analyses done in the latter study suggested dimensions of satisfaction with health, income, residence, and social leisure time. In general, however, the individual domains treated separately have been most useful in assessing quality of life, particularly as used in needs assessment or program monitoring. A major research issue concerns the relationship between perceived quality of life and the objective environmental qualities that compose each domain of perceived quality (Campbell et al., 1976). This question has been addressed at some length elsewhere (Lawton, 1983) and will not be pursued here.

Psychological wellbeing, like perceived quality of life, reflects the quality of one's inner state and has both cognitive and affective components (Andrews & McKennell, 1980). However, psychological wellbeing is more global and less clearly tied to the separate domains of everyday life than is perceived quality of life. Psychological wellbeing is a subjective sense of overall satisfaction and positive mental health that is commonly thought to be the best indicator of unobservable constructs such as self-esteem or ego strength.

The relative conceptual neatness of the perceived quality of life sector is not repeated in the psychological wellbeing sector. Literature reviews have made clear the diversity in conceptions of psychological wellbeing (George & Bearon, 1980; Lawton, 1975; Lawton, 1982b) that have been advanced by researchers in this area. Such constructs go by many names. A recent review (Lawton, 1982b) suggests that there are four dimensions that recur in the research of different investigators;

these dimensions have been shown to be valid both in a discriminant sense and in their relationships with other outcomes:

(1) neuroticism or negative affect — a diverse group of dysphoric feelings such as anxiety, depression, agitation, worry, and so on (Bradburn, 1969; Lawton, 1977);
(2) positive affect — feelings of active pleasure, usually linked to a relatively short and recent period of time (Bradburn, 1969);
(3) congruence between desired and attained goals — only one of five dimensions posited to define life satisfaction, but the only one to show up consistently as different investigators have factored the Life Satisfaction Index of Neurgarten, Havighurst, and Tobin (1961); and
(4) happiness — traditionally measured using a single item (Bradburn, 1969; Lawton, 1977) although such a factor has also appeared in multiple item sets (Lawton & Kleban, 1982). Some research (Bradburn, 1969; Kozma & Stones, 1980) has suggested that happiness may itself be an outcome of the net of positive and negative affects.

The nongerontological history of psychometrics is constructed of attempts to determine the factorial dimensionality of the psychological wellbeing domain, ranging from approaches that include both symptoms of distress and personality characteristics (Cattell, 1950) to those emphasizing psychopathology (Ellsworth, 1957) and those that include both psychological wellbeing and perceived quality of life (Andrews & Withey, 1976). Some efforts have been made to determine the joint factor structure of instruments measuring psychological wellbeing among the elderly, as in Kozma and Stone's (1980) combination of the Affect Balance Scale (Bradburn, 1969), the Life Satisfaction Index (Neugarten et al., 1961) and the Philadelphia Geriatric Center Morale Scale (Lawton, 1975) or Morris, Wolf and Klerman's (1975) combination of the Philadelphia Geriatric Center Morale Scale and the Zung Depression Scale (1965). However, none have yet done such research using multiple items assembled so as to represent systematically each of any large number of presumed dimensions such as the four named above.

Testing Two Models of Wellbeing

Recent research done by Kleban and myself (1982) did make such an attempt. In addition to items representing the above four constructs and measures, the literature led us also to represent the following aspects of psychological wellbeing in an item pool designed to explore the dimensionality of psychological wellbeing: age-related morale, perceived cognitive functioning, denial, futurity, psychological symptoms, self-esteem, self-rated health, and social desirability. These additional domains were chosen to represent those previously used dimensions of wellbeing that we judged also to have some coherent construct validity. Notably absent from this collection are "morale" and "life satisfaction," constructs that we suggest are themselves multidimensional and therefore to that extent lacking in conceptual clarity. Our research dealt with subjective wellbeing as a whole and therefore also included items representing the following domains from the sector of perceived quality of life: residential satisfaction, quality of social relationships (family and friends separately), and perceived quality of time use.

Subjects were 285 older people from four groups putatively ordered in terms of their mental health. The first question was whether factor-analytic methods could reproduce the dimensions that constituted the input for the item pool. The overall answer was simple: They did not. Exactly what was produced requires a more complex answer. Exploratory factor analysis produced 13 principal factors, as named in Table 4.1. Two of the strongest factors plus two weaker ones reproduced the four replicated dimensions named above: Happiness and negative affect (strong) and positive affect and congruence (weaker). Also reproduced were denial (with some mixture of social desirability), self-rated health, and two perceived quality of life dimensions — residential satisfaction and perceived quality of time use. No factors resembling age-related morale, perceived cognitive functioning, futurity, psychophysiological symptoms, or perceived quality of family interaction or friends interaction were obtained. The Rosenberg Self Esteem Scale (1965) divided six of its items into two separate factors. Two minor factors named social ease and wish to move also appeared.

At this point, a few rational regroupings of items were made to provide greater face homogeneity for a few item clusters and to preserve the Bradburn Positive Affect Scale and the Rosenberg Scale in the interest of maintaining some comparability with other research resulting from their widespread use. Finally, despite their failure to be defined as psychometric clusters, items appearing to note psychophysiological symptoms, perceived quality of family interaction, and perceived quality of friends' interaction were grouped and used as separate scales because they are so uniformly considered usable constructs. Scores obtained by unit weighting items on these 14 groups of items were subjected to a principal-components analysis with orthogonal rotation, resulting in the second-order factor structure shown in Table 4.1 (loadings reflected where appropriate so as to give desirable characteristics a positive loading).

The first second-order factor seems to be the familiar subjective distress factor, led by negative affect but also including some dimensions viewed as close to the core of the personality, such as self-esteem

TABLE 4.1 Rotated Two-Factor Solution of Second-Order Component Analysis of Indices of Subjective Wellbeing

	I *Interior Wellbeing*	*II* *Exterior Wellbeing*
Negative affect	75	38
Psychophysiological symptoms	72	21
Expression/denial of negative affect	67	−02
Self-esteem	67	22
Self-rated health	62	38
Satisfaction with family	52	09
Congruence	51	04
Social anxiety	.51	10
Happiness	64	60
Residential satisfaction	13	70
Positive affect	24	61
Time use	31	60
Wish to move	−04	59
Satisfaction with friends	50	57

and congruence. The clusters composing the second factor force us to find a construct name to describe the high loadings on residential satisfaction, positive affect, perceived quality of time use, wish to move, and satisfaction with friends. This task is not difficult. Four domains are from the sector of perceived quality of life, that is, sources of satisfaction that lie outside oneself. The fifth positive affect is one of the domains that replicated findings have put in the psychological wellbeing domain. I shall argue that the seond-order factors can be called interior wellbeing and exterior wellbeing, respectively.

I have thus far deliberately omitted happiness, with its high and nearly equal loadings on both factors, from consideration. Happiness in fact links the two factors. The set of loadings in Table 4.1 represents a moderately accurate confirmation (in a totally different context) of Bradburn's (1969) classic findings that while positive affect and negative affect were both related to happiness, they were unrelated to each other — the two-factor conception of psychological wellbeing. Because of the solid replicability of the positive and negative affect factors and their relationship to happiness, one may look at these domains as "marker" variables in our present data around which other less well-replicated dimensions group. If factor 2 represents an outer focus for psychological wellbeing, factor 1 may be thought of as an inner focus for psychological wellbeing. Of course, the independence of the two factors is only partial and there are exceptions to the clear assignment of domains to the inner and the outer sector. For example, the negative affect and self-rated health factors also have minor loadings on exterior wellbeing. Satisfaction with friends, an exterior domain, carries a loading almost as high on interior wellbeing while satisfaction with family, certainly a domain of life outside the person, loads on interior but not on exterior wellbeing. Despite these deviations, however, the results do show some general conformity to the two-factor conception of psychological wellbeing advanced by Bradburn. The results of the first-order factor analysis also support the suggestion that a distinction between the sector of psychological wellbeing and the sector of perceived quality of life is meaningful in that there was almost no "crossing over" of any item designed as an indicator for one sector to a factor that represented the other sector (1 item out of the total of 89 did so).

If negative affect and positive affect constitute core indicators of two different kinds of experience, it then seemed useful to consider how these two factors of psychological wellbeing were related to a third sector of the good life — behavioral competence. (A more extended discussion of this relationship may be found in Lawton, 1983). A further word about this construct is in order. Competence is measurable in the domains of health, functional health (activities of daily living), cognition, time use, and social behavior (Lawton, 1972). An interview-based assessment instrument, the Philadelphia Geriatric Center Multilevel Assessment Instrument (MAI; Lawton, Moss, Fulcomer, & Kleban, 1982) was constructed to assess systematically behavioral competence in each of these domains. Competence is defined in objective and normative terms, that is, the assumption is made that quality of behavior in a domain can be arrayed in an order that by common consensus could be evaluated on a positive-to-negative continuum (Lawton, 1972). While I have asserted that "basic competence" is a quality that resides in the person, we have few indicators of such pure competence and perforce must lean on performance rather than competence as the source of our measurable indicators.

Because behavior is always conducted in some environmental context with its unique affordances and constraints, behavioral competence (performance) must be viewed as an outcome of the person-environment transaction. Nonetheless, the relative strength of personal versus environmental determinants of competent performance may vary. Thus it is possible to group types of behavioral competence into rough inner-determined and outer-determined subgroups. Functional health is more strongly determined by the inner person factor of biological health, while social behavior may be more contingent on the supply of environmental opportunities. Thus the theoretical assertion made above that the two aspects of psychological wellbeing were composed of elements that differ along a continuum of interior to exterior aspects

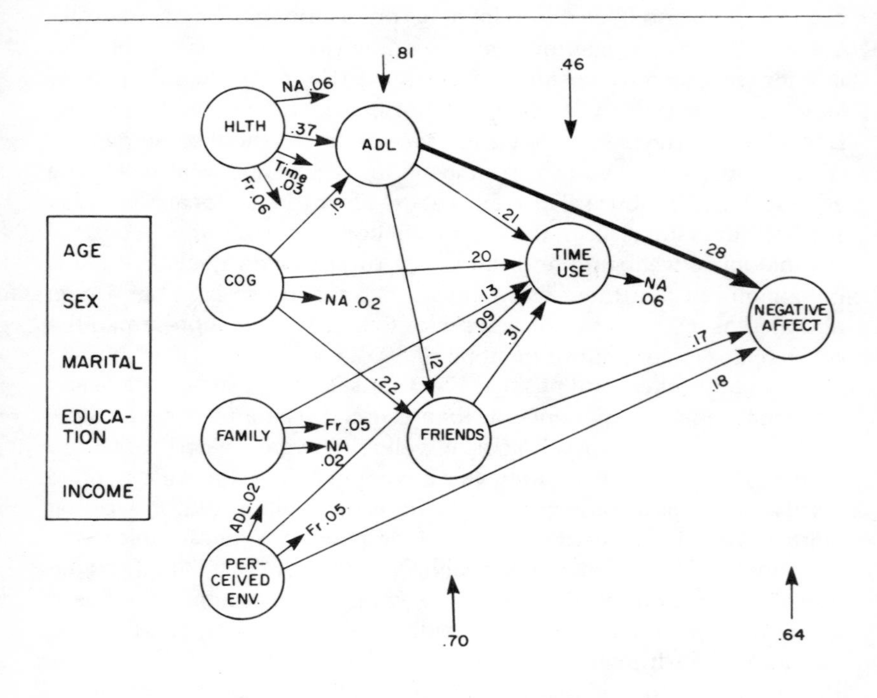

Figure 4.1 Path Model for Negative Affect

of experience is paralleled by the hypothesis that positive and negative affect are, in turn, differentially determined by interior and exterior aspects of behavioral competence. This general hypothesis was tested by path analyses in which four specific hypothesis were made: That physical and functional health, the two inner domains of behavioral competence that are most closely related to the self, would be most closely related to negative affect. The exterior aspects of behavioral competence more closely associated with environmental resources — that is, time use, family interaction, and friends' interaction — would be most closely related to positive affect (cognition was hypothesized to be unrelated to either domain of psychological wellbeing, while perceived environment was expected to be related to both).

Figures 1 and 2 show the results of a full path analysis, with nonsignificant paths indicated by short arrows and the hypothesized paths by heavy arrows. As usual, there was good news and bad news. As

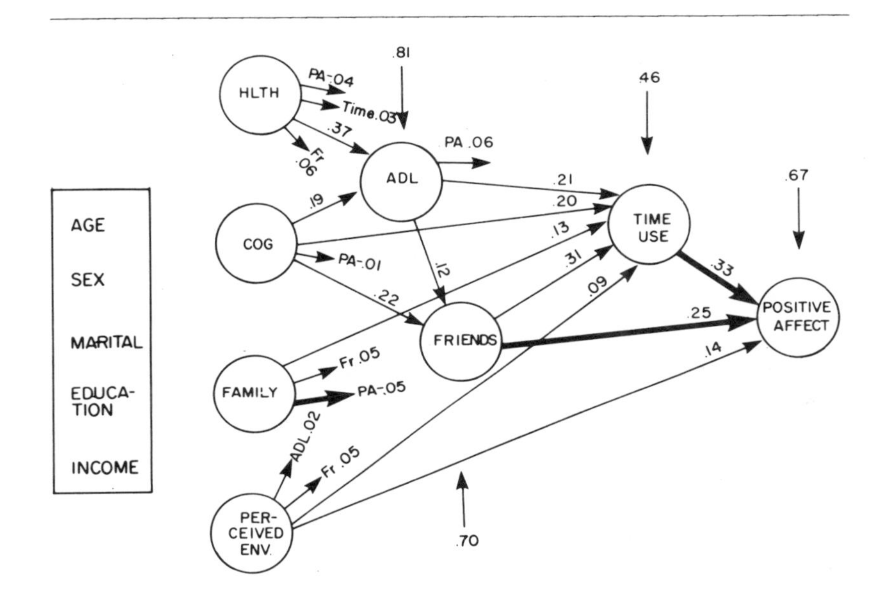

Figure 4.2 Path Model for Positive Affect

hypothesized, negative affect was predicted by functional health but not by family interaction or by time use. Counter to the hypothesis, a significant direct path was observed from friends' interaction to negative affect. Similarly, three of the four hypotheses regarding positive affect were confirmed: Time use and friends' interaction showed significant paths to positive affect, while health did not. Contrary to prediction, family interaction showed no direct path to positive affect.

A replication, with different indicators of the same independent variables (minus cognition and funtional health) was done in the 1975 *Myth and Reality of Aging* sample (National Council on the Aging, 1975; N = 2797). All of the hypotheses were confirmed with this larger and more representative data set with the exception that health did show a marginally significant (beta = .077) direct relationship to positive affect. Again, while the hypothesized mutual relationships were not perfectly confirmed, the suggested pattern seemed generally upheld. The strength of the findings is increased by replication across the data sets.

To recapitulate thus far, indicators of interior psychological wellbeing and exterior psychological wellbeing cluster separately, with the latter cluster showing a stronger link to social behaviors and perceived quality of life. In turn, classic indicators of these two clusters also appear to be differentially related in a hypothesized causal sequence to behavioral manifestations of inner and outer competence.

Life Events

Behavioral competence refers to the evaluated performance of the person in relation to inner or outer events. How about the events themselves? In my conception of the good life, life events along with "resources" (Carp, 1979) and other "environmental press" included in the ecological model proposed by Nahemow and myself (1973) belong in the sector that I refer to as "objective environment." Viewed more closely, however, events do not always logically belong in the category of the objective environment. In common parlance, "life events" include both those events that "happen" to a person (external or objective environment) and those to which the person's behavior contributes or causes (person-environment interaction). Two areas of inquiry are relevant to the present discussion, the differential effects of positive and negative events and of events ascribed to internal or external causes.

Positive and Negative Events

Considerable recent research (Dohrenwend, 1974; Zautra & Reich, 1980, in press) has been devoted to the differential effects of positive and negative events on psychological and somatic outcomes, as contrasted with the life-change hypothesis (Holmes and Rahe, 1967), which suggests that it is the amount of change per se rather than the positive or negative quality of the change that affects outcome. Thus for the present discussion it is relevant to inquire about whether events that vary in positive versus negative quality are differentially related to the inner and outer aspects of psychological wellbeing.

Zautra and Reich (in press) reviewed the complete body of research that differentiated between positive and negative events, dividing their review into effects on "psychiatric distress" (negative affect) and on "positive affect measures of wellbeing" (positive affect, pleasantness of daily events, and perceived quality of life). A highly regular pattern was found whereby negative events were virtually always related to the negative affect class of outcome and postive events to the positive affect class. Positive events were almost never related to negative affect, and negative events were related to positive affect in less than half the instances. These results suggest that negative events reach more deeply into the psychological interior of the person than do positive events. This conclusion is consistent with Kleban's and my findings that self-esteem and congruence, as well as psychological distress, loaded on the negative affect factor.

Before accepting this neat parallel between negative and positive events and affects, however, the neglected factor of time must be considered. It may be that the difference in the way positive and negative events affect wellbeing is partly a function of the relative time duration and permanence of the effects of the events that are commonly classified into the two categories. The ususal life events lists, especially those events relevant to the older person, are heavily loaded with events whose effects (often negative) can be presumed to be of long duration: retirement, bereavement, residential relocation, change in household structure, or illness of spouse. These phenomena hardly classify as "events." All of them involve long-term changes in self-perception, role, the expectations of others, and to some extent perceived quality of life. Positive events are often emphemeral. A search of some of the most frequently used events schedules for all ages (Holmes & Rahe, 1967; Lindenthal & Pepper, 1971; Sarason, Johnson, & Siegel, 1978) and the elderly (Kiyak, Liang, & Kahana, 1976) shows few age-relevant events that are unconfounded with outcome and at the same time are positive and have high probability of having long-term effects. Most negative events are losses whose long-term negative effects are known and predictable (some such events, of course, for example, retirement, a move, or the loss of a destructive personal relationship, may in fact be perceived positively). It is more difficult to be certain how enduring the effects of apparently positive events may be, for example, the marriage of a child or an increase in income. Thus it seems to me that before concluding that negative events bear an essential causal relationship to negative affect that is not shared in an opposite way by positive events, we must make certain by studying the effects of events of equal expected duration that we are comparing similar phenomena. Schulz (1982) has called our attention to the inverse relationship between the intensity and duration of affects and has related these variations to the locus of the effects of emotional expression. Further comparative study of "daily hassles" and "uplifts" (Kanner, Coyne, Schaefer, & Lazarus, 1981) that are more equal in duration and intensity is indicated.

With this reservation in mind, the relationships laid out by Zautra and Reich (in press) do seem to be consistent with Bradburn's two-factor theory of psychological wellbeing. Everyday, perhaps short-lasting, events based on the person's transactions with the external world can produce pleasant feelings that may or may not coexist with psychological outcomes on another dimension — the positive mental health to negative affect continuum suggested to vary with longer-duration states, especially those associated with negative events.

Personal Causation

A second dimension of events derives from their degree of external versus internal origin. DeCharms (1968) has named events in which the person participates as a causal agent "origin" events as contrasted with "pawn" events (those imposed externally). Zautra and Reich (1980, in press) found some "crossing over" of the effects of positive and negative events on the parallel domains of positive and negative affect when taking account of the origin-pawn distinction. That is, there were tendencies for positive events to be associated with negative affect when the events occurred gratuitously, without orgin behavior by the person — perhaps a partial explanation of the observed tendency of some life changes to cause distress even when the changes appear to be positive.

This research is only one example out of many attesting to the major importance of the sense of personal causation. Experiments by Schulz (1976) and Langer and Rodin (1976) induced a sense of personal control and the opportunity to actually exert some control over some aspects of their daily lives by nursing home residents, with apparent favorable results on health. Gatz (1979) and George (1979) found that events that were expected and those perceived as chosen were associated with more favorable psychological outcomes. Reid and Ziegler (1977, 1981) found that both the expectancy and the desire for control were associated cross-sectionally and prospectively with psychological and health outcomes.

Is the sense of personal causation itself controlled by factors in the external, objective environment? Certainly the experimental interventions introduced by Schulz (1976) and Langer and Rodin (1976) were, ironically, not produced by the subject; to accept their results as the authors interpret them requires one to see a two-stage process whereby a pawn event (a set toward an opportunity for personal control created by the E in the S) leads to origin behavior, which then becomes the therapeutic agent. Perhaps this sequence produced an "illusion of control" (Lefcourt, 1973). In any case, it does seem that the extent to which origin behavior can occur hinges partly on the resources, the barriers, and the contingencies of the external environment.

Just as clearly, however, the person must contribute to origin behavior. I suggest that origin behavior is at one and the same time the result of all the positive aspects of self, an expression of behavioral competence, and in turn a cause of further ego strength and behavioral competence. Thus whether one can be the origin of events depends both on the environmental context and on whether one has a sense of competence in the domain of behavior in question.

Personality

The question of what is stable in human behavior or whether there is such an entity as "personality" has been debated for a long time, and I am not knowledgeable enough on the issue or argue either way. However, a stream of lifespan research by Costa and McCrae (1976, 1977, 1980, this volume) using personality inventories has made amply clear that there are enduring aspects of the person represented by the introversion/extraversion and neuroticism factors much studied by personality researchers (Cattell, 1950; Eysenck & Eysenck, 1954). Research by Costa and McCrae (1980) dealing with the relationships between these two higher-order personality factors (positive and negative affect) and happiness deserve consideration in some detail. These authors' results affirm another facet of the two-factor conception of psychological wellbeing and their differing antecedents. Costa and McCrae first determined the bivariate relationships between scores on seven subscales of the Buss and Plomin (1975) EADI-III Temperament Survey, the Bradburn scales, and a set of presumed indicators of happiness. In general, all seven temperament scales were related to the happiness measures, but the temperament scales were related differentially to the Bradburn scales. While the relationships were not totally regular, four "negative" temperaments — general emotionality, fear, anger, and poor inhibition of impulse — were most strongly related to the negative affect scale. By contrast, the sociability, tempo, and vigor temperaments were related most strongly to positive affect. The similarity of these two clusters of temperaments to neuroticism and to introversion-extraversion, respectively, is apparent. These two higher-order personality factors were then measured directly with the Eysenck (1954) and Cattell (1950) inventories. The associations between extraversion and positive affect and between neuroticism and negative affect were repeated. Thus Costa and McCrae concluded that while extraverts were likely to experience life with more affectively positive experiences, they were no more or less likely than introverts to experience negative affect. In their acceptance of Bradburn's averaging concept of happiness as the net of positive and negative affect, Costa and McCrae say that

> low Neuroticism introverts and high Neuroticism extraverts may have similar levels of life satisfaction of happiness, but they achieve this result in utterly different ways. The former are seldom depressed but

> just as seldom elated. The latter are prone to both extremes and reach "average" satisfaction only because there is as much satisfaction as dissatisfaction in their lives. (p. 676)

Finally, these authors demonstrated that prospectively measured neuroticism and introversion-extraversion predicted negative and positive affect scores, respectively, over a ten-year period.

Costa and McCrae argued that their results supported the potency of personality as a determinant of both types of psychological wellbeing. Bradburn's (1969) analysis of the correlates of positive and negative affect led him to conclude that life events were the primary determinants of positive affect. I shall also suggest that intrapersonal factors, which include *both* interior behavioral competence and self-evaluations, are the primary determinants of negative affect. On the other hand, a true personality trait is represented in the introversion-extraversion factor, which functions as a filter through which external events and the outward behaviors of the person are evaluated.

It would be possible to argue that both of the basic second-order personality factors are filters through which events are processed. On the one hand, those who are more open to stimulation from the environment seek and respond to those social and other externally satisfying behaviors events that elevate day-to-day mood. On the other hand, those with neurotic personalities find events and situations that confirm their long-term poor adjustment. I find the conclusion regarding extraversion quite tenable, but the conclusion regarding neuroticism is less satisfactory; as discussed below.

Introversion-Extraversion as a Filter

Introversion-extraversion is a true enduring personality characteristic that channels our relationship to the self and the external world. (Schulz, 1982, suggests that this personality type represents the member of longest duration of the broad class of mental activities that he calls affects.) Introversion represents a tendency to assimilate external events and transactions into the enduring conception of self. Extraversion by contrast is associated with stronger focus on what happens to the person from day to day. Thus events with short-term consequences (hassles and uplifts, for example) and whose pawn versus origin character is also shorter-lived are more likely to influence the mood of the extravert than of the introvert. The net psychological wellbeing of the introvert is more refractory to short-term events and affects. Happiness for the introvert is achieved through the self and only secondarily through the cumulative daily experiences that elevate or depress mood. Happiness for the extravert is behavioral competence as evidenced in the activities of everyday life, particulary as they involve other people and as they generate satisfaction with the domains by the quality of life sector.

Neuroticism as an Outcome

In my view, longer-term satisfaction with self, events, and one's performance in the domains of life quality *is* positive mental health and its opposite is neuroticism, negative affect, and other forms of psychopathology. In this sense neuroticism is not a personality trait, it is an outcome. To determine that measures of mental health "predict" negative affect (Bradburn, 1969) seems to me to be tautological. The ease with which psychometric research has separated neuroticism and introversion-extraversion very possibly may come from their being two totally separate components of the person-environment system.

A rejoinder to this argument has been offered by McCrae (1983), however, who suggested that neuroticism and introversion-extraversion were traits whose analagous "states" (Spielberger, 1972) were negative affect and positive affect. McCrae also cites evidence that "openness to experience" is a trait of the filtering type that is statistically independent from introversion-extraversion. These positions are worthy of serious consideration.

Conclusion

In summary, this chapter attempted to impose some greater order on the psychological wellbeing domain by determining its factorial dimensions. Two second-order factors emerged, which were named interior wellbeing and exterior wellbeing. As hypothesized, negative affect was better predicted by intrapersonal factors (such as functional health) than by exterior environmental transactions (such as time use or friends' interaction), while the opposite pattern was observed for the predictors of positive affect. Further discussion of other investigators' work suggests that interior wellbeing may be associated with the absence of negative events and a sense of personal causations, while exterior wellbeing is associated with positive events. Finally, the argument was made that the familiar second-order personality factor neuroticism was a subjective psychological outcome closely related to negative affect. By contrast, introversion-extraversion is suggested as a personality trait that filters experience in such a way that introverts experience events to the extent that they affect the self, while the extravert experiences both positive and negative events more directly.

The bottom line is that there are many routes to psychological wellbeing of which person versus environment, origin versus pawn, introversion versus extraversion, the domains of behavioral competence, and the domains of perceived quality of life represent major way stations. I am most unhappy with happiness as the ultimate criterion and most frustrated at the recalcitrance of the self to measurement in a way that is at least moderately independent of behavioral competence or psychological wellbeing. Finally, as amply demonstrated by all research, the distinctions among elements are always abstractions. In the real world (represented by irregularities such as the dissonant elements in the Lawton and Kleban second-order factors; the cross-modality effects noted by Zautra and Reich; or the lack of complete parallelism between personality and affect in Costa and McCrae) we have continua rather than categories and reciprocal, assimilative effects rather than causal paths.

References

Andrews, F. M. & McKennell, A. C. (1980). Measures of self-reported wellbeing: Their affective, cognitive, and other components. *Social Indicators Research, 4,* 127-155, 1-39.

Andrews F. M. & Withey, S. B. (1976). *Social indicators of well-being.* New York: Plenum.

Botwinick, J. (1978). *Aging and behavior.* Second edition. New York: Springer.

Bradburn, N. M. (1969). *The structure of psychological wellbeing.* Chicago: Aldine.

Buss, A. H., & Plomin, R. (1975). *A temperament theory of personality development.* New York: John Wiley.

Campbell, A., Converse, P. E., & Rodgers, W. L. (1976). *The quality of American life: perceptions, evaluations, and satisfactions.* New York: Russell Sage Foundation.

Carp, F. M. (1979). Effects of the living environment on activity and the use of time. *International Journal of Aging and Human Development, 9,* 75-91.

Cattell, R. B. (1950). *Personality: A systematic theoretical and factual study.* New York: McGraw-Hill.

Costa, P. T. & McCrae, R. R. (1976). Age differences in personality structure: A cluster-analytic approach. *Journal of Gerontology, 31,* 564-570.

Costa, P. T. & McCrae, R. R. (1980). Influence of extraversion and neuroticism on subjective wellbeing: Happy and unhappy people. *Journal of Personality and Social Psychology, 38,* 668-678.

Costa, P. T. & McCrae, R. R. (1977). Age differences in personality structure revisited: Studies in validity, stability, and change. *International Journal of Aging and Human Development, 8,* 261-275.

deCharms, R. (1968). *Personal causation.* New York: Academic Press.

Dohrenwend, B. P. (1974). Problems in defining and sampling the relevant population of stressful life events. In B. S. Dohrenwend and B. P. Dohrenwend (Eds.), *Stressful life events: Their nature and effects.* New York: John Wiley.

Ellsworth, R. B. (1957). The MACC Behavioral Adjustment Scale. Beverly Hills, CA: Western Psychological Services.

Eysenck, H. T. & Eysenck, S. B. (1964), *Eysenck Personality Inventory Manual.* San Diego: Educational and Industrial Testing Service.

Fischer, C. S. (1982). *To dwell among friends: Personal networks in town and city.* Chicago: University of Chicago Press.

Gatz, M. (1979, November). Unsolicited events: Ready or not here I come. Paper presented at the annual meeting of the Gerontological Society, Washington, DC.

George, L. K. (1979, November). Dimensions of events: Diamonds in the rough. Paper presented at the annual meeting of the Gerontological Society, Washington, DC.

George, L. K. & Bearon, L. B. (1980). *Quality of life in older persons: Meanings and measurement.* New York: Human Sciences Press.

Gurin, G., Veroff, J., & Feld, S. (1960). *Americans view their mental health.* New York: Basic Books.

Herzog, A. R. & Rodgers, W. L. (1981a). Age and satisfaction: Data from several large surveys. *Research on Aging, 3,* 142-165.

Herzog, A. R. & Rodgers, W. L. (1981b). The structure of subjective well-being in different age groups. *Journal of Gerontology, 36,* 472-479.

Holmes, T. H. & Rahe, R. H. (1967). The Social Readjustment Rating Scale. *Journal of Psychosomatic Research, 11,* 213-218.

Kanner, A. D., Coyne, J. C., Schaefer, C. & Lazarus, R. (1981). Comparison of two modes of stress measurement: Daily hassles and uplifts versus major life events. *Journal of Behavioral Medicine, 4.*

Kiyak, A., Liang, J., & Kahana, E. (1976, August). A methodological inquiry into the schedule of recent life events. Paper presented at the Annual meeting of the American Psychological Association, Washington, DC.

Kozma, A., & Stones, M. J. (1980). The measurement of happiness. *Journal of Gerontology, 35,* 906-912.

Langer, E. & Rodin, J. (1976). The effects of choice and enhanced personal responsibility for the aged. *Journal of Personality and Social Psychology, 34,* 191-198.

Lawton, M. P. (1972). Assessing the competence of older people. In D. Kent, R. Kastenbaum, and S. Sherwood (Eds.), *Research, planning and action for the elderly.* New York: Behavioral Publications.

Lawton, M. P. (1975). The Philadelphia Geriatric Center Morale Scale: A revision. *Journal of Gerontoloy, 30,* 85-89.

Lawton, M. P. (1977). Morale: What are we measuring? In C. Nydegger (Ed.), *Measuring morale: A guide to affective assessment.* Washington, DC: Gerontological Society.

Lawton, M. P. (1982a). Competence, environmental press, and the adaptation of older people. In M. P. Lawton, P. G. Windley, & T. O. Byerts (Eds.), *Aging and the environment: Theoretical approaches.* New York: Springer.

Lawton, M. P. (1982b). The well-being and mental health of the aged. In T. Field, A. Stein, H. Quay, L. Troll, & G. E. Finley (Eds.), *Review of human development.* New York: John Wiley.

Lawton, M. P. (1983). Environment and other determinants of wellbeing in the aged. *Gerontologist, 23,* 349-357.

Lawton, M. P. & Kleban, M. H. (1982). Psychological wellbeing in the aged: Factorial and conceptual dimensions. Philadelphia Geriatric Center.

Lawton, M. P., Moss, M., Fulcomer, M., & Kleban, MH. (1982). A research and service-oriented Multilevel Assessment Instrument. *Journal of Gerontology, 37,* 91-99.

Lawton, M. P. & Nahemow, L. (1973). Ecology and the aging process. In C. Eisdorfer and M. P. Lawton (Eds.), *Psychology of adult development and aging.* Washington: American Psychological Association.

Lefcourt, J. M. (1973). The function of the illusions of control and freedom. *American Psychologist, 28,* 417-425.

Lewin, K. (1935). *Dynamic theory of personality.* New York: McGraw-Hill.

McCrae, R. R. (in press). Extraversion is not a filter, neuroticism is not an outcome: A reply to Lawton. *Experimental Aging Research.*

Morris, J. N., Wolf, R. S., & Klerman, L. V. (1975). Common themes among morale and depression scales. *Journal of Gerontology, 30,* 209-215.

Myers, J. K., Lindenthal, J. J., & Pepper, M. P. (1971). Life events and psychiatric impairment. *Journal of Nervous and Mental Disease, 152,* 149-157.

National Council on the Aging (1975). *The myth and reality of aging in America.* Washington DC: National Council on the Aging.

Neugarten, B. L., Havighurst, R. J., & Tobin, S. S. (1961). The measurement of life satisfaction. *Journal of Gerontology, 16,* 134-143.

Reid, D. W. & Ziegler, M. (1977). A survey of the reinforcements and activities elderly citizens feel are important for their general happiness. *Essence, 2,* 5-24.

Reid, D. W. & Ziegler, M. (1981, November). Longitudinal studies of desired control and adjustment among the elderly. Paper presented at the annual meeting of the Gerontological Society, Toronto.

Rosenberg, M. (1965). *Society and the adolescent self-image.* Princeton NJ: Princeton University Press.

Sarason, I. G., Johnson, J. H., & Siegel, J. M. (1978). Assessing the impact of life changes: Development of Life Experiences Survey. *Journal of Consulting and Clinical Psychology, 46,* 932-946.

Schulz, R. (1976). Effects of control and predictability on the physical and psychological well-being of the institutionalized aged. *Journal of Personality and Social Psychology, 33,* 563-573.

Schulz, R. (1982). Emotionality and aging: A theoretical and empirical analysis. *Journal of Gerontology, 37,* 42-51.

Spielberger, C. D. (1972). Anxiety as an emotional state. In C. D. Spielberger (Ed.), *Anxiety: Current trends in theory and research* (Vol. 1). New York: Academic Press.

Zautra, A. & Reich, J. (1980). Positive life events and reports of well-being: Some useful distinctions. *American Journal of Community Psychology, 8,* 657-670.

Zautra, A. J. & Reich, J. W. (in press). Life events and perceptions of life quality. A review of findings. *Journal of Community Psychology.*

Zung, W. W. K. (1965). Self-rating despression scale. *Archives of General Psychiatry, 12,* 63-70.

5

Personal Adjustment, Wellbeing, and Life Events

BERTRAM J. COHLER
ANDREW M. BOXER

Across the adult years, feelings of wellbeing are of central importance in determining psychological adjustment. Evaluation of mental health should include not only factors associated with psychiatric impairment including the major psychiatric syndromes, but also so-called positive mental health. Feelings of enhanced psychological wellbeing or morale — an important indicator of positive mental health — are closely associated with the changing social context across adult-

AUTHORS' NOTE: This manuscript is an abbreviated and revised version of an earlier report, "Mental Health and Aging: Life Course Perspectives," submitted to the Senior Consultant panel, Behavior Sciences Cluster Review, National Institute of Mental Health, 1983. The second author was supported by a Predoctoral Fellowship, National Institute of Mental Health T32 MH14668, Clinical Research Training Program in Adolescence, jointly

hood, including experienced congruity between one's present position in the course of life and that which is expectable among members of a particular society. The present chapter is focused upon morale, mental health, and the nature and timing of life events as well as role transitions across the adult years. In addition, consideration is given to the implications of these issues for individuals' feelings of continued wellbeing that result from changes in their understanding of their place in the course of life, characteristic of middle and old age.

Psychological Wellbeing and Mental Health

As a result of intensive longitudinal investigations of adulthood and the aging process, particularly in regard to psychological changes over the second half of life (beginning in the fourth decade), there has been increased appreciation of the complexity of issues related to the study of personal adjustment over the life course. Diachronic studies, such as those at Berkeley's Institute for Human Development (Eichorn, Clausen, Haan, Honzik, & Mussen, 1981), have supported Kagan and Moss's (1962) observations regarding so-called "sleeper effects" in development in which the relationship between such factors as morale and aspects of social context significantly associated at one point in the course of life might show little association, or even a negative association, at another point.

Studies of particular lives over time, as those reported by Vaillant (1977) or Osherson (1980), show the variety of ways available to persons for preserving their feelings of wellbeing when confronted by adverse life events. These studies also suggest that persons experiencing the greatest discontinuity over time in sources of satisfaction, and observed to show the greatest amount of life change, also showed less satisfactory adjustment. Recent findings have further contributed to an understanding of the numerous factors associated with feelings of psychological wellbeing (see Lawton, this volume, for a detailed discussion). Further, investigations of "successful" aging have demonstrated the variety of ways in which older persons are able to maintain morale and have led to a rethinking of traditional criteria for understanding mental health in adulthood (Palmore, 1981).

---

sponsored by the Department of Psychiatry, Michael Reese Hospital and Medical Center; and the Committee on Human Development of the University of Chicago. The authors also gratefully acknowledge the Laboratory for the Study of Adolescence, Department of Psychiatry, Michael Reese Hospital and Medical Center, Chicago, Illinois.

Psychological wellbeing in adulthood includes the related, but not necessarily identical, elements of positive morale, happiness, and life satisfaction. As originally used to discuss successful aging (Neugarten, Havighurst, & Tobin, 1961), life satisfaction referred to a complex balance of personal wellbeing, zest or enthusiasm for life, acceptance of personal responsibility for one's own life, sense of congruence between desired and realized goals, positive self-image, and cheerful mood (Neugarten, Havighurst, & Tobin, 1961). This measure of life satisfaction appears to be most closely related to subjective perceptions of adequate health (Palmore & Luikart, 1972; Edwards & Kleemack, 1973; Larson, 1978), although Lawton (1982) suggests it may also be a measure of experienced congruence between expectations and present sources of satisfaction.

There is currently much debate as to whether these related elements of life satisfaction may be regarded as a single construct. Based on findings such as those by Adams (1969) that delineate separate factors within the life-satisfaction measure, George (1979) and Lawton (1982) maintain that life statisfaction should be narrowly defined as separate from morale and happiness; while Herzog, Rodgers, and Woodworth (1982) in a reanalysis of findings from several national survey studies report that happiness and life satisfaction appear to measure a similar underlying concept. Questions have also been raised regarding the inclusion of several related concepts as a single construct of life satisfaction. Adams (1969) reports that separate factors can be identified within the life-satisfaction measure, while Lawton (1982, and this volume) suggests that the construct of life satisfaction includes both more and less general factors.

In our view, life satisfaction includes concepts related to both morale and happiness (George, 1979). Morale, a term first used in studies of aging by Kutner, Fanshel, Togo, and Langner (1956) to refer to personal confidence and enthusiasm (George, 1979; Lawton, 1982), should, however, be differentiated from happiness (Bradburn, 1969) defined as a ratio of positive to negative feelings that are independent dimensions of mood. Lawton (1982) suggests that happiness refers to a variable of affect, while life satisfaction and morale represent cognitive or self-evaluative elements that are so global that their meaning in research is ambiguous.

For purposes of the present dicsussion, life satisfaction, morale, and happiness may be thought of as components of a larger, more generalized concept of wellbeing or positive self-integrity and cohesiveness (Bradburn, 1969; Lawton, 1982). This sense of psychological wellbeing includes the perception that the course of life is roughly that which had been anticipated and on-time in terms of expectable life events and role transitions; for example, health problems are experienced as no worse than those of others of the same age and do not interfere in mobility. As a consequence of these feelings of wellbeing, individuals are able to preserve an outlook on the future characterized by cheerfulness and appropriate optimism or confidence that life challenges may be mastered and that fears and tensions may be contained.

Across the first half of life, as persons look forward to challenges yet to be mastered, their sense of wellbeing may be based both on changes in self and in social surround. Somewhat later in life, with the realization of the very finitude or boundedness of life itself (Munnichs, 1966; Marshall, 1981), there is a change in focus from looking forward to looking backward, considering life attainments in terms of the relative balance between cherished goals that have been reached and disappointments experienced. Additional effort is required to reconcile hopes and attainments. Increasingly across the second half of life, efforts at maintenance of a sense of wellbeing depend upon the success of reminiscence activity directed at the reconciliation of goals and attainments, resulting in accumulated experience of a past made congruent with the present.

Psychological Wellbeing and Social Time in Adulthood

Findings from a number of cross-sectional studies (e. g., Fiske, 1980; Andrews & Withey, 1976) have suggested that variations in wellbeing across adulthood are not *directly* related to such demographic characteristics as chronological age or social status. Rather, findings from these studies suggest that psychological wellbeing is mediated by such aspects of the social context of adult lives as the nature and extent of adult responsibilities; individuals' histories of both expected and eruptive life events; and, in particular, the extent to which the course of adult life follows a timetable based on a socially shared set of expectations. These findings demonstrate the value of considering adjustment as a dialectical process involving changes in adult lives within the context of an every changing social context (Riegel, 1979) and highlights the complex relationship between psychological wellbeing and aging.

At least within our own society, the course of life is understood as a progression through a series of "life-stations" (Neugarten & Hagestad, 1976; Riley, Johnson & Foner, 1972) or socially defined tasks, stages, or strata, each of which is accompanied by a particular set of expectations regarding performance as well as sanctions for nonperformance. Further, because of a shared understanding of the life cycle as finite or bounded, there is also consensual agreement regarding the ages at which persons must progress across the several stations of life.

Life Course, Social Timing, and Psychological Wellbeing

Shared expectations regarding role transitions and life events are important elements in the continuing evaluations that persons make of their own lives in order to maintain a story or narrative of life that provides an account of the life history that is perceived as coherent or internally consistent. (Cohler, 1982). It is as a result of the very structure of myth and story in Western civilization that such accounts are expected to have beginnings, middles, and ends (Ricouer, 1977; Cohler, 1982). Lives are expected to follow the same structure as other narratives, using remembered past, experienced present, and presently anticipated future as the elements of this continuing, coherent, account of the course of one's own life (Weber, 1955; also see McAdams, this volume). Foremost among the elements employed in the continuing revision of the personal narrative is that concerning one's present place in the expectable course of life.

While it is possible to attain consensus among persons regarding the expectable course of life in the same manner as in evaluating prestige in measuring social status (Warner, 1959; Blau & Duncan, 1967), this timetable shifts across cohorts, reflecting sociohistorical change. However, within particular cohorts there is general agreement on the timetable for specific role transitions such as finishing school, marriage, birth of first child, grandparenthood, death of own parents, retirement, widowhood, and so on.[1]

When life events happen too "early" or too "late" in terms of what is expected, there are important implications for maintenance of psychological wellbeing. Widowhood is perhaps the best example of the deleterious impact of such off-time events (Blau, 1973; Lopata, 1972). At the present time, wives are expected to outlive husbands, and to become widows first in their late sixties or early seventies. Women becoming widows at this expectable time have a chance to learn to be a widow from others who have already experienced this event (anticipatory socialization). With the arrival of on-time widowhood, there are also others who are available as role colleagues to be of help in dealing with this event. However, when widowhood happens early (i.e., off-time) to a woman in her thirties, there are few friends available to help her negotiate this event and little opportunity to learn how to prepare for and adjust to this role. The fact of being off time, disturbing in itself, is further intensified by this lack of support from significant others.

It should be noted that both positive as well as negative and adverse events may lead to lowered morale and decreased sense of wellbeing if taking place too early in the course of life. Career promotions at too early an age can lead to a foreshortened sense of career; a major problem among creative scientists is the phenomenon of a rapid career advancement due to youthful discoveries that can lead, in mid-life, to feelings of career stagnation.

Implications of the timing of life events and role transitions for continued psychological wellbeing must always be considered in terms of such aspects of social differentiation as social status, sex, and age, defined by place in the timetable of the liffe course rather than by chronological age. For example, Neugarten and Hagestad (1976), summarizing findings from studies of timing and social timetables, note that higher social status is associated with delayed completion of education as well as delayed assumption of such characteristic adult roles as those of spouse and parent. While, in general, events taking place too late in life—as contrasted with those taking place too early—tend to have a less adverse impact upon morale, circumstances associated with social differentiation lead to qualification of that statement, such as those concerning the timing of the advent of parenthood among men and women. Many higher status women presently postpone marriage and often parenthood as well until they are well settled in their careers (Daniels & Weingarten, 1982). As a consequence of the "biological clock," which limits the years during which women are able to bear children, delay of marriage and parenthood may create pressure for women later in the childbearing years concerning the necessity of realizing this event before it is "too late." Men feel little of this life-course "squeeze" as a result of late (off-time) assumption of the parental role. As Nydegger (1980) has noted, men may be better able to accept the parental role later in life because after they have become more confident of their career success and more settled in life they may feel able to devote greater time and energy to the task of caring for young children.

While problems of being off time, either too early or too late, in expectable role transitions and life events are not uncommon, persistent and extreme asynchronization in many spheres of life may cause time relationships to become distorted and disordered (Cain, 1964; Seltzer, 1976). Such dislocations may seriously affect psychological wellbeing, such as among refugees or among persons surviving disasters, who are forced to start over in life. Problems in being seriously off time in many spheres of life may snowball, making it increasingly difficult to "catch up" with age mates within a cohort. This problem is often faced by verterans returning home from war, as well as discharged psychiatric patients and released prisoners.

Particularly in the case of disasters, war, and illness, society allocates a certain number of "idiosyncracy credits" (Hollander, 1964; Neugarten

& Hagestad, 1976). However, in time these credits are "used up" as persons are able to get back on time, such as among recurrently hospitalized persons with major mental disorders (Zubin & Spring, 1977). Among these psychiatric patients, the very fact of being off time may lead to a lowered sense of wellbeing and associated sense of stigma (Clausen, 1981), apart from the disturbing intrusion of particular forms of mood or thought disorder. At least a part of the distress these recurrently hospitalized psychiatric patients express may actually be due to problems of being off time for the course of expectable adult lives, rather than as a result of the disturbance itself (Cohler & Ferrono, 1983).

Aging, Social Relations and Psychological Wellbeing

To date, the impact of aging itself as a factor associated with the meaning of social context has been less well appreciated than either social status or sex, although all three forms of social differentiation are important in understanding the importance of timing and social context for psychological wellbeing. For example, findings from a number of studies have suggested that the availability of a circle of kindred and friends plays an important buffering role in reducing the otherwise stressful impact of adverse life events, such as illness or expectable role transitions (such as widowhood) taking place across the second half of life (Henderson et al., 1981; Mueller, 1980). Indeed, one of the reasons why life events may be adverse is precisely because they disrupt long-term social relations. In particular, the continued availability of family members is believed to be particularly important for older persons in reducing the otherwise adverse impact of illness and role losses, including the deaths of spouse and friends. At least in part, this view of the supportive role of family for older persons emerges from a view of aging as inevitably a time of increased loneliness that can be reduced by continuing contact with kindred.

Family Relations and Social Support

Much of what is known about social support, particularly relations among family members, as a buffer in times of personal crisis has been based on studies of persons across young and middle adulthood. There has been little comparative study of the role of social relations in determining morale across the second half of life, recognizing that the function of social relations for the maintenance of psychological wellbeing might not be equivalent across the adult years. Findings from studies of intergenerational relations among older grandparents and their younger offspring and grandchildren (Cohler & Grunebaum, 1981) as well as the study of middle-aged and older persons in an urban community (Cohler & Lieberman, 1980) suggest that position in the life course affects the experience of continuing relations among family members.

Young adults, newly married and beginning their family, look to their own middle-aged and older parents for advice and assistance, including continued socialization into adult roles. As important as continuing ties with parents are for young adults, these requests may be less positively acknowledged by middle-aged and older grandparents. At the outset, it should be noted that, contrary to popular stereotype, American families remain highly bonded across generations. Intergenerational studies of the family across social strata and within diverse subcultures in American society show that the modal American family is a modified extended one in which the generations live apart but share resources and assistance (Litwak, 1960; Shanas, 1979; Sussman, 1965; Uzoka, 1979). Shanas's survey findings show that more than four-fifths of urban residents have visited with their older parents within a week prior to the survey. In spite of age, the flow of resources and assistance is still primarily from the older to the younger generations within the family, with findings from a national survey study showing that more than half of persons over age 80 continue to provide material assistance for their middle-aged offspring (Harris & Associates, 1975).

Findings such as those reviewed here show quite clearly that the extent of contact among relatives in contemporary urban society in which not only frequent contact but also sharing of resources across generations is the norm. Much less is known about the affective quality of these continuing family contacts than the frequency of visits (Troll, Atchley, & Miller, 1979); however, at least within older generations, it is clear that feelings of loneliness and social isolation are much less salient than had been assumed. Particularly in late life with increased role-loss and the death of close friends the range of available social ties does shrink, but only among those who previously were most gregarious is there an impact upon feelings of wellbeing (Lowenthal & Robinson, 1976). Findings reported by Lowenthal (1964), Lowenthal and Robinson (1976), and Medley (1976, 1980), show quite clearly that older persons do not necessarily feel less satisfied with opportunities available for continuing social relations than earlier in the course of life.

Across the seocnd half of life, at least among recent cohorts of less well educated older adults, persons increasingly prefer modes of relating to others in a manner characterized by greater formality, closer ties to a smaller number of significant others, and lessened investment of time and effort in social relations than has been found in studies of morale and social relations among younger adults. Fiske (1980) reports a positive association between the extent of positive morale among older persons and the extent to which persons are able to reduce overall social investments to a small number of confidants, while Snow and Crapo (1982) report that older men reporting higher morale have fewer close relationships with others.

The grandparental role is a particularly problematic one for many older persons. As Rosow (1976) has noted, the advent of grandparenthood is not a role that middle-aged and older persons elect for themselves; often the advent of grandparenthood serves as an additional reminder for older persons of the fact of their own aging. Further, the grandparent role is, of necessity, a strained an formal role. Grandparents are unable to have access to their grandchildren except with consent of the parents; often it is the parents themselves who initiate such requests at times convenient for them but not for the grandparents who are not seen as having other obligations or interests. Particularly within working-class families where kinship obligations are extensive and somewhat more complex than within middle-class families (e.g., Rainwater & Handel, 1964; Bott, 1971), the demands imposed on grandparents for providing emotional support for other generations in the family become especially burdensome.

Consistent with this perspective, several studies have reported negative associations between morale and the extent of contact with adult offspring among late middle-aged and older grandparents (e.g., Kutner et al., 1956). However, other investigators report essentially no relationship between morale of older persons and the extent of their family contacts (e.g., Beckman, 1981). Rosenmayr and Kockeis (1963) have suggested that, overall, the mode of relationship with family members most enchancing of feelings of wellbeing is that of "intimacy at a distance" in which contacts are formal, distant, and not felt as costly of scarce time and effort.

It is possible that the impact of continuing family contacts upon a sense of wellbeing differs somewhat among older men and women. Gutmann (1975, 1977), George and Bearon (1980), and Sinnott (1982) have suggested that there may be a shift in sex roles after mid-life. Women increasingly prefer to seek instrumental and executive activities as a source of satisfaction seen in an increased investment in work or career, while, consistent with the findings of Tamir (1982), men are increasingly likely to view interpersonal relations as a major source of life satisfaction, turning away somewhat from prior investments in work or career. This shift appears to be partly a result of the end of that phase of the adult life course marked by active parenting, when men feel particular responsibility for providing for the economic security of the family and women feel particular responsibility for emotional support and day-to-day management of the household.

Findings supporting this position have been reported by Palmore and Luikart (1972) who note that friendship ties are particularly important as a source of positive morale among older men, and by Medley (1976) and R. Sears (1977) who report that among older men, maintenance of family ties is associated with increased morale. Wood and Robertson's (1978) detailed review of findings regarding sex differences in the association of family ties and morale, and findings from the study by Mancini, Quinn, Gavigan, and Franklin (1980) provides little support for assuming differences among men and women in the extent of satisfaction provided by family ties, at least as reflected in the role of grandparent.

Aging and Feeling of Wellbeing

Although social relations are less important than has been assumed in the maintenance of wellbeing among older persons (Tobin & Neugarten, 1961; Larson, 1978), there is little evidence of an overall decline, in feelings of wellbeing and in morale among older persons, except among the much less well educated (Bradburn & Caplovitz, 1965). Reviewing findings from three national survey studies, Andrew and Withey (1976) found that except in the areas of health and parent-child relations, feelings of wellbeing remain quite stable across adulthood. Campbell, Converse, and Rodgers (1976) note that while younger persons report greater happiness than older persons, perhaps reflecting greater optimism regarding the future, older persons report greater feelings of life satisfaction.

However, in his study of men particularly on time within their cohort for the expectable course of life events, Harry (1976) reports a linear relationship between aging and reports of happiness; especially among men after mid-life, fewer family constraints was identified as a particularly important factor leading to increased happiness. Concern with health as well as the extent to which health interferes in mobility appears particularly important as a factor related to feelings of wellbeing among men (e.g., Palmore & Kivett, 1977; Medley, 1980; Mussen, Honzik, & Eichorn, 1982).

There has been much less longitudinal than cross-sectional investigation of sources of wellbeing across the adult years. Findings reported to date have been based largely on the follow-up of the men and women originally a part of Terman's (Terman, Burks, & Jensen, 1930) study of giftedness, the Duke longitudinal research (e.g., Palmore, 1981) and, most significantly, continuing studies of the now middle-aged men and women of their older parents followed from earliest childhood at the Institute for Human Development at the University of California at Berkeley (Jones et al., 1971; Eichorn et al., 1981). Following up gifted older adults last studied more than twenty-five years earlier by Terman and Oden (1959), R. Sears's (1977) analysis of determinants of life satisfaction among men suggests that a sense of optimism and feelings of enhanced self-worth were the most salient predictors of a continued sense of wellbeing over time.

While to some extent the maintenance of feelings of wellbeing across the second half of life may be predicted on the basis of earlier life adjustment, it is not necessarily the case that persons showing positive morale in later life have consistently maintained such morale across the adult years. Discontinuity and the capacity for change, due in part to changing socially shared definitions of both person and setting, seem to be important in maintaining morale over time. In a study of the older parents of the middle-aged persons followed in the longitudinal research at the Institute for Human Development, Maas and Kuypers (1974) report that women studied at ages 30 to 70 showed greater stability than men in life satisfaction and adjustment over a 40-year interval, with those women least well adjusted in late life showing the greatest stability over time. Men least satisfied with their lives at age 30 were also most likely to report a lack of life satisfaction at age 70.

Finally, it is important to distinguish between aging and cohort effects, that is, between effects due to aging itself and those that are the result of growing up and living within a particular historical period. Felton and Shaver (this volume) address this issue in some detail.

Conclusion

Findings from both a number of cross-sectional and longitudinal studies across the adult years have shown that feelings of psychological wellbeing and accompanying positive morale are largely cohort specific, as defined in terms of particular sociohistorical events, perceived place in the life course within a particular cohort, and present social context. As Cohler (1983) has suggested, too often it is assumed that factors contributing to feelings of wellbeing and morale across the first half of life will contribute in the same manner to morale across the second half of life.

As a consequence of shared understandings of social timetables including that regarding the expectable duration of life, with the advent of mid-life there is a growing realization that more time has already passed than is left to be lived, leading to an increased personalization of death (Neugarten & Datan, 1974) as well as an appreciation of the very finitude of life. However, the social timing of expectable adult roles may alter this increased awareness of finitude (Marshall, 1981). For example, late off-time entry into such expectable adult roles as parenthood is likely to lead to a later awareness of the crisis of finitude, typically sometime during the years between 45 and 55, when there is a dramatic transformation in the perception of self and place in the course of life (Cohler, 1982). While this increased personalization of death (Neugarten & Datan, 1973) leads to a greater preoccupation with self, it need not lead to lowered morale.

Continuing relations with a small number of confidants with whom there is a continuing, reciprocal, intimate relationship and symmetrical expectations on the part of each partner seems to foster psychological wellbeing across the course of life (Lowenthal & Haven, 1968; Wood & Robertson, 1978; Liang, Dvorkin, Kahana, & Mazian, 1980; Strain & Chappell, 1982). However, if middle-aged persons with full role-portfolios (Hagestad, 1974) experience many demands and expectations from a large number of significant others, such demands may conflict with developmentally determined needs for increased time for self, leading to lowered morale and a reduced rather than enhanced sense of wellbeing as a result of continuing social relations in adulthood (Cohler & Lieberman, 1980).

These problems may be particularly pronounced among working-class women who, as kin-keepers for a large extended family (Firth, Hubert, & Forge, 1970), are particularly burdened with demands and expectations from kindred. Among men, it is more likely that social relations across the second half of life will be voluntary rather than obligatory, and that these relations will be characterized by shared intimacy and feelings of support and concern on the part of others including children and grandchildren rather than the demands for assistance without reciprocal support that so often characterize the relations of middle-aged and older women with kindred. However, much more study is required of the nature and quality of social relations across the second half of life as associated with psychological wellbeing or morale in order to understand both the differential effect of social relations in the lives of men and women and those aspects of interpersonal ties most likely to facilitate or to disrupt wellbeing among middle-aged and older persons.

Note

1. Research on age norms (e. g., Neugarten, Moore & Lowe, 1965) has illuminated the varying degrees of constraint or regulation which these norms provide over individuals and social groups. Such research has demonstrated that individuals carry with them a set of assumptions and expectations which serve proscriptive and prescriptive

functions with regard to age-appropriate human conduct. However, it is extremely difficult to investigate agents of socialization as they operate and are perceived, or their processes of transmission. The role of *reference groups* is enormously complicated since individuals have multiple reference groups to which they are bound. Current research leaves us with the question of which reference groups exhibit what degree of age constraints for which individuals, as they move through a complex social system which is graded not only by age, but by sex, social class, and a number of other factors which help give shape to the course of human lives.

References

Adams, D. L. (1969). Analysis of a life satisfaction index. *Journal of Gerontology, 24,* 470-474.

Andrews, F., & Withey, S. (1976). *Social indicators of well-being: Americans' perceptions of life quality.* New York: Plenum.

Beckman, L. (1981). Effects on social interaction and children's relative inputs on older women's psychological well-being. *Journal of Personality and Social Psychology, 41,* 1075-1086.

Blau, P. M., & Duncan, O. D. (1967). *The American occupational structure.* New York: John Wiley.

Blau, Z. (1973) *Old age in a changing society.* New York: Franklin Watts.

Bott, E. (1971). Family and social network (2nd ed.). London: Tavistock Press. (Original work published 1957)

Bradburn, N. (1969). *The structure of psychological well-being.* Chicago: Aldine.

Bradburn, N., & Caplovitz, D. (1965). *Reports on happiness: A pilot study of behavior related to mental health.* Chicago: Aldine.

Cain, L. (1964). Life-course and social structure. In R. Faris (Ed.), *Handbook of Modern Sociology* (pp. 272-309). Chicago: Rand McNally.

Campbell. A., Converse, P., & Rodgers, W. (1976). *The quality of American life.* New York: Russell Sage Foundation.

Clausen, J. (1981). Stigma and mental disorder: Phenomena and terminology. *Psychiatry, 44,* 287-296.

Cohler, B. (1982). Personal narrative and life-course. In P. Baltes & O. G. Brim, Jr. (Eds.), *Life-Span Development and Behavior* (Vol., pp. 205-229) New York: Academic Press.

Cohler, B. (1983). Autonomy and interdependence in the family of adulthood: A psychological perspective. *The Gerontologist, 23,* 33-39.

Cohler, B., & Ferrono, C. (1983). Schizophrenia and the adult life course. In N. Miller & G. Cohen (Eds.), *Schizophrenia and Aging.* New York: The Guilford Press.

Cohler, B., & Grunebaum, H. (1981). *Mothers, grandmothers, and daughters.* New York: John Wiley.

Cohler, B., & Lieberman, M. (1980) Social relations and mental health: Middle-aged and older men and women from three European ethnic groups. *Research on Aging, 2,* 445-469.

Daniels, P., & Weingarten, K. (1982). *Sooner or later: The timing of parenthood in adult lives.* New York: Norton.

Edwards, J., & Kleemack, D. (1973). Correlates of life satisfaction: A reexamination. *Journal of Gerontology, 28,* 497-502.

Eichorn, D., Clausen, J., Haan, N., Honzik, M., & Mussen, P. (1981). *Present and past in middle life.* New York: Academic Press.

Firth, R., Hubert, J., & Forge, A. (1970). *Families and their relatives: Kinship in a middle class sector of London.* New York: Humanities Press.

Fiske, M. (1980). Tasks and crises of the second half of life: The inter-relationship of commitment, coping, and adaptation. In J. Birren & R. B. Sloane (Eds.), *Handbook of Mental Health and Aging,* (pp. 337-373). Englewood Cliffs, NJ: Prentice-Hall.

George, L. (1979). The happiness syndrome: Methodological and substantive issues in the study of social-psychological well-being in adulthood. *The Gerontologist, 19,* 210-216.

George, L., & Bearon, L. (1980). *Quality of life in older persons: Meaning and measurment.* New York: Human Sciences Press.

Gutmann, D. (1975). Parenthood: Key to the comparative study of the life-cycle. In N. Datan & L. Ginsberg (Eds.), *Life-span developmental psychology: Normative life-crises,* (pp. 167-184). New York: Academic Press.

Gutmann, D. (1977). The cross-cultural perspective: Notes toward a comparative psychology of aging. In J. Birren & K. W. Schaie (Eds.), *Handbook of the psychology of aging* (pp. 302-326). New York: Van Nostrand-Reinhold.

Hagestad, G. O. (1974) Middle-aged women and their children: Exploring changes in a role relationship. Unpublished doctoral dissertation, University of Minnesota.

Harris, L., & Associates. (1975). *The myth and reality of aging in America.* Washington, D. C. National Council on the Aging.

Harry, J. (1976). Evolving sources of happiness for men over the life cycle: A structural analysis. *Journal of Marriage and the Family, 38,* 289-296.

Henderson, S., Byrne, D., & Duncan-Jones, P. (1981). *Neurosis and the social environment.* New York: Academic Press.

Herzog, A., Rodgers, W., & Woodworth, J. (1982). *Subjective well-being among different age groups.* Ann Arbor: The University of Michigan Press.

Hollander, E. (1964). *Leaders, groups, and influence.* New York: Oxford University Press.

Jones, M. C., Bayley, N., MacFarlane, J., & Honzik, M. (Eds.). (1971). *The course of human development.* Waltham, MA: Xerox Publishing.

Kagan, J., & Moss, H. (1962). *Birth to maturity.* New York: John Wiley.

Kutner, R., Fanshel, D., Togo, A., & Langner, T. (1956). *Five hundred over sixty: A community survey on aging.* New York: Russell Sage Foundations.

Larson, R. (1978). Thirty years of research on the subjective well being of older Americans. *Journal of Gerontology, 33,* 109-125.

Lawton, M. P. (1982). The well-being and mental health of the aged. In T. Field, A. Huston, H. C. Quay, L. Troll, & G. Finley (Eds.), *Review of human development, (pp. 614-628).* New York: John Wiley.

Liang, J., Dvorkin, L., Kahana, E., & Mazian, F. (1980). Social integration and morale: A reexamination. *Journal of Gerontology, 35,* 746-757.

Litwak, E. (1960). Geographical mobility and extended family cohesion. American *Sociological Review, 25,* 385-394.

Lopata, H. (1972). *Widowhood in an American city.* Cambridge, MA: Schenkman.

Lowenthal, M. F. (1964). Social isolation and mental illness in old age. *American Sociological Review, 29,* 54-70.

Lowenthal, M. H., & Haven, C. (1968). Interaction and adaptation: Intimacy as a crucial variable. *American Sociological Review, 33,* 20-30.

Lowenthal, M. F., & Robinson, B. (1976). Social networks and isolation. In R. Binstock & E. Shanas (Eds.), *Handbook of aging and the social sciences,* (pp. 432-456). New York: Van Nostrand.

Mancini, J., Quinn, W., Gavigan, M., & Franklin, H. (1980). Social network interaction among older adults: Implications for life satisfaction. *Human Relations, 33,* 543-554.

Maas, H., & Kuypers, J. (1974). *From thirty to seventy: A forty-year longitudinal study of adult life-styles and personality.* San Francisco: Jossey-Bass.

Marshall, V. (1981). *Last Chapters: A sociology of death and dying.* Belmont, CA: Wordsworth.

Medley, M. (1976). Satisfaction with life among persons sixty-five years and older. *Journal of Gerontology, 31,* 448-455.

Medley, M. (1980). Life satisfaction across four stages of adult life. *International Journal of Aging and Human Development, 11,* 193-209.

Mueller, D. (1980). Social networks: A promising direction for research on the relationship of the social environment to psychiatric disorder. *Social Science and Medicine, 14A,* 147-161.

Munnichs, J. (1966). *Old age and finitude: A contribution to psychogerontology.* New York: Karger.

Mussen, P., Honzik, M., & Eichorn, D. (1982). Early adult antecedents of life satisfaction at age 70. *Journal of Gerontolgy, 37,* 316-322.

Neugarten, B., & Datan, N. (1973). Sociological perspectives on the life cycle. In P. Baltes & W. Schaie (Eds.), *Life-span developmental psychology: Personality and socialization,* (pp. 53-69). New York: Academic Press.

Neugarten, B., & Datan, N. (1974). The middle years. In S. Arieti (Ed.), *The American handbook of psychiatry, (Vol. 5, Rev. ed.,* pp. 592-608). New York: Basic Books.

Neugarten, B., & Hagestad, G. (1976). Age and the life course. In R. Binstock & E. Shanas (Eds.), *Handbook of aging and the social sciences,* (pp.35-55). New York: Van Nostrand.

Neugarten, B., Havighurst, R., & Tobin, S. (1961). The measurement of life satisfaction. *The Journal of Gerontology, 16,* 134-143.

Neugarten, B., Moore, J., & Lowe, J. (1965). Age norms, age constraints, and adult socialization. *The American Journal of Sociology, 70,* 710-717.

Nydegger, C. (1980). Role and age transitions: A potpourri of issues. In C. Fry & J. Keith (Eds.), *New methods for old age research: Anthropological alternatives,* (pp. 127-145). Loyola University of Chicago: Center for Urban Studies.

Osherson, S. D. (1980). *Holding on or letting go: Men and career change at midlife.* New York: The Free Press.

Palmore, E. (1981). *Social patterns in normal aging: Findings from the Duke longitudinal study.* Durham, NC: Duke University Press.

Palmore, E., & Kinett, V. (1977). Change in life satisfaction. *Journal of Gerontology, 32,* 311-316.

Palmore, E., & Luikart, C. (1972). Health and social factors related to life satisfaction. *Journal of Health and Social Behavior, 13,* 68-80.

Rainwater, L., & Handel, G. (1964). Changing family roles in the working class. In A. Shostak & W. Gomberg (Eds.), *Blue collar world: Studies of the American worker.* Englewood Cliffs, NJ: Prentice-Hall.

Ricoeur, P. (1977). The question of proof in Freud's psychoanalytic writings. *Journal of the American Psychoanalytic Association, 25,* 835-872.

Riegel, K. (1979). *Foundations of Dialectical Psychology.* New York: Academic Press.

Riley, M., Johnson, M., & Foner, A. (Eds.). (1972). *Aging and society, Volume III: A sociology of age stratification,* (pp. 198-235). New York: Russell Sage Foundation.

Rosenmayr, L., & Kockeis, E. (1963). Predispositions for a sociological theory of action and the family. *International Social Science Journal, 15,* 410-426.

Rosow, I. (1976). Status and role change through the life span. In R. Binstock & E. Shanas (Eds.), *Handbook of aging and the social sciences,* (pp. 457-482). New York: Van Nostrand-Reinhold.

Sears R. (1977). Sources of life satisfactions of the Terman gifted men. *American Psychologist, 32,* 119-128.

Seltzer, M. (1976). Suggestions for examination of time-disordered relationships. In J. Gubrium (Ed.), *Time, roles, and self in old age,* (pp. 111-125). New York: Human Sciences Press.

Shanas, E. (1979). Social myth as hypothesis: The case of the family relations of old people. *The Gerontologist, 19,* 3-9.

Sinnott, J. (1982). Correlates of sex roles of older adults. *Journal of Gerontology, 37,* 587-594.

Snow, R., & Crapo, L. (1982). Emotional bondedness, subjective well-being and health in elderly medical patients. *Journal of Gerontology, 37,* 609-615

Strain, L., & Chappell, N. (1982). Confidants: Do they make a difference in quality of life? *Research on Aging, 4,* 479-502.

Sussman, M. (1965). Relationships of adult children with their parents in the United States. In E. Shanas & G. Streib (Eds.), *Social structure and the family: Generational relations,* (pp. 62-92). Englewood-Cliffs, NJ: Prentice-Hall.

Tamir, L. *Men in their forties: The transition to middle-age.* New York: Springer.

Terman, L. M., Burks, B., & Jensen, D. (1930). *Genetic studies of genius, Vol. III: The promise of youth; follow-up studies of a thousand gifted children.* Stanford, CA: Stanford University Press.

Terman, L. M., & Oden, M. H. (1959). *Genetic studies of genius, Vol. V: The gifted group at mid-life.* Stanford, CA: Stanford University Press.

Tobin, S., & Neugarten, B. (1961). Life satisfaction and social interaction in the aging. *Journal of Gerontology, 16,* 344-346.

Troll, L., Miller, S., & Atchley, R. (1979). *Families in later life.* Belmont, CA: Wadsworth.

Uzoka, A. The myth of the nuclear family: Historical background and clinical implications. *American Psychologist, 34,* 1095-1106.

Vaillant, G. (1977). *Adaptation to life.* Boston: Little Brown.

Warner, W. L. (1959). *The living and the dead.* New Haven: Yale University Press.

Weber, M. (1955). *The Protestant ethic* (T. Parsons, Trans.). New York: Scribners. (Original work published 1905)

Wood, V., & Robertson, J. (1978). Friendship and kinship interaction: Differential effects on the morale of the elderly. *Journal of Marriage and the Family, 40,* 367-375.

Zubin, J., & Spring, B. (1977). Vulnerability—A new veiw of schizophrenia. *Journal of Abnormal Psychology, 86,* 103-126.

III

HISTORICAL INFLUENCE ON EMOTION DEVELOPMENT

A pervasive theme in lifespan developmental psychology is that sociohistorical changes impact upon individuals and affect their psychological development, thus marking each cohort in a unique way. Two chapters in this section bring this perspective to bear in their analyses. Felton and Shaver examine cohort effects in wellbeing and Gelfond analyzes the varying incidence of a clinical syndrome over the past century.

In their chapter Felton and Shaver argue that distinct cohort-specific experiences impact on beliefs, attitudes, role assignments, and social comparison standards — factors that are related to wellbeing judgments. To the extent that emotions are related to socially conditioned beliefs, needs, attitudes and values (i.e., the motivational and cognitive determinants of emotional experience), reported feelings of wellbeing can be expected to vary across cohorts. The authors examine the evidence available from longitudinal data sets and find that while the evidence is not definitive, it is supportive of the thesis and thus bears further examination in future research.

The chapter by Gelfond presents a model for examining the relationship between sociohistorical events and clinical symptoms, taking the fluctuating incidence of agoraphobia among women as a formal case. Although agoraphobia is commonly defined as a fear of open space, it is here conceived of as a fear of public spaces. The increased incidence of agoraphobic women is interpreted as the result of increasing pressure on women to work outside of the home for which they were earlier socialized — home representing a familiar safe place, public spaces representing an alien threat. She argues that the rather dramatic change in women's status, together with the impersonal nature of contemporary public spaces makes those who do not know how to be alone vulnerable to the symptoms of agoraphobia. Other clinical entities may also bear such a dialectical analysis.

6

Cohort Variation in Adults' Reported Feelings

BARBARA J. FELTON
PHILLIP SHAVER

The concept of wellbeing has been central to gerontology ever since researchers at the University of Chicago (Cavan, Burgess, Havighurst, & Goldhamer, 1949; Havighurst & Albrecht, 1953; Neugarten, 1963) introduced the notion of "successful aging." Implying that old age inevitably presents people with unhappy exigencies to which they must adapt, the concept of successful aging has served as the cornerstone of investigations aimed at understanding why some adults fare well as they pass through middle age and late life, while others (including some who were previously well adjusted) encounter increased difficulty or suffer emotional maladjustment. Scientific interest in this issue, as well as society's humane and pragmatic concerns, pointedly raise the question, How well are the elderly doing?

Research on the wellbeing of older as compared with younger Americans has produced a complicated set of answers to what at first

AUTHORS' NOTE: We are grateful to Joseph Veroff and the editors of this volume for helpful comments on an earlier draft of this chapter.

might seem a straightforward question. Some of the answers offer direct clues about elderly Americans' health and happiness, but others reveal problems inherent in measuring something as subjective and multifaceted as "wellbeing" and in comparing levels of this elusive emotional state across ages and age cohorts. For example, an intriguing and frequently replicated finding is that older people, by and large, live in what might be called "more unhappy" circumstances than younger people (the elderly have lower incomes and more chronic illnesses, for example, and more frequently experience the death of a close friend), yet — especially in recent years — the elderly report levels of wellbeing at least as high as those of younger adults. How can this paradox be explained?

One answer might lie in the universal process of aging. As people grow older, perhaps they become less worldly, more self-contained, less future-oriented, and more content with reflecting on events rather than participating in and controlling them. Perhaps they lower some of their expectations and standards, part company with earlier desires, and — to the extent that satisfaction is "calculated" as a difference between wishes and perceived actualities — truly are happier in old age. On the other hand, it seems likely that subjects in existing studies represent not just different age groups but substantially different cohorts, each with its own unique formative experiences and historically conditioned dominant concerns. According to this view, age differences in wellbeing might be due as much to cohort differences in values, expectations, and preferred coping strategies as to anything general about the aging process.

The viability of the cohort explanation of age differences in wellbeing is the main concern of this chapter. The idea that historical changes affect individuals' psychological development, hence marking each cohort in special ways, has been a persistent theme in lifespan developmental psychology, a subdiscipline that has articulated persuasive reasons for expecting cohort differences, especially in attitudes and cognitive skills (Cutler & Kaufman, 1975; Schaie, 1970). Less attention has been paid to the possibility of cohort differences in emotional wellbeing during old age, but the general logic of cohort analysis would seem to apply. As we will show, judgments of life satisfaction are based on potentially identifiable cognitive processes; and these processes are likely to be shaped by historical influences and current cultural contexts. Our approach — necessarily rather abstract and speculative at this point, given the paucity of available data — will be to consider subjective wellbeing in light of a certain subset of recent emotion theories. These theories, some of which focus on the cognitive determinants of emotion and coping responses, offer insights into the ways in which cohort differences in beliefs, attitudes, values, and preferred coping strategies might explain cohort differences in reported life satisfaction.

Measures and Determinants of Subjective Wellbeing

The most extensive investigation of life-satisfaction measures to date has been conveniently summarized by Andrews and Withey (1976) in *Social Indicators of Well-Being: Americans' Perceptions of Life Quality.* All of the points we wish to make concerning self-reports of wellbeing can be illustrated by their findings, and these points are generally compatible with other research on life satisfaction (e.g., Bradburn, 1969; Campbell, Converse, & Rodgers, 1976; Lawton, 1982).

In designing their own measure of life satisfaction, the "Delighted-to-Terrible" (or DT) scale, Andrews and Withey assumed that the

> quality of life is not just a matter of the conditions of one's physical, interpersonal and social setting but also a matter of how those are judged and evaluated by oneself and others. . . . Leave the situations of life stable and simply alter the standards of judgment and one's assessed quality of life could go up or down according to the value framework. It may well be that subjective quality of life is better understood by studying the nature and determinants of value structures than by assessing the more objective conditions of living. (1976, p. 12)

Indeed, when Andrews and Withey correlated measures of objective circumstances with measures of either global wellbeing or wellbeing in specific life domains (e.g., ratings of satisfaction with annual income), the resulting relationships were consistently weak. As we will discuss shortly, emotion theorists have come to a similar conclusion. It is usually not possible to say that certain external circumstances "cause" a person to feel angry, happy, or sad. Instead, researchers must consider how these external circumstances are perceived — as just or unjust, for example, or as better or worse than what the person in question was seeking. Thus, an emotional reaction depends as much on a person's definition of justice, or on his or her hopes and expectations, as it does on objective conditions. Life-satisfaction ratings, being in some sense aggregations of emotional experiences, are similarly dependent on personal standards, needs, and expectations — variables that may be influenced by cohort-related forces.

One of Andrews and Withey's most interesting discoveries was that immediate personal concerns are much more important in determining overall life satisfaction than are evaluations of more distant circumstances, such as the quality of local or national government. Personal issues include one's own recent level of fun and enjoyment, feelings of self-efficacy, the belief that one makes a contribution to other people's lives, being dependable, honest, and sincere. Based on several cluster and multidimensional scaling analyses, Andrews and Withey determined that domains of life are organized in ways that parallel subjects' major social roles, and that these roles can be arrayed along a dimension of distance from the self: After one's identity or self comes one's family roles, then one's roles as friend and worker, next one's roles as consumer, citizen of a local community, and finally, citizen of the United States.

> The concept of roles as an organizer of sets of evaluations about aspects of life serves to reduce the multiplicity and variety of facets of life than an individual faces. It is of considerable theoretical interest that this concept of social roles ties as closely as it does to the empirically derived structure of perceptions. (1976, p. 42)

It is especially interesting given our present task because, as we will show, important cohort differences in life satisfaction derive from changes in the salience and availability of social roles.

Andrews and Withey noted that satisfaction was particularly high for life domains close to the self, and that people tended to see themselves as better off than their neighbors in those domains. This suggests parallels with research on self-esteem (summarized by Meyers, 1983, chap. 3) indicating that people attain positive self-feelings by imagining that their sense of humor is better than the next person's, that they are an unusually loyal and good friend, and so on. We maintain that the similarity between life satisfaction and self-esteem judgments can actually be *felt:* If asked, "How has your life been going lately?" we can often virtually feel ourselves recoiling from a negative conclusion and searching actively for evidence to bolster a positive reply. This suggests that one of the major issues for research should be not simply *how satisfied* people are (especially since at least 70 percent of Americans typically say they are satisfied), but what individual and group differences exist in the *bases* of satisfaction or dissatisfaction. This is an area in which cohort differences can be expected.

Another of Andrews and Withey's discoveries was that the combined effects of respondents' evaluations of various life domains could account very well for overall levels of reported wellbeing. The success of the linear additive model

> suggests that somehow individuals . . . "add up" their joys and sorrows about specific concerns to arrive at a feeling about general wellbeing. It appears that joys in one area of life may be able to compensate for sorrows in other areas; that multiple joys accumulate to raise the level of felt wellbeing; and that multiple sorrows accumu-

late to lower it. (1976, p. 122; for further elaboration of these points, see McKennell & Andrews, 1980)

Thus, one way a person of any age in almost any life circumstance can attain a reasonably high level of satisfaction is to emphasize joys and try to deny or deemphasize sorrows.

Despite our .emphasis on potential disparities between objective reports of life circumstances and subjective reports of wellbeing, it is obvious that not all Americans are equally happy or satisfied with life. Just how *do* people go about deciding how satisfied they are? Andrews and Withey chose three domains of life that differ in closeness to the self — personal accomplishments, house or apartment, and national government — and attempted to predict global ratings of these domains (on their DT scale) from six kinds of more specific ratings with varying frames of reference: (1) need satisfaction; (2) social position ("considering your age and position in life"); (3) fairness; (4) resource input ("considering the money, time, and energy being put in"); (5) others' feelings (how others would feel); and (6) ease of change ("considering what it would take to bring about a change"). In each of the three domains, the best three predictors of global satisfaction (together accounting for virtually all of the reliable variance) were, in order of importance, *need satisfaction, fairness,* and *social position.* It seems reasonable to conclude, then, that people generally make life satisfaction ratings with three criteria in mind: How well are my needs being met? (The answer will obviously be affected by a person's particular, perhaps cohort-based, conception of needs.) How fair are my life outcomes? (This depends on the person's conception of what is fair, and seems not to be based primarily on resource inputs.) And, How satisfactory is my situation given my age and social position? In other words, people of different ages relativize their judgments based on what they believe is reasonable for their age or cohort, a process that can be expected to reduce differences in life satisfaction due to age and other demographic characteristics.

How Feelings Are Generated and Reported

The Role of Cognition

Considering that life-satisfaction researchers from Bradburn (1969) through Andrews and Whithey (1976) to Lawton (1982; see also McKennel & Andrews, 1980) have found that global satisfaction ratings are predictable from summary measures of positive and negative affects while these positive and negative summary measures fail to correlate highly with each other, it is important to take into account how affects themselves are generated. If there are cohort differences in life satisfaction, presumably there are also cohort differences in the frequency of certain affects and perhaps also in the causes of the dominant affects. Fortunately, recent theorizing about emotion has illuminated the cognitive determinants of emotional experience, so it is easier today than it would have been just a few years ago to say how cohort differences in beliefs, expectations, and values might influence positive and negative feelings and thus affect life satisfaction.

Several promising models of the cognitive or judgmental basis of emotion have been formulated (e.g., Abelson, 1983; Dahl, 1979; de Rivera, 1977, 1981; Roseman, 1979). For our purposes it matters little which of these proves to be more correct; it is the set of features held in common by all such models that interests us. Each theory is based on the assuption that *judgments* precede and cause discretely different emotions. According to Roseman's theory, for example, "the 13-or-so basic emotions" arise from judgments arrayed along five dimensions: (1) motivational state (wish, desire); (2) situational outcome; (3) probability; (4) agency (self, other, circumstances); and (5) legitimacy (fairness, deservingness). The motivational-state and situational-outcome dimensions correspond to what Andrews and Withey called "need satisfaction"; people experience joy, pleasure, or happiness when they get what they want. They feel distress when they "get what they don't want," in Roseman's terms; relief when they avoid feared or unwanted outcomes; and sadness or sorrow when they fail to get what they want. This part of Roseman's theory is similar to Andrews and Withey's claim that "quality of life is not just a matter of conditions of one's physical, interpersonal, and social setting [what Roseman calls outcomes] but also a matter of how those are judged and evaluated" (in terms of needs, desires, and expectations, according to Roseman).

When outcomes are uncertain — that is, when their "probability" is less than one — we speak of hope and fear rather than joy, relief, sadness, and distress. If the causal agent involved is impersonal, the six terms mentioned so far suffice; but when an outcome is attributed to another person, the attributor speaks of liking or love, disliking or hatred. If the agent is oneself, the emotion is likely to be pride or regret. Finally, legitimacy or fairness combined with agency affects whether a person feels angry toward others or guilty about his or her own actions.

In Andrews and Withey's analysis of life-satisfaction judgments, fairness also plays an important role. People's satisfaction or dissatisfaction with particular life domains depends not only on how well their needs in those domains are or are not being met, but also on how fair they consider this state of affairs to be. The third important life-evaluation criterion mentioned by Andrews and Withey, "age and social position," presumably affects what people believe are legitimate desires. Thus, the cognitive dimensions that determine specific emotions, according to Roseman's (1979) theory, are the same ones that enter into ratings of subjective wellbeing. Whether we think of global judgments as summaries of already existing affects (as Bradburn, 1969, did) or as affects in their own right (literally, feelings about life as a whole), it is clear that cohort differences in wishes, beliefs about fairness, and choice of comparison standards (e.g., reference groups) might influence subjective wellbeing.

Cherlin (1981), summarizing demographic research by Easterlin (e.g., 1980), provides a good example of this kind of cohort-specific influence: "It could have happened . . . that single young men [born in the 1920s and 1930s and married in the 1940s and 1950s] would spend their paychecks on themselves and that young couples would use all of their extra money to buy bigger houses, more furniture, and the like." That most members of the 1920s cohort chose not to do this was, according to Cherlin and Easterlin, an effect of growing up during the Great Depression. "A person's [desired] standard of living . . . is determined by the material conditions he or she experiences during childhood and especially during adolescence" (Cherlin, 1981, p. 61). Feeling no great need for bigger houses and fancy furnishings, the Depression-era adolescents, once grown up, chose instead to invest in larger families, which had the effect of producing a baby boom. It may also have influenced the standards — materialistic or nonmaterialistic, for example — against which members of this cohort, now entering old age, judge their daily experiences (i.e., generate their most frequent emotions) and rate the overall quality of their lives. If this kind of cohort-based standard-setting is the rule rather than the exception — and assuming that biases toward positive self-ratings are not so great as to wipe out all group differences — we have reason to expect cohort differences in life satisfaction during old age.

Secondary Appraisal and Coping

The cognitive processes highlighted in Roseman's theory — the ones that cause or generate affects — are commonly referred to in the emotion literature as "primary appraisals" (Arnold, 1960). Also important are the individual's attempts to *cope,* both with the environmental situation causing the emotion and with the positive or negative feeling itself. Feelings are initiated by an appraisal of the kind Roseman has outlined, but they can be altered by "secondary appraisals" (redefinitions of the situation and reconsideration of the range of possible responses) and by active attempts to alter either the environment or the initial feelings. The mental scramble one undertakes to find evidence to support a happy self-rating is one kind of coping effort. While we do not have space for a detailed treatment of coping processes (see Lazarus & DeLongis, 1983, for a recent review dealing specifically with the elderly), we need to bear in mind that cohort differences might appear not only in primary emotional experiences but also in the processes of coping with emotions and reporting them to unfamiliar interviewers.

The Theoretical Case for Expecting Cohort Effects

That historical change can shape cohorts and thus profoundly affect individual development is a fundamental tenet of lifespan developmental psychology (e.g., Baltes, Cornelius, & Nesselroade, 1978). As expressed in Riegel's dialectical theory (1979), personal development is a result of the crises and catastrophes that inevitably occur as the individual and, simultaneously, his or her immediate social setting and larger society undergo change. Baltes (1979) cites "normative history-graded influences" as one of the three antecedent factors determining development. The conviction that historically fluctuating external events affect psychological development across the life span is, in fact, so central to the developmental perspective that in describing it Baltes (1979) paraphrases Anastasi's (1958) classical paper on the nature-nurture issue: "The central question is not, 'How much cohort variance?' but rather, '*How* do historical and ontogenetic factors interact in codetermining individual development?'" (pp. 270-271).

Sociological theories of social structure and individual development go beyond statements of the importance of historical events to suggest that it is historical shifts in the relationship between roles and role occupants that determine change and stability in both society and individuals. According to Riley's formulation of age-stratification theory (Riley, 1976), changes in the composition of successive cohorts and in the timing of age-related events shape society's age stratification system, as do historical changes in the numbers and kinds of roles available to people of different ages. Distinctive cohorts emerge as society's ways of allocating individuals to roles and socializing them to perform those roles shift (Riley, 1976). This fits well with our earlier observation, based on Andrews and Withey's (1976) work, that domains of life satisfaction correspond closely to available roles, thus making it likely that the *sources* of wellbeing, if not its mean levels, are different for different cohorts.

Neugarten and Datan (1973) argue that historical events affect personality development primarily through their impact on the timing of events in the life cycle. Their suggestion that social change has its impact on individual development by altering normative expectations about the appropriate timing of life-cycle events coincides with historical sociology's conception of the interplay between historical events and individual development (Elder, 1978; Hareven, 1978; Hogan, 1981). Norms defining the appropriateness of one's behavior and social position might affect wellbeing by influencing judgments of need satisfaction and legitimacy which, according to Roseman's (1979) model, determine the nature of emotional experience.

Political attitude researchers have explored cohort effects in somewhat different terms. Cutler and his colleagues (Cutler, Lentz, Muha, & Riter, 1980), summarizing findings from many studies of political and social attitudes, proposed that more general and less personal attitudes are relatively impervious to change over the life span and thus exhibit cohort effects (at least in cases where different cohorts have different general attitudes because of historical conditions early in their lives). More specific and proximate attitudes — those tied directly to personal experience — are more subject to change, according to these authors. This post hoc interpretation provides an organizing framework for data showing that older cohorts of adults have changed little in the direction of society's recent increased liberalism (Glenn, 1980), tolerance of ideological nonconformity (Cutler & Kaufman, 1975; Nunn, Crickett, & Williams, 1978), and positive attitudes toward the admission of Communist China to the United Nations (Glenn, 1974), while they have changed in step with society when it comes to attitudes toward legalized abortion (Cutler et al., 1980) and the women's movement (Cutler, 1983).

Sears (1983), taking a slightly different position, has noted the relative stability of adults' "symbolic predispositions," particularly party identification, liberalism (or conservatism), and racial attitudes. These predispositions seem to develop in adolescence or early adulthood and remain stable thereafter. According to studies reported by Sears and his colleagues, these predispositions often override immediate personal calculations of costs and gains.

It is beyond the scope of this chapter to investigate the details of Cutler's and Sears's arguments. For our purposes, it is sufficient to note that to the extent that cohorts differ in the attitudes prevailing during their formative years, they may differ later in life as well. And, to the extent that fundamental beliefs and attitudes enter life-satisfaction considerations, we should expect to find cohort differences in either levels of satisfaction, the cognitive-judgmental bases of satisfaction, or both.

While all of these theoretical perspectives suggest that psychological variables ought to be shaped by historical events, none deals specifically with subjective wellbeing. Nevertheless, we think it is reasonable to infer that two areas of influence are most significant for cohort differences in wellbeing: (1) social beliefs and attitudes, and (2) social roles. Thinking back on our brief summary of Roseman's model of emotion generation, it is easy to see how beliefs, attitudes, and expectations (cognitive variables, in short) could influence feelings and in turn influence cohort differences in life satisfaction. Reflecting on Andrews and Withey's discovery that life satisfaction is organized around a person's major roles suggests that role availability and role-related rewards and costs — factors that change substantially with history — may also significantly affect an entire cohort's "calculation" of life satisfaction. Taken together, cognitive variables and role-related variables (both of which have been shown to change over time and to mark particular cohorts) could easily affect people's judgments concerning needs and need satisfaction, legitimacy or fairness, and the appropriateness of life's outcomes given one's age and social positions — the major judgments affecting life satisfaction, according to Andrews and Withey (1976).

Evidence for Cohort Effects in Psychological Wellbeing

Despite the existence of approximately twenty-five years' worth of data on American adults' subjective wellbeing, few direct investigations of cohort effects have been attempted. This is due in part to the lack of well-articulated theories but also to important technical difficulties. Cross-study comparisons can be treacherous, because measures of well being differ from study to study, and mismatches between age categories and times of data collection can prevent the construction of cohort-analytic tables (Glenn, 1977). More critically, currently intractable statistical problems make it virtually impossible to infer cohort effects to the exclusion of age or period effects (Glenn, 1976, 1981; Mason, Mason, Winsborough, & Poole, 1973; Rodgers, 1982a). Still, several suggestive studies do exist, and it is part of our task to make some sense of them.

One of the most intriguing clues in the literature regarding cohort effects on wellbeing is the changing correlation between age and wellbeing — variously measured — in large-scale representative survey studies conducted at different times. As Glenn (1980) and Witt, Lowe, Peek, and Curry (1980) have noted, in studies based on data collected before 1970 (e.g., Bradburn & Caplovitz, 1969; Gurin, Veroff, & Feld, 1960) the correlation between age and wellbeing is negative, supporting the conventional wisdom that happiness declines with age. Studies based on data collected in the early 1970s (e.g., Alston, Lowe, & Wrigley, 1974; Edwards & Klemmack, 1973; Spreitzer & Snyder, 1974), in contrast, find no relationship between age and wellbeing. And, more surprising still, studies based on data collected more recently (e.g., Clemente & Sauer, 1976; Czaja, 1975) show that older people are actually happier or more satisfied than younger adults.

Witt et al. (1980) examined this historical trend in 17 national studies that had used the same single-item happiness measure over two decades. They confirmed that from 1948 through 1965, the correlation between age and happiness was, while weak, consistently negative, ranging from −.113 to −.062. (The small size of these coefficients is compatible with Andrews and Withey's finding that demographic variables in general do not explain much variance in wellbeing, probably because of the powerful role of psychological as compared with situational determinants.) In studies conducted in 1966 and 1972, however, Witt et al. found that the correlation went from negative to near zero, and then in 1973 emerged as slightly positive — a pattern which has persisted ever since.

While Witt et al. decided that the early negative correlations might have been due to methodological artifacts, the negative-to-positive shift in the relationship between age and the single-item happiness measure has been interpreted substantively by other analysts (e.g., Glenn, 1980; Rodgers, 1982b). Rodgers's analyses, in particular, were based on data selected to be free from some of the methodological problems cited by Witt's group, yet still turned up the same negative-to-positive correlational shift over the 1957-1978 period. Glenn (1980) found a similar pattern in 14 studies conducted since 1946 and decided that it was due to cohort effects. Interestingly, he warned that it is not safe to conclude that negative effects of aging hinted at in earlier studies have disappeared in recent years, but that instead "cohort effects have come to mask negative age effects" (p. 632). According to Glenn, the influx of increasingly discontent younger cohorts provides the most plausible explanation of the changing pattern of correlations. Older respondents may not have gotten more content, but changes at the low end of the age continuum have caused a potentially misleading change in the correlation coefficient.

In the most intensive investigation of recent sociohistorical changes in wellbeing, Veroff and his colleagues (Veroff, Douvan, & Kulka, 1981; Veroff, Kulka & Douvan, 1981) concluded that stability over the period 1957 to 1976 was much more striking than change. Despite increases in worrying and in problems judged by respondents to be relevant for help, most indicators of subjective mental health showed no change over this socially tumultuous twenty-year period, leading the authors to conclude that evaluations of wellbeng occur in a sociohistorical context and are influenced by people's comparisons with reference groups and historically relative standards, in addition to being moderated by individuals' considerable adaptive skills. What *did* change over the period were the bases of people's satisfaction judgments. Veroff, Douvan, and Kulka (1981) called their book *The Inner American* to emphasize that in 1976, compared with 1957, Americans based their evaluations of wellbeing more on personal, psychological issues and less on public role performances.

In their examination of age-related influences on wellbeing, Veroff and his colleagues found more convincing evidence for aging effects than for cohort influences, and the aging effects proved to be fairly complex (see also Costa & McCrae, 1982). Older people were less happy, less optimistic about their future, less likely to cite the present as the happiest time of their life and more likely to perceive some past period as happier. On the other hand, these same people reported being more completely satisfied with life and were less likely to say that they'd experienced a nervous breakdown or felt overwhelmed by problems. Life cycle differences (e.g., foreseeing a shorter "future," living under relatively stable conditions) rather than cohort differences seem likely to be responsible for these age effects.

Still, there were some effects of cohort. Cohort differences appeared in people's styles of seeking help. People who were middle aged in 1957 and old in 1976 remained consistently self-reliant despite a shift among younger groups toward seeking help for personal problems. Similarly, the cohort of adults young in 1957 emerged as distinctive in consistently placing greater importance on being a parent; the newly arrived adult cohorts were unique in breaking sharply with negative attitudes toward people who decided not to marry; and younger women were similarly distinct in placing much more importance on careers. In line with the work of Sears (1983) and Cutler et al. (1980), Veroff and his coauthors concluded that where cohort effects appear in subjective indicators of mental health, "the measures probably reflect either expressive styles [we would say 'coping styles'] or value commitments made in late adolescence or early adulthood as part of young people's consolidation of values. This early commitment may be impervious to further social change" (p. 541).

(We might note that this resistance to change is probably due as much to social as to psychological stability. Sears [1983] points out that social relationships are much more stable after early adulthood, and that while only six percent of Americans between 25 and 31 have lived at their current address for ten years or more, almost two-thirds of those past retirement age have done so. Moreover, people of all ages tend to socialize with similar aged peers, so their social comparisons and evaluations of information are biased in favor of consistency with cohort members.)

Herzog, Rodgers, and Woodworth (1982) have attempted to explain the recent small positive correlation between age and wellbeing in a somewhat different way. Using general life satisfaction and satisfaction in several domains as criteria and examining studies spanning the years from 1971 to 1978, they found it likely that both cohort and aging play a role in determining the positive correlation. Without directly (i.e., statistically) searching for cohort effects, Herzog et al. (1982) decided that, of the four factors capable of explaining some part of the relationship, two — religiosity and social desirability (both of which may be fundamental according to Cutler and Sears) — were probably linked to cohorts, an interpretation consistent with our emphasis on cohort-linked beliefs, attitudes, and values. The other two factors, a decline in the number of life events and time spent in one location, were plausibly thought to be matters of age rather than cohort.

Clearer evidence for cohort effects emerges from Rodgers's (1982b) analysis of survey data spanning the years 1957 to 1978, including the results reported by Veroff et al. Rodgers found age-by-period interaction effects, implying cohort differences. Specifically, cohorts of adults born before 1903 have had consistently lower happiness levels than adults born subsequently, and their average happiness level has slowly increased over time. A very different pattern emerges for the cohort born between 1923 and 1942; their happiness levels declined between the late 1950s and the early 1970s, suggesting that "whatever it was that produced the period effect during the 1960s, those factors had the greatest influence on the younger members of the adult population." The "period effect" to which Rodgers refers was a societal shift toward "postmaterialistic" values. Older cohorts, along with younger uneducated and lower income adults, have experienced increased happiness levels corresponding closely with improved economic conditions, while the 1923-1942 cohort was more affected by the societal shift in values than by material conditions. This is consistent with Veroff et al.'s finding that between 1957 and 1976 economic concerns were mentioned less frequently as a source of happiness or unhappiness while distress with community, government and world problems received greater mention. Rodgers finds this trend most characteristic of those adults born after 1923, who, despite material circumstances equal to or better than those of other cohorts, experienced a decline in happiness during the late 1960s.

Other evidence supports the contention that the economic lives of the cohort of adults born before 1900 were different from the economic lives of those born later. Well before recent investigations of life satisfaction, Cain (1967) had identified what he called a psychological "watershed" — a sharp discontinuity in the life experiences of the cohort of adults born between 1900 and 1909 and those of earlier cohorts. Compared to the cohort born between 1890 and 1899, the favored 1900-1909 cohort received more education and had lower fertility rates, greater freedom from stringent sexual mores, lower unemployment rates, greater earnings, a shorter workweek, fewer jobs involving physically taxing labor, and a smaller percentage of immigrants. This cohort directly experienced no wars, may have fared better than other cohorts during the Depression, held lucrative defense jobs during World War II, and had fewer children to educate. Cain portrays the social context of these people's early adulthood as rapidly changing but fairly benign: The major social and political events — women's suffrage, prohibition, the rapid increase in the availability of automobiles, radio and movies — coincided with a general repudiation of the previous social order, a move away from social Darwinism, and the abatement of "Protestant ethic" ideologies.

The effect of changing economic circumstances seems to be partly due to relative deprivation, as indicated by Rodgers's (1982b) finding that the impact of changing economic conditions was greater for adults with less education. But economic conditions are also important as they shape values and beliefs about the causes of economic wellbeing (Rodgers, 1982a). Moen (1978) found a difference between the pre- and post-1900 cohorts' willingness to accept help and explained the greater prevalence of the "nonacceptor syndrome" among the older cohort as due to differences in norms that accompanied economic shifts in these people's lives. The pre-1900 birth cohort grew up in an era that, despite material difficulties, stressed individualism and "promised rewards to anyone who worked hard" (p. 299). The elderly born after 1900 were socialized to New Deal attitudes, according to which poverty was seen as a societal rather than an individual problem.

Historical changes in these values also show up in the cohort difference in coping styles documented by Veroff et al. Their findings reflect a continuation of the historical movement away from self-reliance and toward the use of others — both friends and helping professionals — in solving personal problems. Recall that Veroff et al. found the cohort of people who were middle aged in 1957 and "elderly" in 1976 to be less inclined than subsequent cohorts to use informal helping as a means of handling worries and unhappiness. Like younger people, they remained constant over the twenty-year period in their help-seeking preferences, contributing to a cohort effect which Veroff et al. call "a cultural shift toward personal informality" (p. 539). In addition, the elderly cohort of 1976 emerged as distinctly self-sufficient in their reliance on formal (i.e., professional) providers. They seem to have been as immune to the cultural trend toward reliance on psychological experts as they were to the growing tendency to reveal problems to friends.

Concluding Comments

There is no doubt that certain cohorts are distinctive in certain respects, and that this distinctiveness can tentatively be linked to patterns of beliefs (including beliefs about what is needed and what is fair or just), role assignments, and social comparison standards — factors that are related to wellbeing judgments, according to Andrews and Withey (1976), and that can easily be tied to models of emotion generation like Roseman's (1979). Still, the causal road from historical influences to individual feelings and wellbeing judgments is rocky indeed; it is still a long way from being fully documented or understood. Our "case for cohort variation in adults' reported feelings" is, then, an argument for plausibility and potential value, not a cut-and-dried position built on irrefutable or powerful findings. Our hope is that we have been able to point out some of the most promising areas to investigate if one wants to look for such cohort effects.

One such area is the domain of socially conditioned needs, beliefs, attitudes, and values — the motivational and cognitive determinants of emotional experience, according to Roseman. Evidently, important beliefs, standards, and attitudinal predispositions are laid down in adolescence and early adulthood, and these in turn form the basis of emotional reactions all through later life. Most of the existing research on these relatively stable dispositions is aimed at understanding political orientations; much less is known about personal beliefs and attitudes, which are more relevant to evaluations of personal wellbeing.

A charming if minor example of probable cohort differences in personal beliefs or standards appears in B. F. Skinner's recent lecture to the American Psychological Association:

> Among the signs [of fatigue on this list] are several I find helpful. One is an unusual use of profanity or blasphemy. . . . When I find myself saying "damn," I know it is time to relax. (That mild expletive is a sign of my age as well as of my fatigue; I have never felt right about the scatological language of young people.) (1983, p. 241).

What Skinner calls a sign of his age is actually a mark of his cohort; today's young people will probably be just as blasé about scatological language during their old age as they are in their youth. Since the major life domains determining satisfaction are personal and microsocial, not societal (Andrews & Withey, 1976), we need to know more about the stable beliefs and desires against which personal realities are judged.

Another area in which cohort differences in wellbeing (or, at least, in the bases of wellbeing) can be found is connected with social roles. All psychological phenomena linked to social roles ought to be susceptible to cohort effects, as historical changes producing cohort effects are likely to consist, societally, of shifts in social role allocation and, at the individual level, of shifts in the role choices available and the timing of social role assumption (Hogan, 1981; Neugarten & Datan, 1973; Riley, 1976). Bryant and Veroff's (1982) recent comparison of the influences of sex and history on wellbeing offers a current illustration to supplement the ones we have mentioned already. Examining data for married adults in the 1976 *Mental Health in America* study, Bryant and Veroff found that sex differences in the structure of wellbeing that were evident in 1957 had virtually disappeared by 1976. One of the major historical shifts of the period centered around men's increased involvement with parenting and women's increased reliance on work-role performance as bases for evaluating personal adequacy. Although the evidence is still very incomplete, it is reasonable to suggest on the basis of this and other studies that cohort effects appear more strongly in the role-based *elements* of the happiness "equation" than in the overall level of happiness itself.

One of the ways in which evaluations of life satisfaction can be made simpler, and probably more positive for most people, is to narrow the standard of comparison to similar others — including, prominently, members of one's own subjective cohort or reference group. We may not be wealthy, influential, or blessed with leisure time compared to some people, but this fact becomes almost irrelevant if we narrow our considerations to include only what other early middle-aged academics are experiencing. By the same token, an elderly self-evaluator may be missing some of the joys of the 20-year-old, but this is hardly relevant if the standard of comparison is other elderly people, perhaps even just the subclass of elderly people who went to school at a certain place and time. More needs to be known about these social comparison standards because, as Andrews and Withey (1976) have shown indirectly, they act as relativizers and buffers between objectively observable conditions, such as impaired health or reduced income, and subjective judgments of wellbeing.

Cohort effects should also be measurable in the area of coping, as we suggested earlier. Not all people strive to maintain satisfaction in the same ways. Besides the possibility that certain cohorts learn to favor certain coping techniques (leaning on a psychotherapist, praying, getting drunk or high), recent research indicates that adults' choices of coping strategies are linked to the nature of the problems they face (Folkman & Lazarus, 1980). This suggests that to the extent that different cohorts experience different stresses, they may also exhibit different coping strategies. Veroff, Kulka, and Douvan (1981) showed that when older and younger adults' perceptions of their problems were equated, older people were no less likely to seek formal help. Therefore, the more promising site for cohort effects may be in problem definition rather than coping per se.

A general problem in delineating cohort differences is that they often appear in the form of interactions, not main effects. Rodgers (1982a) suggests that current events have different consequences for people at different stages of life and for people who grew up under different historical circumstances. People born during the Depression, for example, when fertility rates were low, have experienced different career opportunities than adults born in the high-fertility era following World War II. Another form of complex interaction involves differential exposure: Elder (1974, 1979) found the negative psychological consequences of the Depression to be specific to boys of economicaully deprived families with obvious marital distress. Along with evidence for more rapid response to social trends on the part of more educated adults, these findings suggest that cohort effects might be easier to document if we defined as cohorts such groups as "the college-educated 1930s cohort," "the 1960s cohort of employed women," and "Vietnam era veterans."

Cohort effects may not be equally likely in all generations. Jones (1980) argued that the generation that came of age in the 1960s was a special group — unusually large because of the postwar baby boom and unusually situated in time. Consistent with Mannheim's (1952) original conception of "generations," this notion is still largely untestable given that we have available too few studies over too short a time period; the life span of survey research is still shorter than the lives of most of the people whose life satisfaction reports we wish to understand. It is noteworthy, however, that among the analyses considered in this chapter the evidence for cohort effects is strongest in cases where a longer time period was examined. This can be taken as a hint that as we collect more data, over a period of several decades, the task of identifying cohort differences in life satisfaction will become somewhat easier.

Another complexity that will have to be addressed is the role played by individual differences within cohorts — individual differences that reflect the consequences of idiosyncratic historical events as well as the consequences of various genetic and developmental processes. Longitudinal studies reveal that neuroticism is highly stable across later adulthood and significantly predictive of negative affects ("unhappiness") 10 years hence; extraversion is also quite stable and reliably related to positive affects (Costa & McCrae, 1980). Maas and Kuypers (1974) found that poorly adjusted 30-year-olds were likely to be poorly adjusted 40 years later. As yet there are no birth-to-death studies involving these variables, but it is at least possible that genetic temperaments account for some of the documented adult stability. If so, these personal tendencies, which are clearly related to life satisfaction, will count as substantial error variance in studies of cohort influences on wellbeing unless they are explicitly measured.

Finally, more research needs to be directed at the process by which people generate wellbeing assessments. We have suggested certain similarities between this and the process of emotion generation outlined recently by Roseman, Abelson, Dahl, and de Rivera, among others. We have also suggested that happiness or satisfaction assessments closely parallel self-esteem judgments, which have been shown to be highly biased in a positive direction. More needs to be known about the degree of distortion and defensiveness that enters publicly stated life-satisfaction assessments. Our own guess is that people, at least in our culture, either feel personally responsible for a negative evaluation of their life course and hence are highly motivated to avoid a self-damning conclusion, or simply find it more functional to view themselves as content. More than 70 percent of adult survey respondents manage to describe themselves as at least "satisfied," despite the myriad complaints we all utter and listen to daily. We cannot ignore the possibility that subjective measures should not be the court of last resort when it comes to assessing the wellbeing of America's elderly, or of any other group.

In general, one of the most interesting and challenging tasks facing lifespan developmental psychology is incorporating a sophisticated understanding of emotion. Toward the end of life when, according to Erikson (1982), each person faces a crisis of "integrity versus despair," he or she must somehow survey life's options, choices, and outcomes and say either, "This has been good; for the most part life was as it should be," or "This is despicable but it cannot be corrected at this late date." Surely there are no more poignant emotions than these which summarize the feelings of a lifetime. It is surprising how little we know about them.

References

Abelson, R. P. (1983). Whatever became of consistency theory? *Personality and Social Psychology Bulletin, 9,* 37-54.

Alston, J. P., Lowe, G. D., & Wrigley, A. (1974). Socioeconomic correlates of four dimensions of self-perceived life satisfaction. *Human Organization, 33,* 99-102.

Anastasi, A. (1958). Heredity, environment, and the question "How." *Psychological Review, 65,* 197-208.

Andrews, F. M. & Withey, S. B. (1976). *Social indicators of well-being.* New York: Plenum.

Arnold, M. B. (1960). *Emotion and personality, Vol. 1: Psychological aspects.* New York: Columbia University Press.

Baltes, P. B. (1979). Life-span developmental psychology: Some converging observations on history and theory. In P. B. Baltes & O. G. Brim (Eds.), *Life-span development and behavior* (Vol. 2). New York: Academic Press.

Baltes, P. B., Cornelius, S. W., & Nesselroade, J. R. (1977). Cohort effects in developmental psychology: Theoretical and methodological perspectives. In W. A. Collins (Ed.), *Minnesota symposium on child psychology* (Vol. 11). Minneapolis: University of Minnesota.

Bradburn, N. M. (1969). *The structure of psychological well-being.* Chicago: Aldine.

Bradburn, N. M. & Caplovitz, D. (1969). *Reports on happiness: A pilot study of behavior related to mental health.* Chicago: Aldine.

Bryant, F. B., & Veroff, J. (1982). The structure of psychological well-being: A sociohistorical analysis. *Journal of Personality and Social Psychology, 43,* 653-673.

Cain, L. D., Jr. (1967). Age status and generational phenomena: The new old people in contemporary America. *Gerontologist, 7,* 83-92.

Campbell, A., Converse, P. E., & Rodgers, W. L. (1976). *The quality of American life.* New York: Russell Sage Foundation.

Cavan, R. S., Burgess, E. W., Havighurst, R. M., & Goldhamer, H. (1949). *Personal adjustment in old age.* Chicago: Science Research Associates, Inc.

Cherlin, A. J. (1981). Explaining the postwar baby boom. *Social Science Research Council Items, 35,* 57-63.

Clemente, F. S., & Sauer, W. J. (1976). Life satisfaction in the United States. *Social Forces, 54,* 621-631.

Costa, P. T., Jr., & McCrae, R. R. (1980). Influence of extraversion and neuroticism on subjective well-being: Happy and unhappy people. *Journal of Personality and Social Psychology, 38,* 668-674.

Costa, P. T., Jr., & McCrae, R. R. (1982). An approach to the attribution of aging, period, and cohort effects. *Psychological Bulletin, 92,* 238-250.

Cutler, S. J. (1983). Aging and changes in attitudes about the women's liberation movement. *International Journal of Aging and Human Development, 16,* 43-52.

Cutler, S. J., Lentz, S. A., Muha, M. J., & Riter, R. N. (1980). Aging and conservatism: Cohort changes in attitudes about legalized abortion. *Journal of Gerontology, 35,* 115-123.

Cutler, S. J. & Kaufman, R. L. (1975). Cohort changes in political attitudes: Tolerance of ideological nonconformity. *Public Opinion Quarterly, 39,* 69-81.

Czaja, S. J. (1975). Age differences in life satisfaction as a function of discrepancy between real and ideal self-concepts. *Experimental Aging Research, 1,* 81-89.

Dahl, H. (1979). The appetite hypothesis of emotions: A new psychoanalytic model of motivation. In C. E. Izard (Ed.), *Emotions in personality and psychopathology.* New York: Plenum.

de Rivera, J. (1977). A structural theory of the emotions. *Psychological Issues Monograph No. 40.* New York: International Universities Press.

de Rivera, J. (1981). The structure of anger. In J. de Rivera (Ed.), *Conceptual encounter: A method for the exploration of human experience.* Washington, D.C.: University Press of America.

Easterlin, R. A. (1980). *Birth and fortune: The impact of numbers on personal welfare.* New York: Basic Books.

Edwards, J. N., & Klemmack, D. L. (1973). Correlates of life satisfaction: A re-examination. *Journal of Gerontology, 24,* 497-502.

Elder, G. H., Jr. (1974). *Children of the Great Depression.* Chicago: University of Chicago Press.

Elder, G. H., Jr. (1978). Approaches to social change and the family. *American Journal of Sociology, 84* (Special supplement).

Elder, G. H., Jr. (1979). Historical change in life patterns and personality. In P. B. Baltes & O. G. Brim, Jr. (Eds.), *Life-span development and behavior* (Vol. 2). New York: Academic Press.

Erickson, E. H. (1982). *The life cycle completed: A review.* New York: Norton.

Folkman, S., & Lazarus, R. S. (1980). An analysis of coping in a middle-aged community sample. *Journal of Health and Social Behavior, 21,* 219-239.

Glenn, N. D. (1976). Cohort analysts' futile quest: statistical attempts to separate age, period and cohort effects *American Sociological Review, 41,* 900-904.

Glenn, N. D. (1977). *Cohort analysis.* Beverly Hills, CA: Sage.

Glenn, N. D. (1980). Values, attitudes, and beliefs. In O. G. Brim, Jr., and J. Kagan (Eds.), *Constancy and change in human development.* Cambridge: Harvard University Press.

Glenn, N. D. (1981). Age, birth cohorts, and drinking: An illustration of the hazards of inferring effects from cohort data. *Journal of Gerontology, 36,* 362-369.

Gurin, G., Veroff, J. & Feld, S. (1960). *Americans view their mental health,* New York: Basic Books.

Hareven, T. K. (1978). *Transitions: The family and the life course in historical perspective.* New York: Academic Press.

Havighurst, R. J., & Albrecht, R. (1953). *Older people.* New York: David McKay.

Herzog, A. R., & Rodgers, W. L. (1981). Age and satisfaction: Data from several large surveys. *Research on Aging, 3,* 142-165.

Hogan, D. P. (1981). *Transitions and social change: The early lives of American men.* New York: Academic Press.

Jones, L. Y. (1980). *Great expectations.* New York: Ballantine.

Lazarus, R. S. & DeLongis, A. (1983). Psychological stress and coping in aging. *American Psychologist, 38,* 245-254.

Lawton, M. P. (1982). *The varieties of well-being.* Address presented to the American Psychological Association, August 26.

Maas, H. S., & Kuypers, J. A. (1975). *From thirty to seventy.* San Francisco: Jossey-Bass.

Mannheim, K. (1952). The problem of generations. In P. Keckskemeti (Ed.), *Essays on the sociology of knowledge.* New York: Oxford University Press. (Originally published, 1928)

Mason, K. O., Mason, W. M., Winsborough, H. H., & Poole, W. K. (1973). Some methodological issues in cohort analysis of archival data. *American Sociological Review, 38,* 242-258.

McKennell, A. C., and Andrews, F. M. (1980). Models of cognition and affect in perceptions of well-being. *Social Indicators Research, 8,* 257-298.

Meyers, D. G. (1983). *Social psychology.* New York: McGraw-Hill.

Moen, E. (1978). The reluctance of the elderly to accept help. *Social Problems, 25,* 293-303.

Neugarten, B. L. (1963). Personality changes during the adult years. In R. G. Kuhlen (Ed.), *Psychological backgrounds of adult education.* Chicago: Center for the Study of Liberal Education.

Neugarten, B. L., & Datan, N. (1973). Sociological perspectives on the life cycle. In P. B. Baltes & K. W. Schaie (Eds.), *Life-span developmental psychology: Personality and socialization.* New York: Academic Press.

Nunn, C. A., Crickett, H. J., & Williams, J. A. (1978). *Tolerance for nonconformity: A national survey of Americans' changing commitment to civil liberties.* San Francisco: Jossey-Bass.

Riegel, K. F. (1979). *Foundations of dialectical psychology.* New York: Academic Press.

Riley, M. W. (1976). Age strata in social systems. In R. H. Binstock & E. Shanas (Eds.), *Handbook of aging and social sciences.* New York: Van Nostrand Reinhold Co.

Rodgers, W. L. (1982). Estimable functions of age, period, and cohort effects. *American Sociological Review, 47,* 774-787. (a)

Rodgers, W. L. (1982). Trends in reported happiness within demographically defined subgroups, 1957-78. *Social Forces, 60,* 826-842. (b)

Roseman, I. (1979). *Cognitive aspects of emotion and emotional behavior.* Paper presented at the annual meeting of the American Psychological Association, September.

Schaie, K. W. (1970). A reinterpretation of age related changes in cognitive structure and functioning. In L. R. Goulet & P. B. Baltes (Eds.), *Life-span developmental psychology: Research and theory.* New York: Academic Press.

Sears, D. O. (1983). On the persistence of early political predispositions: The roles of attitude object and life stage. In L. Wheeler & P. Shaver (Eds.), *Review of personality and social psychology (Vol. 4).* Beverly Hills, CA: Sage Publications.

Skinner, B. F. (1983). Intellectual self-management in old age. *American Psychologist, 38,* 239-244.

Spreitzer, E., & Snyder, E. E. (1974). Correlates of life satisfaction among the aged. *Journal of Gerontology, 29,* 454-459.

Veroff, J., Douvan, E., & Kulka, R. A. (1981). *The Inner American: A self-portrait from 1957 to 1976.* New York: Basic Books.

Veroff, J., Kulka, R. A., & Douvan, E. (1981). *Mental Health in America: Patterns of help-seeking from 1957-1976.* New York: Basic Books.

Witt, D. D., Lowe, G. D., Peek, C. W., & Curry, E. W. (1980). The changing association between age and happiness: Emerging trend or methodological artifact? *Social Forces, 58,* 1302-1307.

7

Agoraphobia and Personal Crisis

MARJORIE GELFOND

> Making decisions became overwhelming. I hadn't even decided whether getting married had been the right decision, much less getting divorced.
>
> Being on an escalator or an elevator in a store was really terrifying because once you made the decision you couldn't really turn around. The same thing was true on highways, and so I would always take another route because I didn't want to have to commit myself until I got to the next exit.
>
> Then getting into the car and going to town became a problem. Gradually, the environment just became too overwhelming. I don't think I left the neighborhood for almost a year.
>
> (Valerie, age 30)

It is a curious fact of history that the first two clinical accounts of agoraphobia appeared within a year of one another, in 1870 (Benedikt) and 1871 (Westphal). Each identified it as a man's disorder. Today, an increasing amount of attention is being devoted to agoraphobia and, by all accounts, the vast majority of agoraphobics are women. Can these matters be explained away as mere artifacts of research and reportage, or is it possible that both the time of the initial appearance of the disorder, and the changes in size and composition of the group reflect important social changes?

The present examination of agoraphobia departs from others' conceptions of the problem as a solely intrapsychic phenomenon. Here, it is set into a framework that takes the changing social situation of women into account. Further, the "disorder" (a word which itself will begin to seem not quite appropriate) is seen here as an outcome of earlier experiences common to women that culminate in a developmental crisis of adulthood.

Agoraphobia has traditionally been defined as a fear of open spaces or, literally, as a fear of the marketplace. Its major symptoms include intense anxiety upon leaving home, often accompanied by the physiological symptoms of arousal such as palpitations and tremors, chronic anticipatory anxiety, and ideation centered on losing control of oneself or even of dying of a heart attack. In addition, many agoraphobics evidence symptoms of depression, depersonalization, obsessive-compulsive concerns, and claustrophobia.

Generally regarded as the most debilitating of the phobias, the reports of its prevalence vary dramatically. One survey (Agras, Sylvester, & Oliveau, 1969), using a stratified sample of the residents of Burlington, Vermont, reported a rate of 6.3 per 1000. Another study (Langer & Michael, 1963) quoted the figure of 280 per 1000.

While the usual criticism of widely varying prevalence rates involves an apparent lack of rigor in identification, this criticism may hide a real phenomenon evidenced by the higher figures — namely, that a considerable number of individuals find that going out elicits mild apprehension at best and severe panic at worst. Although discrete, rigorously defined categories of "Xs" and "non-Xs" are unquestionably tidier to deal with statistically and intellectually, it may well be more illuminating to endure the messiness of seeing agoraphobic fears as falling along a continuum of severity. Doing so sheds light on the situation of a generation of women adapting to the rapid liberalization of feminine sex roles and to a changing relationship with the public world.

Epidemiological Considerations

Researchers today are in agreement that 80 to 90 percent of agoraphobics are women, and that the most common times of onset are during mid-adolescence and especially between the late twenties to early thirties (Marks & Gelder, 1966; Marks & Herst, 1970). This is, in itself, noteworthy as it is the only phobia that typically begins in adulthood.

No other consistent pattern emerges in terms of intelligence, socioeconomic status, birth order, number of siblings, stability in the parental family, marital stability, or level of education, all of which have been examined.

Most studies report that a majority of agoraphobics are married, a fact that in itself is of uncertain significance considering that most adult women are married. On the other hand, a broader view of the literature on the mental health of women reveals a disproportionately high number of married women who have diagnosed neuroses when compared with both men and with nonmarried women (Gove, 1980). This raises the question of whether there are differences of either a chacterological or situational nature that might contribute substantively to the development of a mid-life phobia in married women.

Etiological Theories

Freud made early mention of agoraphobia, referring to it as "topophobia," a fear of spaces. He offered two explanations. In one, he described the disinhibiting qualities of open spaces, found threatening insofar as they invite one to indulge in sexual activity (1959). In the other, he interpreted his own apprehensions about traveling as a regressive fear of separation from the maternal figure, symbolically represented by the house (Jones, 1961).

Later psychoanalytic writers most frequently elaborated the theme of separation fears. Frances and Dunn (1975) applied Margaret Mahler's notion of separation/individuation to their explanation of agoraphobia. This involves the assumption tht physical separation is a necessary precursor of psychological separation, something which, in turn, must precede the establishment of an autonomous identity. Thus, the agoraphobic's inability to leave home, an environment which again is said to represent the mother, is interpreted as the individual's failure to establish an autonomous identity.

The early behavioral literature invokes the paradigm developed by John Watson in his induction of an experimental phobia in Little Albert. Watson interpreted the phobic's seemingly irrational fear as a conditioned response to stimuli that have become incidentally associated with a fear-producing situation.

Joseph Wolpe's more recent interpretation (1970) takes into consideration certain social factors. He reports the disorder to occur most typically in unhappily married women, "low in self-sufficiency," who possess a fantasy of liberation but who are unable to symbolically and literally leave the home for fear of "falling into a social abyss" (p. 299).

The assertion that social factors play a part in the relatively high incidence of neurosis among women is central to the theories of such writers as Gove (1980), Jessie Bernard (1971), and others who see the housewife role as one of low status, as boring, emotionally confining, and as contributing little to self-esteem. Robert Seidenberg (1973) applied this to his explanation of a woman's agoraphobic symptoms in an article entitled, "The Trauma of Eventlessness."

British psychiatrist Isaac Marks (1966) considers the socially conditioned avoidance of fear-producing stimuli to be a factor, especially for women. Marks further suggests that busy places can produce overarousal which, for some, can be anxiety provoking.

While a number of writers have contended that agoraphobia is really a form of masked depression, this would seem to obfuscate the reality of a distinct symptomatology, writing it off instead as unimportant or uninterpretable. The temptation to do so is considerable, as it is difficult to comprehend how the environment to which one has been exposed because birth could suddenly become the object of a phobia.

Other researchers have offered physiological theories, explaining agoraphobia as an outcome of temporal lobe epilepsy (Roth, 1959) or as a disorder involving the production of neurotransmitters (Sweeney, 1983). In general, however, physiological theories, including genetic ones, have not gained wide acceptance in the field.

Each of the above theories offers a possible clue into the causes of agoraphobia, yet many questions are left unresolved. Of these, a few seem especially pertinent. First, why are so many agoraphobics women? Teaching girls to avoid "fear-producing stimuli" may well be a cultural phenomenon, but how does the world beyond home become a fear-producing stimulus?

Is the fear of the outside merely fortuitous, is home only a maternal representation, or is it possible that environments themselves can be important sources of affect, particularly for women?

Finally, is it just the situational predicament of being unhappily married that triggers the disorder, or can this be seen (like depression in women) as possibly the outcome of early developmental experiences?

Rethinking the Problem

Perhaps we might begin by noting that the fear of open spaces is a misconceptualization of the problem. In fact, the most frequently reported symptoms involve anxiety elicited by going away from home, traveling, sitting in traffic, being alone, walking on narrow streets, and being in crowds, according to a study by Snaith (1968). Snaith's subjects ranked the fear of large open spaces a lowly ninth. Similarly, Burns and Thorpe (1977) found that 96 percent of their sample found waiting on line in a department store more anxiety arousing than any of a list of other situations.

In short, it appears that it is not *open* spaces but *public* spaces that elicit negative affect, and it seems more plausible to view the difficulty as one of constraint rather than of disinhibition as Freud had supposed.

Let us further consider the meaning of home. The idea of "coming home," of "never being able to go home again," and of playing a game "on the home field" all embody some very concrete meanings regarding the psychological comfort of an environment in which there is a close fit between identity and setting.

The very notion of the weary traveler, coping with a gnawing homesickness, feeling emotionally drained from being away from what is most familiar, lends a clear sense that, apart from any historical, symbolic representations, places can be powerful sources of affect that can support or undermine the sense of self.

Many people also experience a growing reluctance to leave home after being there for even as brief a time as a few days. Dislodging oneself for a return to work after a holiday is something many people find difficult, as much because of the leaving as because of what they must return to.

If one likens the agoraphobic's fear of going out to the traveler's homesickness, it is obvious that agoraphobia is more than a peculiarity of the few with uncertain identities or accidentally unpleasant associations to the outdoors. The notion of home as representing only mother hardly does justice to the web of feelings and associations that individuals accumulate over time. That home may inspire feelings of competence, identity, and being at ease can be considered as contemporary responses rather than historical ones.

Conversely, "leaving home" conveys a sense of autonomy and self-sufficiency but also of having to brave the social and physical elements. Thus, while walking out the front door, either to run an errand or to leave a marriage, may have some symbolic weightiness, the present reality of the public environment, its familiarity or unfamiliarity, its crowdedness, social demands, requirement of vigilance, and so on are all aspects that can elicit feelings of competence or helplessness, challenge or apprehension, and can be draining or rejuvenating, depending largely on one's background of preparedness.

Insofar as women have acquired a different relationship with home and public environments than men, we may have a first clue into the overrepresentation of women among agoraphobics.

Agoraphobics as Women

> When I graduated from high school, I was given a choice of one of two things: Becoming a secretary or being an airline stewardess . . . those were the only two "adventures" that my parents would give me the money for. . . .
>
> When I broke up with my husband and went back to live with my parents, I felt very dependent and childlike . . . I led myself to believe that I would have led a very contented life just sitting in the house with them all the time. I seemed always to be waiting for their approval before it was okay to go out.
>
> (Valerie)

Dialetics and Disorder

Heretofore, only clincians have attempted to understand this perplexing disorder. In applying a trait dynamic theory that emphasizes such qualities as dependency and identity-related conflicts, or a physiological theory that attributes the problem to an internal malfunction, the importance of the sociohistorical context in which women's roles have undergone dramatic change has been overlooked.

One might do better to stand back from the thick of individual symptoms and personal history, examining instead the evolution of public life and women's relationship with it. Klaus Riegel's (1979) paradigm of a dialectical psychology, reached by integrating lines of individual psychological and biological development with the alterations in social and physical conditions, provides a circumspect view that can be applied to the problem of women with agoraphobia.

Riegel hypothesized that synchronization among the various individual, social, and physical processses is sometimes achieved at the expense of one or another of them. For example, the development of an intense child-centered family life as the central element in community organization could only occur if women subordinated their personal needs to those of the family. A social movement that strives toward the emancipation of women will then produce within the social system a state of disequilibrium, or what Riegel called a "crisis of desynchrony."

Whereas most theorists see disequilibrium as a force that interferes with individual and social functioning, Riegel asserted that it is a necessary condition for critical changes and, ultimately, progression to a higher level of synthesis. Indeed, he claims that this progression can only occur when coordination among the parts is replaced by "a sufficient degree of autonomy that is reflected in mutual appreciation and respect" (p. 12), something that applies well to women's changing circumstances.

At the personal level, however, stress often accompanies a state of disequilibrium. The appearance of increasing numbers of agoraphobic women is a product of this stress. Because of women's change in status, and because environments themselves have been transformed over time, the once comfortable fit between women and the home environment has become less so. The home setting which before seemed safe, may now seem confining. Simultaneously, environments outside the home that may not even have been represented in women's life space, now present new opportunities, but demand a repertoire of behaviors that some women have not yet acquired.

Thus, it appears that Gove's understanding of neurosis in women as a consequence of women's status as lowly housewife is less true than is the increasing possibility that women can be or should be more than housewives, but are ill prepared for new roles.

Women and Environments

Despite widely diverging theoretical backgrounds, there has been remarkable agreement among clincians regarding the basic personality profile of the agoraphobic woman. She is described as someone with strong dependency needs and fundamental acceptance of the traditional feminine role. She also appears to fit into Rae Carlson's (1971) description of women whose cognitive style is well suited to the communal world of home and neighborhood. Here, says Carlson, psychological wellbeing rests upon shared rather than individualized identity; the sense of self is embedded in the intimate context of home life, with the neighborhood an extension of the home. In contrast, men assume the impersonal and distanced stance demanded by the public, working world. Identity and environment here remain separate.

In view of the goals set for women, which continue to be centered around home life, it is not surprising that home has special, affect-laden meanings for women that are considerably different than those for men. The close relationship that develops between competence and positive affect can be seen here. Socialized to function in the home setting, the traditional woman becomes deeply invested in the place where the physical and social attributes illuminate her sense of self.

Several researchers (e.g., Saegert & Winkel, 1979; Csikszentmihalyi & Rochberg-Halton, 1981; Hayward, 1979) found that women perceived the home as a personalized place, a place that expressed their identity and supported self-clarifying activities, a setting for important relationship, and where they have control. Women tended to respond to the affective qualities of the home—the amount of light, color and design.

In contrast, men responded to home more cognitively than affectively, identifying it as a physical structure, a commodity, a locational backdrop for activities, a possession or repository for possessions and as a place associated with childhood. And while women selected as their most meaningful objects those that evoked feeling because of some aesthetic and/or interpersonal attribute, men chose those that were primarily instrumental. Women selected such items as pictures, plants, and collections; men selected sports equipment, vehicles, power tools, trophies, and firearms — all of which refer to outside activities.

One may further assert that womens response to environments in general is more suffused with affect than men's, who react in a more intellectualizing and distanced fashion. Beyond Carlson's notion of identity, there are considerable variations in one's entire relationship with environments, associated, for example with age, sex, and culture. It is this factor that confounds the clinician who, in seeking to understand space-related fears begins with the assumption that environments have largely objective qualities.

Illustrative of the sex differences in environmental relationships, one study found that when husbands and wives were asked to develop cognitive maps of places, the wives used home as their point of orientation; the husbands used abstract coordinates (Everitt & Cadwallader, 1972).

How then might women, especially traditional women, react to public settings? These are the settings they have been warned against. Not only are girls made aware early on the myriad dangers of physical hazard and strangers but, compared to boys, they are more often restricted to a closer home range, checked on, supervised, required to adhere to a curfew, and transported from place to place (Saegert & Hart, 1978). In general, women are treated successively from childhood to supervision, chaperonage, and escortage when outside the home. Taboos against women going alone to such places as parks and recreation areas, restaurants, bars, theaters, or anywhere after dark are not long gone. They continue to reverberate in women's reluctance to travel unaccompanied to these places.

Thus, while the symbolic meaning of places might account for the agoraphobic's fear of going out, the more parsimonious explanation is that the socialization process for women, particularly traditional women, results in their finding psychological anchorage at home and in viewing the public world as one that allows little sense of safety, control, or competence. The agoraphobic's conflicts are not merely played out in the context of the environments but are elicited by the relationship she has with them.

The Capacity To Be Alone

An important, related matter involves the capacity to be alone. Many people view periods of aloneness as both pleasurable and necessary for their emotional wellbeing. Aloneness can even be imbued with a sense of excitement that comes, perhaps, with the young child's discovery of hiding places. Aloneness, privacy, and secrecy are all intimately related to one another and tend to be regarded, when they are of one's own volition, as having this certain pleasurable and sometimes special quality.

The personally experienced need to be alone is seldom reflected in the literature of a culture that often equates aloneness with pathology and stultifies the developmental impulse to learn to be alone contructively, both in private and in public. The choice of aloneness comes about when the individual feels capable of functioning alone. Doing so enhances one's autonomy and competence.

That the capacity as well as the need to be alone require early practice is well illustrated by an observation made by Isaac Marks (1966). He reported a high incidence of agoraphobia among minority group women who had been relocated from their single room tenement homes to housing in a different area of the city. The homes to which they were moved had several rooms, yet many of the women continued to occupy a single room with the rest of the family. The women were described as being fearful of doing anything alone. These "symptoms," however, might readily be understood as a consequence of a socialization process in which aloneness was a rare experience for the women and are less well interpreted as form of individual psychopathology.

Entire cultures, in fact, such as can be found in India, might be described as having "agoraphobic" tendencies insofar as their use of space, like that of these women, assures that they will seldom be alone. A study of Chandigarh (Brolin, 1976), the fashionably modern, Western-style capital of Punjab, revealed that residents saw the parks, which remain largely unused, as a foreigner's conception of desirable recreational space. Women, who customarily require their husband's escort in such public places, stay in the limited area in front of their homes to socialize, watch their children at play, and do their chores.

Inside, homes designed to reflect the Western valuing of privacy by having several bedrooms are found to have numerous members sharing rooms with one room that would be left vacant were it not for the constant stream of houseguests that frequent the Indian home.

The fear of being alone is not problematic to individuals in societies, past or present, where one is seldom if ever left alone. It is only when setting demands change and one is suddenly confronted with the prospect of aloneness that those least prepared for it by their past experiences will find themselves unable to tolerate it. Conversely, I should find it altogether stressful, given my own background, to find myself, let us say, in a hospital ward sharing a room with several others, trying to do in a relatively public place many of the things that I am accustomed to doing alone. Should we call these forms of psychopathology, generated solely by internal conflicts, or shall we say also that the conflict flows from circumstances made untenable by the way the person has been socialized? Further, to the extent that girls in urbanized Western cultures are discouraged from being independent explorers of new places while boys are encouraged to explore, girls will have a greater tendency to remain in familiar surroundings, especially if alone, whereas boys will be more likely to seek out unfamiliar places. Commonly in adulthood, this preference can be seen during times of stress, when women retreat to the bedroom but men go out.

For the agoraphobic woman, then, early socialization would have afforded little chance for her to learn to function competently alone outside of home and the immediate neighborhood. Her inability to be alone in the unfamiliar territory beyond the home and neighborhood (which many can tolerate) reflects her assumption that she cannot function there unless accompanied by a familiar other. And, instead of assuming the distanced relationship with her surroundings described by Carlson, as typical of men, she feels inescapably a part of it, becoming overwhelmed as she begins to experience herself as well as her surroundings as unfamiliar.

In sum, the socialization process results in the agoraphobic feeling unable to cope with the constraints of the public world and thus, paradoxically, she feels trapped outdoors but liberated inside her home.

Developmental Issues and Agoraphobia

We might now return to the question of why agoraphobia appears in women initially during adolescence and early middle age. Many writers on the subject of adolescence have made note of the discontinuities characteristic of the developmental process in modern societies. Whereas traditional societies prepare children gradually to assume adult roles, little provision is made for that here. During the adolescent years there is an increasing demand for autonomy that follows a relative absence of opportunities to rehearse.

Second, adolescence is typified by a growing need for privacy. In contrast to the young child, for whom the essential compenent of privacy is physical separation, for the more mature individual it evolves into a psychological phenomenon. As the ability to internalize certain elements of the outside world while screening out others improves, the adolescent articulates an inner world. However, for those adolescents who have had only a limited opportunity to learn to utilize aloneness, there is a continuing vulnerability to external circumstance. Because the agoraphobic individual is unable to withdraw psychologically from her surroundings into an inner world, the constant impingement on consciousness of the environment without respite contributes to the sense of being inundated and, ultimately, exhausted. Having to stand on line presents itself as an ordeal rather than a chance to think things over.

Adolescence, then, is a critical juncture at which time earlier developmental weaknesses result in problems of adaptation to specific sets of demands. The adolescent girl's lack of prior experience in negotiating the public world manifests itself now when the sudden requirement for autonomous activity in the public context produces agoraphobic symptoms.

Later adulthood, the second period in which agoraphobic symptoms appear, is similarly characterized by the assumption of adult responsibilities, and most notably involves the willingness to commit oneself to marriage, parenthood, and/or career. Here again, however, early protectionism has limited women's opportunities to develop the full range of roles, affects, and skills. The possibilities for an expanded sense of self have been foreclosed prematurely by the constraints of the feminine role.

Interestingly, one is readily struck by the self-assurance and liveliness many agoraphobic women in the home. Despite symptoms that often have been present since adolescence, the majority have maintained a marriage, established a family, and manage to conduct a fairly active social life. A number of women even report running home-based businesses. Although one might readily assume that remaining at home for years would be stifling, most of these women have adapted well enough to obtain many of the gratifications of a more normal life.

To return, finally, to the question of how the size and composition of the agoraphobic population has changed since the nineteenth century let us consider the matter of social change.

Few eras were more aptly named than the age of the Industrial Revolution. One of the most far reaching of the changes it brought was the break between public and private life. It has been suggested that this break required a corresponding need to develop public and private selves, each with its own set of roles and attitudes, but that such an adaptation could only result in an identity crisis. Gadlin (1974) believes that his led to the emergence of people as an autonomous beings, defined internally rather than by their surroundings.

Such an assertion, however, can apply only to the men of the era, who were forced to straddle the two separate worlds of work place and home. It could not apply to women, who lived their lives for the most part in the private sphere.

It was in this context of rapid industrialization and urbanization during the mid- to late nineteenth century that the first accounts of agoraphobia were published and in which the problem was described as one affecting men. One can see in this, using Riegel's formulation, how lines of individual development in men changed to accomodate social changes. The intervening crisis of desynchrony, however, also produced a new situationally appropriate symptomatology.

The predicament of the Victorian male presaged the current social situation of women. The last fifteen years also have consituted a period of rapid social change in which substantial numbers of women have begun full-time employment, undergone divorce, and assumed the responsibilities of single parenting. It is a time in which traditional feminine pursuits have been most aggressively challanged by options to seek careers instead of just work, and to establish a life-style that demands a far more active public life.

There is much evidence suggesting that women's emotional wellbeing has improved significantly with these expanded commitments. The enhancement in self-esteem resulting from the move into the public sphere is something that Gove, Bernard, and Seidenberg might have predicted. Nonetheless, women have not arrived at the kind of autonomous self-definition that we have said may typify the post-Industrial male. Some women have attempted to adapt by carrying their private roles into the public context, maintaining their housewifely role in the workplace; others seem to have entirely renounced their traditional private selves in both public and private worlds. In any case, it is clear that traditional child-rearing practices have not caught up with women's changing social circumstances, and have left a proportion of women ill prepared for the entry into public life. The shrinking number of women who remain in the now half-deserted suburbs of daytime whose early experiences prepared them for homemaking are exposed to increasing pressure to abandon that setting for the workplace. One would predict that among those who capitulate some will be added to the ranks of agoraphobics.

Lastly, the very character of public life has changed since the Industrial Revolution. Once permeated with a sense of familiarity and community, it has acquired a new aura of alienation and even danger. Thus aloneness, which before had scarely been a circumstance to be encountered anywhere, has now become an attribute of public places. And while the unfamiliarity and anonymity that now characterize it may be liberating to some, it places new demands on the individual in terms of the capacity to function competently and comfortably alone.

References

Agras, S., Sylvester, D., & Oliveau, D. (1969). The epidemiology of common fears and phobias. *Comprehensive Psychiatry, 10*(2), 151-156.

Benedikt, V. (1981). Uber Platzschwindel. Allgemeine Wiener Medizinische Zeitung, 1870. Cited in A. Mathews, M. Gelder, & D. Johnston *Agoraphobia: Nature and treatment.* New York: Guilford Press.

Bernard, Jessie, (1971). The paradox of the happy marriage. In V. Gornick & B. Moran (Eds.) *Woman in sexist society.* New York: Basic Books.

Brolin, Brent (1976). *The failure of modern architecture.* New York: Van Nostrand-Reinhold.

Burns, L. E. & Thorpe, G. L. (1977). Fears and clincial phobias: Epidemiological aspects and the national survey. *Journal of International Medical Research, 5,* Supp. (1), 132-139.

Carlson, Rae (1971). Sex differences in ego functioning: Exploratory studies of agency and communion. *Journal of Consulting & Clinical Psychology, 37*(2), 267-277.

Csikszentmihalyi, M. & Rochberg-Halton, E. (1981). *The meaning of things.* Cambridge: Cambridge University Press.

Everitt, J. & Cadwallader, M. (1972). The home area concept in urban analysis. In *EDRA 3,* Los Angeles: University of California.

Frances, A. & Dunn, P. (1975) The attachment-autonomy conflict in agoraphobia. *International Journal of Psychoanalysis, 56,* 435-439.

Freud, Sigmund (1959). *Inhibitions, symptoms, and anxiety.* New York: Norton.

Gadlin, Howard (1974). *Private lives and public order: A critical view of intimate relations in the United States.* Paper presented at Conference on Close Relationships, Amherst, MA.

Gove, Walter (1980). Mental illness and psychiatric treatment among women. *Psychology of Women Quarterly, 4*(3), 345-362.

Hayward, D. Geoffrey (1977). *Psychological concepts of home among urban middle class families with young children.* Unpublished doctoral dissertation, the City University of New York.

Jones, Ernest (1961). *The life and work of Sigmund Freud.* New York: Basic Books, 1961.

Langer, T. S. & Michael, S. T. (1963). *Life stress and mental health.* New York: Macmillan.

Marks, Isaac (1966). *Fears and phobias.* London: Heinemann Press.

Marks, I. & Gelder, M. (1966) Different ages of onset in varieties of phobia. *American Journal of Psychiatry, 123,* 218-221.

Marks, I. & Herst, E. (1970). A survey of 1200 agoraphobics in Britain. *Social Psychiatry, 5,* 16-24.

Riegel, Klaus (1979). *Foundations of dialectical psychology.* New York: Academic Press.

Roth, M. (1959). The phobic anxiety depressionalization syndrom. *Proceedings of the Royal Society of Medicine, 52,* 587-595.

Saegert, S. & Hart, R. (1978). The development of environmental competence in girls and boys. In M. Salter (Ed.), *Play: Anthropological Perspectives.* Cornwall: Leisure Press.

Saegert, S. & Winkel, G. (1980). The home: A critical problem for changing sex roles. In G. Wekerle, R. Peterson, & D. Morley (Eds.), *New space for women.* Boulder: Westview Press.

Seidenberg, Robert (1973). The trauma of eventlessness. In J. Miller (Ed.), *Psychoanalysis and women.* New York: Penguin Books.

Snaith, R. P. (1968). A clinical investigation of phobias. *British Journal of Psychiatry, 114,* 673-697.

Sweeney, Donald (1983 February 22). *Agoraphobia.* Paper presented at Psychopharmacology for Psychologists Conference, Fair Oaks Hospital.

Westphal, C. (1981). Die Agoraphobie: Eine neuropathische Erscheinung. Archiv fur Psychiatrie und Nervenkrankheiten. Cited in A. Matthews, M. Gelder, & D. Johnston. *Agoraphobia: Nature and treatment.* New York: Guildford Press.

Wolpe, Joseph (1970). Identifying the antecedents of an agoraphobic reaction: A transcript. *Journal of Behavior Therapy and Experimental Psychiatry, 1,* 299-304.

IV

EMOTION AND PERSONALITY

The chapter by Costa and McCrae provides a bridge between the previous chapters dealing with the general construct of psychological wellbeing on the one hand, and individual personality on the other. He notes that although few younger individuals look forward to old age, research has consistently shown that the elderly do not differ markedly from younger adults in subjective wellbeing. In part, this is because individuals adapt to their life circumstances; in part, because wellbeing is powerfully influenced by stable personality traits in the domains of neuroticism and extraversion. New data from 350 men and 256 women in the Augmented Baltimore Longitudinal Study of Aging are used to confirm, extend, and modify a model of personality and subjective wellbeing, and longitudinal analyses over 10-to 23-year intervals show that wellbeing can be predicted by antecedent personality. Some implications of this fact for the assessment of wellbeing in old age are discussed, and it is noted that the quality of life for older persons may be better than commonly is assumed.

In the chapter by McAdams, the relationship between the affective themes of intimacy and power motivation and personal identity is explored. McAdams examines identity at mid-life as observed from the personal life story — a personalized myth constructed consciously and unconsciously by the individual in late adolescence and adulthood. According to McAdams, by providing a coherent narrative framework within which the disparate events of a person's life can be embedded and given meaning, the life story integrates past and present with an envisioned future so as to confer upon the individual that sense of inner sameness and continuity which Erikson maintains is at the heart of ego identity. Research with actual life stories indicates that love and power images — personified and idealized images of the self — are intrinsic aspects of adult identities.

The chapter by Malatesta and Culver examines the interplay between affective experiences, personality dynamics, and the normative life tasks and demands of adulthood by following the lives of a cohort of 59 college-educated women from late adolescence into middle adulthood. Content analysis of projective and autobiographical material showed that affective themes of anger, fear, and sadness occurred with moderate frequency over the four waves of data collection, but the primary affect for any given wave varied across waves from anger during adolescence to sadness during the peak child-rearing years to anxiety during years involved in resuming or developing careers. Top-ranking themes of achievement and affiliation during adolescence placed in different rankings over the years. The pattern of obtained results was taken as support for the thesis that thematic content developed in childhood and/or adolescence (as part of the personality) maintains and periodically regains eminence during later years, that these themes collect around an affective core, and that adult life roles tend to overwhelm and obscure primary themes at certain developmental periods.

Finally, using a role-theoretical approach with a socioanalytic perspective, the chapter by Hansson, Hogan, and Jones examines the relationship between emotional and personality processes and the experience of becoming old. In this framework emotional portrayal and control competencies are seen as being related to the attainment of status and popularity vis-á-vis one's reference group and the roles one plays. Role contraction in old age creates reduced group expectations, standards, and structure. The authors show how reduced role opportunity can be held to account for a host of changes that have typically been associated with aging, such as interiority and diminished emotional competencies, but perhaps are more appropriately assigned to role changes.

8

Personality as a Lifelong Determinant of Wellbeing

PAUL T. COSTA, Jr.
ROBERT R. McCRAE

Despite the folk wisdom implicit in such sayings as "money can't buy happiness," one of the most difficult lessons for students of wellbeing to learn has been the relative independence of objective and subjective wellbeing (Lawton, this volume). Most of us firmly believe that we would be happier if we had better health, greater prestige, lower taxes, or more security. The life stories of a hundred movie stars or lottery winners notwithstanding, we feel certain that we would appreciate our new-found blessings and live happily ever after if only we got whatever it is we currently want.

Conversely, we expect we would be less happy if we had poorer health, lower status, less money, fewer friends. And since all these — together with decline in sexual vigor, loss of physical beauty, and the imminence of death — are associated with age, most of us regard the approach of old age with attitudes ranging from resignation to gloom to desperation. Surely old people must be among the most unhappy of all groups!

Yet survey research has shown again and again that the elderly are not particularly unhappy — in fact, they may be more satisfied with life than are younger men and women (Andrews & Withey, 1976; Campbell, Converse & Rogers, 1976; Herzog, Rodgers, & Woodworth, 1982). Should that be taken as evidence that life is better for the aged than we imagined, that there are compensatory gains? Does it suggest that their responses to measures of subjective well-being are meaningless, mere rationalizations, a brave but false front intended to deny the inevitable? Or is happiness perhaps determined by other factors that do not change with age?

These questions are of more than academic interest, but even as intellectual problems they are fascinating. Their answers depend on an understanding of the relations between environment and cognition, cognition and affect, affect and personality. None of these is fully understood, but in recent years considerable progress has been made. This chapter will review some of the evidence and present results of new studies confirming, extending, and in some cases modifying a model of personality and subjective wellbeing we have been developing over the past few years. Our new data come from the Augmented Baltimore Longitudinal Study of Aging (ABLSA; McCrae, 1982), a well-educated, generally healthy, community-dwelling group of volunteers who cover the full adult age range and have been studied for as much as 25 years. Other research, done here (Costa, McCrae, & Norris, 1980; Lawton, this volume) and abroad (Warr, Barter, & Brownbridge, 1983) supports the generalizability of the basic model.

Wellbeing, Social Desirability, and Adaptation

Before we attempt to explain the paradox of happiness in old age, we should be sure that the reports that create it are trustworthy. When self-report results contradict experimenter expectations, social desirability or defensive responding is often urged as an explanation of the discrepancy. Tamir (1982), for example, thinks that her failure to find much evidence of a mid-life crisis can be accounted for by socially desirable responding in middle-aged men; and Herzog, Rodgers, and Woodworth (1982) raise this as a possible explanation for the reported high life-satisfaction of the elderly. Because most research on wellbeing is done using self-reports (and must be if subjective wellbeing is the variable of interest), this charge would be serious if supported.

But there are at least three good reasons for doubting that it is true. First, despite widespread beliefs, social desirability as a response style has rarely proven to be a significant threat to the validity of self-report measures (Dicken, 1963; McCrae & Costa, 1983b). Second, the hypothetical distortion we attribute to the elderly would also have to be attributed to minorities, the poor, the undereducated, and many other groups who might be supposed to be lower in wellbeing, but who show relatively small differences in most studies (e.g., Andrews & Withey, 1976). When so many groups that should be unhappy are not, some process more fundamental than mere responding bias is suggested. Third, there is an alternative explanation that plausibly accounts for the general lack of age differences: adaptation theory.

Adaptation level (Helson, 1964) is a general theory of perception that holds that an individual's estimation of quantity depends on his or her recent experience rather than on absolute standards. A brass band may sound "loud" to a devotee of chamber music, but not to a rock musician. The same model has been extended to more abstract perceptions, including satisfaction with housing, perceived health, and general wellbeing (Brickman & Campbell, 1971). According to this model, changes in the quality of life lead to increases in happiness only temporarily, until the neutral point of comparison has been reset. Brickman and Campbell refer to this phenomenon as the "hedonic treadmill," and they imply that the rising standard of living that America enjoyed in the fifties and sixties could not be expected to produce a concommitant rise in wellbeing. The good news, of course, is that the declining standard of living of recent years has brought less misery than it would have had we not all adjusted our expectations downward.

Brickman, Coates, and Janoff-Bulman (1978) gave a dramatic example of the power of adaptation by comparing lottery winners with paraplegics and showing little difference in wellbeing. A more persuasive test of adaptation level theory would utilize a longitudinal design: We would predict large initial differences between groups who had recently experienced tragic or fortunate events, followed by gradual readjustment to a neutral point. In the absence of such studies, adaptation level theory remains an attractive and intuitive hypothesis.

Note, however, that his theory calls for a reinterpretation of most measures of psychological wellbeing. Wellbeing has been measured as satisfaction in different areas of life, as a balance of positive to negative affects (Bradburn, 1969), or as a simple avowal of happiness (Gurin, Veroff, & Feld, 1960). But all these indices of subjective wellbeing have customarily been interpreted as reflections of the objective quality of life. Happy, satisfied people must be leading rewarding lives — or so it was assumed. But if we take adaptation level theory seriously, we will interpret these signs differently. We will say instead that, compared to the recently established neutral point, happy and satisfied people are better off than they were. Happiness becomes entirely relative, and the basis of comparison is recent past experience. We could not, under this theory, tell whether the quality of life was good or bad in any absolute sense; we could only infer that it had recently improved or deteriorated. As long as negative age-changes are sufficiently gradual, they might have no noticeable impact on subjective wellbeing.

Personality and Wellbeing

Although there is doubtless a good deal of truth in this model of happiness, there are also some serious flaws. Studies of the stability of happiness show that something else must be going on as well.

If wellbeing were nothing but temporary perturbations around a neutral point, then we would expect most individuals to be unhappy as often as happy. In fact, retest correlations of wellbeing measures ought to be consistently negative because the happier one is today, the higher the neutral point becomes and the more likely one is to be unhappy tomorrow. Happiness could be sustained only for the fortunate few whose lives every day in every way were getting better and better.

Yet data from a number of studies clearly show that, while not immutable, happiness is relatively stable in individuals. We recently readministered a battery of wellbeing mesures to our ABLSA subjects after an interval of two years. The battery included the Bradburn (1969) Affect Balance Scales, which yield separate scores for Positive Affect (PAS), Negative Affect (NAS) and the difference of these two, Affect Balance; a Satisfaction Index that asks whether subjects are not at all, somewhat, or very satisfied with 14 areas of living (housing, city, government, work, leisure, appearance, sex, health, marriage, family, finances, friends, self-respect, and faith); and the Delighted-Terrible (D-T) scale of Andrews and Withey (1976), a single item that asks subjects to evaluate their life as a whole. Retest correlations for these five measures range from .47 to .63 ($N = 473$, $p < .001$). Similar values have been reported elsewhere for different intervals (Costa & McCrae, 1981; Palmore & Kivett, 1977). Wellbeing indicators may well be sensitive to short-term changes in life quality, but they are also influenced by more enduring conditions.

As Bradburn and others have consistently demonstrated, positive affect and negative affect are independent contributors to global wellbeing. In part this appears to be because the external events that elicit them are independent (Warr, Barter, & Brownbridge, 1983), like the hygenic and intrinsic factors that have been identified as contributors to job satisfaction (Herzberg, Mausner, & Snyderman, 1959). But another reason for their independence is that positive affect and negative affect are differentially related to the two personality dimensions of extraversion and neuroticism. We believe the influence of these personality dimensions contributes to stability in wellbeing.

In data from Boston's Normative Aging Study (Costa & McCrae, 1980a), we showed that Positive Affect Scale (PAS) scores in a large sample of adult men were consistently related to personality traits that together formed the broad domain of extraversion. Negative Affect Scale (NAS) scores were unrelated to extraversion, but were predicted by traits in the domain of neuroticism. Affect Balance scores, along with other global measure of wellbeing (hopelessness, personal security, and life-satisfaction index) were related positively to extraversion and negatively to neuroticism.

Wellbeing and Personality in Adult Men and Women: New Data

In our more recent research we have employed a new instrument — the Neuroticism-Extraversion-Openness (NEO) Inventory — to assess personality (Costa & McCrae, 1980c; McCrae & Costa, 1983a). The NEO inventory provides scores on six different facets or aspects for each of three distinct, global domains of personality. Domain scores for neuroticism, extraversion, and openness, are formed by summing the respective six subscales. The inclusion of separate facets allows us to determine which specific aspects of neuroticism and extraversion are responsible for the associations with wellbeing.

The right-hand panel of Table 8.1 shows the relations between NEO scales and wellbeing measures administered in 1979 to a sample of 350 men aged 25 to 91. As hypothesized, PAS is related chiefly to traits in the domain of extraversion, NAS to traits in the domain of neuroticism. Both extraversion and neuroticism are associated with overall wellbeing, whether measured as affect balance, satisfaction, or the single-item D-T scale.

An examination of specific facets shows that all of the neuroticism facets or traits, especially anxiety and depression, are related to wellbeing. Individuals who are chronically anxious, hostile, depressed, self-conscious, impulse-ridden, and vulnerable to stress are (not surprisingly) likely to have an unfavorable affect balance and to be dissatisfied with life. In the case of extraversion, the relationships seem more differentiated. Interpersonal warmth leads to greater happiness, but mere gregariousness often does not, despite the fact that these two

TABLE 8.1 Correlations Between Self-Reported NEO Scales and 1979 Wellbeing Measures

	Men[a]					Women[b]				
NEO Scales	*PAS*	*NAS*	*Balance*	*Satisfaction*	*D-T Scale*	*PAS*	*NAS*	*Balance*	*Satisfaction*	*D-T Scale*
Anxiety	-14**	40***	-37***	-35***	-36***	-18**	34***	-35***	-27***	-29***
Hostility	-09	32***	-27***	-28***	-24***	-13*	34***	-32***	-29***	-31***
Depression	-20***	44***	-44***	-43***	-42***	-28***	59***	-59***	-41***	-44***
Self-consciousness	-10	32***	-29***	-27***	-27***	-16*	38***	-36***	-31***	-30***
Impulsiveness	06	29***	-15**	-23***	-12*	-08	39***	-32***	-30***	-24***
Vulnerability	-23***	20***	-29***	-31***	-30***	-19**	43***	-42***	-34***	-40***
Neuroticism	-15**	45***	-41***	-42***	-38***	-23***	54***	-52***	-42***	-43***
Warmth	23***	-11*	23***	22***	25***	17**	-10	17***	24***	23***
Gregariousness	14*	00	09	06	11*	05	00	03	10	05
Assertiveness	24***	-13*	24***	17**	17**	19***	-11	19**	19**	16**
Activity	30***	00	20***	10	04	16**	13*	01	08	06
Excitement seeking	14**	13*	01	-05	01	05	20**	-11	-09	-07
Positive emotions	40***	-01	28***	22***	35***	39***	-12*	33***	25***	35***
Extraversion	36***	-02	26***	17**	22***	28***	01	17***	20**	21***
Fantasy	06	23***	-12*	-15**	-06	-04	23***	-19**	-14*	-15*
Aesthetics	20***	05	10	09	08	25***	00	15*	01	06
Feelings	24***	18***	04	08	09	08	21***	-10	-04	00
Actions	13*	02	08	07	13*	17**	-01	12	12	04
Ideas	14*	02	08	06	04	09	-06	10	04	01
Values	04	18***	-09	-04	-09	03	04	-01	-09	-09
Openness	21***	18***	02	03	05	15*	10	02	-03	-03

NOTE: Decimal points omitted.
a. N = 350 for Bradburn scales; 344 for Satisfaction; 342 for D-T Scale.
b. N = 256 for Bradburn scales; 256 for Satisfaction; 250 for D-T Scale.
*$p < .05$
**$p < .01$
***$p < .001$

aspects of sociability are highly correlated. Assertiveness and the predisposition to experience positive emotions consistently correlate with happiness and life satisfaction, but excitement seeking (which is akin to Zuckerman's sensation seeking, 1979) does not. Activity is related to positive affect, but not to life satisfaction.

As in all our previous studies on this topic, the data in the right panel of Table 8.1 derive only from men. Can the same model be applied to women? The left-hand panel of Table 1 suggests that it can. Personality data from 256 women aged 24 to 96 are presented here, and the same general pattern is found. In this sample, the relation between NAS and neuroticism is exceptionally high ($r = .54$); correlations with extraversion are comparable to those found in men. As in men, depression is the facet contributing most to the prediction of NAS; warmth, assertiveness, and positive emotions are most strongly related to PAS.

The data from both men and women call for a reinterpretation of the relations between extraversion and wellbeing. In many respects extraversion appears to be a more complex dimension that neuroticism, compounding the conceptual difficulties that arise from its frequent confusion with the Jungian concept of the same name (McCrae, 1983). Eysenck and Eysenck (1963) argued that sociability and impulsivity were identifiable components of a larger extraversion factor, and factor analyses of the NEO Inventory (McCrae & Costa, 1983a) found dominance, affiliation, and impulsivity components. Excitement seeking and gregariousness — elements placed in the impulsivity component — do not appear to be related to subjective wellbeing. This suggests that the arousal associated with thrill-seeking and the social stimulation of crowds does not contribute to wellbeing. Instead, friendliness, self-confidence, and cheerfulness appear to be the key facets of extraversion responsible for the association. (Incidently, these distinctions show the potential utility of the multifaceted approach to measuring personality domains embodied in the NEO Inventory.)

Wessman and Ricks (1966; Wessman, 1977) point out that hedonic level — the average level of day-to-day mood — is independent of mood variability. They found that individuals who experienced the most dramatic mood shifts were neither more nor less happy than stable individuals. They were, however, characterized by such personality traits as imagination, enthusiasm, and openness, whereas less moody individuals were rigid, cautious, and closed. Openness to experience seems to have similar effects on subjective wellbeing. Individuals who are open to experience seek variety and novelty, and have an appreciation for the intrinsic value of experience itself. Such people are likely to be more sensitive than others to both positive and negative experiences, and in previous studies openness has been shown to be related to both PAS and NAS, but not to affect balance (McCrae, 1983). Examination of Table 8.1 supports this hypothesis in men, and partially supports it among women. Openness to aesthetic experience is particularly associated with PAS; openness to fantasy with NAS. Openness to feelings, appropriately, is positively related to both, as is overall openness.

Avoiding Artifacts: A Second Opinion on Personality

The relations of extraversion and neuroticism to subjective wellbeing are, from one point of view, not surprising. People who are chronically depressed and anxious are likely to be unhappy; those who are friendly, self-confident, and cheerful are likely to be happy. But on a topic where so many of our expectations are wrong, these basic relationships stand out. Andrews and Withey, for example, report that family life-cycle stage, age, income, education, race, and sex together account for only 8 percent of the variance in wellbeing. From Table 8.1 we can see that extraversion alone accounts for about the same amount of variance, and neuroticism accounts for as much as 27 percent. Personality is probably the strongest known predictor of wellbeing.

But Lawton (personal communication, April, 1983) has pointed out that there is a potential confound in these comparisons. In all our studies to date, self-reports of personality have been correlated with self-reports of wellbeing. Any biases that affect responses to one will probably also affect the other. This is particularly problematic in the case of Bradburn's scales, where key words — "anxious", "excited", "lonely", "proud" — often are also found in the items of personality inventories. The peculiarities of each individual's vocabulary may act across instruments to inflate the correlations. At a more fundamental level, both instruments draw on the individual's particular view of him- or herself and of the surrounding world, and it is always a matter of question how well individuals know themselves or at least how accurate their self-reports are.

If we are interested in subjective wellbeing, of course, we have no choice but to ask the individual directly. If I claim to be unhappy, who can dispute it? Self-reports are virtually unavoidable in this context (Carp, 1977). But personality is different. Although inner thoughts and experiences are among the most important indicators of personality, they are by no means the only manifestations. Neuroticism, extraversion, and openness to experience ought to show up in overt behaviors, in interpersonal relationships, in the expression of emotions, in attitudes and values. An observer with sufficient familiarity should be able to rate an individual's personality even without access to inner experience, and the literature on the correspondence between self-reports and ratings confirms this expectation (McCrae, 1982).

Observer ratings are not infallible either. Raters may be biased themselves, or poor observers, or prone to the kinds of response styles (like acquiesence) that may distort self-reports. But they do have the clear advantage of being an independent source of data. While response biases may inflate correlations between one self-report and another, they restrict correlations between self-reports and observer ratings by introducing unshared error variance. The correlations in Table 8.1 may represent the upper bound of the personality-wellbeing relationship; correlations with rated personality would provide a lower bound.

Table 8.2 provides just such correlations using ratings made by husbands and wives of subjects on a third-person version of the NEO Inventory (see McCrae, 1982, for details). Correlations are somewhat smaller than in self-report studies, but the pattern of results is strikingly similar. All the neuroticism facets are related to wellbeing, as are warmth, assertiveness, and positive emotions from the extraversion domain. Spouse-rated neuroticism appears to be a much better predictor than extraversion; even PAS is more strongly related to neuroticism than to extraversion. Perhaps the absence of joy is interpreted by external observers as a sign of maladjustment. The openness scales also show the same pattern seen in self-reports, although the correlation of total openness with NAS does not reach significance.

Judging from these correlations, facets of extraversion account for about 5 percent of the variance in wellbeing, and neuroticism for about 14 percent. Once again, these compare favorably with demographic predictors.

The Enduring Influence of Dispositions

The importance to adult development of the relation between personality and wellbeing stems from the fact that personality dispositions are extraordinarily stable in adulthood. A series of longitudinal studies (Block, 1977; Costa & McCrae, 1977; Costa, McCrae, & Arenberg, 1980; Leon, Gillum, Gillum, & Gouze, 1979) have shown that objectively measured personality dispositions routinely show retest correla-

TABLE 8.2 Correlations Between Spouse-Rated NEO Scales and 1979 Wellbeing Measures in Men and Women

NEO Scales	*PAS*	*NAS*	*Balance*	*Satisfaction*	*D-T Scale*
Anxiety	-23***	30***	-35***	-26***	-31***
Hostility	-17**	24***	-27***	-28***	-26***
Depression	-25***	38***	-41***	-29***	-35***
Self-consciousness	-23***	24***	-31***	-16**	-28***
Impulsiveness	-10	22***	-21***	-29***	-19**
Vulnerability	-19**	29***	-32***	-21***	-36***
Neuroticism	-24***	36***	-40***	-32***	-37***
Warmth	21***	-06	18**	22***	20***
Gregariousness	12*	02	07	05	10
Assertiveness	10	-05	10	03	07
Activity	06	06	00	-03	04
Excitement seeking	02	07	-03	-12*	-02
Positive emotions	21***	-07	18**	15**	26***
Extraversion	19***	-01	13*	08	17**
Fantasy	04	20***	-10	-15*	-07
Aesthetics	15*	06	06	00	01
Feelings	05	19**	-09	-03	-02
Actions	09	01	05	04	06
Ideas	07	-07	10	02	11
Values	12*	05	04	03	06
Openness	14*	10	02	-02	04

NOTE: N = 296 for Bradburn scales; 291 for Satisfaction; 287 for D-T Scale. Decimal points omitted.
*$p < .05$
**$p < .01$
***$p < .001$

tions of .70 or higher over intervals of 6 to 30 years, and that stability is found equally in young and old adults. In addition, studies on mean level differences in personality (Costa & McCrae, 1978; Douglas & Arenberg, 1978; Siegler, George, & Okun, 1979) have consistently shown little or no change in the average level of traits. As Dibner remarked, "At any point in time, a person is more like he has always been than he is like peers of his age group. A mature, nonneurotic younger person is likely to be a well-adjusted older person. The neurotic aged were most likely neurotic through much of their lives" (1975, p. 80).

To the extent that wellbeing depends on personality, it follows that an individual's wellbeing can be predicted years in advance by assessment of personality. Psychologists are not prophets, and we cannot predict whether life will hold wealth or poverty, health or illness, love or loss. But if our model is correct, we can predict how individuals will evaluate whatever life circumstances they encounter, whether they will be happy or unhappy with their lot (cf. Conley, in press).

This is a bold claim, but one supported by data. In the Boston longitudinal study, extraversion and neuroticism scores from the Sixteen Personality Factor Questionnaire (Cattell, Eber, & Tatsuoka, 1970) were significantly related to wellbeing measures administered 10 years later (Costa & McCrae, 1980a). Scores from the Guilford-Zimmerman Temperament Survey (GZTS; Guilford, Zimmerman, & Guilford, 1976) predicted happiness, life satisfaction, and personal adjustment to aging over 6- and 12-year intervals in the BLSA sample (Costa, McCrae, & Norris, 1980). The wellbeing batteries administered in 1979 and 1981 provide another opportunity to test this prediction.

Table 8.3 gives the correlations between GZTS scores collected in the period from 1959 to 1969 with wellbeing data collected 10 to 23 years later. The mean predictive interval for the first administration is 15.6 years; it is 17.7 years for the second. To interpret the findings, it is necessary to note that factor analyses (Costa & McCrae, in press) have shown that general activity, restraint (reversed), ascendance, and sociability load on a factor of extraversion; emotional stability, objectivity, friendliness (or low hostility), and personal relations (and to a lessor extent, masculinity) define the opposite pole of a neuroticism factor. Thus, Table 8.3 shows that three of the extraversion scales — general activity, ascendance, and sociability — are related to wellbeing, and especially PAS; all of the neuroticism scales except masculinity are related to wellbeing, and especially NAS. These correlations are not markedly different in magnitude from contemporaneous measures, and provide a strong retrospective-predictive replication of the findings.

The GZTS restaint scale (reversed) most closely resembles the excitement seeking facet of the NEO Inventory and, like excitement seeking, is an aspect of extraversion unrelated to wellbeing. The GZTS thoughtfulness scale loads on an openness to experience factor, and is related to PAS (in 1981) and NAS (1979) but never to gobal wellbeing. Despite a lapse of nearly two decades and the use of an entirely different instrument, even the details of the personality-wellbeing model appear to be replicated.

Personality, it appears, is a lifelong determinant of subective wellbeing. Individuals high in neuroticism are likely to see the problems of middle age as a "crisis" (Costa & McCrae, 1978); they will worry about increasingly poor health (Costa & McCrae, 1980b); they will be frustrated and disappointed by retirement, and are at risk for depression and Erikson's (1950) "despair" in old age. If, however, they are closed

TABLE 8.3 Correlations Between GZTS Scales Administered 1959-1969 and Wellbeing Measures from Two Administrations

GZTS Scales	*PAS*	*NAS*	*Balance*	*Satisfaction*	*D-T Scale*
1979 Wellbeing administration					
General activity	20**	−03	16*	11	04
Restraint	−06	−06	00	14*	02
Ascendance	18**	−11	19**	09	17*
Sociability	23***	−14*	25***	15	23*
Emotional stability	24***	−34***	39***	33***	34***
Objectivity	07	−23***	20**	28***	22***
Friendliness	10	−24***	22***	26***	18**
Thoughtfulness	05	15*	−07	−05	−05
Personal relations	05	−27***	21**	17*	10
Masculinity	−06	−13*	04	08	05
1981 Wellbeing administration					
General activity	18*	−13*	23**	18*	17*
Restraint	−05	−03	−02	08	07
Ascendance	28***	−13*	28***	17*	17*
Sociability	30***	−09	27***	20**	11
Emotional stability	09	−17*	21*	33***	31***
Objectivity	03	−19*	16*	28***	22**
Friendliness	−04	−12	08	23**	20*
Thoughtfulness	23**	04	09	−01	05
Personal relations	−07	−03	−02	14	05
Masculinity	−07	00	−04	04	04

NOTE: N = 214-239 for 1979 wellbeing administration; 158-182 for 1981 administration. Decimal points omitted.
*$p < .05$
**$p < .01$
***$p < .001$

to experience, these affects may be blunted a bit; if they are extraverted, then their sorrows may be offset by the joy, warmth, and excitement that tend to accompany this disposition.

Fortunately, most people are not high in neuroticism, and survey research shows that a full 35 percent consider themselves "very happy" (Gurin, Veroff, & Feld, 1960). Adjusted introverts are likely to meet the challenges of aging with equanimity; and adjusted extraverts will show the *joie de vivre* that make many older men and women an inspiration to the rest of us.

These are sweeping generalizations, and have a fatalistic quality that will probably be unwelcome. They do not bring words of encouragement about aging to those who need it most — the unhappy young and middle aged. But they do appear to accurately reflect the facts, and those who would understand affect in adult development cannot afford to ignore them. We need to consider both the implications and the limitations of these generalizations in order to fully appreciate them.

Reassessing the Quality of Life in Old Age

Enduring personality dispositions have important effects on wellbeing, particularly since they operate year-in, year-out over the entire adult life span. On the other hand, at any given time personality variables appear to account for no more than a quarter of the variance in wellbeing. Even allowing for unreliability of measurement, it is clear that a substantial portion of variance must be accounted for by something else. We have pointed out the classic error of assuming that subjective wellbeing mirrors objective life quality; we must also warn against the danger of dismissing wellbeing as nothing but chronic complaining or groundless optimism.

What does it *mean* when an old woman tells us she is perfectly happy living alone, or an old man complains that local transportation systems do not meet his needs? Do these comments reflect real assets or deficiencies in their environments? Should they be taken at face value, and used as the basis for interventions to enchance life quality? Do they represent only recent and relative changes in quality of life, as adaptation theory would suggest? If so, different evaluations could be expected as time passes. Or are they chiefly reflections of long-standing dispositions, equally impervious to the assaults of an unsympathetic world, and to the assistance of benevolent social institutions? Until research clarifies these issues, we will be on shaky ground in employing subjective wellbeing as the only criterion.

One alternative is to disregard wellbeing entirely. Rosow (1977) has argued that subjective wellbeing is essentially irrelevant as a basis for social policy decisions: We ought to improve the quality of life for individuals whether they appreciate it or not. There is much to be said for this position, but its implementation depends on our ability to identify aspects of the good life. More importantly, given limited resources we must be able to prioritize them, but we have no guarantees that our priorities correspond to those of older individuals. And how, without consulting him or her, can we design programs best suited to the specific needs of each individual?

There must be a middle ground between uncritical acceptance and complete disregard of subjective judgments of satisfaction. Several possibilities suggest themselves. Responses to individual items in a life-satisfaction index may represent the joint influence of external circumstances and personal dispositions; when added together, the external circumstances may vary and cancel out, while the personal dispositions will emerge as the main determinant of total score. The influence of objective circumstances is likely to be most pronounced when specific areas of satisfaction or dissatisfaction are addressed. For example, satisfaction with health declines with age, even though overall satisfaction does not (Campbell, Converse, & Rodgers, 1976). An intervention to improve the diet of older people ought to result in improved satisfaction with food, and possibly with health, but probably would not noticeably affect global morale (cf. Carp, 1977).

Even specific judgments, however, are made against the individual's subjective standards, and these are influenced to an unknown degree by processes of adaptation and by characteristic levels of optimism or pessimism. It might be more informative to ask individuals to evaluate their life quality against other objective situations. The wealthy are not much happier than the poor, but, given the choice, we'd rather be rich; and that choice is perhaps a better indicator of the value of money than is any rating of satisfaction. Individuals may be better able to evaluate the quality of life and suggest ways of improving it through such comparisons.

Another Look at Old Age

Discussions of adaptation level and of the influence of personality on satisfaction easily lead to the impression that subjective judgments are narcotics that lull us into accepting the inevitable. This chapter may have reinforced the prevalent notion that life after 60 really is miserable even though older people may feel satisfied, but such an impression would be unwarranted.

No one would deny that the elderly in America face a number of stresses. Often economic resources are limited, with little prospect of improvement. Friends and relatives die, health and vigor decline, memory begins to fail. But no age is without its drawbacks, and in many respects, the ills of old age have been exaggerated.

For example, most older people have frequent and rewarding contact with younger family members (Troll, Miller, & Atchley, 1979). They enjoy the blessings of grandparenthood without the responsibilities of parenthood. As most gerontologists — but few laypersons — know, only about 5 percent of those over 65 are institutionalized, with most older Americans living in their own homes. Retirement, once thought to be enforced idleness, is enjoyed by many individuals as a time for leisure and as much or little productive activity as they care for. If and when we devise an absolute measure of life quality independent of the subjective judgment of the individual and its personality determinants, we may well find that old age is the happiest time of life.

References

Andrews, F.M, & Withey, S.B. (1976). *Social indicators of well-being: Americans' perception of life quality.* New York: Plenum.

Block, J. (1977). Advancing the psychology of personality: Paradigmatic shift or improving the quality of research. In D. Magnusson & N. S. Endler (Eds.), *Personality at the cross-roads: Current issues in interactional psychology.* Hillsdale, NJ: Lawrence Erlbaum.

Bradburn, N.M. (1969). *The structure of psychological well-being.* Chicago: Aldine.

Brickman, P., & Campbell, D.T. (1971). Hedonic relativism and planning the good society. In M.H. Appley (Ed.), *Adaptation level theory: A symposium.* New York: Academic Press.

Brickman, P., Coates, D., & Janoff-Bulman, R. (1978). Lottery winners and accident victims: Is happiness relative? *Journal of Personality and Social Psychology, 36,* 917-927.

Campbell, A, Converse, P.E., & Rodgers, W.L. (1976). *The quality of American life: Perceptions, evaluations, and satisfactions.* New York: Russell Sage Foundation.

Carp, F.M. (1977). Morale: What questions are we asking of whom? In C.N. Nydegger (Ed.), *Measuring morale: A guide to effective assessment.* Washington, DC: Gerontological Society.

Cattell, R.B., Eber, H.W., & Tatsuoka, M.M. (1970). *The handbook for the sixteen personality factor questionnaire.* Champaign, IL: Institute for Personality and Ability Testing.

Conley, J.J. (in press). The hierarchy of consistency: A review and model of longitudinal findings on adult individual differences in intelligence, personality, and self-opinion. *Personality and Individual Differences.*

Costa, P.T., Jr., & McCrae, R.R. (1977). Age differences in personality structure revisited: Studies in validity, stability, and change. *Aging and Human Development, 8,* 261-275.

Costa, P.T. Jr., & McCrae, R.R. (1978). Objective personality assessment. In M. Storandt, I.C. Siegler, & M.F. Elias (Eds.), *The clinical psychology of aging.* New York: Plenum.

Costa, P.T., Jr., & McCrae, R.R. (1980a). Influence of extraversion and neuroticism on subjective well-being: Happy and unhappy people. *Journal of Personality and Social Psychology, 38,* 668-678.

Costa, P.T., Jr., & McCrae, R.R. (1980b). Somatic complaints in males as a function of age and neuroticism: A longitudinal anlaysis. *Journal of Behavorial Medicine, 3,* 245-257.

Costa, P.T., Jr., & McCrae, R.R. (1980c). Still stable after all these years: Personality as a key to some issues in adulthood and old age. In P.B. Baltes & O.G. Brim (Eds.), *Life span development and behavior* (Vol. 3). New York Academic Press.

Costa, P.T., Jr., & McCrae, R.R. (1981). Stress, smoking, and psychological well-being: The illusory benefits of smoking. *Advances in Behavior Research and Therapy, 3,* 125-150.

Costa, P.T., Jr., & McCrae, R.R. (in press). Concurrent validation after 20 years: Implications of personality stability for its assessment. In J.N. Butcher & C.D. Spielberger (Eds.), *Advances in Personality Assessment,* Vol. 4. Hillsdale, NJ: Lawrence Erlbaum.

Costa, P.T., Jr., McCrae, R.R., & Arenberg, D. (1980). Enduring dispositions in adult males. *Journal of Personality and Social Psychology, 38,* 793-800.

Costa, P.T., McCrae, R.R., & Norris, A.H. (1981). Personal adjustment to aging: Longitudinal prediction from Neuroticism and Extraversion. *Journal of Gerontolgy, 36,* 78-85.

Dibner, A.S. (1975). The psychology of normal aging. In M.G. Spencer & C.J. Dorr (Eds.), *Understanding aging: A multidisciplinary approach.* New York: Appleton-Century-Crofts.

Dicken, C. (1963). Good impression, social desirability, and acquiescence as suppressor variables. *Education and Psychological Measurement, 23,* 699-720.

Douglas, K., & Arenberg, D. (1978). Age changes, cohort differences, and cultural change on the Guilford-Zimmerman temperament survey. *Journal of Gerontology, 33,* 737-747.

Erikson, E.H. (1950). *Childhood and society.* New York: Norton.

Eysenck, S.B.G., & Eysenck, H.J. (1963). On the dual nature of extraversion. *British Journal of Social and Clinical Psychology, 2,* 46-55.

Guilford, J.S., Zimmerman, W.S., & Guilford, J.P. (1976). *The Guilford-Zimmerman Temperament Survey handbook: Twenty-five years of research and application.* San Diego, CA: EdITS Publishers.

Gurin, G., Veroff, J., & Feld, S. (1960). *Americans view their mental health.* New York: Basic Books.

Helson, H. (1964). *Adaptation-level theory.* New York: Harper & Row.

Herzberg, F., Mausner, B., & Snyderman, B.B. (1959). *The motivation to work.* New York: John Wiley.

Herzog, A.R., Rodgers, W.L., & Woodworth, J. (1982). *Subjective wellbeing among different age groups.* Ann Arbor: Institute for Social Research, University of Michigan.

Leon, G.R., Gillum, B., Gillum, R., & Gouze, M. (1979). Personality stability and change over a 30 year period-middle age to old age. *Journal of Consulting and Clinical Psychology, 23,* 245-259.

McCrae, R.R. (1982). Consensual validation of personality traits: Evidence from self-reports and ratings. *Journal of Personality and Social Psychology, 43,* 293-303.

McCrae, R.R. (1983). Extraversion is not a filter, neuroticism is not an outcome: A reply to Lawton. *Experimental Aging Research. 9,* 73-76.

McCrae, R.R., & Costa, P.T., Jr. (1983a). Joint factors in self-reports and ratings: Neuroticism, extraversion, and openness to experience. *Personality and Individual Differences, 4,* 245-255.

McCrae, R.R., & Costa, P.T., Jr. (1983b). Social desirability scales: More substance than style. *Journal of Consulting and Clinical Psychology. 51,* 882-888.

Palmore, E., & Kivett, V. (1977). Change in life satisfaction: A longitudinal study of persons aged 46-70. *Journal of Gerontolgy, 32,* 311-316.

Rosow, I. (1977). Morale: Concept and measurement. In C.N. Nydegger (Ed.), *Measuring morale: A guide to effective assessment.* Washington, DC: The Gerontological Society.

Siegler, I.C., George, L.K., & Okun, M.A. (1979). Cross-sequential analysis of adult personality. *Developmental Psychology, 15,* 350-351.

Tamir, L. M. (1982). *Men in their forties: The transition to middle age.* New York: Springer.

Troll, L. E., Miller, S. J., & Atchley, R. C. (1979). *Families in later life.* Belmont, CA: Wadsworth.

Warr, P. Barter, J., & Brownbridge, G. (1983) On the independence of positive and negative affect. *Journal of Personality and Social Psychology, 44,* 644-651.

Zuckerman, M. (1979). *Sensation seeking: Beyond the optimal level of arousal.* New York: Lawrence Erlbaum.

9

Love, Power, and Images of the Self

DAN P. McADAMS

In a dramatic account of a crisis in ideology and identity encountered as an adult, essayist and social critic Joan Didion writes, "We tell ourselves stories in order to live" (1979, p. 11). Didion describes a critical period in her life cycle when she was moved, by personal experiences and certain historical events of the late 1960s and early 1970s, to rewrite the story that had hitherto served to make sense of her life. "Certain of these images did not fit into any narrative I knew," she writes (p. 13), resulting in a radical transformation of old values, expectations, and a narrative line formulated during what was now seen as a bygone era of naivete. From the standpoint of her own life experience, Didion speaks of what Erik Erikson (1959, 1968) would term identity and identity change. According to Erikson, identity is a personalized construction or integration of past, present and an anticipated future, first attempted in adolescence, which aims at "inner sameness and continuity" (Erikson, 1963, p. 261) while promising to provide adult lives with coherence, direction, and purpose. Didion suggests, and other students of adult development would concur (Gould, 1980; Levinson, 1978), that identity formation and reformation extend well into adulthood. She further implies that the products of the process, our identities per se, take the form of narrative.

My associates and I have adopted Didion's metaphor of narrative in our investigations of identity at mid-life. We have conceived of identity as a *life story* — a personalized myth constructed consciously and unconsciously by the individual in late adolescence and adulthood. By providing a coherent narrative framework within which the disparate events of a person's life can be embedded and given meaning, the life story integrates past and present with an envisioned future so as to confer upon the individual that sense of inner sameness and continuity that Erikson maintains is at the heart of ego identity. Like stories in literature, therefore, identities can be understood in terms of setting, characters, scenes, and theme. This chapter focuses on the story element of character. In our life-story model of identity, the major characters in the narrative are termed *imagoes.*

The purpose of this chapter is to explore the main characters inhabiting the stories that people tell themselves in order to live. These characters or imagoes are personified and idealized images of the self. Working in narrative concert with other story elements such as setting, scene, and theme, imagoes perform self-defining actions and engage in self-defining conflicts that determine the plot lines of human identities. In this chapter, I introduce the imago as a significant component of adult identity. Drawing upon extensive interviewing and projective testing undertaken with 50 mid-life adults (30 women and 20 men), I will first recall initial observations concerning personified self-images in these data. After a brief review of concepts related to the imago in the writings of Jung, Sullivan, Berne, and others, I will return to the mid-life data to describe our coding and classification of the different types of imagoes observed in life stories. Two superordinate themes — love and power — serve to organize the various types of imagoes discovered. I will then present the major hypothesis of this work: That intimacy (McAdams, 1980b) and power motivation (Winter, 1973), as assessed via the Thematic Apperception Test, are significant predictors of the salience of imagoes emphasizing love and those emphasizing power, respectively. Following a review of the meaning and measurement of intimacy and power motivation, I will present some preliminary findings suggesting support for the main hypothesis. Finally, I will use case examples to illustrate love imagoes and power imagoes functioning as personified and idealized self-images in adult identities.

Imagoes

Initial Observations

Our 50 mid-life adults, ranging in age from 35 to 49 years, were recruited from evening classes taught at a university in the Chicago area. The sample is predominantly white (94 percent) and middle class, with 70 percent of the subjects having obtained at least a bachelor's-level degree. Fifty-eight percent of the subjects were married at the time of initial assessment. Median family income (1981-1982) was between $30,000 and $40,000. Participating in two two-hour sessions, each subject was asked to think about his or her life as if it were a book and to divide the life into its major chapters, entitling and describing each. Other questions concerned significant experiences and turning points in one's life, one's vision for the future, heroes and role models, philosophy of life, and the underlying theme of the person's life story. This life-story interview lasted between one and two hours for each subject. All interviews were tape-recorded.

Listening to the interviews, we were initially struck by the fairly common appearance of two discordant images of self, or imagoes, in many of the subjects' accounts. Although our subjects were generally deemed relatively "normal" and well adjusted, numerous men and women described their past lives and their hopes for the future *as if* they were inhabited by "multiple personalities" or discordant subselves, typically two of these posed as opposites on some fundamental dimension. In stories of self that generally bespoke very little pathology but marked multiplicity of self-conception, our subjects explicitly or implicitly connected these divergent imagoes to specific significant others in their lives (e.g., heroes, role models, friends), specific childhood experiences that seemed to serve as origin myths for personified images of self, and specific biographical epochs in which a particular imago was ascendant in behavior and experience while the other appeared to lie dormant.

Consider the following brief example. One 39-year-old man, an editor at a publishing house, unmarried, well travelled, and earning what he considered a very modest salary (around $15,000 annually), repeatedly described himself as the "artist." Creative, imaginative, somewhat Bohemian but always refined, the artist image integrated a host of expressed values (aesthetics, culture, good taste), interests (classical music, visual arts, literature, gourmet cooking), avocations and activities (writing children's literature, teaching arts and crafts in schools and churches, making beautiful things), role models and heroes (an older mentor, his mother), and biographical events illustrating the perceived "birth and growth" of the artist imago. Yet, a second imago had recently manifested itself with a vengeance. Described as an opposite or at least contrary image of self vis-à-vis the artist, the "successful, worldly, money maker" had of late assumed a dominant place in the subject's aspirations for the future. Taking stock of his life in his late 30s, the subject had tentatively decided that he wanted to make money and accumulate material possessions more than he wanted to be the artist. A number of biographical elements could be likewise connected to this second imago. The two images of self, therefore, defined a central conflict or tension in this man's life story, a conflict that might variously be described as that between art and reality, aesthetics and economics, transcedent beauty and worldly pragmatics. The subject implied that a major goal for the future was to integrate in some way these two discordant imagoes.

Theoretical Background

In drawing upon theory to inform our initial observations concerning imagoes, we have reviewed a number of similar concepts in the literatures of personality and clinical psychology, although no single formulation appears identical to our conceptualization of a personified and idealized image of self. The term "imago" was sometimes used by Carl Jung (1943) in reference to his structural concept better known as the archetype. Archetypes were conceived as universal thought forms charged with emotion. Located in that inherited repository of phylogenetic memory called the collective unconscious, archetypes were sometimes classified in terms of paired opposites, such as the case of the anima or feminine archetype in men and the animus or masculine archetype in women. The mandala was Jung's symbol for the unity of self — an accomplishment usually saved for mid-life — in which all pairs were reconciled in psychic harmony. At mid-life, according to Jung, individuals ideally called upon hitherto hidden (unconscious) elements of their personality and integrated them with the conscious elements of the ego. This pairing of opposites, termed individuation, was seen as the sine qua non of maturity in the adult years.

Jung catalogued a variety of archetypes which included the hero, the wise old man, the earth mother, the demon, the child, birth, rebirth, death, power, and magic. The first five are personified but the latter five are more abstract or conceptual. (The earth mother is a person; death is a concept.)

Harry Stack Sullivan (1953), on the other hand, focused exclusively on personified images in his concept of the personification. A personification was conceived as an image that an individual has of him- or herself *or of another person,* an amalgam of feelings, attitudes, and expectations growing out of childhood experiences of need gratification and struggles with anxiety. Examples include the "good mother," the "bad mother," the "good me," and the "bad me."

Related concepts appear in the writings of modern object-relations theorists and ego psychologists. Fairbairn (1952) writes of internalized objects that are either excitatory, rejecting, or neutral and that are each cathected by (attached to) different parts of the ego. In Fairbairn's object-relations theory, the interaction among conflicting interpsychic objects (the internal) shapes the interaction between the person and the real-life others (the external) who correspond, in a sense, to these internalized objects. In his psychology of the self, Kohut (1971) lays emphasis on idealized images of the good love object that have been built up through family interactions and that are often projected onto the analyst in therapy. Jacobson (1964) writes of the "wished-for self image" that is considered an autonomous part of the ego made up of those valued and admired qualities and attributes that are associated with significant others and that the individual longs to make his or her own. Finally, Eric Berne (1972) and other proponents of transactional analysis describe three personified "ego states" — the parent, child, adult — each associated, in many cases, with characteristic patterns of interaction, gestures, mannerisms, facial expressions, intonations, and verbal utterances.

Our concept of the imago is at the same time more general and more specific than these other concepts. Unlike Jung's structural components of the collective unconscious, life-story imagoes are by definition personified and exist not as part of a phylogentic collectivity but rather as highly personalized, idiosyncratic images defining how a person is different from others as well as similar to them. Like characters in good fiction, imagoes are carefully crafted by the author — the person constructing identity — to be highly individualized. Unlike Sullivan's personifications, imagoes refer solely to images of self, although images of others may be incorporated into images of self. The writings of Fairbairn, Kohut, Jacobson, and Berne all set forth specific propositions concerning the development of various personified images (internalized objects, wished-for self images, ego states) and concerning their structure and function that are not essential to our conceptualization of imagoes in life stories. At present, we do not know how imagoes develop. They are structured as personified and idealized images of self, highly individualized and created to play roles in specific life stories. Their function is that of character in narrative.

Coding and Classification

Impressed with the rich diversity of personified self-images presented by our mid-life subjects, we endeavored to derive a rudimentary classification system within which imagoes might be ordered. We have tentatively settled on a taxonomy grounded in the mythology of Ancient Greece. On one level, the gods and goddesses of the Greek pantheon represent projected personifications of what the Greeks understood as fundamental human propensities and strivings. Larger and more powerful than mortals, the Greek deities made love and war, experienced rage, envy, and joy, and performed acts of heroism and ignominy in ways that were remarkably human. Each of the major deities, futhermore, personified a distinctive set of personality traits that were repeatedly manifested in the myths and legends in which his or her behavior can be observed. We chose 12 major gods and goddesses as our models for imagoes. Taken together the group embodies well most of the idealized and personified self-images we have observed in our sample of mid-life adults.

The Greek prototypes for imagoes are organized along the two independent thematic lines of power/agency/mastery/conquest and love/communion/care/surrender. Class 1 imagoes are power imagoes: Zeus, the omnipotent and omniscient source; Hermes, the swift traveller; and Ares, the warrior. Class 3 imagoes are love imagoes: Demeter, the caregiver; Hera, the friend; Aphrodite, the lover. Class 2 imagoes combine power and love: Apollo, the healer/artist/protector; Athene, goddess of peace and prudence; and Prometheus, the revolutionary. Finally, Class 4 imagoes are "low" in both power and love: Hestia, the homemaker; Hepheastus, the worker; and Dionysius, the escapist.

Our coders for the life-story interviews first familiarized themselves with the Greek taxonomy of imagoes. An imago scoring manual described in detail each of the four classes of imagoes, the 12 types, and a number of possible variants of each type. The coders then listened to a full interview and wrote an objective and detailed summary of the information provided by the subject. Next, the coders listened to the interview a second time in order to classify the dominant self-image presented by the subject into 1 of the 12 types. Once a primary imago was identified, the coder listened for evidence of a second self-image that was posed in some way as an opposite of the first. This second self-image was termed an anti-imago. For each primary imago identified, the coders completed an imago description sheet that asked for all of the following information: imago type, brief summary of the imago's primary features, associated personality traits, associated significant other (hero, role model, etc.), how the significant other(s) relate(s) to the imago, biographical event giving birth to the imago, four events in which the imago was "displayed" in behavior, associated wishes and goals, brief description of associated anti-imago, behavioral evidence for anti-imago, and nature of the conflict between the imago and anti-imago. The imago description sheets provide a format for the organization of evidence supporting a particular imago interpretation. Specifying answers for every question on the sheets was not a necessary prerequisite for scoring an imago nor was it necessary to find an antagonistic anti-imago. Scorers were instead encouraged to do the best they could in completing the forms, with the understanding that such an inquiry was highly exploratory and therefore required a good deal of flexibility and tolerance for ambiguity.

Two independent coders, blind to all other information on the subjects, scored the 50 life-story interviews for imagoes. Given the substantial interpretive effort required to identify imagoes, it is not surprising that scoring reliability figures have thus far been only moderate. For the 50 subjects in the present study, two trained coders agreed on the general class (Class 1, 2, 3, or 4) of the primary imago 68 percent of the time (34 out of 50; Cramer's $\phi = .51$). In the 16 cases of disagreement, a third independent scorer listened once to the interview and decided between the two imago classes.

For our entire sample of 50 adults, primary imagoes were classified as Class 1 in 11 cases (22 percent), Class 2 in 7 cases (14 percent), Class 3 in 12 cases (24 percent), and Class 4 in 20 cases (40 percent). For the men, the distribution was 10 percent Class 1, 30 percent Class 2, 15 percent Class 3, and 45 percent Class 4. For women, 30 percent Class 1, 3 percent Class 2, 30 percent Class 3, and 37 percent Class 4. A contrasting anti-imago was identified in 70 percent (35 out of 50) of the cases.

Love and Power

Motives

As significant components of identity, imagoes should connect in meaningful ways to certain salient personality dispositions assessed by independent methods. Our main hypothesis in this work is derived from an expectation that human *motives* should bear close association to imagoes. Motives are emotionally toned cognitive clusters centered around preferred experiences and goals (McAdams, 1982a; McClelland, 1971; Winter, 1973). Sharing conceptual space with Izard's (1978) "affective-cognitive structures," motives link patterns of affect and thought by suggesting general experiential goals imbued with positive affect. Motives are conceived as internal dispositions in persons who energize, direct, and select behavior in certain situations (McClelland, 1971). We submit that one's life story or identity shapes and is shaped by one's most prominent motive dispositions. This is to say, there should be a thematic connection between the kinds of personified self-images displayed by men and women at mid-life and the dominant motives energizing, directing, and selecting their daily behavior.

The two motives of central concern in the present investigation are intimacy (McAdams, 1980) and power (Winter, 1973). Resembling David Bakan's (1966) concept of *communion,* which he posits as one of two fundamental tendencies of all living forms, the intimacy motive is an affectively toned cognitive cluster centered around the preferred experience of close, warm, and communicative exchange with another. The goal state of the motive is to feel *close* to another. The power motive, on the other hand, resembles Bakan's other fundamental tendency, *agency,* and is defined as an affectively toned cognitive cluster centered around the preferred experience of feeling strong and having impact. The goal state is to feel *strong* vis-à-vis others. Both motive dispositions are measured via content analysis of story responses provided to the Thematic Apperception Test (TAT). Detailed scoring manuals complete with practice stories and exercises for each of the two motives assure very high interscorer reliability (McAdams, 1980a; Winter, 1973). In the present inquiry into imagoes, we predicted that strong intimacy motivation, assessed via the TAT, would be associated with imagoes of love (Classes 3 and 2) whereas strong power motivation would be associated with imagoes of power (Classes 1 and 2). Relatively weak intimacy *and* power motivation should be associated with imagoes low in love and power (Class 4).

Intimacy Motivation

The intimacy motive scoring system for the TAT was developed by McAdams (1980) in a series of experiments in which TAT stories written under "intimacy-arousal" conditions (conditions emphasizing joy, harmony, and communication in interpersonal interaction) were compared to those written under neutral classroom conditions. The thematic categories consistently differentiating between stories written under the two conditions came to comprise the scoring system for intimacy motivation. The system is comprised of ten thematic categories each of whose presence (score +1) or absence (score 0) in each story is assessed. Examples of the scoring categories are Positive Affect (+A: a relationship facilitates joy, happiness, etc.); Dialogue (Dlg: characters engage in reciprocal and noninstrumental communication); Time-

Space (TS: a relationship goes beyond usual temporal or spatial limitations); Commitment or Concern (CC: character helps another or exhibits loyalty to another); and Surrender (Sr: characters surrender control in interpersonal relations).

A number of recent studies have bolstered the construct validity of TAT-scored intimacy motivation. Sampling daily thought, behavior, and affect over the course of a week, McAdams and Constantian (1983) found strong positive correlations between intimacy motivation assessed via the TAT and (1) interpersonal thoughts, (2) conversation and letter-writing behavior, and (3) positive affect experienced in the presence of others. Intimacy motivation has also been associated with (1) warm and friendly behavior in a psychodrama (McAdams & Powers, 1981); (2) peer ratings of "warm," "loving," "sincere," "natural," and "nondominant" (McAdams, 1980b); (3) significant autobiographical recollections highlighting themes of love, dialogue, helping, and tender touch (McAdams, 1982a; McAdams et al., 1981); (4) greater self-disclosure and listening in interactions with friends (McAdams, in press); and (5) higher levels of smiling and laughter among college women in a one-on-one interview (McAdams & Jackson, 1983). In a longitudinal study of mid-life men, TAT intimacy motivation at age 30 was positively correlated with indices of overall psychosocial adjustment (including job and marital satisfaction) determined at age 47 (McAdams & Vaillant, 1982). In college samples, women occasionally score slightly higher than men on intimacy motivation, though these sex difference typically do not reach statistical significance (McAdams, 1982b).

Power Motivation

The general procedure followed in the development of the power motive scoring system for the TAT was very similar to that employed in the derivation of the intimacy system. In a series of arousal experiments in which stories written under conditions designed to make subjects feel strong were compared to those written under neutral conditions, Winter (1973) derived a scoring system comprised of 11 thematic categories, each of whose presence (score +1) or absence (score 0) in a story is assessed. Examples of the scoring categories are Power Imagery (PowIm: a character is concerned about establishing, maintaining, or restoring impact, control, or influence over others); Prestige Increase (Pa+: characters concerned with power goals are described in ways which heighten their status); Instrumental Activity (I: a character engages in overt or mental activity in order to attain the power goal); Block in the World (Bw: a character encounters an obstacle to power goal); and Positive Goal Anticipation (Ga+: a character expects to gain power).

The numerous studies supporting the construct validity of the power motive have been reviewed in McClelland (1975), Winter (1973), and Winter and Stewart (1978). Power motivation has been related to a host of behavioral and experiential indices suggesting an overriding concern for mastery, influence, and having an impact on one's world. Power motivation has been associated with (1) attaining positions of leadership in college (Winter, 1973); (2) entering careers entailing the direct influence of other people's behavior (Winter & Stewart, 1978); (3) dominance in decision-making groups (Fodor & Smith, 1982); (4) accumulation of prestige possessions (McClelland, 1975); (5) angry outbursts among young men (McClelland, 1975); and (6) significant autobiographical recollections emphasizing themes of mental or physical strength, vigorous activity, and heightened prestige (McAdams, 1982a). High power motivation in men has also been associated with instability in heterosexual love relations, although this does not appear to be the case for women (Stewart & Chester, 1982). Few other sex differences in power motivation have consistently appeared.

Imagoes of Love

The purest love imagoes are those personified images of self as caregiver (Demeter), friend (Hera), and lover (Aphrodite). These are what we have termed Class 3 imagoes. They are indeed the most interpersonal of imagoes in that they are defined in terms of intimate relationships with others. Mid-life adults whose life stories were marked by the actions and interactions of Class 3 imagoes tended to frame their narratives in relational terms, often structuring their life chapters around the most significant interpersonal relationships in their lives rather than, say, around life accomplishments or instrumental pursuits. Class 2 imagoes also emphasize love/communion/care/surrender, but these images of self are also marked by a theme of power/agency/mastery /conquest. We hypothesized that higher intimacy motivation, assessed via the TAT, would be associated with Class 3 and 2 imagoes. Our analyses provided support for the prediction. Mean intimacy motive score (standardized) for adults classified into each of the four imago classes were 57.9 for Class 3, 53.1 for Class 2, 47.8 for Class 1 (low love, high power), and 45.6 for Class 4 (low love, low power). The mean differences among the four groups were significant ($F[3,46] = 5.31$ $p < .01$), with Class 3 imagoes having significantly higher intimacy motivation than Classes 1 and 4 combined ($p < .001$), and the two classes of love imagoes (Classes 2 and 3) scoring higher than Class 1 and 4, the two classes of imagoes not emphasizing love ($p < .01$).

Illustrating one prominent love imago, Dean K. tells a life story in which the major personified image of self is the *caregiver.* A 36-year-old engineer with a wife and three children, Dean has lived his entire life in a southwest-side Chicago neighborhood. It is the same neighborhood in which his parents, too, have lived their entire lives, and their parents before them. Dean describes the neighborhood as working class and extremely stable, an extended but close-knit network of friends, family, and families of friends, most of whom were born and most of whom will probably die on the same city block. This neighborhood was the setting for what Dean reconstructs as the idyllic chapter of his childhood and youth: a time of happiness, close family, and many friends. As an adult he has sought to nurture a family life that recaptures the warmth and closeness of his childhood. With respect to his children, he believes that he has been successful. But his relationship with his wife has been less smooth, and he now acknowledges that he would have left her long ago if he were not completely devoted to his children.

In Dean's life story, the caregiver imago is kind, modest, sympathetic, caring, and somewhat self-effacing. It is reflected in his reports of the greatest moments in his life (the birth of his children, especially his daughter who is "the jewel of my life"), his greatest aspirations for the future (to "make my marriage work" in order to "save the children"; to have another child), and his present involvement as scoutmaster and manager of a little league baseball team. The caregiver speaks most clearly in Dean's answer to the question "What is the major theme of your life story?" He responded, "To be there for others." And the imago is also reflected in Dean's statements that it is his children and his friends who provide for his life the most satisfaction. In Dean's life story, the caregiver imago appears to be placed in opposition to a somewhat suppressed anti-imago that our coders have described as the "drifter" or the "wanderer." This is the part of Dean, as it were, which would love to leave his southwest-side neighborhood behind and escape to the mountains where he could devote his life to photography. It is the children, Dean concludes, that keep him from going.

Sara N. is a 43-year-old Catholic nun who, better than any of our other mid-life subjects, epitomizes the imago of the *lover.* She tells a beautiful life story in which two ostensibly antagonistic images of self — the passionate lover and the ascetic nun — arise very early and subsequently fuse in her adult years into an image of self as the passionate, loving woman of God. A foreshadowing of the integration of these two — an event that Sara deems highly symbolic — was her conversion in preadolescence to the Catholic faith. She states that she became a Catholic on Valentine's Day.

The lover imago has its roots in Sara's relationship with her grandmother before the age of nine. Never very close to either of her parents (both of whom were fundamentalist Protestants), Sara considered her grandmother her first heroine. She was "the perfect human being," states Sara, "loving, independent, feisty, committed to God and to others." After joining the religious order, Sara joined her faith and her passion to become, in the eyes of others as well as her own, the "earthy one" — the nun steeped in the world and people rather than abstractions and the dogma of the church. Sara describes many very close friendships in unabashedly passionate terms and states that these serve as the greatest source of satisfaction in her life. She also found herself involved in romantic relationships in her earlier years, relationships that she describes as laden with passion and pathos. In one case, she fell in love with a priest as he was deciding to leave the religious life. She, on the other hand, had decided to enter the religious life largely because of the example he set for her as a priest. Thus, she declined his proposal of marriage and became a nun.

Sara's dream for the distant future is to set up a religious community in Wyoming where people can live in peace with each other and with God. She speaks of ministering to others both in her work as a school counselor and in her play. Summing up, she states, "I see my life as becoming more and more integrated — to be able to be a space for ministry in my work and with friends, and to enable people to grow and be who they are." Her life theme, in her words: "a lot of living, dying, and loving."

Imagoes of Power

The purest power imagoes are those personified images of self as the omniscient one (Zeus), the swift traveller (Hermes), and the warrior (Ares). These are what we have termed Class 1 imagoes. Mid-life adults whose life stories were marked by the actions and interactions of Class 1 imagoes tended to highlight the overlapping themes of self-assertion, self-expansion, conquest, master, agency.

Unlike Class 2 imagoes, these pure power imagoes generally bespeak a sense of agency unmitigated by major concerns for relationships. This is not to say that adults displaying these images of self are ruthless or Machiavellian. Rather, they choose to frame their life stories around significant agentic actions rather than communal relationships with others. We hypothesized that higher power motivation, assessed via the TAT, would be associated with Class 1 as well as Class 2 imagoes. Again, we obtained some empirical support for this hypothesis. Mean power motive scores for adults classified into each of the four imago classes were 59.3 for Class 1, 51.7 for Class 2, 47.5 for Class 3, and 45.6 for Class 4. The mean differences among the four groups were significant ($F [3,46] = 6.16$, $p < .01$), with Class 1 imagoes having significantly higher power motivation than Classes 3 and 4 combined ($p < .001$), and Classes 1 and 2 having higher power motivation than Classes 3 and 4 ($p < .01$).

In the life story of Rebecca K., the central character is the *swift traveller* (adventurer/explorer/pioneer). Rebecca is a 38-year-old, divorced, social worker who has travelled the world over. Structured in an episodic style reminiscent of the picaresque novel, Rebecca's life story reads like a romantic adventure in which the heroine's incessant search for new places, new experiences, and new people defines the major plot lines. In describing her philosophy of life, Rebecca states, "It is the journey that matters, not the arrival. I will not stop running; I'll refuse until I'm in a wheel chair." The peak experiences in her life are frequently set in exotic, far-away places, like Mexico and the Orient. There are illicit love affairs, experiments with drugs, tempestuous relations with lovers and friends, strange foods, strange customs, and captivating conversations. The traveller imago arises early in the life story when Rebecca finds that she is continually "moving against" the nuns in her Catholic elementary school. Although the nuns don't appear to appreciate her endless questions and frequent explorations into the forbidden, Rebecca continues to cultivate the new-formed imago, reinforced by her mother who insists that she not be intimidated by the nuns and Rebecca's aunt (one of her heroines) who "believed in trying new things."

Rebecca left for Mexico shortly after high-school graduation — a move that she, in retrospect, describes as "running away." This is by no means the last instance of running away. Although she has held the same job for the last eight years, Rebecca continues to travel, regularly visiting Latin America where she has some very dear friends. In Rebecca's life story, physical travel mirrors the psychological/spiritual journey she perceives. In her eyes, she is ever-expanding, ever-growing, ever-changing. "Life is a journey," she adds. Stasis breeds boredom and ennui. With adventure and constant movement comes sophisticated in-the-world wisdom which she contrasts to the idealistic abstractions of her adolescence and early adult years. This contrast hints at what our coders saw as the central anti-imago in Rebecca's life story — the "naive idealist" who as a very young child (before the nuns) played the role of the good little girl and who as an adolescent sought to "save the world." Indeed, the anti-imago survives in Rebecca's efforts "to do some good for a few people" in her role as social worker. Yet, in the next breath, she states that she would love to scrap all of that and take off again for Mexico, this time without returning.

A different sort of power imago is observable in the life story of Tom H. The major character in Tom's narrative is Ares, the noble *warrior.* Tom is a 43-year-old communications worker employed by the police department who, like Rebecca, is divorced. Growing up in a southeast-side Chicago neighborhood during World War II, Tom recalls a number of significant events in his very early years associated with war, death, and authority. His earliest memories concern the air raid sirens and the childhood fear of "imminent invasion" in the regular air raid drills organized by Chicago neighborhoods. The unexpected death of his grandmother and his dog, the latter killed by a speeding automobile, were two early events associated with a feeling of rage vis-à-vis those who were larger, stronger, and in authority. In 1943, Tom's family moved to a farm community outside Chicago which, Tom reports, resulted in considerable stress. The major conflict in Tom's new community, as he saw it, was between the "farm kids" and the displaced "city kids." He describes his role in the conflict as that of diplomat: "I was like Henry Kissinger doing shuttle diplomacy," negotiating fragile peace treaties between warring factions. Tom found himself assuming a similar role in the wake of family arguments.

All of Tom's heroes in childhood were war heroes. Quick to link his own life history to contemporaneous world events (the beginning of the Korean War, the construction of the Berlin Wall, the assasination of John F. Kennedy), Tom describes the glory years of high school when he attended a military academy and his subsequent "first big failure" at Notre Dame University where he repeatedly battled a host of authority figures, unwittingly cultivating the role of the "rebel." Soon after dropping out of college, Tom enlisted in the Air Force and began another glory chapter as the good soldier. His life story since then is a roller-coaster ride from periods of glory when he is being the noble warrior (as a "good citizen," dedicated politician) to times of depravity and shame when he fails to live up an implicit warrior code — a regimen of conformity, impulse control, and spartan austerity — and falls into heavy drinking and generally irresponsible behavior. The latter refers to an anti-imago that, in keeping with the martial tone of the story, might be termed the "deserter" or the "traitor." This anti-imago is the main character in Tom's chapters of failure — Notre Dame, drinking, his divorce, periods of unemployment. In sum, Tom's life story is a saga of warfare in which the noble warrior is victorious when he is strong enough to keep the internal forces of dereliction and depravity under raps while channelling aggressive impulses into the arts of preparing for war, negotiating treaties between warring factions (Henry Kissinger), and sometimes making war so as to keep the peace. The noble warrior is the vanguard of domestic tranquility whose work and whose life bespeak peace through strength.

Conclusion

This chapter has covered quickly a good deal of unfamiliar ground concerning love, power, and images of the self in adulthood. The major construct proposed — the imago — exists in the life stories that constitute adult identities as an idealized and personified image of self assuming the role of character in narrative. I have described two qualitatively different classes of imagoes. Love imagoes, such as the "caregiver" and the "lover," are images of self as intimately intertwined with others. Life story data from 50 mid-life adults suggest initial support for the hypothesis that love imagoes are associated with high intimacy motivation as assessed via the TAT. Power imagoes, such as the "swift traveller" and the "noble warrior," emphasize the individual's acts of strength and mastery over others (and over self). Our mid-life data further suggest a positive correlation between these kinds of self-images and high power motivation assessed via the TAT.

Psychologists would do well to look more closely at the content and the structure of adult's conceptions of who they are. In adopting the story metaphor for identity and in proposing imagoes as life-story characters, we have taken initial steps down one particular path of inquiry. It is our belief that the understanding of affective development in adulthood could be furthered if other investigators would take similar steps.

References

Bakan, D. (1966). *The duality of human existence.* Boston: Beacon Press.

Berne, E. (1972). *What do you say after you say hello?* New York: Grove Press.

Didion, J. (1979). *The white album.* New York: Simon & Schuster.

Erikson, E. H. (1959). Identity and the life cycle: Selected papers. *Psychological Issues,* Vol. 1, No. 1, pp. 5-165. New York: International Universities Press.

Erikson, E. H. (1963). *Childhood and society* (2nd ed.). New York: Norton.

Erikson, E. H. (1968). *Identity, youth and crisis.* New York: Norton.

Fairbairn, W. R. D. (1952). *Psychoanalytic studies of the personality: The object relations theory of personality.* London: Routledge & Kegan Paul.

Fodor, E. M., & Smith, T. (1982). The power motive as an influence on group decision making. *Journal of Personality and Social Psychology, 42,* 178-185.

Gould, R. L. (1980). Transformations during early and middle adult years. In N. J. Smelser & E. H. Erikson (Eds.), *Themes of work and love in adulthood.* Cambridge, Mass.: Harvard University Press.

Izard, C. E. (1978). On the ontogenesis of emotions and emotion-cognition relationships in infancy. In M. Lewis and L. A. Rosenblum (Eds.), *The development of affect.* New York: Plenum.

Jacobson, E. (1964). *The self and the object world.* New York: International Universities Press.

Jung, C. G. (1953). The psychology of the unconscious. In *Collected works,* Vol. 8. Princeton: Princeton University Press. (First German edition, 1943)

Kohut, H. (1971). *The analysis of the self.* New York: International Universities Press.

Levinson, D. (1978). *The seasons of a man's life.* New York: Knopf.

McAdams, D. P. (1980a). *Scoring manual for the intimacy motive.* Unpublished manuscript, Loyola University of Chicago.

McAdams, D. P. (1980b). A thematic coding system for the intimacy motive. *Journal of Research in Personality, 14,* 413-432.

McAdams, D. P. (1982a). Experiences of intimacy and power: Relationships between social motives and autobiographical memory. *Journal of Personality and Social Psychology, 42,* 292-302.

McAdams, D. P. (1982b). Intimacy motivation. In A. J. Stewart (Ed.), *Motivation and society.* San Francisco: Jossey-Bass.

McAdams, D. P. (in press). Human motives and personal relationships. In V. Derlega (Ed.), *Communication, intimacy, and close relationships.* New York: Academic Press.

McAdams, D. P., Booth, L., & Selvik, R. (1981). Religious identity among students at a private college: Social motives, ego stage, and development. *Merrill-Palmer Quarterly, 27,* 219-239.

McAdams, D. P., & Constantian, C. A. (1983). Intimacy and affiliation motives in daily living: An experience sampling analysis. *Journal of Personality and Social Psychology, 45,* 851-861.

McAdams, D. P., & Jackson, R. J. (1983). *Intimacy motivation, reciprocity, and nonverbal behavior in college women.* Paper presented at Midwestern Psychological Association Convention, Chicago.

McAdams, D. P., & Powers, J. (1981). Themes of intimacy in behavior and thought. *Journal of Personality and Social Psychology, 40,* 573-587.

McAdams, D. P., & Vaillant, G. E. (1982). Intimacy motivation and psychosocial adjustment: A longitudinal study. *Journal of Personality Assessment, 46,* 586-593.

McClelland, D. C. (1971). *Assessing human motivation.* Morristown, NJ: General Learning Press.

McClelland, D. C. (1975). *Power: The inner experience.* New York: Irvington.

Stewart, A. J., & Chester, N. L. (1982). Sex differences in human social motives: Achievement, affiliation, and power. In A. J. Stewart (Ed.), *Motivation and society.* San Francisco: Jossey-Bass.

Sullivan, H. S. (1953). *The interpersonal theory of psychiatry.* New York: Norton.

Winter, D. G. (1973). *The power motive.* New York: The Free Press.

Winter, D. G. & Stewart, A. J. (1978). The power motive. In H. London and J. E. Exner, Jr. (Eds.), *Dimensions of personality.* New York: John Wiley.

10

Thematic and Affective Content in the Lives of Adult Women

Patterns of Change and Continuity

CAROL ZANDER MALATESTA
L. CLAYTON CULVER

As noted in the introduction to this volume, discussions of emotional *development* are usually limited to the early years of life. This is in large measure attributable to the bias of paedogenesis in psychological thinking (Averill, this volume), as well as the great success with which adults

AUTHORS' NOTE: This study was supported by a Radcliffe Research Scholars grant awarded to the first author, funded by the Andrew W. Mellon Foundation. We are indebted to Abigail Stewart for giving us access to the data set on which our analysis was made and to the staff at the Henry Murray Center, especially Nancy Bower, for their

manage to conceal their emotions. The emotional behavior of adults is governed by constituitive and regulative rules (Izard, 1971, 1977; Tomkins, 1962; Averill, this volume). Regulative rules are largely proscriptive and focused on modulation and restraint of expressive behavior. This dampened expressive behavior makes adults appear less emotional than children, although appearance can be deceiving, as we shall see. In the present study we are not so much concerned with public behavior as with the individual's experience of emotion. Here we examine the incidence of affective content in women's descriptions of their lives. We also trace the prominence and continuity of particular affective themes from late adolescence into middle adulthood, and examine the relationship between situational variables and the affective content of experience.

One of the best ways of studying change and continuity in human development is via longitudinal data. Despite the growing numbers of longitudinal studies of personality development and the assumed linkage between personality and affective functioning (Plutchik, 1965; Izard, 1971, 1977), few researchers have exploited these data sets for an investigation of emotional dynamics. Neugarten's (1977) review of the literature of longitudinal studies of personality development in the adult years indicates that the primary targets of research have been egocentrism, dependency, introversion, dogmatism, rigidity, wellbeing, cautiousness, conformity, ego strength, risk taking and decision making, need achievement, locus of control and creativity — precious little about the emotional content of experience. An exception is an early study by Kagan (1961) using data from the Fels longitudinal files. Reasoning that the tendency to ascribe affect to TAT characters might represent a preferred mode of perceptual organization and a prepotent tendency to conceptualize the social environment and subjective experience in terms of affect labels, Kagan examined the stability of affect attribution to projective media over an eight-year period of time. The results showed significant intraindividual consistency for Rorschach material and a trend towards the same for TAT, between the ages of 17 and 25. It would be interesting to see whether such trends might persist over longer periods of time and whether the stabilities are evident in other material such as autobiography (Combs, 1947). Another interesting question is the issue of continuity in the use of certain *types* of

---

hospitality and kind assistance during the period we were in Cambridge making use of the data set. We thank Melanie Albin, Barbara Baer, Patricia Bass, and Friderike Heuer for their assistance in coding. Thanks are also due Mary Joan Gerson for a critical reading of an earlier draft of the manuscript.

affective expression, for example, the continuity of anger versus anxiety themes.

Finally, another relatively unexplored area is the relationship between affective states and the developmental demands found in the normative life tasks. In an idiographic study of the life of Virginia Woolf, Haviland (1983) found that from late adolescence to adulthood there was a cognitively related shift in Woolf's personality organization that resulted in the organization of affects and situations into certain salient themes. This shift assumedly was linked to other ontologic changes accompanying development, such as the emergence of formal operational thinking and adult task demands. In addition, Haviland found that the alliance between affective and thematic material was an outstanding aspect of Woolf throughout her life. Each of her major themes of affiliation, control, and ability had closely associated affective components. For example, ability themes were linked to shame, contempt, and emotionality, while affiliative themes were closely tied to joy and distress.

The findings for the case of Virginia Woolf may have more general applicability. As Denenberg (1981) has noted, the single case can provide interesting leads for generating developmental hypotheses that then can be tested with larger samples. Haviland's analysis of Woolf suggests that developmental *per se* and changes accompanying development (such as the assumption of new adult roles) will cause a shift in the thematic content of an individual's life, making certain issues more salient and emotionally charged than others.

The present chapter builds upon the two foregoing studies. First, we sought to extend Haviland's work and examine the interplay of affective and life themes over the adult years in a larger group of individuals. Second, extending the work of Kagan, we wished to determine the prominance of certain types of emotion expression at different developmental epochs. Third, we wanted to examine the interplay between affective experiences and normative life tasks and demands.

Method

In order to explore the above we needed a longitudinal data set that provided data on individuals over a long enough period of time to permit assessment of stability or change, and measures on individuals that included standard affective measures as well as other verbal material that could be content analysed for life themes and use of affective terminology. The data set for Abigail Stewart's Longitudinal Study of the Life Patterns of College Educated Women, archived at the Henry

Murray Center, Radcliffe College, offered the ideal opportunity to explore the issues delineated above, inasmuch as it followed women for 19 years and included four waves of measurement — TAT protocols, narrative autobiographical data, and measures of anxiety and depression (Stewart, 1975, 1978, 1980; Stewart & Salt, 1981). The data set is described in more detail below.

The Original Sample

The original subjects for this study were the class of 1964 of a prestigious women's college in the Eastern United States. In 1960 a battery of six TAT cards were administered to all the freshmen at this school. Ten years after graduation, in 1974, these women were contacted and asked to complete a "Life-Patterns Questionnaire, "containing questions about their backgrounds, college experiences, activities since graduation, and future aspirations. In 1976 another questionnaire was sent ot those subjects who had responded in 1974 with questions regarding health and life changes during the preceding two years, as well as open-ended questions regarding important life events and future plans; in addition, depression and anxiety scales were embedded in the questionnaire. In 1979, these subjects were once again recontacted to obtain current demographic data as well as descriptions of major events in the past and aspirations for the future. The attrition rate from wave to wave remained fairly constant with about 23 percent of the sample lost through geographic relocation or failure to return the questionnaires in each successive wave.

Data Used in the Present Study

1960 wave. The only data available at this time were typed TAT protocols on virtually all of the members of the class of '64 (N=242). The protocols, as well as narrative autobiographical data gathered in the next three waves, were all subsequently content analyzed as described in the next section.

1974 wave. Of the information solicited from the Life-Patterns Questionnaire at this time, we used the open-ended narrative account of the high and low points of the previous ten years. The question asked about both events and feelings concerning those events.

1976 wave. A paragraph description of important events and feelings in the preceding year was used as the data base for this wave. We also obtained a printout of the subjects' scores on the Zung self-rating anxiety scale (1971) and Zung self-rating depression scale (1965).

1979 wave. The narrative material from this wave concerned a description of the subjects' high and low points over the previous years.

It should be noted that in each of the latter three waves similar information was requested (i.e., information regarding important life events and the subjects' feelings about them) so that differences in *content* gathered over these three waves is unlikely to be due to method variance. Analysis of variance on total word count over the last three sets of data disclosed no significant differences, demonstrating that the subjects generated the same *amount* of material in each successive sample, and assumedly similar amounts of investment in the task.

Coding of Life Themes and Affective Content

The TAT stories and open-ended responses were content anlayzed according to standard procedures (Krippendorff, 1980). The content categories, consisting of personality themes and situational themes as well as affective statements, come from Haviland (1982), with some adaptation. Haviland's system included 29 possible themes. Of her original themes, four — affiliation, lack of affiliation, success, and lack of success — were expanded so as to take into account more referential information. We distinguished six types of affiliation: affiliation with an unspecified family member or simple references to the "family"; affiliation with husband, affiliation with lover, and affiliation with colleagues, children and relatives. Lack of affiliation was partitioned into loneliness, lack of affiliation with unspecified family member, lack of affiliation with husband, children, other relatives, lover, and colleagues. For the success and lack of success categories we distinguished among themes having to do with one's own success, that of one's lover or husband and that of one's children. These subcategories for success and lack of success proved to be so infrequent as to be subsequently dropped.

Frequencies of themes were tabulated for use in assessing the important thematic and affective concerns of the subjects, making the somewhat standard assumption that the frequency of the appearance of a theme in narrative material is an index of the dynamic importance of the theme in the person's life (Baldwin, 1942; Haviland, 1983). A description of some of the more frequent themes follows. (The complete coding manual can be obtained from the authors.)

Affiliations: All affiliations involve references to liking another person, enjoying joint activities, meeting with the other person, comraderie, and so on.

Lack of affiliation: Concerns about not having, or losing, a friendship or intimate relationship, including the mention of divorce or separation.

Anger/aggression: The mention of feeling angry, mad, irritated, bitter, annoyed, or an act of aggression, including fights, arguments, and quarrels. Themes of murder or mayhem (usually in TAT protocols) were included here. References to "conflict," "struggle," or "hassle" were not coded in this category because of the ambiguity of meaning in the contexts in which they occured.

Depression/sadness/unhappiness/distress: The mention of feeling sad, unhappy, depressed, blue, gloomy, or discouraged. Feeling upset was not included because of its vagueness.

Fear/anxiety: The mention of feeling anxious, tense, fearful, nervous, uneasy; also included were references to the feeling of being under stress or strain if it appeared, contextually, to reference a state of anxiety.

Success/recognition/achievement: The concern with achievement, receiving recognition or striving; effort directed towards attaining something of recognizable importance; a meritorious act. Reference to whether one actually succeeds is not needed.

Lack of success/recognition/achievement: The mention of or concern with the lack of success in a job, school or endeavor; lack of achievement or failure, including losing a job, being unemployed, getting poor grades.

Four coders trained to a group reliability of at least 80 percent for each theme, using practice material. Then one pair of coders assumed responsibility for coding half the actual protocols, the other the remainder. Coders were assigned the same subjects for each of the four waves of data but were kept uninformed as to which data were from which subjects; waves and subjects were interleaved in a random fashion. Repeated intercoder reliability checks for each team as well as cross-team reliability checks to avoid "drift" from the original system all proved that coding reliably stayed well above 80 percent, with an average reliability of 86 percent. Category reliabilities were also calculated. Any category whose reliability fell below 80 percent was dropped from subsequent analysis. The reliability formula used in this study was number of agreements on type of theme divided by number of agreements plus disagreements.

Subjects

There were complete protocols for 59 subjects. Demographics of the sample are noted below.

(1) Employment status: According to the Hollingshead scale (Hollingshead, 1975) 37 percent of the sample (as per 1979 data) rated as having professional jobs, 19 percent managerial, 20 percent menial, 10 percent technical, 8 percent administrative, and 3 percent clerical. There were no data on 2 percent. Of their husbands, 50 percent were employed in professional occupations, 15 percent in administrative positions, 8 percent in technical jobs, 2 percent in managerial positions, 1 percent in menial labor, 2 percent in clerical positions, and there were no data on 17 percent.
(2) Marital status: At the time of the 1979 sample, 76 percent were married, 17 percent were divorced or separated, and data were unavailable on 7 percent. The average length of the marriage was 11

years. Of the married sample 34 percent had been divorced at least once, and 66 percent had remained married to their original spouse.

(3) Age: The average age of the subjects was 36 years old in 1979.

(4) Children: In 1960, one woman had a one-year-old child; all the other subjects were childless. By 1974, 42 of the 59 subjects had at least one child. The average subject had a mean number of 2.12 children (S.D. = .94). The mean age of the children was 4.63 years, median = 5, S.D. = 3.14, modes = 2 and 5. By 1976, 43 subjects had children. The average subject had a mean of 2.35 children (S.D. = 1.09). The mean age for these 101 children was 5.89 years, median = 6, S.D. = 3.58, modes = 4 and 7. By 1979, 47 subjects had children. The average subject had a mean of 2.36 children (S.D. = 1.19). The mean age in 1979 for these children was 8.23 years, median = 8, S.D. = 4.01, modes = 10 and 7.

The above data indicate that although these women are typical of their birth cohort in many ways, their high level of employment in the professions makes them somewhat atypical. There is also some evidence of skewness in a comparison of respondants and nonrespondents. Although Stewart and Salt (1981) report that the 96 subjects in the 1976 wave did not differ significantly from the 26 nonrespondents from the 1974 sample on any demographic or personality variables assessed either at the original testing in 1960 or at the time of the first follow-up in 1974, there is evidence of difference between the 1976 and 1979 samples. Zung anxiety and Zung depression scores were available on all 96 subjects from the 1976 wave data collection. Wave four in 1979 included 59 of these subjects. Most of the remaining 37 subjects dropped out or could not be located; there were also a few who were not included in the present study because there were missing data in one or more of the earlier waves. A t-test on the means of the Zung anxiety and depression scores disclosed significant differences for the respondents and nonrespondents. Subjects with complete data for the four waves had significantly lower depression and anxiety scores than did the nonrespondents. The mean anxiety rating for the respondents was 38.1 (S.D. = 6.45) and for the nonrespondents was 41.7 (S.D. = 8.22), yielding a t value of 2.36, df = 94, $p < .02$. The mean depression rating for the respondents was 37.8 (S.D. = 7.54) and for the nonrespondents was 42.2 (S.D. = 8.05), yielding a t value of 2.69, df = 94, $p < .008$.

The statistics for the respondents on the Zung scale scores can best be interpreted with reference to data on the standardization groups (Zung, 1965, 1971). The figures on depression for the present sample compare favorably with the standardization group mean of 33 with a range of 25-45 (S.D. not reported). A clinically depressed group had a mean of 74 and a range of 63-90. The range for the present sample

(29-56) does not overlap with this. The figures on anxiety are also comparable, although somewhat elevated. The mean for the standardization group was 33.8 (S.D. = 5.9); a group of patients diagnosed as having "anxiety disorder" obtained a mean of 58.7 (S.D. = 13.5)

The foregoing demographic information on the subjects in this study indicates that they are typical of their cohort in some ways and atypical in others. Nonetheless, they may disclose trends and patterns that will shed light on affective processes. The attrition rate over the years has been moderate; if attrition has been greater among those who actually exhibit the most change, a spurious impression of greater stability will be manifest than would otherwise be the case in the general population. For these and other reasons, we take an exploratory stance with respect to the conduct of this study, and recommend caution in generalizing the results beyond the immediate subjects.

Results and Discussion

We report the results of the coding of 25 categories of thematic and affective content (see Table 10.1). Six of the original themes had very low frequencies; those that accounted for less than one percent of the total thematic pool were dropped from further analysis. The themes that were eliminated were age, control, confidence, lack of affiliation with family, lack of affiliation with children, and lack of affiliation with relatives. The low rates in these categories may reflect the lack of concern for these themes in our sample of subjects, or conversely, conflictual areas to be avoided.

Frequency and percentage of themes. Table 10.1 indicates the frequency with which each theme appeared in the data summed across subjects and across waves. Success/recognition/achievement is far and away the top-ranking theme. Of interest to those who view affect as the primary motivational system in humans (e.g., Tomkins, 1962; Izard, 1977) is the prominence of affective themes among the top-ranking themes. Of the four affects coded in this study, three of them rank in the top half of the distribution with anger in the third rank, fear in the sixth, and depression in the eleventh. Table 10.2 provides a breakdown of the relative rankings of these themes within each wave; at this point it is noted that there are certain changes in the prominence of particular themes over the years spanning the four waves, that is, from 1960 when the subjects where about 17 years old to 1979 when they were about 36 years old. We take up a discussion of these shifts momentarily. Before we do that, however, it is worth noting once again the relative promi-

TABLE 10.1 Frequency and Percentage of Themes Summed Over Subjects and Waves

Theme	*Frequency*	*Percentage*
Success/recognition/achievement	350	10.69
Affiliation with lover	253	7.73
Anger/aggression	246	7.51
Dominance/power	240	7.33
Lack of success	169	5.16
Fear/anxiety	154	4.70
Affiliation with husband	149	4.55
Illness/health concerns	147	4.49
Affiliation with children	145	4.43
Competence/ability	139	4.24
Depression/sadness	128	3.91
Nurturance	125	3.82
Affiliation with colleague	122	3.73
Death	118	3.60
Independence	99	3.02
Lack of affiliation with husband	93	2.84
Affiliation with family	79	2.41
Dependency	71	2.17
Lack of affiliation with lover	69	2.11
Birth	60	1.83
Sex/sensuality	48	1.47
Regret/guilt/shame	43	1.32
Affiliation with relatives	38	1.16
Loneliness	37	1.13
Lack of affiliation with colleague	36	1.10

nence of affective themes. A major affect ranks in the top four (out of 25) thematic categories in each wave. Also, the primary affect for any given wave varies across waves, from anger in 1960 to sadness/depression in 1974, to fear/anxiety in 1976 and 1979.

Figure 10.1 depicts how the rankings of themes changed over successive waves, providing a sense of how ontological variables vary with thematic content, as discussed below. (Only the top 16 themes plus birth are plotted: Values are expressed within each wave as a ratio of total frequency for each theme summed across subjects, to total frequency for all themes.)

Shifts in thematic content over the years. Wave 1960 represents the scores derived from TAT material when the subjects were 17 years old. The five top-ranking themes are success, anger/aggression, dominance/power, affiliation with lover, and lack of success. The appearance

TABLE 10.2 Rank Order of Themes by Waves

Wave 1960	*Wave 1974*	*Wave 1976*	*Wave 1979*
Success	Depression/sadness	Affiliation (children)	Success
Anger/aggression	Lack of affiliation (husband)	Success	Illness
Dominance/power	Success	Fear/anxiety	Affiliation (lover0
Affiliation (lover)	Affiliation (children)	Nurturance	Fear/anxiety
Lack of success	Competence	Affiliation (lover)	Competence
Affiliation (husband)	Illness	Affiliation (husband)	Depression/sadness
Independence	Birth	Illness	Affiliation (children)
Nurturance	Death	Dominance/power	Affiliation (colleague)
Affiliation (colleague)	Affiliation (lover)	Dependency	Death
Affiliation (family)	Affiliation (husband)	Anger/aggression	Anger/aggression
Competence	Dominance/power	Competence	Dominance/power
Fear/anxiety	Fear/anxiety	Death	Affiliation (husband)
Lack of affiliation (lover)	Lack of success	Depression/sadness	Lack of affiliation (husband)
Death	Nurturance	Affiliation (relatives)	Birth
Affiliation (children)	Anger/aggression	Affiliation (colleague)	Dependency
Depression/sadness	Affiliation (colleague)	Lack of success	Lack of success
Loneliness	Dependency	Sex/sensuality	Nurturance
Regret/guilt/shame	Lack of affiliation (lover)	Birth	Affiliation (relatives)
Dependency	Independence	Lack of affiliation (husband)	Affiliation (family)
Sex/sensuality	Regret/guilt/shame	Loneliness	Independence
Lack of affiliation (colleague)	Sex/sensuality	Independence	Lack of affiliation (lover)
Illness	Lack of affiliation (colleague)	Affiliation (family)	Sex/sensuality
Lack of affiliation (husband)	Affiliation (relatives)	Regret/guilt/shame	Regret/guilt/shame
Affiliation (relatives)	Loneliness	Lack of affiliation (lover)	Lack of affiliation (colleague)
Birth	Affiliation (family)	Lack of affiliation (colleague)	Loneliness

of success and lack of success as top and fifth to the top ranking themes comes as no surprise, given that this is a sample of young women entering the freshman class of a prestigious and competitive women's college. The conjoint presence of success, power, and affiliation themes among the top ranking themes is also not very startling as these themes are considered as three primary human motives by David McClelland (1951). There is cause for comment, however, since McClelland's concepts about motivation and empirical work were grounded originally in observations of men, and here we are dealing with *women's* projections to TATs.

When we single out the affective themes — anger, fear, sadness, and shame/guilt, we find that anger predominates, with fear and sadness/depression as rather low frequency themes, and shame the lowest. (The latter is not shown in Figure 10.1 because it is among the lowest ranking themes across waves.)

In light of literature on the TAT indicating that sadness/depression is the most commonly elicited affect (Eron, 1963), possibly owing to the gloomy cast to most of the pictures, the preponderance of anger/aggression themes in the present data is striking. Perhaps in this instance anger/aggression is best seen as part of an assertiveness/aggressivity component closely allied to power/dominance. In fact, the two themes of anger/aggression and power/dominance are significantly correlated ($r = .28$, $p < .05$). The prominence of power and aggression themes among these women may reflect the same traits that were selected favorably for in admission to this competitive top-ranking women's college. Notably, anger/aggression themes recede dramatically over the successive years.

One could argue that TAT "pulls" for the darker emotions and allows expression of content that is normally socially unacceptable. Anger is possibly one of the most socially proscribed affects for women. One could also argue a "parental imperative" interpretation for the data (Gutmann, 1975). David Gutmann has asserted, largely on the basis of cross-sectional, cross-cultural research that with the onset of the child-rearing years, women suppress the more aggressive, masculine aspects of themselves and act out the more passive, nurturant, dependent qualities that foster the optimal development of offspring. In Gutmann's view, aggressive, dominant traits in young mothers are potentially lethal to the marital relationship and emotional security of children. In the present longitudinal investigation, as predicted by the theory, anger and dominance recede and stay down during the child-rearing years. Unfortunately, method (TAT versus autobiographical material) is confounded with the ontological variable so that we remain uncertain as to the

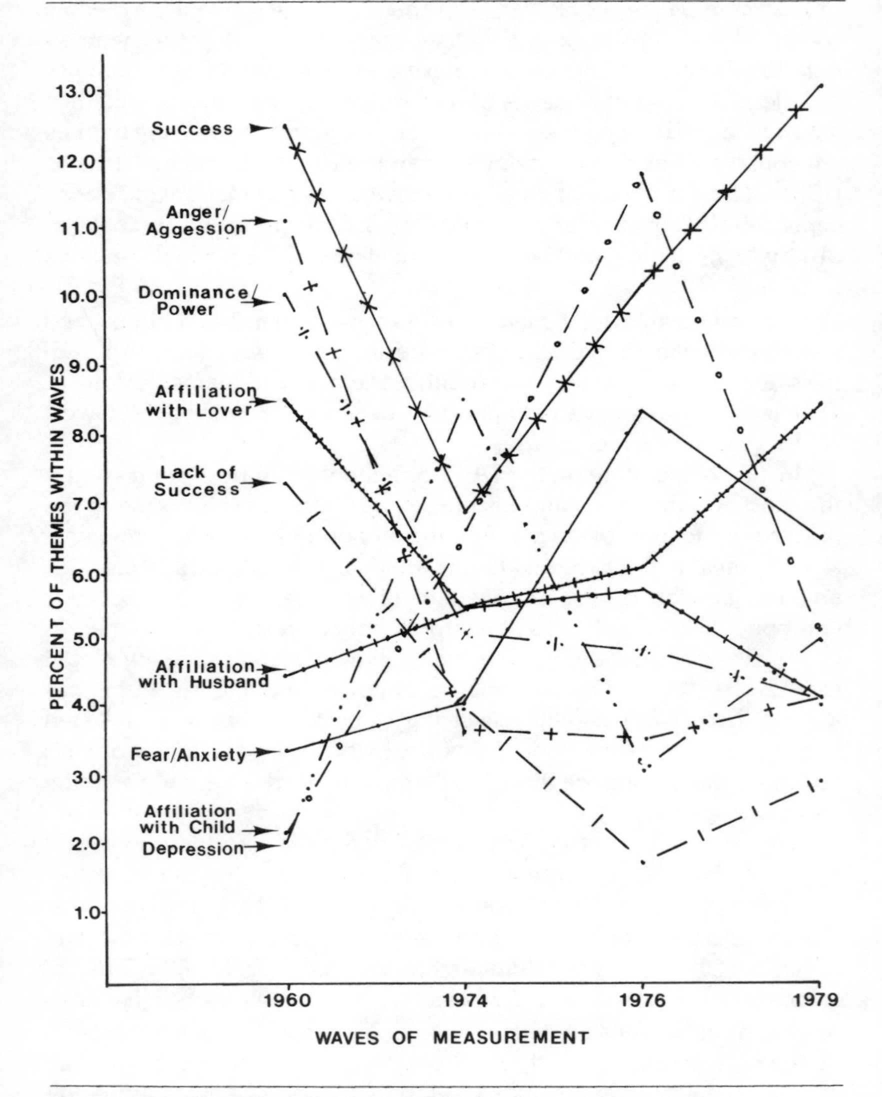

Figure 10.1 Ranking of Themes Within and Across Ages

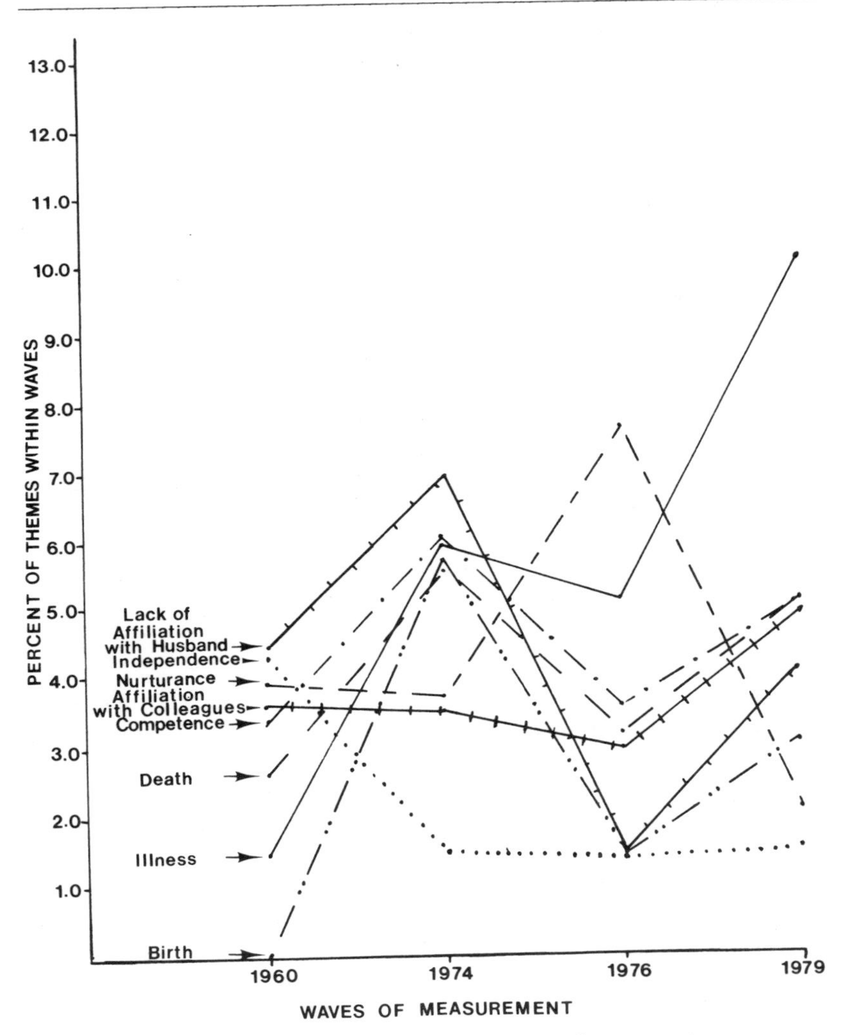

NOTE: The 17 themes are plotted on two graphs rather than on one to facilitate reading.

Figure 10.1 Continued

unique contribution of the parental imperative. We do note, however, that the reduction in dominance/power and anger/aggression themes coincide with an increase in birth and nurturance themes. Also note that independence themes drop way down as well. Successive waves of data on these same women as they move beyond the child-rearing years may help resolve the issue.

1974. At the time that these women were recontacted, in 1974, they were 31 years of age and most had married. Almost all had at least one child, the average being two, and most of these were preschool-age children. The data gathered during this time then, reflect the important events and emotional feelings of what are the peak child-rearing years. Examining Figure 10.1 we see that success is still a high frequency theme but now it is superceded by depression as the primary theme.

A number of studies have indicated that mothers of young children are prone to high rates of dysphoria (Patterson, 1980; Campbell, Converse & Rodgers, 1976; Hoffman & Manis, 1978). Stress, depression, anxiety, and feelings of isolation and helplessness are not uncommon. The direct and indirect causes are less readily identified, and reasons are likely to vary as a function of the demographics of the sample in question. Patterson (1980) found that rearing both normal and socially aggressive children provides mothers with high rates of aversive events. Observations in the home and laboratory showed minor aversive events occurred as often as once every three minutes when the mother was dealing with normal preschoolers; major conflicts occurred as often as three per hour. This study also found that the younger the child, the higher the density of these events; in addition, socially aggressive boys provided over two times as great a density of aversive events. Such statistics make it easy to see how dysphoria could be generated.

Another potential cause has been identified by Blood and Wolfe (1960); these investigators found patterns indicating that a wife's power in family decisions diminishes with the birth of the first child although it rises in later stages. When we examine the data in the present study, another reason comes to the fore, and this may have something to do with the unique nature of the sample under consideration. In examining the pattern of intercorrelations we find that depression is significantly correlated with independence ($r = .34$, $p < .008$) and lack of success ($r = .35$, $p < .007$). This would suggest that it is not so much the *presence* of children that is distressing so much as the fact that young children pose obstacles for the pursuit of achievement-oriented objectives.

Themes of anxiety also show up during this wave, but to a lesser extent; and they are allied with different thematic material, in this case, themes of affiliation (affiliation with lover, $r = .28$, $p < .03$, and affiliation with relatives, $r = .28$, $p < .03$).

1976. The women in our sample are now 33 years old, and their children are generally of school age. Birth themes have declined and themes concerning affiliation with children now attain eminence. The proportion of success themes is greater now than it was in 1974. Depression themes have receded but in their place we find a preponderance of anxiety themes. Depression is still allied with lack of success ($r = .29$, $p < .03$), but now anxiety has also joined in linkage with lack of success ($r = .43$, $p < .0008$).

1979. The women are now 36 years old and some 34 percent of the married women have divorced. Depression has gone up somewhat for the sample. However, unlike the case in 1974, depression is not linked to lack of success, but instead is correlated with death themes describing loss of parents and relatives ($r = .47$, $p < .0002$) and lack of affiliation with lover ($r = .28$, $p < .03$). The reason for the lack of association between depression and lack of success becomes evident from an examination of other themes. Success is now once again reestablished as the top ranking theme just as it was in 1960 when these women are college freshmen. The difference, of course, is that instead of fantasy projections of success, these women are talking about and feeling proud of their recent accomplishments — developing skill in a new job as a therapist, opening a law firm, publishing a book, receiving an advertising award. Experiences of fear/anxiety have receded but still constitute the chief affectively negative experiences, and these are correlated with both affiliative and success themes (affiliation with lover $r = .41$, $p < .002$; success, $r = .41$, $p < .002$; lack of success, $r = .40$, $p < .002$). As noted earlier, over one-third of the sample have become divorced or separated and many have reestablished intimate relationships with men as reflected in the third ranking theme "affiliation with lover." This relationship is commonly one of some ambivalence, as judged by its linkage with both anxiety and depression; it elicits some of the most affectively charged language found in the autobiographical material. One woman, for example, described a current relationship as generating "violent uhappiness."

To recapitulate, depression is correlated with independence and lack of success in 1974, with lack of success again in 1976, and with death and lack of affiliation themes in 1979. The alliance of anxiety and certain themes also shifts over the three waves of autobiographical data. Anxiety is linked with affiliative relationships in 1974, with lack of success in 1976 and with both success and affiliation themes in 1979.

While the anxiety theme is always correlated with the top ranking projections of 1960 (i.e., success or lack thereof, and affiliative relationships with men), the patterns is somewhat different over the years; and this changing pattern, we suspect, is largely attributable to ontological changes linked to family structure and its relation to work. Thus we see that the primary affects of anxiety and depression are closely associated with their primary motives of success and affiliation as defined by TAT projections obtained in adolescene. The ontological/family changes that "organize" affects and these trait/situational themes are those of managing intimate relationships, rearing children, and finding arenas for the fulfillment of personal needs for accomplishment and recognition. This delicate balancing act is one faced by more and younger cohorts of women and hence these patterns may be more generalizable than at first foreseen.

Collective Profile of the Lives of Women Moving from Adolescence into Mid-Life

As adolescent women entering a competitive college in the fall of 1960, we have a portrait of a cohort of bright, achievement-oriented, aggressive young women who are seeking to balance intellectual and affiliative needs as they prepare for the adult years ahead. By the time they are into their early thirties many of them have fulfilled the traditional roles expected of the 1943 birth cohort of women (i.e., marrying and having babies). Like many young mothers they show high rates of depression. Depressive motifs cooccur with a high frequency of themes describing struggles over restriction of freedom and denial of access to opportunities for achievement and recognition. It is of interest to note that achievement strivings were *not,* as popularly assumed, channelled into vicarious enjoyment of the achievements of husband or children. There were a negligible number of instances where subjects mentioned achievements of spouse, lover, or children, and instead a preponderance of themes describing their own successes or attempts to achieve success and recognition. By 1976 mothers are raising older children, many of whom have begun school; the focus of interest and energy is now on affiliative relationships with these older children and resumption or plans to resume interrupted careers. Coinciding with this change in orientation there is a decrease in depressive motifs and an increase in the experience of anxiety. By 1979, with the attainment of achievement and career goals, themes of nurturance and affiliation with children have declined; anxiety has fallen and depression remains relatively low. These women appear to have navigated early mid-life and its vicissitudes rather expertly, fulfulling many of the traditional roles of women while eventually holding true to their dominant thematic concerns of success/achievement and affiliation. Note that all of this occurs in fairly rapid order by conventional standards; this remarkable group of women is disproportionately represented in the professions, and many have achieved a good deal of eminence in their fields by the time they are 36 years old.

The scores of these women on the Zung anxiety and depression scales are somewhat elevated over standardization groups, but not markedly so. However, despite the fact that they are clinically well within normal bounds on these affective scales, their autobiographical material demonstrates that their lives are far from conflict free; and themes of anger, fear, and depression appear with moderate frequency. The dominant entering theme of this group of women — success/recognition — fluctuates over the child-rearing years. Beginning high and then receding, it reemerges as the most dominant theme once again 19 years later. It is perhaps noteworthy that the affective themes of depression and anxiety are typically correlated with themes of frustration and attainment of the success motive over the years.

Summary and Conclusions

The findings of the present investigation are in accord with other recent work on the patterns of women's lives during successive life stages. First, we have verified two propositions tentatively suggested by Haviland's (1982) idiographic analysis of the life of Virginia Woolf: (1) thematic content developed in childhood and/or adolescence (in this case success/recognition) maintains or periodically regains eminence during later years, and (2) thematic content is bounded by strong emotional feelings.

Second, the present study also highlighted the importance of life-stage factors in the relative salience of themes and in the tendency of ontologic roles to overwhelm and obscure primary themes at certain developmental periods. A similar finding has recently been reported by Krogh (1982). This investigator studied two groups of women at different life stages, mothers of preschool children and mothers with school-age children. She examined shifts in these women's motivational hierarchies, specifically shifts in the achievement and nurturance motives during these two life stages involving the family. The results supported the thesis that women's motives change in relation to changes in their life stages. That is, women with very young children indicated that their children and their children's welfare was more central to them than did women who had older children, although children were still very much an important part of their lives. The women's achievement concerns also were found to change as a function of life stage; when change in the importance of achievement goals occurred, the change was in the direction of those goals becoming less important to women with younger children and more important to those with older children. In sum, there was an increase in the need to nurture during the early child-rearing years and a decrease in the achievement motive, with a reversal of this pattern in the later years among those who showed change. These findings, as well as those of the present investigation offer empirical support for the speculations of Kuhlen (1964) and McClelland (McClelland & Winter, 1969) concerning the liklihood of motivational change in adulthood related to situational change. The results of these two studies also coincide with findings of a cross-sectional study by Baruch (1967), demonstrating that the nAch scores of Radcliffe graduates were related to their age and family situation. The present investigation represents one of the first *longitudinal* demonstrations of the interplay between personality and motivational variables on the one hand, and situational variables on the other, in the context of women's lives; it included the *affective* dimension of experience, which proved to be an important feature.

Finally, we have demonstrated the utility of looking at the broader contex of lives when attempting to examine the interface between personality functioning and affect. By coding a wide range of common life-thematic concerns, ranking them and tracking changes in the relative ranks over an extended period of time, we have a better perspective on "primary themes." Had we just lcoked at the 1964 data we might have concluded that success themes were most central to these women. Had we just looked at the 1976 data we might have decided that child-rearing and affiliation themes are most central to their lives. Instead we get a picture of the dynamic interplay between affiliative and achievement strivings in the context of real-life role demands, as well as a view of how these changes elicit strong affective reactions.

References

Baldwin, A. L. (1965). A method for investigating the single personality. In E. A. Southwell & M. Merbaum (Eds.), *Personality: Readings in theory and research.* Belmont, CA: Wadsworth.

Baruch, R. (1967). The achievement motive in women: Implications for career development. *Journal of Personality and Social Psychology, 5,* 260-267.

Blood, R. O. & Wolfe, D. M. (1960). *Husbands and wives: The dynamics of married living.* New York: The Free Press.

Campbell, A., Converse, P. & Rodgers, W. (1976). *The quality of American life.* New York: Russell Sage Foundation.

Combs, A. W. (1947). A comparative study of motivations as revealed in thematic apperception stories and autobiography. *Journal of Clinical Psychology, 3,* 65-75.

Denenberg, V. H. (1979). Paradigms and paradoxes in the study of behavioral development. In E. B. Thoman (Ed.), *Origins of the infant's social responsiveness.* Hillsdale, NJ: Lawrence Erlbaum.

Eron, L. D. (1965). A normative study of the thematic apperception test. In B. I. Murstein (Ed.), *Handbook of projective techniques.* New York: Basic Books.

Gutmann, D. (1975). Parenthood: A key to the comparative study of the life cycle. In N. Datan & L. H. Ginsberg (Eds.), *Life-span developmental psychology: Normative life crises.* New York: Academic Press.

Haviland, J. M. (1983). Personality development from childhood to young adulthood: Thinking, feeling and self in Woolf's writing. In C. E. Izard, J. Kagan, & R. Zajonc (Eds.), *Emotions, cognitions, and behavior.* New York: Cambridge University Press.

Hoffman, L. W. & Manis, J. D. (1978). Influences of children on marital interaction and parental satisfactions and dissatisfactions. In R. M. Lerner & G. B. Spanier (Eds.), *Child influences on marital and family interaction.* New York: Academic Press.

Hollingshead, A. B. (1971). Four-factor index of social position. Yale University.

Izard, C. (1971). *The face of emotion.* New York: Appleton-Century-Crofts.

Izard, C. (1977). *Human emotions.* New York: Plenum Press.

Kagan, J. (1961). Stylistic variables in fantasy behavior: The ascription of affect states to social stimuli. In J. Kagan & G. S. Lasser (Eds.), *Contemporary issues in thematic apperceptive methods.* Springfield, IL: Charles C. Thomas.

Krippendorff, K. (1981) *Content analysis: An introduction to its methodology.* Beverly Hills, CA: Sage.

Kuhlen, R. G. (1968). Developmental changes in motivation during the adult years. In B. L. Neugarten (Ed.), *Middle age and aging.* Chicago: University of Chicago Press.

McClelland, D. C. (1951). *Personality.* New York: William Sloane Associates.

McClelland, D. C. & Winter, D. G. (1969). *Motivating economic achievement.* New York: The Free Press.

Neugarten, B. L. (1977). Personality and aging. In J. E. Birren & K. W. Schaie (Eds.), *Handbook of the psychology of aging.* New York: Van Nostrand-Reinhold.

Patterson, G. R. (1980). Mothers: The unacknowledged victims. *Monographs of the Society of Research in Child Development, 45* (5).

Plutchik, R. (1962). *The emotions: Facts, theories, and a new model.* New York: Random House.

Stewart, A. J. (1978). A longitudinal study of coping styles in self-defining and socially defined women. *Journal of Consulting and Clinical Psychology, 46,* 1079-1084.

Stewart, A. J. (1980). Personality and situation in the prediction of women's life pátterns. *Psychology of Women Quarterly, 5,* 195-206.

Stewart, A. J. & Salt, P. (1981) Life stress, life-styles, depression, and illness in adult women. *Journal of Personality and Social Psychology, 40,* 1063-1069.

Tomkins, S. (1962). *Affect, imagery, consciousness: Vol. I, The positive affects.* New York: Springer.

Zung, W. W. K. (1965). A self-rating depression scale. *Archives of General Psychiatry, 12,* 63-70.

Zung, W. W. K. (1971). A rating instrument for anxiety disorders. *Psychosomatics, 12,* 371-379.

11

Affective Processes and Later Life Changes

A Socioanalytic Conceptualization

ROBERT O. HANSSON
ROBERT HOGAN
WARREN H. JONES

Theories of emotion, like theories of personality, motivation, or behavior disorders, should broaden our understanding of the social nature of human kind. Such theories should be placed in the proper context — they should be ecologically valid and should predict behavior and experience across the span of our lives. The present volume, with its focus on emotion in adult development, presents an opportunity to integrate perspectives. This chapter represents one such integration.

Specifically, in this chapter we explore the relationship between emotional and personality processes and the experience of growing old. We will argue, from a role-theoretical perspective, that (1) emotions, like other personality processes, can be usefully conceptualized as instrumental role enactments, and (2) they develop and change in response to one's level of status and acceptance in society. Our argument draws upon two propositions from recent emotion theory. The first is that specific emotional patterns evolve as they become adaptive in a social context, where they serve to stimulate and focus appropriate cognitive and behavioral activity (see. Izard, 1978; Izard & Beuchler, 1980; Malatesta & Izard, this volume). Although this theme typically occurs in discussions of how patterns of emotion develop in infants and young children, we will focus on what becomes of such responses if they become unnecessary or maladaptive in old age. The second proposition, that emotions can be viewed as transitory social role enactments, was developed in a notable paper by Averill (1980, and also this volume). He suggested that to express an emotion toward another person (e.g., anger or love) is to enter into a temporary social relationship with that person; consequently, emotional reactions are governed by the rules and expectations that are learned in one's sociocultural environment. We will attempt to place Averill's proposition about such interactions in the context of socioanalytic theory (Hogan, 1982), which takes a similar view regarding the nature of personality but which makes some specific predictions regarding personality and emotional development in youth and old age.

In the first section we present the socioanalytic perspective. The second section reviews some of the psychological demands of growing old, paying particular attention to the implications of role loss for one's social identities. The third section briefly discusses the tasks of adapting to old age, and the final section speculates about age-related changes in personality, emotional responsivity, and criteria for self-esteem and adjustment.

Socioanalytic Theory

Our theoretical perspective is presented in detail elsewhere (Hogan, 1982). The principal assumptions, however, are outlined below. First, people are seen as having evolved as group-living animals; moreover, the social structure of every human group is organized in terms of a status hierarchy. Individual survival and prosperity thus depend upon achieving relative status and acceptance within one's group. Second, we assume that three primary needs or drives profoundly influence human social behavior: (1) a need for social approval, (2) a need for status, and (3) a need for predictability and structure. Third, we assume that the psychological demands of these motivational propositions are such that they can only be satisfied through continued and structured social interaction.

Socioanalytic theory proposes six basic dimensions of interpersonal performance that are relevant to successful attainment of status and acceptance in society. These performance factors should be valued by almost every group, because they promote group productivity and solidarity. Moreover, these characteristics (intellectance, adjustment, ascendancy, self-control, sociability, and likeability) are consistent with factor analytic studies of the structure of traits (Hogan, 1982).

There are, of course, vast differences in adult personality, and these are, in turn, associated with differences in status and acceptance in one's group. Socioanalytic theory focuses on the developmental processes that shape those differences and their consequences for an individual's self-image and personal identity. Quite early in development, children learn that social interaction provides attention and other social rewards in a structured and predictable fashion. They quickly progress from primitive, parent-baby interactions where the roles and the rules for interaction are handed down by adults, to play interactions with other children where roles are developed and assigned by negotiation and consensus. In the process they learn that social roles are the vehicles for social interaction, and that the roles and the rules that govern interaction are social constructions. In very general terms, these are the processes underlying the development of adult personality.

We conceptualize personality in terms of two broad structures. The first, *character structure*, is comprised of the rules, values, and expectations internalized during the socialization process in early childhood. Character structure is the aspect of personality of which we may be the least conscious but which may be the most stable. The second, *role structure,* forms in early adolescence and is comprised of one's beliefs about the rules, values, and expectations of one's peer group. Character structure, then, becomes a generally unconscious component of adult personality, reflecting one's deeply held values and moral beliefs. Role structure, however, is more conscious, and is usually reflected in one's strategies for dealing with reference groups to achieve one's goals. The congruence between character and role structure can be problematic, especially during times of rapid social change.

A major problem in life is to negotiate the most advantageous identity one can, given the parameters and constraints of the social environment. Several aspects of this process should be distinguished. *First,* over time we develop self-images that we would also like our social groups to believe. *Second,* we also internalize the expectations of significant others (our reference groups) and guide our actions specifically so as to earn their praise and avoid their censure. *Third,* as a consequence of our self-images and reference groups, our interactions largely consist of self-presentations or stylized role peformances wherein we attempt to project an image that will result in attention and approval. *Finally,* over time. our self-images and self-presentational strategies become automatic and unconscious. They are the end products of personality development, and reflect our developmental history, our self-presentational methods, the demands of our reference groups, and the degree to which we are motivated to comply with their demands. Because our self-presentations reflect a social consensus regarding our various talents and their importance to the other members of a group, it follows that these personality characteristics may decline or change if such social demands change. We shall return to this point and its implications for personality change in old age because a parallel argument can be made regarding changes that may occur in emotional control and responsivity.

Averill's Constructivist View of Emotion

Averill's (1980, this volume) constructivist view of emotion and socioanalytic theory are conceptually rooted in a symbolic interactionist framework. Averill describes the responses of infants to emotion-inducing situations as being initially devoid of cognitive content. Children must therefore acquire in the developmental process appropriate means for discriminating between and labelling emotions. Children's play thus promotes the development of both emotional and social competence. Children, for example, will play at being angry; in so doing they try on emotions, faces, and feelings to determine how well they wear them, and how they affect other people. Averill suggests that active experimentation with emotion in the context of other social learning experiences not only builds skills, but also allows children to learn the meaning of different emotions, and degrees of emotion with respect to broader social, moral, and aesthetic systems. Such efforts therefore provide an opportunity to learn what the cultural group defines as the "appropriate" response to the question, "How should I feel in this situation?" Thus, the progression of jealousy, for example, may be guided not only be feelings of threat or loss, but also by cultural notions of how I ought to feel when someone "poaches" what is rightfully mine.

Averill also points out that there is usually an object for an emotion —a person, event, or entity about which one is fearful, joyous, or angry. When the object is a person or a group, emotion is not just a matter of labelling arousal. Rather, in becoming angry with someone, for example, one enters into a social relationship with that person. Such relationships are governed by traditional views of how one ought to feel in these circumstances, by one's role-taking ability, and by the depth of one's involvement in the scene that is taking place. Averill adds that, as with other kinds of role performances, we often monitor our emotional reactions with respect to the manner and appropriateness with which we are responding, as defined by the expectations of the group; in this way we obtain feedback regarding the effectiveness of our portrayals.

We noted earlier that role playing ability and self-presentational skill are associated with achieving status and acceptance in one's cultural group. Specifically, socioanalytic theory suggests that appearing bright, self-confident, leaderlike, dependable, sociable, and friendly will in the long run lead to status and popularity. Successful identities will therefore be composed of some form and combination of those characteristic dimensions. But where do emotional portrayals fit into such a theoretical perspective? Izard (1978) and others have suggested that among infants specific emotional patterns develop as they become adaptive vis-à-vis their caretakers. We would suggest that from early adulthood, those emotional portrayals that serve important functions in the cultural group will be valued and encouraged. The most important functions concern solving group tasks and socioemotional problems. This generalization is, of course, a commonplace in other areas of psychology. The group dynamics literature, for example, highlights these two functions as problems for group leaders, and the sex roles literature has always emphasized instrumental and communal roles as core personality constructs. Competent portrayals of affection, empathy, or joy, for example, should facilitate communication, cooperation, and cohesion within a group. Similarly, competent portrayals of fear, anger, or outrage may at times be useful in rallying the group's defensive posture or in facilitating the achievement of the group's external goals. In addition, competency in controlling one's emotions and effectively avoiding being drawn into wasteful emotional interactions will occasionally be important for the achievement of group goals.

As usual, novelists seem more attuned to this process than are psychologists. Consider the following examples from John Le Carre's recent novel, *The Little Drummer Girl* (1983). In the first example, Charlie (the drummer girl) is being interrogated by Israeli agents; she doesn't like the interrogation; at the same time, however, she is "being herself":

> Her anger swept over her like a red-hot sea. It lifted her, it cleansed her. . . . she let it take command of her entirely, while she herself, that tiny gyroscopic creature deep inside that always managed to stay upright, tiptoed gratefully to the wings to watch. Anger suspended her bewilderment and dulled the pain of her disgrace; anger cleared her mind and made her vision brilliant. Taking a step forward, she lifted her fist to swipe at him.

This ploy didn't work; consequently, "There was only one way out for her, so she took it. Hunching her shoulders, she dropped her face dramatically into her hands and wept inconsolably until . . . Rachel came forward from the window and put her arm around her shoulder" (p.137).

Later in the novel, Charlie is interrogated by agents of the PLO; now, however, she is working for the Israelis and is putting on a performance. In this case she had just been told that her fictional lover was murdered by the Israelis:

> She had her head sideways and she was resting her cheek on her clenched fist, so that the stream of her tears ran across her face instead of down it . . . Helga manhandled her to the sofa, where she lay again, her face buried in the prickly cushions and her hands locked over her face, weeping as only the bereaved and children can. Turmoil, anger, guilt, remorse, terror: she perceived each one of them like the phases of a controlled, yet deeply felt performance. I knew; I didn't know; I didn't dare allow myself to think. You cheats, you murdering Fascist cheats, you bastards who killed my darling lover in the theatre of the real.
>
> She must have said some of this aloud. Indeed she knew she had. She had monitored and selected her strangled phrases even while the grief tore at her: *You Fascist bastards, swine, oh Jesus, Michel.* (p. 275)

These are examples of very competent emotional performances. They are similar in their competence; they differ in their goals and dynamics. In the first instance Charlie is not consciously dissembling; in the second case she is dissembling, however she is careful not to be too conscious of doing so.

Competency is broadly defined, then, as being able to *rise to the occasion;* social and emotional role-playing competencies are an important part of the process. From the perspective of socioanalytic theory, then, appropriate emotional portrayals (like personal identity, self-presentation, and reputation) are social constructions. In the same way, competencies that develop in response to social demands should change when such social demands change.

It should be clear, then, that it is the reference group's needs and values (or one's perceptions thereof) that influence the development of interpersonal and emotional competency. We turn now to the implications of this model for understanding life transition and systematic patterns of change in old age, particularly in response to those group needs and values that remain relevant in later life.

The Demands of Growing Old

Personal Domains of Decline and Loss

Although subject to wide variability, old age is ultimately associated with systematic, individual decline and loss. In addition to decreased physical health and function, declining sensory capacity (eyesight, hearing), widowhood, and loss of income are often associated with decreased mobility and decreased access to supportive social interaction.

Role Change Across the Life Span

We concur with Averill's general analysis of the development and refinement of emotional portrayals. The socioanalytic perspective, however, provides a more general context for understanding personality development (as manifested in self-image, sense of identity, and self-presentational skills and behaviors), *and* emotional competencies (or emotional control). The guiding influence for both is the extent to which the evolution and refinement of self-presentations (portrayals) is instrumental in attaining status and acceptance within one's cultural group. Although the socioanalytic perspective is useful for understanding personality and emotional development in old age, it provides an incomplete account of the major role changes across the adult life span. One further integrative step is therefore necessary.

Rosow (1976) proposes a useful taxonomy of role-types and speculates about role change across the life span. His model postulates three substantive role-types (institutional, tenuous, and informal), the first two of which are critical for a socioanalytic analysis of aging. Consistent with sociological role theory, Rosow distinguishes between a status, defined as "a position in a social structure" and a role, defined as "the pattern of activity intrinsic to that position" or behavioral expectations for a person in that status (1976, p. 458). At any time a person occupies multiple statuses or social positions; and within each, he or she may interact with numerous others. Role-types differ in the extent to which they involve associated status and roles. An *institutional* role-type has a well-defined (institutionalized) status within society (occupational, family, political, social, etc.) for which there are relatively clear behavioral expectations (roles). *Tenuous* role-types have clearly defined status positions but lack clear roles. Such status-positions may be titular, symbolic, or token and entail no real function or responsibility. Tenuous role-types may also include statuses that are vulnerable to "role emptying"; in such cases a status loses (over time) its original rights and responsibilities. The role of a parent, for example, follows this pattern. In other cases the status position may be lost, and this will be followed by the loss of the associated roles, as in the case of widowhood, retirement, or disability. Such loss may result in a dramatic decrease in opportunity for social participation. For the elderly, there are fewer opportunities for role replacement or role succession; thus the process seems irreversible.

Rosow makes several additional points about this form of role loss that are consistent with the socioanalytic perspective, and the general theme of this chapter. First, role loss excludes older adults from the mainstream of society, and in doing so, devalues them. By being outside the mainstream, former sources of self-esteem and personal reward are withheld from them. Second, old age signals for the first time the systematic loss of status for all persons so classified. Similarly, for the first time major role transitions do *not* lead to increased responsibility or access to opportunity and reward. Moreover, for the first time, people enter a phase of life for which they have not been socialized. Finally, in agreement with Neugarten and Hagestad (1976), Rosow suggests that the transition to old age leads to reduced structure and predictability. As old people have fewer responsibilities, there are fewer defined expectations or standards for their behavior, performance, and attitudes.

By plotting across the life span the relative importance of and level of involvement in his role-types, Rosow can graphically portray the psychological significance of the various changes that occur. Institutional role involvement increases in importance from childhood through late middle age, and then begins to decline precipitously. Tenuous role involvement, on the other hand, follows an inverted-U function, being relatively high in one's childhood, decreasing through middle age and then increasing dramatically with old age.

Tasks of Adaptation in Old Age

The gerontological literature describes in detail the developmental tasks of old age (see George, 1980; Pfeiffer, 1977). Successful aging is viewed in terms of how well one adapts to changing circumstances and statuses and whether one finds ways to meet one's basic needs without undue disruption or suffering (Pfeiffer, 1977). Pfeiffer has identified a number of physical, cognitive, and emotional skills that facilitate adaptation. He points, for example, to the ability to replace lost social relationships with new ones. Also important is the ability actively to retain important personal functions, to retrain temporarily lost capacities (e.g., following a stroke or prolonged illness), and, when necessary, to learn to make do with less. There are broader tasks as well. One must come to terms with new limitations on the range of instrumental activities that can be successfully pursued. Similarly it is important to acknowledge limitations on the kind of responsibilities that one can assume, and to deal with any guilt arising from a declining ability to assume earlier responsibilities. With these declines, one must also reassess one's values and find new sources of life purpose and meaning to replace older ones.

Such issues may be most relevant, however, for those persons in their mid-seventies and beyond (Butler, 1975). The consensus among gerontologists seems to be that (at least in the current cohort) one's sixties and early seventies are not marked by *dramatic* declines (Hickey, 1980). Similarly, few of the so-called "young-old" think of themselves as old.

The practical circumstances of advanced old age suggest a number of factors that might influence one's ability to *rise to the occasion* (to demonstrate competence) in coping with the declines and disruptive events in one's life or within one's major cultural groups. These circumstances also suggest several mechanisms that may ease the transition. For example, by their mid-seventies, most people have already adjusted to significant levels of loss in terms of health, income, immediate family and friends, and meaningful occupational and civic roles. Experience may provide opportunity for learning and practicing various coping strategies. Also, by this age such events as widowhood may be less unexpected, and many people will have had opportunities to "rehearse" for widowhood (Glick, Weiss, & Parkes, 1974), and for other significant role changes. Moreover, one's friends, who are also potential social models, are, by this age, more likely to have progressed through important periods of adjustment, and this will provide opportunities for adaptive social comparison. Finally, evidence from the literature on widowhood suggests that older women feel less pressured by family and friends to take immediate steps after the loss of a spouse to make significant adjustments (changes) in their lives in terms of housing, finances, new friends, and so on (Lopata, 1979). Thus, for older persons, *external* pressures to demonstrate continued competence and successful adaptation may be less intense.

Age-grading. In most cultures, individuals are systematically categorized on the basis of salient forms of ascribed status. Gender and age are perhaps the most basic kinds of ascribed status and they determine in large part an individual's access to social roles. Age-graded norms further define "age-appropriate" behavior within social, family, occupational, and civic roles. To the extent that individuals are willing to comply with age-graded norms, they should experience increased structure, predictability, and acceptance in social interaction. The reader may recall that structure, predictability, and approval were posited earlier (within the socioanalytic perspective) as primary needs influencing human behavior. Neugarten and Hagestad (1976) suggest that age norms regarding social behavior are widely recognized as "social timetables"; if these are internalized, they then provide an individual with a "social clock" against which to evaluate his or her progress through the life course. They argue further that role transitions at any age are less traumatic if they are perceived as happening on time. They add, however, that age expectations appear to be more clearly delineated and more strictly enforced during early adulthood; such expectations demand less of middle-aged and older individuals. From this perspective, then, an important source of structure and predictability (critical to personality and emotional development) appears to become less useful in old age.

Predictions for Change in the Individual

Personality. Rosow (1976) concludes that advanced old age (especially after age 75 or so) is a time of general and systematic role contraction when even such roles as parent lose their function and status. He further argues that any remaining role behavior "has relatively little effect on other persons and is thereby socially inconsequential" (p. 465). The implications of this are twofold. First, because the active role involvement of older adults within the cultural group is significantly reduced, they will be faced with fewer normative expectations coming from the group. Older adults should, therefore, be under less pressure to negotiate their identities or public self-images with important others. Second, Rosow concludes that "for the first time in life, the elderly are excluded from central functions and social participation on which self-conceptions and self-esteem are based." That is, to the extent that roles contract and lose their status or function, elderly people will lose the opportunity to negotiate or renegotiate their social identities (p. 467).

The point, then, is that as we become older and lose competencies, socially mediated demands for dealing with decline and with disruptive events in one's life may become less intense. Similarly, the criteria for evaluating one's self-worth (which are the products of social consensus) may also become less relevant when these criteria are no longer tied to important role enactments within the social group. As legitimate opportunities for interaction are withdrawn from an individual, adventitious interactions with social and occupational others also lose their meaning and utility. In losing role opportunities, an individual thus loses the structure that facilitates interaction, the predictability that a role provides in the interaction, and, of course, the opportunity for interaction in the first place. Remaining interactions are less likely to be guided by mutual consensus, and should become unproductive and short-lived. Other people will no longer be an important source of predictability or reward.

Social responsiveness. With increasing age we might therefore expect to find decreasing social responsiveness. This is a particularly important point, because we regard interpersonal and emotional competencies as social responses to the demands of social environments. The result of age-related changes should then be a flattening of personality profiles *and* emotional portrayals, and, eventually, competencies. The theme is one of a decreased need to cope or rise to occasions, to serve the group, to negotiate a positive identity, to internalize group-valued personality characteristics, to retain a repertoire of adaptive emotional competencies, or to maintain emotional control. Consistent with such speculation, Neugarten (1977) concluded on the basis of hundreds of cross-sectional studies of personality change in old age that the one replicable personality change with age (in old age) is an increase in "interiority." Interiority refers to a general decrease in one's attention to the demands and evaluations of others and a reduced susceptibility to social reinforcers (Maehr & Kleiber, 1981).

Still another theme has to do with emotional responsiveness to threat. Stress theorists (e.g., Lazarus & DeLongis, 1983) emphasize the importance of the process of threat appraisal in stress management. Threat is considered to reside in the "eye of the beholder", in part as a function of one's needs, experiences, perceptions of coping resources (secondary appraisal), and so on. We would also argue that one's perceptions of the cultural group's demands for continued competence and coping efforts is an important aspect of the threat appraisal process. To the extent that older adults perceive such demands to be reduced, their emotional responsivity to many kinds of the threat should also be flattened. Although the socioanalytic perspective suggests that the threat of social isolation or group censure should generally be stressful, the foregoing discussion suggests that the circumstances of old age may make them less stressful.

In a manner analogous to the role of social comparison processes in times of stress, emotional comparison allows one to judge how much of an emotional reaction (e.g., fear, grief) is normative and adaptive in a particular circumstance. A recent study of older widows (Hansson, Hicks, & Mihelich, 1982) found a very interesting pattern (consistent with the point of this chapter) in subjects defined as young-old as contrasted with "old-old" groups (ages 60-72 versus ages 73-90). In this study the old-old exhibited what appeared to be a narrowing focus (or need) for emotional-social comparison at the time of their spouse's death. The younger group viewed emotional comparisons as useful only to the extent that they included a wide range of comparison others (including some nonwidows); in contrast, the older group found comparisons helpful only in relation to similar others (other widows). We interpret the broader response of the younger group as reflecting a continuing concern for social integration across a broad spectrum of roles. In this study, having been able to compare feelings with others was significantly related to long-term adjustment and self-esteem only among the younger group of widows.

Changing criteria for self-esteem and adjustment. Feelings of self-worth tend to reflect evaluations of one's current attributes, competencies, and levels of success. In adapting to old age, however, it may be necessary periodically to reassess one's criteria for self-evaluation. As a person begins to lose competencies and spheres of influence, it may be quite adaptive to drop them as criteria for self-evaluation (Saul, 1974).

This process may be facilitated in part by what Butler (1968) called the life review. The life review is a natural, cognitive activity in which older persons reexamine their lives, recall and integrate both positive and painful events, and place their recollections in a (hopefully positive) philosophical perspective. An extended temporal framework for evaluating the worth of one's life might take the place of *immediate* competencies as criteria for self-esteem.

Socioanalytic theory also provides an account of how older people maintain self-esteem. We have outlined how a person's identity and the criteria for evaluating his or her worth are social constructions to begin with, and how what rises in response to environmental demands should also fall when such demands are withdrawn. Individuals negotiate self-images and self-presentations designed to enhance their status and acceptance within important roles. This ritualized process of identity negotiation and self-presentation facilitates group interaction because it provides some predictability and control for all parties in the interaction. Predictability and control in turn allow all members of the group to achieve mutually satisfying instrumental pursuits (Athay & Darley, 1981).

Older adults experience decreased demands for competence and effective self-presentation when the cultural group begins to devalue their contribution and to restrict their access to key roles in the group. Identity negotiations and maintenance become less critical because there is less demand for predictability and cooperation in instrumental pursuits. We have already described a number of adjustment mechanisms that may ease the transition into old age with its eventual declines and losses.

We have gathered some data regarding the hypotheses that the availability of (1) personal and social competencies, and (2) continuing, satisfying social roles will be related to adjustment and self-esteem among the young-old but not among the old-old. Preliminary findings from our widowhood samples suggest the following: (1) Being in good health, having more education, and having positive instrumental and communal/expressive competencies are related to measures of adjustment and self-esteem among women aged 60-72 but not among those aged 73-90. The presence of sufficient income is, however, related to adjustment in the old-old; as we noted earlier, however, life success defined in terms of income is often associated with personal soundness. (2) Similarly, satisfactory involvement with children, family, friends, and clubs or organizations is substantially related to adjustment only among the young-old. Only the quality of one's involvement with one's religion is related to adjustment among the old-old.

Stability of personality. The final issue to be discussed concerns the stability of personality. Many leading gerontologists (McCrae & Costa, 1982; Neugarten, 1977) conclude that personality traits are generally quite stable over time. Traits, however, reflect the observers' view of personality. From the actor's perspective, there is an element of flexibility in personality, particularly when one views it as a social construction, the result of developmental sequences that reflect evolving methods for achieving status and acceptance in the cultural group. We have also proposed that in old age, with changing group demands and role contraction, personality from the actor's perspective may change. There is no contradiction between seeing personality — defined as one's social reputation — as remaining quite stable across the lifespan, while viewing another part (the structures that produce the reputation) as responsive to changing environmental demands.

Conclusion

There are five points from the preceding discussion that we would like to emphasize. First, we concur with Averill's (1980) constructivist view of emotion as a transitory role enactment. Second, we believe that a role-theoretical approach to emotion can be more fully explored within a socioanalytic perspective; here emotional portrayal and control competencies are seen as being related to the attainment of status and popularity vis-à-vis one's reference group. Third, certain emotional competencies will be more important than others for attaining status and acceptance within the cultural group. Fourth, recent theory regarding the manner in which role opportunity and involvement change across the life span suggest a pattern of substantial role contraction and emptying in old age, which in turn results in reduced group expectations, standards, and structure. Finally, in response to decreased role opportunity and decreased demands to cope for oneself or the group, older individuals typically experience (1) decreased social responsiveness, consistent with what Neugarten (1977) has called interiority; (2) diminished emotional competencies; (3) reduced responsiveness to social stressors and reduced need for social comparison; (4) changed criteria for self-esteem involving a shift from social to internal appraisals; and (5) reduced predictability with respect to characteristic personality or emotional patterns.

In closing, we note that in all these matters there are great individual differences, and those differences are themselves a function of competence. Consider the best 60- or 70-year-old golfers and tennis players in the country. Those people outperformed the other members of their age cohorts at every point in the developmental cycle. As it is in sporting games, so it is in the game of life. Some people become old, in the sense of a pronounced decline in their social and emotional competencies, in their 50s and early 60s. Others (e.g., Freud, Picasso, Einstein, Stravinsky, Bertrand Russell, Thomas Hardy, G.B. Shaw) maintain substantial competency to the ends of their lives. But they always were at the head of the class.

References

Athay, M., & Darley, J. M. (1981). Toward an interaction centered theory of personality. In N. Cantor & J. F. Kihlstrom (Eds.), *Personality, cognition, and social interaction.* Hillsdale, NJ: Lawrence Erlbaum.

Averill, J. R. (1980). A constructivist view of emotion. In R. Plutchik & H. Kellerman (Eds.), *Emotion: Theory, research, and experience.* New York: Academic Press.

Butler, R. N. (1968). The life review: An interpretation of reminiscence in the aged. In B. L. Neugarten (Ed.), *Middle age and aging: A reader in social psychology.* Chicago: University of Chicago Press.

Butler, R. N. (1975). Why survive? Being old in America. New York: Harper & Row.

George, L. K. (1980). *Role transitions in later life.* Belmont, CA: Brooks/Cole.

Glick, I. O., Weiss, R. S., & Parkes, C. M. (1974). *The first year of bereavement.* New York: John Wiley.

Hansson, R. O., Hicks, C. H., & Mihelich, M. H. (1982, August). Age, access to coping resources, and adjustment to widowhood. Paper presented at the meeting of the American Psychological Association, Washington, DC.

Hickey, T. (1980). *Health and aging.* Belmont, CA: Brooks/Cole.

Hogan, R. (1982). A socioanalytic theory of personality. In M. Page & R. Dienstbier (Eds.), *Nebraska Symposium on motivation.* Lincoln: University of Nebraska Press.

Izard, C. E. (1978). On the ontogenesis of emotions and emotion-cognition relationships in infancy. In M. Lewis & L. A. Rosenblum (Eds.), *The development of affect.* New York: Plenum Press.

Izard, C. E., & Buechler, S. (1980). Aspects of consciousness and personality in terms of differential emotions theory. In R. Plutchik & H. Kellerman (Eds.), *Emotion: Theory, research, and experience.* New York: Academic Press.

Lazarus, R. S., & DeLongis, A. (1983). Psychological stress and coping in aging. *American Psychologist,* 245-254.

Le Carre, J. (1983). *The little drummer girl.* New York: Knopf.

Lopata, H. Z. (1979). *Women as widows: Support systems.* New York: Elsevier.

Maehr, M. L., & Kleiber, D. A. (1981). The graying of achievement motivation. *American Psychologist, 36,* 787-793.

McCrae, R. R., & Costa, P. T. (1982). Self-concept and the stability of personality: Cross sectional comparisons of self-reports and ratings. Journal of Personality and Social Psychology, *43,* 1282-1292.

Neugarten, B. L. (1977). *Personality and aging.* In J. E. Birren and K. W. Schaie (Eds.), *Handbook of the psychology of aging.* New York: Van Nostrand Reinhold.

Neugarten, B. L., & Hagestad, G. O. (1976). Age and the life course. In R. H. Binstock & E. Shanas (Eds.), *Handbook of aging and the social sciences.* New York: Van Nostrand Reinhold.

Pfeiffer, E. (1977). Psychopathology and social pathology. In J. E. Birren & K. W. Schaie (Eds.), *Handbook of the Psychology of Aging,* New York: Van Nostrand Reinhold.

Rosow, I. (1976). Status and role change through the life span. In R. H. Binstock & E. Shanas (Eds.), *Handbook of aging and the social sciences.* New York: Van Nostrand Reinhold.

Saul, S. (1974). *Aging: An album of people growing old.* New York: John Wiley.

V

EMOTION AND INTERPERSONAL INTERACTION

In this section Cornelius offers a rule model of adult emotional expression that is an extension and elaboration of Averill's social constructivist theory (this volume). He argues that one of the things we learn as we are growing up, is to monitor our social performances, including interpersonal emotional performances. This will involve becoming aware of how one assigns meaning to events and contextualizes one's actions. (Empirical examples of social weeping and intimacy are offered to demonstrate how emotiôn responses can be studied as meaningful social performances.) Cornelius suggests that one of the more interesting kinds of changes observed in adult development involves changes in individuals' awareness of their emotional performances (meta rules of performance). The rule model he presents affords one means of exploring this proposition further.

In the next chapter Halberstadt examines the issue of how adult patterns of emotional expressivity or inexpressivity are acquired, stressing the role of family as the primary socializing unit. She demonstrates that not all social training concerning the emotions is directed at emotion inhibition and that in some families the emphasis is on emotion exaggeration rather than suppression. The two types of familial patterns appear to contribute to adult personal styles and these styles are related to differential interpersonal communication skills and patterns of social perception.

In a study of the facial expressivity of young, middle-aged, and older adults, Malatesta and Izard find that adults (at least adult women) are surprisingly expressive under emotion induction conditions, with little age-related difference in sheer amount of expressive activity. However, this expressivity was characterized by a high incidence of dissimulated or masked emotion, emotion blends, and fragmented or partial versions of expressions, leading to high decoder inaccuracy. Moreover, the incidence of these "noisy" expressions increased with age of subject. The findings were taken as support for the thesis that adults attenuate and transform their emotion signals to suit a variety of personal and interpersonal purposes. That these signal transformations are more often seen in older people suggests that older people may be at risk for distortion of meaning in interpersonal contexts.

12

A Rule Model of Adult Emotional Expression

RANDOLPH R. CORNELIUS

Emotional Expression as Intelligent Performance

Emotional expression never occurs in a vacuum. Emotions are complex social behaviors that are played out within a rich tapestry of interpersonal interaction. In fact, it may be said that emotions are forms of social interaction in and of themselves (Averill, 1980; Cornelius, 1981). The expression of emotions consists of more than simple momentary facial expressions or bodily movements; our emotions are holistic patterns of behavior elaborated in both time and space. As Averill (1980) argues, emotions may be likened to transitory social roles that derive their form and meaning from the social context (both micro and macro) within which they occur. That is, "emotional expression" consists of a variety of behaviors that are rendered meaningful as expressions of emotion by their interpersonal and social context.

AUTHOR'S NOTE: I would like to thank Janet Gray and Alison Nydick for their helpful comments on earlier versions of this manuscript, and Carol Malatesta and Carroll Izard for their superb editing. My thinking on these matters has benefited greatly from the many

The present chapter presents an attempt to develop a framework for the study of emotions as meaningful social performances. The focus of the model is on how social actors' rules for meaning and action make certain forms of social interaction possible. The model presented here draws heavily on the social constructivist theory of emotion developed by Averill (1980, and this volume) and the theory of interpersonal communication and interaction developed by Pearce and Cronen (1980) which they call the coordinated management of meaning. I demonstrate how these two theories may be used complementarily to develop a model of emotional expression as intelligent social performance, based on the thesis that emotional expression is a form of social action governed by rules followed by intelligent (that is, thoughtful but not necessarily logical) social actors.

Such an approach is particularly appropriate in a volume such as this, with its focus on *adult* development. Space does not permit a full account of the utility and generative capacity of rule models of social life. However, as Averill's contribution to this volume (see Chapter 2) illustrates, an analysis of the development of emotions in adulthood in terms of rules provides important insights into this long-neglected process. Rule models of social interaction would seem to be especially germane to investigations of change in adulthood, as they take into account the cognitive complexity of adults in modeling change (see Pearce & Cronen, 1980, pp. 290-301). Although the model I describe in this chapter presupposes a fair degree of cognitive sophistication and thus is most applicable to adults, there is really no reason why such an approach could not be used, with some modification, to explore the affective lives of children as well. In fact, through the use of rule models it may be possible to construct a unified approach to the study of emotional development in both adults and children (see Averill, this volume). A description of such an approach, even in outline form, however, is beyond the scope of the present discussion.

Emotions as Transitory Social Roles

The approach developed here involves what may be called *semantic ecology*, the study of how the activities of social actors are related to their semantic environment, in short, how acts are rendered meaningful

---

discussions I have had with James Averill, Vern Cronen, and Barnett Pearce over the past three years. A good part of the theoretical development of the model presented here is drawn from portions of my dissertation (Cornelius, 1981), and I would like to acknowledge James Averill, Barnett Pearce, Ronnie Janoff-Bulman, and Howard Gadlin for their kind help on that project.

by their social context. A central assumption of this approach is that emotions are not meaningful in and of themselves, but only as they are embedded with a context, specifically, an interpersonal/social context.[1]

A crucial feature of the present approach, one that differentiates it from other approaches to the study of emotional expression, is its focus on episodes of interaction. An episode is a relatively well defined, socially constituted, bounded pattern of interaction between two or more social actors. Episodes may be thought of as "meaningful wholes" in which the specific manner in which individuals behave within the episode is given meaning by reference to the episode as a whole (see below). The approach taken here bears certain similarities to that developed by Forgas (1979) in his studies of the cognitive structure of interaction episodes. The two approaches differ, however, in that Forgas's (1979) investigations deal with the perceptual/evaluative dimensions of episodes, while the approach I take focuses on the ways in which specific acts are made meaningful within episodes.[2]

The approach I describe here takes it for granted that the most interesting aspect of emotions is their social nature, and a major assumption of the approach is that emotions are, in a very real sense, social constructions. That is, they do not exist "in nature," apart from their social context, or to put it another way, they do not, as Rorty (1980) says, "form a natural class." Rather, emotions are given their coherence and very identity as emotions by the ways in which society organizes them as "social events." The point of view most compatible with this approach as far as the study of emotions goes is that embodied by Averill's (1980, and this volume) social constructivist theory of emotions.

Emotions as Individual and Social Constructions

According to Averill's (1980) theory, emotions may be thought of as transitory social roles, as *patterns* of behavior that are given both intra- and interpersonal coherence by means of learned social rules. In this view, emotions are constructions in two ways. They are constructions of the individual in that they are based on his or her appraisal or interpretation of the situation. At the same time, emotions are social constructions in that the manner in which the individual comes to appraise situations, the form that the individual's behavior takes in response to his or her appraisal of the situation, and the individual's interpretation of his or her own behavior while emotional are socially, rather than biologically, given.

Central to Averill's theory is the notion that when individuals are behaving emotionally they are following rules (see Averill, 1982 and this volume, for a more detailed explanation of the theory). Rules of *appraisal* are rules of meaning, rules that transform the raw data of our sense impressions into meaningful experiences and rules that render various experiences equivalent. Rules of *behavior,* on the other hand, specify what behaviors should follow given that one has interpreted the situation in this or that manner. The distinction is an important one and in fact forms a large part of the way in which Pearce and Cronen conceptualize the rules of social life. Pearce and Cronen, however, have added a new twist to the old distinction; and it is to their theory that I now turn.

The Coordinated Management of Meaning: A Framework for the Study of Emotional Expression as Intelligent Performance

Stimulated by Bateson's (1972) provocative essay on the nature of communication in play, students of communication have assigned increasing importance to the context of various communicative utterances. Bateson's central insight was that every message (utterance, gesture, and hence, act) possesses not only a content but also a comment on how that content is to be interpreted. Thus, Bateson, watching two monkeys at play, realized that the seemingly hostile bite of one of the monkeys carried with its the message, "This is play," or, more precisely, "These actions in which we now engage do not denote what those actions for which they stand would denote" (Bateson, 1972, p. 180). Thus, every communicative act may be seen as being contextualized within what might be called a metacommunication.

Meanings, therefore, are context-dependent. However, the supraordinate context for messages that so interested Bateson does not exhaust the many ways in which an act may be contextualized. What Pearce and Cronen have done is to further specify the context-dependent nature of meanings and hence, communicative acts. Moreover, they have developed a way to model in a precise fashion how social action grows out of the meanings that individuals assign to their own and others' actions.

Meanings and Rules

In coordinated management of meaning (CMM) theory, individuals are seen as possessing "systems of multileveled meanings organized into rules, the primary function of which is to transform raw sensory data into meanings and meanings into action" (Cronen & Pearce, 1981, p. 19). People make sense out of the world, then, by reference to the meanings they possess and the rules that give those meanings coherence and guide appropriate action.

Levels of meaning. According to CMM theory, the various meanings that allow individuals to transform the raw data of experience are systematically arranged within hierarchies where each meaning is embedded within or contextualized by higher order levels of meaning. Meaning, conceptualized in this manner, is actually an emergent property of the system as a whole and not a characteristic of individual elements.

At the lowest level of contextualization is the actual *content* of an action or communication (message) — that is, the information it conveys in isolation from any instructions as to how the information is to be interpreted. The informational content of an action or utterance is embedded within or contextualized by at least five supraordinate levels of meaning. Each lower level of meaning is seen as being contextualized and defined by the level above it.

(1) The immediate contextualization of the content of an action or utterance is the *act* or speech act within which it occurs. This refers to what a person *does* to another by saying or doing something (cf. Austin, 1975). For example, the monkey's bite described by Bateson becomes at this level either a "playful nip" or a hostile gesture. In the same manner, the information conveyed by the utterance "I'm angry" may be modified in a variety of ways by the nonverbal or paralinguistic context of the utterance. Depending on its context, the same utterance may be interpreted as a playful remark or an expression of emotion.

(2) *Episodes,* the next level of contextualization, are experienced by participants as patterned wholes, as "meaningful, total units of social interaction" (Forgas, 1979, p. 44) bounded by more or less well-defined opening and closing sequences and characterized by rules specifying appropriate verbal and nonverbal behavior (see Cronen & Pearce, 1981, p. 21). Emotions, as social roles, may also be contextualized within the boundaries of more inclusive types of episodes. For example, an "angry outburst" or fit of weeping may be contextualized within episodes of hostile confrontation. As contextualizing events, emotions are interesting in that they are reflexive. That is, they may provide context either in an upward or downward fashion. For example, an angry remark may be contextualized within an episode of hostile confrontation between, let's say, marriage partners. The remark, as an expression of anger, is given meaning by the episode in which it occurs. At the same time, the episode "hostile confrontation" acquires part of its meaning from the angry remarks contained within it.[3]

(3) Episodes are embedded within the *relationship* between or among the actors involved in the episode. Meanings at this level consist of an individual's implicit expectations as to the kinds of episodes that should occur between him- or herself and others within the defined relationship. For example, weeping in the presence of another person will be contextualized in different ways and given different meanings depending on whether it occurs within the context of a relationship between marriage partners or between a personnel director and a potential employee.
(4) Encompassing the level of meaning represented by relationships is the *life-script* (cf. McAdams, this volume) or self-concept of the actor. Life-script refers to the expectations a person has about the kinds of relationships, patterns of episodes, acts, etc., he or she should engage in given the way he or she defines him- or herself.
(5) Life scripts are contextualized within "supra-personal" *patterns of culture,* what Berger and Luckman call "symbolic universes" (1966, pp. 92-93). Patterns of culture define humankind's relationship to nature, mind to body, and so on. These are the mythologies of culture, the most general levels of legitimation.

The foregoing levels represent how meanings are contextualized hierarchically. However, this does not exhaust the various ways in which meanings may be contextualized. Account must also be taken of two kinds of *temporal contextualization.*

Temporally antecedent meanings (acts, episodes, etc.) contextualize subsequent meanings. In the simplest case, antecedent conditions may change the probability of occurrence of certain subsequent acts. For example, in our studies of first time avowals of love, Alison Nydick and I have found that saying "I love you" to a person is almost invariably followed by a reciprocal expression of love from that person.

Temporally consequent meanings (e.g., goals and purposes, the consequence or final outcome of an act or series of acts, whether intended or not) may contextualize antecedent meanings. For example, saying "I love you" to a person may serve to legitimate ones past behavior toward that person ("I did it because I love you"). Contextualization by temporally consequent meanings may also take the form of a hierarchy in that we may recognize that a person's actions are guided by immediate episode-dependent goals (e.g., finishing an interaction sequence one has started), as well as more long-term goals (e.g., one's ultimate goal in life).

A model of the ways in which an act may be contextualized hierarchically and temporally is presented in Figure 12.1.

Rules for Meaning and Action

The various levels of meaning that individuals possess are given intrapersonal coherence by means of *rules.* Rules provide structure for

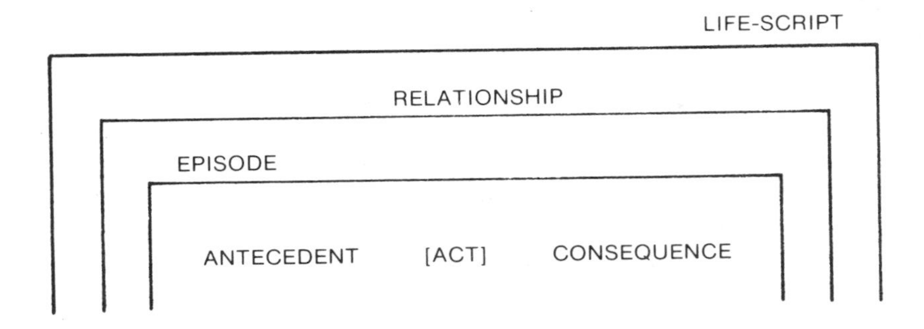

Figure 12.1 Hierarchical and Temporal Contextualization of an Act

meanings and actions through various forms of *entailment,* that is, how one meaning or action is implied by another meaning or action as movement ("If A occurs, do B") or equivalence ("A equals B"). The strength of the entailments among the various meanings and actions that a person possesses is conceived of within CMM theory as being variable.

Pearce and Cronen draw on Von Wright's (1951) system of "deontic" logical operators to express the variable nature of entailment. Using deontic operators, entailment is expressed in terms of the *strength of the relationship* among components of the intrapersonal system of meanings and actions; subjectively, this might be expressed as "degrees of oughtness" connecting the performance of two acts (e.g., the "ought" connecting "Will you?" and "I will" is much stronger when one is involved in a marriage ceremony than when one is being asked to go out for pizza). These entailments thus represent the types of connections that people themselves perceive among their meanings.

The rules that connect the various meanings and actions that a person possesses, and give form to expressions of entailment, are of two types: constitutive and regulative rules. Averill spends considerable time in this volume discussing the nature of constitutive and regulative rules, so I will only very briefly mention the role these rules play within CMM's conception of intrapersonal systems of meaning.

Constitutive rules. Constitutive rules render different meanings and actions equivalent; they specify how meanings at one level count as meanings at another level. For example, the statement "I'm angry" usually counts as a certain type of emotional expression if it is uttered in the context of a hostile confrontation. "I'm angry," however, may count as something quite different if it is contextualized in another way. Thus, constitutive rules specify how the various levels of contextualization outlined above are connected.

Regulative rules. Regulative rules are rules of movement, they specify what actions should or should not be taken given certain antecedent conditions and contexts. In addition, regulative rules specify the consequences of the performances in question. For example, in the context of an intimate relationship, being the recipient of an avowal of love entails that one should follow this utterance with a reciprocal avowal of love in order to maintain the relationship at its present level or bring about positive changes in the relationship. A line of action prohibited by such a rule would be to make light of the remark and treat it as a joke. Because of the reflexive nature of contextualization, such an action might lead one's partner to question the legitimacy of the entire relationship, as the kinds of things that are done at the level of episodes bestow meaning on the relationship level, especially in the formative stages of a relationship (see Cronen et al., 1982, p. 101).

The Logic of Interpersonal Interaction

It should be clear from these examples how interaction based on *interpersonal* rules develops. Interpersonal rule systems are emergent properties of the combination of two or more intrapersonal rule systems. The action resulting from the application of one person's regulative rules in a situation becomes the antecedent condition for the application of another's rules. This means that social interaction is only partly under the control of the individual actors; each brings to a situation a set of meanings and rules that serve to guide his or her own behavior. However, because the combinatory potential of all of the interactants' rule systems is greater in a sense than the sum of its parts, any individual actor may find him- or herself enmeshed in a logic of interaction quite different from that which he or she brought to the situation. One of the implications of this is that people may not always perform the actions they intend to perform. That is, the meanings that guide an actor's behavior in a given situation may combine with those of other actors to produce a logic for action which is different from and supersedes the logic that may have been generated by the individual actor's meanings alone. This important insight gives rise to one of the most crucial aspects of CMM theory — the recognition that the acts performed by individuals in episodes of social interaction are impelled by both the way the individual construes the situation and by the logic of the situation itself. Social action is given its impetus by the "logical necessity" generated by the application of individuals' rule systems and their combination with others' rule systems. Logical necessity is understood to take one of two forms, so-called prefigurative and practical necessity.

Prefigurative and Practical Necessity

According to CMM, at least two types of logical necessity may be identified in the determination of social action. The first, *practical necessity,* involves willful goal-directed activity or the extent to which a person translates his or her wishes or intentions into action. For the purposes at hand, the extent to which a person engaged in an activity in a given situation in order to bring about certain ends would be a measure of practical necessity.

The second form of necessity identified by CMM theory, *prefigurative necessity,* refers to the extent to which certain configurations of meanings "demand" or require certain actions because for the actor (subjectively) "it is the only thing to do."

Practical and prefigurative necessity are conceived of by CMM theory as being expressed by two configurations of entailments within the variable structure of individuals' regulative rules.

The configuration of relationships that define the *prefigurative necessity* exerted by a regulative rule involves how the action implied by the rule is entailed by "preexisting" conditions. These preexisting conditions include the particular antecedent to the act in question, the life script of the actor, the relationship between the actor and others involved and the episode in which the act is embedded. If the strength of these entailments to the specific act implied by the regulative rule is high, then the act is said to be prefigured by the preexisting conditions. For example, a young man, because of the way he defines himself and the kinds of relationships in which he expects to find himself, may feel quite compelled to confess his love to someone he has only known for a short time.

The extent to which actors translate their intentions into goal-directed activity is represented in the configuration of entailments defining the *practical necessity* expressed by regulative rules. These entailments involve how well the consequences of one's actions reflect one's goals; that is, the extent to which the consequences of engaging in a particular act help one to become the person one wants to be (life script), attain the kinds of relationships one would like to have, and the like. In the example cited above, saying "I love you" may be perceived by the young man as a means of bringing about the kind of relationship he would like to share with the other person.

Relative necessity. Prefigurative and practical necessity do not always work in concert. As Pearce and Cronen have pointed out, the predominance of one type of necessity over the other produces characteristic forms of activity. For example, interactions in which prefigurative necessity is very strong and practical necessity is weak tend to be highly ritualized or stereotyped and may be perceived by participants as beyond their control (crying at weddings is a good example). Situations in which practical necessity prevails at the expense of prefigurative necessity may appear to be "enigmatic" to participants or observers; interaction may be perceived here as being relatively uncontrolled by situational constraints, with each participant striving to attain his or her goals regardless of feedback from the others involved — for example, as in arguments that rapidly escalate because neither participant is willing to listen to the other (Cronen & Pearce, 1981, p. 31). The *relative necessity* expressed by each act within the episode may be obtained by comparing prefigurative and practical necessity.

The Structure of Social Action

CMM theory provides us with a model of social interaction based on the meanings individuals impose on events. Social actors make sense out of the world by means of rules for meaning and action. The rules and meanings that people possess are assumed to be organized more or less systematically and it is possible to obtain judgments from people as to the ways in which various meanings entail other meanings and actions. By examining the manner in which actors perceive the various configurations of entailments among the meanings they possess, we may begin to explore the semantic ecology of social action.

A Rule Model of Emotional Expression

The above is a brief outline of the theory I have been using to develop a framework for the study of episodes of emotional expression. The aim of the approach is to study how emotional expression is semantically embedded within the stream of events in episodes of interpersonal interaction. Emotional expression, according to the approach developed here, is an emergent property of social interaction and can only be fully understood by examining the ways in which it is embedded within the larger contexts within which it occurs. The approach may be seen as part of a widespread and growing attempt to explore the fundamental "connectedness" of all social action (see Shotter, 1983); that is, to study the ways in which any social act expresses a relation between itself and what Shotter (after Bohm, 1980; see Shotter & Newson, 1982, p. 38) calls the "implicate order." It should be understood, however, that this exploration of the implicate order is not necessarily a search for the underlying "grammar" or structure of social life because the structure of social life is only partly given by individual actors' rule systems. As Shotter and Newson (1982) point out, social life is the result of

> *joint action,* in which people must interlace what they do with the actions of others. [The] formative influences [of social life] are not wholly there within us to be brought out. The actions of others determine our conduct just as much as anything within ourselves. In such circumstances, the overall outcome of the exchange is simply not up to us [pp. 43-44].

Even though the ultimate product of social action is not the exclusive result of what any one actor brings to the situation, social action is nevertheless grounded in actors' meanings and any exploration of social action must begin with a consideration of the ways in which actors come to regard their own and others' actions as meaningful.

In some sense, calling the approach described here a "rule model" distorts the true nature of the undertaking. Actors' rules are certainly an important part of the model but to speak of rules, especially when discussing emotional expression, is to run the risk of being seriously misunderstood. The rules of social life as conceived of here are *not* akin to, for example, rules of etiquette, but rather are those rules that are constitutive of experience, that actually define or create social reality for us. The rules of emotional expression are those rules that allow us to experience our behavior as meaningful, as part of the context within which it occurs. The aim of a "rule model" of emotional expression, construed in this manner, is to explore the commonalities among individuals in the rules that they employ to render their emotional experience meaningful.

We often assume that all of the actors in a particular social group should share more or less the same rules, and in fact most investigations of the "rules of social life" have concentrated on discovering the kinds of rules that all social actors have in common. However, we must also be attentive to the ways in which individuals differ. One of great strengths of CMM theory is that it may be used in both a nomothetic and idiographic manner. While Pearce and Cronen and their associates have mainly used the theory idiographically to explore the rule systems of individuals or closely related dyads, my own research using the theory has been more nomothetically inclined in that my concern has been to investigate the ways in which certain kinds of emotional performances are made meaningful, averaging across individuals.

Applications of the Model: Empirical Studies of Adult Emotional Expression

Methodology

The methodology involved in exploring the manner in which actors contextualize their emotional performances is quite simple. Subjects are first asked to describe an interaction episode involving another person in which some form of emotional expression played a part. Subjects are asked to describe the particular emotion or expression of emotion of interest (e.g., weeping) and its place in the episode in question. We then ask subjects to describe the boundaries of the episode, that is, how the episode began and how it ended. Most subjects have a very good intuitive grasp of the opening and closing sequences of their interactions with others (e.g., uttering a certain phrase, making a gesture of one sort or another) and although the kinds of things subjects describe may not "objectively" mark the boundaries of the episode, what is of interest to us is not what really happened, but what subjects perceive to have happened, that is, what the meanings of the events in question are for them.

After obtaining a rough outline of the episode from subjects, we ask them to describe the episode in terms of a series or sequence of *acts* on the part of each participant in the episode (e.g., asking a question, embracing, weeping, uttering a particular phrase, etc.). Care is taken to assure subjects that not all episodes need occur in this manner, and that this is merely a convenient way to talk about them. An attempt is made to obtain from subjects verbatim accounts of what was said and done during the episode and not merely a superficial description of the action.

When he or she is finished describing the episode, the subject is asked to rate how he or she perceives the strength of the various entailments among the components of the regulative rules involved in the determination of the acts he or she performed in the episode. Essentially, this procedure involves ascertaining how subjects situate each act within the pattern of possible meanings that may contextualize an act.

As discussed above, the pattern of entailments for any act within an episode may be divided into two clusters — those representing the prefigurative necessity expressed by an act, and those representing the practical necessity expressed by an act. Prefigurative and practical necessity represent, respectively, the degree of reactivity and proactivity expressed by an act (cf. Harris, 1980). The items used to assess subjects' perceptions of the strength of the various entailments expressing both prefigurative and practical necessity are presented in Table 12.1. The cluster of entailments representing prefigurative necessity consists of the

TABLE 12.1 Items Used in Determining the Strength of the Various Entailments for Any Act Within an Episode

Proactive items (items expressing practical necessity)

Act to consequence:

"How much would you say that you [subject's act] in order to bring about a particular response by [the other person present]?"

Consequence to relationship:

"How much would you say that doing [subject's act] in the situation you described helped you bring about the kind of relationship you would like to have with [the other person present]?"

Consequence to life-script:

"How much would you say that doing [subject's act] in the situation you described helped you become the kind of person you would like to be?"

Valence of consequence:

"How much were you pleased with what [the other person present] did or said after you [subject's act]?"

Reactive items (items expressing prefigurative necessity)

Episode to act:

"How much would you say that the situation seemed to require that you [subject's act]?"

Antecedent to act:

"How much would you say that what [the other person present] did or said before you [subject.s act] seemed to require that you do it?"

Relationship to act:

"How much would you say that doing [subject's act] in the situation you described represents or closely reflects what kind of relationship you would like to have with [the other person present]?"

Life-script to act:

"How much would you say that doing [subject's act] in the situation you described represents or closely reflects who you are, that is, the kind of person you see yourself to be?"

NOTE: All questions are answered on a 9-point rating scale (1 = not at all; 9 = very much).

episode to act, antecedent to act, relationship to act, and *life script to act* entailments. These express the extent to which the subject felt compelled to act in the episode by the "logic of events." Subjects are asked to rate the strength of each entailment on a nine-point scale. The cluster of entailments representing practical necessity consists of the *act to consequence,* the *consequence to relationship* and *consequence to life script* entailments, along with what may be called the *valence of the consequence*. All of these entailments express the extent to which the subject engaged in an act in order to bring out some desired outcome.

Once subjects' intuitions about the ways in which their acts are contextualized have been collected, indices of prefigurative and practical necessity for each act are obtained by averaging the four entailment ratings for each type of necessity. An *index of relative necessity* is then derived (in order to assess the relative contribution of prefigurative and practical necessity to each act) by subtracting the index for prefigurative necessity from the index for practical necessity.

Thus, in addition to descriptions of actual interaction episodes, the procedures outlined here yield information on the manner in which subjects contextualize their individual acts in an episode and information on the extent to which any particular act is perceived by subjects as being reactive (loading high on prefigurative necessity) or proactive (loading high on practical necessity).

The Semantic Ecology of Weeping Episodes

In an initial study of the semantic ecology of naturally occurring episodes of emotional expression using CMM theory (Cornelius, 1981, 1982), 38 subjects (18 male and 20 female undergraduate students, 18 to 31 years old with a mean age of 20.4 years) were asked to describe an episode in which they wept in the presence of another person. The aim of the study was to explore the rule structure of episodes of social weeping. Subjects were asked to describe a recent situation involving sadness in which they wept in the presence of a friend or intimate. In order to provide comparisons of sad weeping with other types of episodes, subjects were also asked to describe one of three contrast episodes: (1) an episode involving happiness in which they wept in the presence of another person; (2) an episode involving sadness in which they felt like weeping but did not, also in the presence of another person; or (3) an episode that did not involve emotion, asking a friend or intimate for a favor. Of the subjects 12 were asked to describe sad weeping and asking a favor, 12 were asked to describe sad weeping and happy weeping, and 14 were asked to describe sad weeping and feeling like weeping.

Descriptions of asking a favor were collected in order to provide a nonemotional anchor for the various rating scales used in the study. It was assumed that asking a favor would be perceived by subjects to be voluntary, and hence, would load highly on practical necessity, thus serving as a measure of discriminant validity for the procedure. When the relative necessity indices for sad weeping and asking a favor obtained from those subjects who described both kinds of episodes were compared, asking a favor was in fact found to be proactive and, as expected, sad weeping was found to be reactive (.7 versus −1.5, respectively, where −8 indicates maximum prefigurative necessity and +8 maximum practical necessity). This difference was highly significant ($F[1,10] = 25.99$, $p < .001$). The mean relative necessity index for all of the 38 sad weeping episodes combined was −.9.

On the average, subjects rated their sad weeping as being very strongly related to their life script (*life script to act* entailment = 7.6, where 1 = not at all, 9 = very much; see Table 12.1) and the episode in which it occurred (*episode to act* entailment = 6.8). The consequence of the act was also rated as being quite important to the subject's life script (*consequence to life script* entailment = 6.6). Sad weeping, however, was only weakly related to the immediate consequences of the act (*act to consequence* entailment = 3.4). This latter finding is interesting when compared with subjects' verbal descriptions of the episodes. Content analysis of these descriptions suggested that sad weeping clearly served to change the way the subject and the other person in the episode interacted with one another. In fact, sad weeping almost seemed to be used by subjects in an instrumental fashion at times, often, for instance, changing a situation involving conflict into one involving succor. Thus, even though sad weeping appeared to be quite functional within the episodes, subjects nevertheless perceived their weeping to be reactive, that is, demanded in some sense by the situation. It is also interesting to note in this regard that subjects considered their sad weeping to be uncontrollable and not at all manipulative.

This pattern of results is not all that surprising when considered in the context of Averill's (1980) view of emotions as actions that we interpret as passions. For Averill, the experience of passivity (or in the present context, reactivity) associated with emotions is an interpretation we place on our behavior so as to not be held responsible for what we do while we are emotional. It is probably the case that weeping would not have the kinds of interpersonal effects that it does (e.g., reframing interaction sequences involving conflict as episodes calling for succorance) if it was seen as anything other than involuntary and uncontrollable (see Cornelius, 1981, pp. 137-139).

It is interesting to note in this context that, when all of the 38 sad weeping episodes were combined, a significant difference was found between males and females for their ratings of the *act to consequence* entailment ($F[1,32] = 4.68$, $p. < .05$). Females perceived the entailment to be stronger than did males (4.2 versus 2.6, respectively, where 1 = not at all, 9 = very much). Thus, females saw their sad weeping more as a means to provoke a reaction from the other person than did males, but neither perceived the relationship to be very strong. Aside from some differences in the way males and females subjectively evaluated their sad weeping (women regarded their sad weeping as significantly more angry and self-pitying than did men) and the detail with which the episodes were described (females provided much more detailed descriptions), this was the only sex difference found for subject's descriptions of sad weeping.

There were very few differences among subjects' entailment ratings for sad weeping versus happy weeping and feeling like weeping. On the average, subjects were much more pleased with the consequence of their happy weeping than with the consequence of their sad weeping (8.3 versus 5.4, respectively), but the difference was only marginally significant. Subjects perceived the *episode to act* entailment to be much stronger for sad weeping than for feeling like weeping (7.4 versus 5.7, respectively), but the difference was not significant.

The Semantic Ecology of Confessions of Love

One area of emotional expression that seems to have been all but neglected by students of emotion is that concerned with verbal expressions of emotion. In an attempt to at least partially remedy this state of affairs, Alison Nydick and I have been investigating avowals of love. Specifically, we have been asking subjects to describe the first time they said "I love you" to the person with whom they currently share an intimate relationship. Part of the project involves asking subjects to give us their intuitions as to how the act of saying "I love you" is contextualized within the episode in which it occurs according to the model of emotional expression derived from CMM theory. So far, we have conducted two studies, which, because of sample size limitations, must be considered preliminary (N = 16 for the first study, and N = 18 for the second). Due to limitations on space, only the results from the first study are discussed here.

As one might expect, subjects (3 males and 13 females, 17 to 19 years old with a mean of 18.4 years) saw the act of saying "I love you" as being strongly related to their view of the relationship they shared with the other person and their life script. In addition, saying "I love you" to a person, at least for the first time, almost invariably elicited a reciprocal statement from the person to whom it was said (this was true for 15 of the 16 descriptions we obtained). However, even though saying "I love you" seemed to reliably elicit reciprocal avowals, subjects did not perceive there to be much of a relationship between their avowal and any antecedent acts on the part of the other person (when the other person said "I love you" first) or between their avowal and any consequent acts on the part of the other person (when the subject said "I love you" first), although the valence of the consequence of saying "I love you" was very high.

These latter findings are interesting in that it appears that the subjects we studied were not responding to what seemed to us to be an inherent paradox in the situation. That is, when one says "I love you" to another person, one of the things one is doing is in effect asking the other person for a similar avowal. This amounts to asking for emotional behavior on the part of the other person or, more precisely, requesting spontaneity.[4] On the face of it, this would seem to catch the other person in a paradox, for if he or she goes along with the request and acts emotionally, then he or she is by definition *not* acting emotionally as the emotional behavior is not spontaneous. If the person does not go along with the request, on the other hand, he or she will be seen as not being properly emotional in the situation. Again, these results should not be all that surprising. In many situations, it is probably the case that we must in a sense "seal off" our full awareness of what we are doing in order to be able to interpret our behavior as emotional (V. E. Cronen, personal communication). In situations such as these, we might expect there to be a reflexive relationship between the antecedent and consequent levels of meaning in the regulative rules governing requests for and responses to avowals of love such that a positive (or confirming) response to one's avowal loops back and negates the meaning of that request as a request. This is an intriguing phenomenon that certainly merits further study (as part of our standard interview, we are now asking subjects what would have happened if the other person had *not* returned their "I love you").

Toward an Interpersonal Logic of Emotional Expression

The studies conducted so far using the CMM approach have revealed some of the ways in which acts of emotional expression are related to their interpersonal context. However, these investigations of the semantic ecology of emotional expression must be considered, at best, preliminary. For what we have so far done is to only sketch out one side of the interpersonal equation involved in the performance of expressions of emotion. If it is indeed the case that emotional expression is a property of the interpersonal system that emerges whenever two or more actors' rule systems combine, then it is necessary to shift the focus of our investigations from individual actors' rule systems to the emergent systems themselves. That is, to begin to explore in earnest *episodes* of emotional expression in which the emotion is not seen as a thing located within any one individual actor but as a process that occurs between or among actors. Our own investigations into this process have just begun.

Implications for the Study of Adult Affective Development

As mentioned above, the general approach to the study of social life represented by CMM would seem to be especially fruitful when applied to investigations of adult development. Thus far, unfortunately, few such investigations have been carried out. Nevertheless, a few words may be said regarding the use of the model to study adult development.

Development and change in the affective lives of adults may take place in a variety of ways according to CMM theory. First of all, it must be recognized that change is a ubiquitous feature of social life; social actors continually alter their performances simply by virtue of being "enmeshed" in many different interpersonal rule systems, each with its own demands and contingencies. Thus, we might expect the emotional performances of any given actor to vary considerably in different situations due to situation- and relationship-specific "feeling rules," perhaps of the sort described by Hochschild (1979). But beyond this, and recognizing that individuals construe the world in characteristic ways that lend constancy to their emotional lives, the explanation of change within CMM theory focuses on changes in intrapersonal rule systems, that is, on changes in regulative and constitutive rules.

Changes in regulative rules may come about in two ways. First, changes may occur in the *kinds* of regulative rules that guide an individual's actions. A good example of this kind of change would be the learning of "display rules" for emotional expression as described by Ekman and others (see Ekman and Friesen, 1975). Changes of this type, however, are probably much more important in the development of emotions in children than in adults as we would expect most adults in a given social group to have a more or less well-developed repertoire of emotion rules. If this is indeed the case, adult emotional development would more likely consist of refinements in the *structure* of existing regulative rules rather than the learning of new rules per se.

Structural changes are changes in the strength of the various entailments embodied within regulative rules. Development, in this sense, consists of changes in the way emotional performances are contextualized within an individual's system of regulative rules. Thus, for example, as an individual becomes more deeply involved in a relationship with another person, we might expect the strength of the relationship to act entailment for the act of saying "I love you" for that person to increase while the strength of the antecedent to act entailment for the same act should decrease. Such structural changes in regulative rules may partially account for the individual differences in emotional "style" that Averill (this volume) describes in his discussion of what he calls the heuristic rules of emotion. Individuals who differ in the extent to which a given emotional performance is "demanded" by a given situation could be said to differ in their style of emotional expression.

Changes in constitutive rules are the basis for changes in the meaning of emotional performances. An example of this kind of change from my own research involves the changing meaning of weeping for men. In the course of interviewing men about their weeping it became clear that men (at least in the sample I had gathered) regarded weeping in themselves not as a sign of weakness, as men are stereotypically supposed to regard weeping but, rather, more as a sign of strength. In fact, it appears as if attitudes toward weeping by men have changed so much that some men now regard weeping almost as a sign of their manhood (as in one *New Yorker* cartoon in which a weeping man explains to the woman he is dining with, "Do you know how masculine it is to risk crying?").[5]

The kinds of changes I have discussed so far would allow us to account for changes in the repertoire of emotional performances open to an individual as well as changes in the meaning of those performances. Perhaps the most interesting kind of changes observed in adult development, however, involve changes of an entirely different sort, namely, changes in individuals' awareness of their emotional performances.

It would seem that one of the things we learn as we are growing up is to monitor more closely our social performances, including our emotional performances. From the perspective of CMM, what this involves is becoming aware of how one assigns meaning to events and how one contextualizes one's actions. Thus, we might posit the existence of what might be called "meta-rules" of awareness that govern the extent to which an individual can potentially become aware of the structure of his or her system of rules for meaning and action. In addition to developmental changes, we would expect to find considerable individual variation in the awareness produced by such rules. For example, in our own research we have consistently found that women seem to monitor their social performances much more closely than do men (that is, they can provide much more detailed accounts of their performances).

The foregoing is obviously only a very sketchy description of the ways in which adult affective development is conceptualized within CMM theory. Many questions remain to be answered and many more remain to be asked. Nevertheless, it is hoped that the perspective on adult development provided by CMM can serve as a useful framework within which to investigate this complex and little-understood process.

Notes

1. Taking a broad perspective, the approach elaborated here bears many resemblances to Shotter's attempts to develop an "ecological psychology" (see Shotter & Newson, 1982; Shotter, 1983).

2. This similarity was suggested to me by Barnett Pearce.

3. We might expect, however, that every society provides its members with a more or less restricted range of options for interpreting the content of various kinds of messages; thus, the utterance, "I love you" may have a limited range of possible meanings. That is, it is probably the case that we learn that certain contexts reliably accompany certain kinds of messages and we are apt to come to some confusion when we encounter messages that are out of context or in the wrong context. This notion, in fact, formed the basis of Bateson's analysis of the so-called "double bind" (Bateson et al., 1956; reprinted in Bateson, 1972), a communicative act in which the levels of content and context do not match, epitomized by the parent who says, "I love you" in a harsh or sarcastic tone.

4. I thank Mary Haake for first bringing this to my attention.

5. For another perspective on this, see Burda's (1983) fascinating article, "I'd Rather Cry on a Man's Shoulder."

References

Austin, J. L. (1975). *How to do things with words.* Cambridge: Harvard University Press.

Averill, J. R. (1982). *Anger and aggression: An essay on emotion.* New York: Springer-Verlag.

Averill, J. R. (1980). A constructivist view of emotion. In R. Plutchik and H. Kellerman (Eds.), *Theories of emotion vol. 1* (pp. 305-339). New York: Academic Press.

Bateson, G. (1972). *Steps to an ecology of mind.* New York: Ballantine.

Bateson, G., Jackson, D. D., Haley, J. & Weakland, J. H. (1956). Toward a theory of schizophrenia. *Behavioral Science, 1* (Oct.), 251-264. (Reprinted in Bateson, 1972)

Berger, P. L. & Luckman, T. (1967). *The social construction of reality.* Garden City, NY: Doubleday.

Bohm, D. (1980). *Wholeness and the implicate order.* London: Routledge & Kegan Paul.

Burda, P. C. (1983). I'd rather cry on a man's shoulder. *M. Gentle Men for Gender Justice, 10,* pp. 8-9, 33-34.

Cornelius, R. R. (1982, April). *Weeping as social interaction.* Paper presented at the fifty-third annual meeting of the Eastern Psychological Association, Baltimore, Maryland.

Cornelius, R. R. (1981). *Weeping as social interaction: The interpersonal logic of the moist eye.* Unpublished doctoral dissertation, University of Massachusetts.

Cronen, V. E., Johnson, K. M. & Lannamann, J. W. (1982). Paradoxes, double binds, and reflexive loops: An alternate theoretical perspective. *Family Process, 20,* 91-112.

Cronen, V. E. & Pearce, W. B. (1981). Logical force in interpersonal communication: A new concept of the "necessity" in social behavior. *Communication, 6,* 5-67.

Ekman, P. & Friesen, W. V. (1975). *Unmasking the face.* Englewood Cliffs, NJ: Prentice-Hall.

Forgas, J. P. (1979). *Social episodes: The study of interaction routines.* New York: Academic Press.

Harris, L. M. (1980). *Power, impotence and violence.* Paper presented at the annual convention of the Eastern Communication Association.

Hochschild, A. (1979). Emotion work, feeling rules, and social structure. *American Journal of Sociology, 85*(3), 551-575.

Pearce, W. B. & Cronen, V. E. (1980). *Communication, action and meaning. The creation of social realities.* New York: Praeger.

Rorty, A. O. (1980) Introduction. In A. O. Rorty (Ed.), *Explaining emotions* (pp. 1-8). Berkeley: University of California Press.

Shotter, J. (1983). "Duality of structure" and "intentionality" in an ecological psychology. *Journal for the Theory of Social Behaviour, 13,* 19-43.

Shotter, J. & Newson, J. (1982). An ecological approach to cognitive development: implicate orders, joint action and intentionality. In G. Butterworth and P. Light (Eds.), *Social cognition: Studies in the development of understanding* (pp. 32-52). Chicago: University of Chicago Press.

Von Wright, G. H. (1951). Deontic logic. *Mind, 60,* 1-15.

13

Family Expression of Emotion

AMY G. HALBERSTADT

Everyone has emotions, although not always admitted; and everyone expresses emotions, although not always in ways obvious to others. In addition, there are obvious idiosyncratic differences in the ways that individual adults express their emotions (e.g., Malatesta & Izard, this volume). Many theorists agree that socialization is a major influence upon the degree and patterning of adult emotional expression. How the socialization process occurs, and the ultimate effects of socialization on adult emotional expressivity, interpersonal skills, and perceptions of others have not yet been carefully evaluated, either theoretically or empirically. However, socialization of emotional expression would appear to be a matter of many influences, among them, family, peers, neighborhood, culture, and society.

It seems that the family should be the primary agent for socializing emotional expression, as it is in family situations that an individual must first attempt to communicate needs and desires. The family as a socialization unit for emotional expression is not a surprising notion, and has

AUTHOR'S NOTE: Portions of this chapter are based on a doctoral dissertation submitted to the Johns Hopkins University; I gratefully acknowledge the assistance of Bert F. Green and Judith A. Hall in all phases of that research, and support during that time

been described as such by many writers (e.g., Jones, 1950, 1960; Izard, 1971; Lanzetta & Kleck, 1971; Zuckerman, Hall, DeFrank, & Rosenthal, 1976; Zuckerman, Lipets, Koivumaki, & Rosenthal, 1975) although it has been researched only by Balswick and Avertt (1977) and Malatesta and Haviland (1982).

This chapter reports current findings regarding the (1) family's nature as a socializing unit of emotional expression, (2) the family's influence on the developing individual's emotional styles of behavior and interpersonal communication skills, and (3) the family's influence on the developing individual's perceptions and misperceptions of others who are similar or dissimilar in their socialization of emotional expression.

Regarding the family's role in socializing emotional expression, most researchers hypothesize an inhibiting function. They suggest that the success of family socialization is determined by the degree of expressiveness reduction and imply that all families — indeed, all cultures — place a value on inhibition of emotional expression. In this chapter, it is additionally suggested that some families and some cultures will value exaggeration of emotional expression and will socialize their offspring to express emotions freely and intensely. Expressiveness for these families is not the consequence of failure to socialize but rather is indicative of success in doing so.

Existing evidence certainly indicates that all members of our society are not socialized to inhibit emotions. For example, emotional expressiveness in our society is perceived as characteristic of and generally valued for females (e.g., Broverman, Vogel, Broverman, Clarkson, & Rosenkrantz, 1972; Parsons, 1955; Spence, Helmreich, & Stapp, 1974). Expressiveness has also been described as a valued characteristic for males as well as females among blacks (Kochman, 1981; Lewis, 1975).

It makes sense, then, to explore the socialization of emotional expressiveness from a less judgmental perspective, predicting only that the degree of expressiveness that develops in children will be related to the value for emotional expression inculcated within the family. This, then, is the first set of hypotheses: The norms and values of the family act to encourage or to discourage emotional expression, thereby creating varying atmospheres of emotional expression in which young family members develop.

---

from a National Science Foundation Graduate Fellowship. Thanks are also due to Judith A. Hall, Randolph Cornelius, Bruce C. Milligan, and the editors for their helpful comments on an earlier draft of this chapter.

The second set of hypotheses investigates the impact of the family norms and values for emotional expression upon the interpersonal behavior and skills of the individuals comprising the family unit. Based upon the degree of emotional expression encouraged or discouraged by the family, individual members will develop similarly expressive behavior, and furthermore, will need to practice different interpersonal communication skills in order to interact effectively with other family members.

For this second set, the following hypotheses regarding interpersonal behavior and skills have been formulated: When the family environment is low in expressiveness, individuals must become sensitive to the most subtle displays of emotion in order to relate effectively with other family members. As a consequence of family inhibition, these individuals would become less skilled in expressing emotion but would be more skilled in perceiving emotion. When the family environment is high in expressiveness, individuals do not have to work hard to perceive the emotional states of family members; thus, these individuals would be more skilled in expressing emotion but would be less skilled in perceiving emotion. Specifically, predictions were for (1) greater nonverbal judging skill in individuals whose families inhibit expressiveness relative to individuals whose families value expressiveness, and (2) greater skill in expression of emotion in individuals whose families value expressiveness relative to individuals whose families inhibit expressiveness.

Not only is family expressiveness predicted to affect individuals' interpersonal skills, but its influence is also anticipated in the ways in which individuals perceive the behavior of others. When employing our own ethnocentric views of the world we do not always recognize that others' styles of expression are as appropriate as ours and we tend to judge nonsimilar others somewhat harshly. Thus, this final hypothesis: Individuals coming from families employing similar styles of expressiveness will express more positive attitudes toward each other than will individuals from families employing dissimilar styles of expressiveness.

Thus, the three concerns in this chapter are (1) is inhibition of emotional expression the prevailing norm or do families differ in the value they place on emotional expression; (2) does the family expressive environment influence younger family members' interpersonal behavior and skill; and (3) do individuals' family backgrounds of emotional expression affect initial perceptions of others? To attempt to answer these questions, the author devised a questionnaire tapping expressiveness norms in families and conducted a series of studies to assess individuals' interpersonal communication skills and perceptions of others based on their similar or dissimilar family backgrounds.

Family Socialization of Emotional Expression

Whether expressive individuals have not been successfully socialized by failing to inhibit their expressions, or whether they are revealing the success of their socialization by being openly expressive, can only be indirectly examined, but the results from the questionnaire described below hint at an answer.

The Family Expressiveness Questionnaire (FEQ) went through several stages of development (see Halberstadt, 1983b, for more details). Briefly, 510 college students and 142 parents (mostly mothers) responded to one of three versions of the FEQ, all of which tapped students' recollections of family affect during their childhood or parents' recollections for the same period. For each version subjects rated hypothetical affective scenarios (e. g., spontaneously hugging a family member, or criticizing someone for being late) on one or more scales of 1 to 9 for "not acceptable" to "fully acceptable," "not intense" to "very intense," and "not at all frequently" to "very frequently."

If there is indeed a general norm for inhibition of expression one would suppose that family members would indicate such a value when asked to describe their family's attitudes toward emotional expression. For all three types of questions, students' mean scores were consistently above the middle point of the 9-point scales (for acceptability, weighted mean = 6.09; for intensity, weighted mean = 5.74; for frequency, weighted mean = 5.49), and parents' mean scores were extremely similar. In all cases the weighted mean scores indicated norms of significantly greater expressiveness than expected by chance (for students and parents, median $t = 7.65$, $p < .001$). Although students and parents employed the full range of the scales, the predominance of means above the middle point of the scale suggests that many individuals perceive emotional expressiveness positively.

Asking subjects to be self-aware is often a risky business. It is easy for an investigator to assume that others have thought as carefully and deeply about matters that are only of interest to the researcher. In this case, self-awareness, or actually family-awareness, may be difficult for the subject who is not able to make a comparison with many other family environments or to remember accurately his or her own family environment. Thus, there is likely to be a fair amount of "noise" in the data, indicating some lack of family-awareness, but there is no reason to suspect a particular bias.

To summarize, it seems that more families value expressiveness than disdain it, and further, that behaviorally families do vary substantially in their frequency of expression of emotion.

Family Influences on Interpersonal Behavior and Skill

The next question to be addressed is the manner in which family environment influences individuals' interpersonal behavior and skills. The reader may recall that the socialization hypothesis predicts better nonverbal judging skill for individuals whose families inhibit expressiveness relative to individuals whose families value expressiveness, and better nonverbal sending for individuals whose families value expressiveness relative to individuals whose families inhibit expressiveness. These hypotheses were tested in six studies, all of which employed a measure of family expressiveness and one or more measures of nonverbal behavior and skill. These studies are briefly described in Table 13.1 and below.

In four studies, family expressiveness was measured using one of the forms of the Family Expressiveness Questionnaire (FEQ) mentioned above. In Study 3, students answered one question concerning the freedom of emotional expression in their families; and in Study 5, students answered questions about (1) the severity of parental restrictions against expressing eight emotions, and (2) the strength of emotional expression in the home for those eight emotions.

In these studies, independent judgments of subjects' actual nonverbal behavior and skill were made for three nonverbal channels: voice tone, facial expressions, and body movements. Voice tone was measured by (1) holding word content constant (students said, "I want you to know what I am thinking, I hope you'll understand"); and/or (2) by electronically filtering the words (subjects chose whatever words they preferred, and an electronic voice filter made the words unintelligible while leaving the expressive qualities of the voice more or less intact); and/or (3) random splicing (subjects chose whatever words they preferred, and the tape was spliced into little clips that were then reordered). Facial expressions and body movements were depicted in slides in Studies 2 and 3, in movie form in Studies 4 and 5, and on videotape in Study 6.

The interpersonal behavior and skills measured by the studies were the nonverbal sending and judging of emotion. For nonverbal sending, "spontaneous expression" and "posed encoding" were employed. "Spontaneous expression" applies to the sending that occurred in response to a mood induction, such as "Discuss something as happy or positive as you can, while still feeling comfortable conversing with your

TABLE 13.1 Six Studies Investigating Family Influences on Interpersonal Behavior and Skill

Study	*Investigator*	*N*	*Family Expressiveness*	*Nonverbal Channel*	*Nonverbal Skill*
1	Halberstadt	32, 28	acceptability and intensity	voice tone	sending (posed encoding) and judging
2	Halberstadt (1983)	47	frequency	voice tone and face	judging
3	Hall	36	freedom of emotional expressiveness	voice tone, face and body	judging
4	Taylor	22	frequency	voice tone, face and body	judging
5	Zuckerman	36	lack of restriction and strength of emotion	voice tone, face and body	judging
6	Halberstadt	64	frequency	voice tone and face	sending (spontaneous expression and posed encoding) and judging

partner." The objective of spontaneous sending is to keep the sending (and therefore the situation) as natural as possible, while imposing enough control to assess with confidence the affective content of the sending. These scores are scores of performance rather than of skill or ability, for of interest is not how skilled people can be at expressing but how much they actually do express in a natural everyday setting. Also, in some situations skill might be considered the ability to mask or inhibit nonverbal messages and not the ability to express them. As the subjects did not know that they were being videotaped, the spontaneous expression task seems to provide the optimal balance between natural situations and experimental control.

The second type of sending, "posed encoding," refers to encoding in response to explicit instructions of the experimenter with the subjects' full knowledge that the sending was being recorded. The subjects made conscious and deliberate attempts to be as skillful at sending emotional content as possible. This type of sending thus describes the subjects' optimal skill when consciously attempting to communicate. Posed encoding complements spontaneous expression in that it is a measure of skill, whereas the latter assesses natural expressiveness. These two types of sending are correlated (median r = .43; Cunningham, 1976; Zuckerman et al., 1976; Zuckerman, Larrance, Hall, DeFrank, & Rosenthal, 1979; and in this chapter r = .26, $p < .05$), but this does not preclude a differential degree of relationship between the two types of sending and family expressiveness. Spontaneous expression was examined in Study 6 and posed encoding was examined in Studies 1 and 6.

Nonverbal judging is a conscious attempt to recognize the result of either kind of sending. As in posed encoding, judging describes the subjects' skill in highly controlled and optimal conditions, and it is not known how well the subjects actually apply their skill to judging in real life. Judging and posed encoding are similar to each other in that they are both conscious attempts at skill, but no type of judgment corresponds to spontaneous expression where the subjects are expressing within the context of the situation. A meta-analysis of 19 studies indicates that there is a low and nonsignificant relationship between sending and judging (median r of .16, DePaulo & Rosenthal, 1979). Thus, sending and judging may vary freely with family expressiveness. Judging was examined in all six studies.

Study 6, because of its complexity and importance in analyzing the hypotheses, requires somewhat more detail in description. In this study, 64 undergraduate students chosen for their high or low scores on the FEQ were videotaped without their knowledge while conversing for 15 minutes about happy and sad topics (self-chosen) with one of eight confederates who were students from another university. The confederates also participated in their first session as subjects, and at that time they did not know they were being videotaped. After their initial session, each confederate conversed with eight different subjects as described above. All subjects and confederates were informed that they had been videotaped immediately after that portion of the study and they gave their consent for the videotapes to be used in the research. This constituted the spontaneous expression section of the study. Next, subjects facially and vocally encoded eight communications, two each from four quadrants (positive-dominant, positive-submissive, negative-dominant, negative-submissive). This portion comprised the measure of subjects' posed encoding skill. Videotaped segments of the subjects' happy and sad conversations and posed encoding were observed by four raters who attempted to identify which conversation each segment had occurred in. All vocal segments judged by raters had word content held constant or were electronically filtered, making words unintelligible.

Subjects returned to judge videotaped segments of the confederates' spontaneous expression and posed encoding, recorded during the confederates' initial sessions. Again, all vocal segments had word content held constant or were electronically filtered. This provided the measure of subjects' judging skill of both spontaneous expression and posed encoding. Thus, in Study 6, voice tone and face channels were employed to study both sending and judging, and within sending, both spontaneous expression and posed encoding were examined.

This study was fairly large and included many variables not immediately germane to the hypotheses discussed in this chapter. Some of these variables became relevant, however, when they began to form a "difficulty dimension" that appeared in a series of interactions with family expressiveness. To describe the factors themselves would require too much space, and their importance in this chapter is really in terms of their degree of difficulty, determined by the number of times judges were wrong on an item over all subjects and repetitions of the item. Significant differences in difficulty between two levels of a factor became evident in main effects or interactions not involving subject variables. Which level of a variable was more or less difficult is reported below when the variable interacts with family expressiveness.

One final comment about the nature of these studies is necessary. In all six studies, the experimenters working with the subjects had no knowledge of subjects' scores on either the family expressiveness measure or the nonverbal measures, nor did participants (subjects or confederates) know their own scores or the scores of any other participants.

Family Expressiveness and Sending

Spontaneous Expression

In order to measure the degree to which individuals' own expressiveness was related to family norms for emotional expression, 133 subjects were asked to fill out both the FEQ and the Affective Communication Test (ACT), a measure of expressiveness (Friedman, Prince, Riggio, & DiMatteo, 1980). Although items and conceptualization of expressiveness were somewhat different (Friedman et al. occasionally refer to their scale as measuring "charisma"), these two measures were significantly related ($r = .26$, $p < .01$, two-tailed). This finding supports other questionnaire research with college students (Balswick & Avertt, 1977), and observational research that indicates similarities between infants and mothers in their facial configurations when expressing emotion (Malatesta & Haviland, 1982). As the positive relationship in both questionnaire studies can be accounted for by their common method (e.g., using questionnaires to measure both variables) and the observational study examined infants, Study 6 complements the above work by more directly measuring the influence of family expressiveness on expressive behavior in adults.

The analyses of variance computed for the results in Study 6 reflected the relationship between individuals' expressiveness and their reports of family expressiveness for facial sending only ($F[1,240] = 4.04$, $p < .05$, effect size = $.52\sigma$).[1] As predicted, subjects from high expressive families (mean accuracy = .722) communicated more clearly than subjects from low expressive families (mean accuracy = .631). No interactions with FEQ appeared for facial sending; but for combined voice tone and facial spontaneous sending, a three-way interaction occurred between FEQ (low, high), gender (female, male), and positivity (happy/positive, sad/negative; $F[1,240] = 8.97$, $p < .01$, effect size = $.77\sigma$). This interaction indicates that individuals from more expressive families were more expressive senders in relatively more difficult channels (sad/negative for females, happy/positive for males) compared to those from less expressive families.

Thus, family expressiveness clearly relates to self-expressiveness in facial sending and may also have an impact on self-expressiveness in voice tone.

Posed Encoding

The relationship between posed encoding and family expressiveness was examined in Studies 1 and 6. In Study 1, family expressiveness was measured by the FEQ in terms of acceptability and intensity of emotional expression, and, as predicted, both of these aspects of family expressiveness were related to posed encoding of voice tone (for acceptability, $r[30] = .44$, $p < .01$, two-tailed; for intensity, $r[30] = .39$, $p < .05$, two-tailed).

In Study 6, results from the ANOVA for posed encoding failed to confirm the hypothesis that family expressiveness was positively related to posed encoding. Two three-way interactions with family expressiveness did occur, and their results are worth discussing. In the first interaction, low FEQ subjects (students from less expressive families) were more skilled at sending the easier items ("positive-dominant" and "negative-submissive") but the high FEQ subjects (students from more expressive families) did relatively better at sending the more difficult items ("positive-submissive" and "negative-dominant"; $F[1,840] = 3.96$, $p < .05$, effect size = $.51\sigma$). For the easier items the mean accuracy for low and high FEQ subjects was .396 and .332, respectively; for the more difficult items their mean accuracy was .296 and .293, respectively. In the second interaction, low FEQ subjects were again relatively better at sending the easier items (submissive items communicated in subjects' own words and dominant items communicated when holding word content constant) than the high FEQ subjects, but the high FEQ subjects were relatively better at sending the more difficult items (dominant items communicated in subjects' own words and submissive items communicated when holding word content constant). For the easier items, the mean accuracy for low and high FEQ subjects was .370 and .306, respectively; for the more difficult items their mean accuracy was .318 and .315, respectively ($F[1,840] = 4.16$, $p < .05$, effect size = $.53\sigma$).

In summary, an overall positive relationship between family expressiveness and sending was predicted and this relationship occurred for spontaneous expression. Additionally, a persistent pattern of interactions by type of item and family background appeared across both spontaneous expression and posed encoding. This pattern indicates that high FEQ subjects, who were predicted to send more accurately than low FEQ subjects, had the greater relative advantage at sending the more difficult items, compared to low FEQ subjects, who more accurately sent the easier items.

Judging

All six studies examined the relationship between judging and family expressiveness. Despite the generally small sample sizes and the great variety in methods (voice tone, face, and body sending; and different measures of family expressiveness), the relationship between judging and family expressiveness was always negative although not always significant. To summarize the findings of these six studies a meta-analysis was computed. Meta-analysis allows a researcher to combine statistically the findings of two or more studies investigating essentially the same question, and provides a more powerful summary statement about the findings. The median r for the six studies was .18, and the combined p for the six studies was significant (weighted $z = 2.72$, $p = .003$, one-tailed; Rosenthal, 1978). This indicates clear support for the hypothesis that family expressiveness is negatively related to judging skill; individuals growing up in less expressive families appear more skilled at recognizing emotional communications, possibly because in these kinds of families, skill in recognizing subtle emotional communications is more important for "survival" than it is in more expressive families where emotional expression is abundant and practice isn't necessary.

In light of the fact that the negative relationship between family expressiveness and judging was predicted (Halberstadt, 1983b), Study

6 was also designed to allow further clarification of the negative relationship between family expressiveness and different kinds of judging skill. In this study, spontaneous sending and posed encoding were examined in the voice tone and face channels.

Family Expressiveness and Judging of Spontaneous Expression

The overall relationship between family expressiveness and judging of spontaneous expression was negative but not significant; however, a two-way interaction occurred between FEQ (low, high) and sending condition (talk, listen) in the ANOVA on just facial communications. Subjects from low expressive families judged the more difficult talk conditions more accurately (mean accuracy = .739) than did subjects from high expressive families (mean accuracy = .697), while subjects from high expressive families judged the easier listen items more accurately (mean accuracy = .802) than did subjects from low expressive families (mean accuracy = .781).

Family Expressiveness and Judging of Posed Encoding

The relationship between family expressiveness and judging of posed encoding was negative but not significant. Three interactions, however, were significant and the pattern of their results is worth discussing. In the first interaction, subjects from low expressive families did better on the submissive communications (mean accuracy = .379) compared to subjects from high expressive families (mean accuracy = .325), whereas subjects from high expressive families did better on the dominant communications (mean accuracy = .316) compared to subjects from low expressive families (mean accuracy = .301; $F[1,960] = 5.00$, $p < .05$, effect size = $.58\sigma$). In the second interaction, subjects from low expressive families did better on negative communications (mean accuracy = .429) compared to subjects from high expressive families (mean accuracy = .376), while subjects from high expressive families did better on positive communications (mean accuracy = .267) compared to subjects from low expressive families (mean accuracy = .255; $F[1,960] = 4.90$, $p < .05$, effect size = $.57\sigma$). The third interaction indicates that the advantage low FEQ subjects had in interpreting negative communications was greater in the more difficult voice tone channel than in the easier face channel ($F[1,960] = 3.98$, $p < .05$, effect size = $.52\sigma$).

In summary, an appropriately reversed pattern from the one found in the sending tasks appears to be occurring in both the judging of spontaneous expression and posed encoding. It seems logical that subjects from low expressive families would be better at judging the more difficult items than subjects from high expressive families. Although an *overall* negative relationship between family expressiveness and judging was predicted, a pattern of interactions by type of item and family background appeared. This pattern indicates that low FEQ subjects, who were predicted to perceive more subtle nonverbal communications, were relatively better than high FEQ subjects at judging the more difficult items in spontaneous expression and in the third interaction of posed encoding, in which the low FEQ subjects' advantage for negative items was relatively better for the more difficult, voice tone items.

That low FEQ subjects did better on the more difficult items was not true in the first interaction of posed encoding nor in the second in which subjects of low expressive families were better at the easier, negative communications. However, in the case of the positive-negative dimension, expecting subjects from low expressive families to have less of an advantage for negative communications, because they are easier, actually goes counter to the socialization hypothesis. The hypothesis predicts that individuals from low expressive families need to become more skilled in judging expression in order to "survive" in their families. In terms of "survival," negative communications from other family members would be the most important ones for a child to detect. Whether or not they are relatively easier to judge, the socialization hypothesis should predict that subjects from low expressive families would have the edge over subjects from high expressive families for judging negative expression. Thus, although the pattern of findings was not predicted, the judging data appear consistent with the socialization hypothesis and suggest refinements of the original formulation.

Family Expressiveness and the Sending-Judging Relationship

Family expressiveness and the sending-judging relationship was examined as the concluding series of tests of the socialization hypothesis. Although the previous findings for sending and judging indicated that various aspects of the hypothesis are sound, the final test for the effects of family expressiveness is an analysis of sending and judging across levels of family expressiveness. Accordingly, an ANOVA was computed for each of the four tasks (voice tone and face tasks for both spontaneous and posed communications).

Family Expressiveness and Spontaneous Sending-Judging

For voice tone communications, a four-way interaction occurred ($F[1,240] = 9.79$, $p < .01$, effect size $= .81\sigma$) which, although complicated, is actually quite interpretable. It confirms again that subjects from low expressive families performed relatively better at judging the more difficult items (positive for males, negative for females) relative to sending them, and subjects from high expressive families performed relatively better at sending the more difficult communications (positive for males, negative for females) relative to judging them. Although difficult to understand in one breath, this interaction fits well with the socialization hypothesis.

For spontaneous facial communications, the predicted interaction between family expressiveness and skill (sending, judging) occurred ($F[1,480] = 4.24$, $p < .05$, effect size $= .53\sigma$); subjects from low expressive families were more accurate judges (mean accuracy = .760) than subjects from high expressive families (mean accuracy = .752), and subjects from high expressive families (mean accuracy = .722) were more accurate senders than subjects from low expressive families (mean accuracy = .631). Again, the socialization hypothesis is supported.

Family Expressiveness and Posed Encoding-Judging

For facial communications no new effects appeared, but for voice tone communications an interesting three-way interaction occurred; the predicted relationship of low FEQ subjects judging more accurately than high FEQ subjects appeared, but only for negative communications ($F[1,960] = 11.67$, $p < .001$, effect size $= .88\sigma$).

The reader may recall the earlier emphasis on negative communications as the most important communications for an individual to develop skill in judging. In a home where emotional expressions are suppressed, an individual must work particularly hard at detecting the communications of greater importance and, thus, would become skilled at detecting them. In a home where emotional expression abounds, an individual doesn't have to work hard at detecting important emotions because they are evident, but is more likely to be able to reproduce those communications in ways that are easily understandable to others. Although unexpected, this finding refines the socialization hypothesis very nicely.

To summarize this section, it appears that family socialization for emotional expression does have an important effect on individuals' interpersonal behavior and communication skills. Individuals from more expressive homes are themselves more expressive than individuals from less expressive homes. Individuals from more expressive homes also appear to be more skilled at posing communications, or to have a relatively greater advantage at posing difficult communications compared to individuals from less expressive homes, but the evidence for posed encoding is not as strong as for the other nonverbal behavior and skills influenced by family socialization. Individuals from less expressive homes are the better judges, clearly, and results from Study 6 indicate that the difference in skill between low and high FEQ subjects is even greater for difficult and negative communications.

Perceptions of Others Based on Family Expressiveness

Until this section, discussion has been devoted to the identification of different styles of emotional expression, their development, and the effect of family socialization on individuals' interpersonal behavior and skills in nonverbal communication. It is time to turn to the third consideration — namely, the relationship between one's family background of emotional expression and both actual and perceived personality traits.

A relationship between expressive styles of behavior and specific personality traits was hypothesized as early as the 1930s (Allport, 1937; Allport & Cantril, 1934) but over the years attempts to link expressive styles of behavior with specific personality traits have had varied success. The most recent attempts (Buck, 1975, 1977; Cunningham, 1977; Friedman et al., 1980) have found positive relationships with several characteristics (e.g., extraversion, exhibition, affiliation, and dominance). The studies that employed behavioral measures of expressiveness instead of self-report measures do seem to have found weaker correlations between styles and traits. It appears that stereotypes about expressive people being more friendly, assertive, and outgoing, and about less expressive people as being cool, quiet, and calm certainly exist, and the difference in at least extraversion/introversion may have some basis in reality.

Whether or not some kernel of truth exists within these stereotypes, it is suspected that the influence of the stereotypes themselves is rather weighty in social interaction, and that the stereotypes provoke differential behavior in people accustomed to different expressive styles. Differences between ourselves and others in nonverbal communication are not often consciously noted; and when they are, the concept of different styles is not often invoked as a means of explanation. Rather, our explanations about others often involve attributions about their personalities, and these attributions then affect our interactions with them. It is easy to imagine the misperceptions that abound due to an ethnocentric perspective. If, as suggested, people from different backgrounds are misperceiving each other based on their expectations of appropriate styles of communication, then it follows that it is easier for people to understand individuals from a similar background as well as find them more interpersonally agreeable. Thus, the two hypotheses needing evaluation are (1) that expressive styles are related to personality characteristics, and (2) that individuals prefer interactions with others from similarly expressive backgrounds.

To address these hypotheses, subjects and their partners (confederates) participating in Study 6 were asked to fill out a questionnaire immediately following participation in the spontaneous interaction session of that study (Halberstadt, 1983b). Subjects and their partners filled out the questionnaire in separate rooms so that neither partner would feel constrained about making truthful ratings. Both subjects and confederates made separate ratings for themselves and their partner.

The questions focused on five different categories, each consisting of approximately four questions and all rated on a scale of 1 to 9. These areas were (1) the comfortableness of the preceding social interaction (for oneself and one's partner); (2) the intensity of stories told by oneself and one's partner; (3) the predicted comfortableness and emotional intensity of stories in similar social interactions with one's family; (4) the liking of one's partner and reciprocity of that feeling; and (5) trait-like ratings of the partner on warm, friendly, loud, assertive, outgoing, and excitable dimensions.

Positive relationships between the first three categories and family expressiveness. Compared to individuals from less expressive homes, individuals from more expressive homes should be more comfortable discussing emotional topics, and they were ($r[62] = .21$, $p < .10$, two-tailed); should tell more emotional stories, and by their telling, influence their partner's degree of self-disclosure, and they did (mean $r[62] = .24$, $p < .10$, two-tailed); and should predict greater comfortableness and discussion of more intense topics with their family members, and they did ($r[62] = .60$, $p < .001$, two-tailed). Confederates' observations of the subjects' comfortableness, intensity of stories, and so on supported subjects' assessments although not always significantly.

Pertaining to the relationship between expressiveness styles and personality, subjects from more expressive homes reported greater liking of and reciprocity of that feeling from the confederate, compared to subjects from less expressive homes ($r[62] = .26$, $p < .05$, two-tailed); possibly because they were more comfortable in this particular setting. Also, confederates reported a positive relationship between family expressiveness and the composite score of trait ratings, supporting to some degree the recent studies on personality ($r[62] = .23$, $p < .10$, two-tailed); subjects from more expressive homes were seen as more warm, friendly, loud, assertive, outgoing, and excitable, whereas subjects from less expressive homes were seen as more cool, unfriendly, quiet, mild mannered, reserved, and calm.

To determine whether similar versus different levels of family expressiveness affects perceptions regarding the interactions, a five-way ANOVA was conducted for each of the five categories. Of interest in this chapter is the interaction between confederate FEQ and subject FEQ, which was predicted to be significant for the comfortableness, story intensity, and partner liking categories. Although no significant results appeared for subjects' ratings of comfortableness in the situation nor for ratings of story intensity, subjects did report greater liking for similar confederates ($F[1,44] = 5.29$, $p < .05$, effect size $= .58\sigma$). Also, confederates reported telling more intense stories to and receiving more intense stories from subjects with similarly expressive backgrounds (mean $F[1,48] = 5.68$, $p < .05$, effect size $= .61\sigma$). These results are encouraging, and suggest that social interactions have a greater probability of success when occurring with individuals of similar family backgrounds.

To summarize this section, stereotypes of individuals based on their family backgrounds for emotional expressiveness may have a kernel of truth in them. Also, the perceptions that we have when we meet and interact with other people seem to be at least partially based on the similarity or dissimilarity that we experience in their family socialization for emotional expressiveness.

Conclusions

In the course of the investigations reported in this chapter, the three predictions described earlier have been supported and several new avenues of research have been suggested. It appears that the influence of family socialization on individuals' developing emotional expression has a lasting impact. This socialization works to either encourage or discourage expressive behavior. Further, the specific direction that family socialization takes appears to result in differential expressiveness in adulthood, differential interpersonal communication skills, and differential perceptions of other individuals, based on their similarities and differences in emotional expressiveness. In conclusion, it is not only *what* we feel but *how* we show our feelings that is important. And our styles of expression, skills in communication, and social perceptions are all influenced by the families we grew up in.

Note

1. For all analyses of variance, an aggregated mean square error term was computed (Green & Tukey, 1960) in order to make a more stable error term. The effect-size

estimate reports the size of the effect without influence of sample size and is defined as the difference between the means of the two groups, divided by their common standard deviation. It is useful in assessing how big the difference between two groups actually is; an effect size of .20 is considered small, an effect size greater than .50 is considered visible to the naked eye, and an effect size greater than .80 is considered large (Cohen, 1977).

References

Allport, G.W. (1937). *Personality: A psychological interpretation.* New York: Holt, Rinehart & Winston.

Allport, G. W. & Cantril, H. (1934). Judging personality from voice. *Journal of Social Psychology, 5,* 37-54.

Balswick, J. & Avertt, C.P. (1977). Differences in expressiveness: Gender, interpersonal orientation, and perceived parental expressiveness as contributing factors. *Journal of Marriage & The Family, 39,* 121-127.

Broverman, I.K., Vogel, S.R., Broverman, D.M., Clarkson, F.E., & Rosenkrantz, P.S. (1972). Sex-role stereotypes: A current appraisal. *Journal of Social Issues, 28,* 59-78.

Buck, R. (1975). Nonverbal communication of affect in children. *Journal of Personality and Social Psychology, 31,* 644-653.

Buck, R. (1977). Nonverbal communication of affect in preschool children: Relationships with personality and skin conductance. *Journal of Personality and Social Psychology, 35,* 225-236.

Cohen, J. (1977). *Statistical power analysis for the behavioral sciences, (rev. ed.).* New York: Academic Press.

Cunningham, M.R. (1977). Personality and the structure of the nonverbal communication of emotion. *Journal of Personality, 45,* 564-584.

DePaulo, B.M. & Rosenthal, R. (1979). Ambivalence, discrepancy and deception in nonverbal communication. In R. Rosenthal (Ed.), *Skill in nonverbal communication: Individual differences.* Cambridge, MA: Oelgeschlager, Gunn, and Hain Publishers.

Friedman, H.S., Prince, L.M., Riggio, R.E., & DiMatteo, M.R. (1980). Understanding and assessing nonverbal expressiveness: The Affective Communication Test. *Journal of Personality and Social Psychology, 39,* 333-351.

Green, B.F., Jr. & Tukey, J.W. (1960). Complex analyses of variance: General problems. *Psychometrika, 25,* 127-152.

Halberstadt, A.G. (1983a). Family expressiveness styles and nonverbal communication skills. *Journal of Nonverbal Behavior, 8.*

Halberstadt, A.G. (1983b). *Family socialization of emotional expression and nonverbal communication styles and skills.* Unpublished manuscript.

Hall, J.A. (1978). Unpublished data, Johns Hopkins University.

Izard, C.E. (1971). *The face of emotion.* New York: Appleton-Century-Crofts.

Jones, H.E. (1950). The study of patterns of emotional expression. In M.L. Reymert (Ed.), *Feelings and emotions.* New York: McGraw-Hill.

Jones, H.E. (1960). The longitudinal method in the study of personality. In I. Iscoe and H.W. Stevenson (Eds.), *Personality development in children.* Austin: University of Texas Press.

Kochman, T. (1981). *Black and white styles in conflict.* Chicago: University of Chicago Press.

Lanzetta, J. T. & Kleck, R. E. (1970). Encoding and decoding of nonverbal affect in humans. *Journal of Personality and Social Psychology, 16,* 12-19.

Lewis, D. K. (1975). The black family: Socialization and sex roles. *Phylon, 36,* 221-237.

Malatesta, C. Z. & Haviland, J. M. (1982). Learning display rules: The socialization of emotion expression in infancy. *Child Development, 53,* 991-1003.

Parsons, T. & Bales, R. F. (1955). *Family, socialization and interaction process.* New York: The Free Press.

Rosenthal, R. (1978). Combining results from independent studies. *Psychological Bulletin, 85,* 185-194.

Spence, J. T., Helmreich, R., & Stapp, J. (1974). The Personal Attributes Questionnaire: A measure of sex-role stereotypes and masculinity-femininity. *JSAS Catagglog of Selected Documents in Psychology, 4,* 43 (Ms. 617).

Taylor, M. C. (1979). Unpublished data, Pennsylvania State University.

Zuckerman, M. (1979). Unpublished data, University of Rochester.

Zuckerman, M., Hall, J. A., DeFrank, R. S., & Rosenthal, R. (1976). Encoding and decoding of spontaneous and posed facial expressions. *Journal of Personality and Social Psychology, 34,* 966-977.

Zuckerman, M., Larrance, D. T., Hall, J. A., DeFrank, R. S., & Rosenthal, R. (1979). Posed and spontaneous communication of emotion via facial and vocal cues. *Journal of Personality, 47,* 712-733.

Zuckerman, M., Lipets, M. S., Koivumaki, J. H., & Rosenthal, R. (1975). Encoding and decoding nonverbal cues of emotion. *Journal of Personality and Social Psychology, 32,* 1068-1076.

14

The Facial Expression of Emotion

Young, Middle-Aged, and Older Adult Expressions

CAROL ZANDER MALATESTA
CARROLL E. IZARD

> In age, the passions cool and leave a man at rest . . . when this passion is extinguished, the true kernel of life is gone, and nothing remains but the hollow shell. (Schopenhauer, 1890, pp. 214-215)

> [Old people] resemble children. They have sudden fits of ill temper; they express their feelings violently; they cry easily. (de Beauvoir, 1974, p. 471)

Opinions about the affective life of older individuals tend to take on extreme values. Older people are either seen as theatrically volatile or

AUTHORS' NOTE: We gratefully acknowledge the help of Jeanette Reese Ayars and Karen Callahan in data collection, and Clayton Culver in data analysis. This study was supported by a National Research Service Award (1F32MH08773-10) to the first author.

vacuously blunt and bleached of emotion. Psychologists have at times echoed these same opinions (see Malatesta, 1981, for a review) and sometimes with very little supporting evidence. Remarkably, there is also a dearth of data concerning emotion processes in young and middle-aged adults. Because of the lack of such basic and comparative information, there is little way of gauging whether, in fact, there is precipituous change in emotionality toward the end of the life span.

With a return to interest in empirical exploration of affective processes during adulthood (as exemplified by the work of contributors to this volume), there is promise of movement toward some real data-based understanding of emotion processes in adult development and aging.

There are, of course, a variety of ways to study emotional development in adults. The present chapter reports the results of an investigation of the facial expressions of young, middle-aged, and older adults as they relate emotional experiences. The purpose of the study was *not* to provide a definitive statement about age-related differences in expressive style over the life span, and indeed the cross-sectional nature and restricted sampling within each of the three age groups limits the generality of findings. Instead, we sought to develop a simple, efficacious, emotion-induction procedure for eliciting and recording genuine emotion states in adults under laboratory conditions. A second major purpose was to gather data that might generate fresh ideas about possible developmental trends in emotion expression that could then be explored more fully in subsequent investigations.

We begin with a general review of theory concerning the expression of emotion in adults and then proceed to a discussion of methodological considerations in doing emotions research, including a discussion of the rationale for the present design. Finally, we present a discussion of the results and indicate directions that might be pursued in future investigations.

Theoretical Perspectives on Emotional Expressiveness in Adults

Most writers who have attended to the issue of emotion expression in adults either implicitly or explicitly assume that the ability to modulate affective expression is a mark of maturity (Izard, 1971, 1977; Tomkins, 1962). According to the writings of emotion theorists adult modulation of emotional expression is achieved through three processes: masking, intergradation or blending of different expressions, and miniaturization of expression.

Masking. Masking is a form of emotion modulation that involves either (1) neutralization (the adopting of a blank face with no or little emotion expression) or (2) dissimulation, (covering a particular emotion feeling with an expression that signals a different one). Very frequently, the latter takes the form of masking negative emotion feeling with a positive emotion expression, as in masking fear or anger with a smile (Malatesta, 1982), a socially acceptable and commonly practiced convention in many Western cultures. Other forms of masking or emotion substitution may have a more idiosyncratic form, say masking of fear with contempt or of sadness with anger. Although some study has been made of the smile mask there has been little other systematic research on masking in adults. Saarni, however has initiated a program of research on masking in children (Saarni, 1982).

Blending of emotion signals. Various writers have discussed emotion *blends.* An emotion blend is the result of combining elements of different discrete emotions, such as fear and anger, simultaneously or in rapid succession (i.e., two or more expression changes within a second). The impression created in the observer is one of "mixed emotions." Blends, or intergradation of emotion signals, are thought to be characteristic of primates, especially Old World monkeys and apes and adult humans. In fact, as Ekman, Ellsworth, & Friesen (1982) have pointed out, in early studies of emotion much of the difficulty in establishing that the face contains significant information about emotion resided in the fact that the face can simultaneously convey a variety of emotions or blends, thereby producing observer disagreement.

Miniaturization of expression. Tomkins (1962) has described miniaturization as the process by which innate complex patterned expression is compressed almost to the point of invisibility — that is, so that the emotion is barely perceptible to an observer. Miniaturization can occur by contracting the period of exposure of the expression, for example a rapid flicker of the brow is a temporally attenuated form of the more sustained brow raising that can accompany the interest expression. Expressions are also miniaturized by compressing the physical parameters of the signals; a "thin smile" with only the trace of an upward turning of the corners of the mouth is a physically attenuated form of a full, wide smile. Another type of miniaturization or deintensification discussed by Ekman et al. (1982) consists of "fragmenting" the facial behavior so that only one or two or the usual components of a particular emotional expression occur — for example, only raising the brows under conditions of surprise instead of opening the mouth and widening the eyes as well.

Miniaturization is said to function as a means of avoiding affect contagion, or the spreading of emotion from one individual to another by observance of the other's affect (Izard, 1971, 1977; Tomkins, 1962). Uncontrolled emotion expression conceivably would lead to escalation of feeling states among interactants with subsequent interpersonal strife. Attenuated versions of emotional expressions are assumedly less contagious than full-blown expressions, especially if they cooccur with or rapidly alternate with other emotion signals, thereby potentially obfuscating the signal with "noise" or ambiguity.

The above formulations assume that emotional development, at least in part, consists of acquiring the capacity to conceal through the use of masks, convey nuance or ambiguity through affect blending, and to miniaturize emotion expressions. Such assumptions appear intuitively reasonable. However, there actually has been little empirical study of these capacities and their developmental course. For instance, although we know that the incidence of facial emotion blends increases during the second year of life (Demos, 1982), we know very little about developmental progression beyond that point. There are, however, some interesting leads: Zivin (1982), who has tracked the transformation of two facial signals from preschool into adulthood, finds that adults give more partial versions of them developmentally, thereby supporting the "fragmentation" assumption.

We do not know whether emotion expression patterns developed during childhood remain relatively stable after their acquisition, or whether further refinement occurs during the adult years. In the following section we describe a methodology for examining some of the above questions.

Developing a Methodology for the Study of Adult Emotion Expressions

Initial Considerations

In choosing our eliciting conditions we wanted to be sensitive to issues of ecological validity and task equivalence without compromising the need for experimental control. Some of the methodological considerations and solutions are discussed below.

Ecological validity. The issue of ecological validity in emotions research revolves around the authenticity of evoked emotions and the naturalness of the conditions under which they are elicited. A major criticism of early emotions research was directed at the common use of posed rather than spontaneously generated expressions of emotion in recognition studies; exclusive reliance on artifically evoked expressions precluded definitive conclusions about the ability of people to understand emotional expressions under normally occurring circumstances. While there have been a few attempts to compare posed and spontaneous facial behavior, the results are mixed and inconclusive (Ekman et al., 1982). In the absence of data confirming a relationship between posed and spontaneous expressions, it continues to be preferable to strive for the spontaneous even though such expression-induction is less given to experimental control and more difficult to record. Recent paradigms for eliciting emotion in the laboratory have included the use of electric shock or color slides of emotionally provocative material as the stimuli (e.g., Lanzetta & Kleck, 1970; Buck, 1975). While these eliciting conditions assumedly do generate genuine emotion and certainly permit experimental control, they invite problems with relevance and task equivalence.

Task equivalence. The issue of task equivalence is a particularly troublesome problem in lifespan developmental research and a potential source of threat to internal validity. "Standard" stimuli used with different age groups may have quite different meaning for the different aged subjects. The tasks should also be meaningful and relevant to subjects, and equally meaningful and relevant to each age group. The design we settled on for emotion induction allowed us to at least approach this ideal.

Use of recollected emotion experiences as the emotion-generating stimuli. Recently, the use of imagery has been finding currency as a means of generating emotion states (Schwartz, 1982) and research has demonstrated that asking subjects to visualize an emotion-arousing event and to respond to it as an emotionally significant experience reliably produces facial muscle pattern changes consonant with the expected pattern of discrete emotions. The facial muscle changes are best detected by electromyography, however, rather than by direct visual observation because the appearance changes are often imperceptible. Talking about recollected or imagined emotional events seems to be a somewhat more effective method of producing more obvious changes in emotion expression, at least according to the few studies that have experimented with this method (Exline, Paredes, Gottheil & Winkelmayer, 1979; Buck, personal note, cited in Zuckerman, Hall, DeFrank, & Rosenthal, 1976). Interestingly, Buck found that there was no significant communication of affect when encoders were viewing "emotion-generating" slides; it was only when encoders were talking about their emotional responses to the slides that their faces were decoded above chance. The foregoing suggested to us that a combination of recollected, imaged emotion events, combined with the recounting of them would serve the experimental purposes well.

Methodology

Recording emotion expression. Because emotion expressions in adults are said to be fleeting and subtle, accurate analysis of the expressions requires that the events in question be recorded so that they may be played back at a later date and so that multiple examinations of the material are possible. Videorecording of experimental sessions satisfies these needs; however, care must be taken so that the actual recording is inobtrusive, as subjects may become self-conscious and alter their facial behaviors if they are aware that their facial expressions are under scrutiny.

Measurement of the subjective experience of emotion. Any technique for inducing emotion requires proof of the manipulation's effectiveness. Moreover, as most emotion-eliciting situations and/or events are thought to evoke patterns or blends of emotions (Izard, 1972), it is important to ask for subjective feedback in a form that allows for a range of responses. An evaluation of the subject's own perception of his or her response is especially important in a study of age differences in emotion expression for three additional reasons. In the first place, because symbols or representations of emotion (imagery, memories) can take the place of overt forms of expression and because there may be age-related differences in the ability or preference for inhibiting facial display (perhaps older people are better at this than younger individuals), a demonstration of increase or decrease in the magnitude or form of expression with age does not necessarily imply a corresponding increase or decrease in the subjective experience of emotion. Second, simultaneous measures of facial behavior and subjective reports can yield a measure of the degree of masking or substitution, especially when the face indicates one experience and verbal report another. Third, laboratory studies may seriously underrepresent the capabilities of older individuals if the tasks seem meaningless and fail to engage the attention and motivation of these subjects. Assessment of subjective response is one means of evaluating degree of involvement in the task.

The objective measurement of emotion expression. As it was anticipated that results would confirm the notion that adults often use partial expressions and expression blends, the most appropriate form of evaluation was deemed a facial coding system tailored to component analysis. (Component analysis involves separate analysis of muscle movements in three regions of the face). In addition, because we were mainly interested in facial expressions of *emotion* rather than other movements that are theoretically unrelated to emotion, we needed a system that was expressly designed and validated for this purpose. For these reasons we chose the Maximally Discriminative Facial Movement Coding System (Max; Izard, 1978). Max is a theoretically guided, anatomically based system for coding movement changes related to emotion in three regions of the face. Numerical codes that encode the presence of an appearance change are subsequently translated into emotion signals via a priori formulas provided in the manual. Although the system was originally developed for use with infants, the coding manual specifies that it is also an appropriate vehicle for coding adult faces and includes notes about differences that will be observed in adult faces; in addition, previous experience has demonstrated its feasibility in use with adults (Malatesta & Haviland, 1982). The present chapter includes further comments on the use of Max with adult faces and expands treatment of the differences found in adult versus infant faces.

The Study

Subjects. The subjects were 30 females, 10 in each of three age groups. The mean ages of young, middle-aged, and older subjects were, respectively, 33.3 (SD = 3.9), 55.2 (SD = 4.2), and 68.8 (SD = 2.8) years. They were recruited from local social clubs, recreational centers, and by word of mouth to participate in a study of women's emotional experiences. Subjects in the three age groups were equated on educational level and degree of social contact (defined as number of hours a week socializing with friends). Education level ranged from partial high school to advanced graduate work with the average levels of education for all levels of age groups being partial college. Social contact for young, middle-aged, and older subjects amounted to 10.20 (SD = 6.25), 8.20 (SD = 4.61), and 9.80 (SD = 7.11) hours, respectively.

Procedure and materials. Upon arrival at the laboratory the goals of the study and procedures were reviewed.

Affect induction procedure. A detailed description of the affect induction protocol can be obtained from the authors. In brief, subjects were asked to recall five emotional events, one each for happiness, anger, fear/anxiety, sadness, and affection. Special instructions were given to maximize an authentic recreation of the emotional experiences. Subjects believed that they were communicating with the experimenter through closed-circuit television but were in fact videotaped using a Sony camera fitted with a zoom lens for close-up of upper torso and head while they related their experiences. Immediately following each induction episode subjects were asked to summarize, in one sentence, precisely how the event made them feel. This last procedure provides a brief, condensed episode of the emotion and is referred to as the peak episode. Only peak episodes were subjected to subsequent analysis with Max. In addition, only the anger, fear, and sadness episodes were coded, as the happy episode was used for habituation and the affection episode was included in the sequence to return subjects to a relatively positive state at the conclusion of the experiment.

Rating of subjective experience. Following each individual induction episode subjects were asked to rate their degree of emotional arousal during the induction episode. The emotion rating scale used for manipulation check and assessment of subjective affect intensity was adapted from Izard's (1972) Differential Emotions Scale (DES III) and consisted of ten fundamental emotions with their everyday synonyms. For our purposes the original five-point intensity dimension for each emotion was expanded to a nine-point scale.

Coding of videotapes. The peak episode segments of each subject's tape was coded by the first author who has established reliabilities of above 85 percent with each of the codes. A random sampling of 10 percent of the segments by another trained rater yielded an interrater reliability of 83 percent. A summary of codes used in this study appears below.

Brow region codes, 20: brows raised more than one-half second; *20-0:* brows raised less than one-half second; *21:* one brow higher than other; *23:* inner corners raised; *24:* brows together, slightly down; *25:* brows together, sharply down;

Eye/nose/cheek region codes, 31: eye fissure wide, upper lid raised; *33:* narowed or squinted eyes; *36:* gaze downward, askance; *39:* gaze downward, head tilted back; *42:* nasal bridge furrowed.

Mouth/lips region, head angle, 50: opened roundish mouth; *52:* corners back and slightly *up 53:* open, tense, corners pulled back; *54;* angular squarish; *55:* open tense; *56:* corners drawn downward; *59B:* open, angular, upper lip pulled back; *61:* upper lip raised on one side; *67:* compressed lips; *68:* pursed lips; *75:* lowered head.

The codes were next translated into emotion signals, following the rules outlined in the Max manual. In general, an emotion is predicted by appearance changes in one, two, or three regions of the face. If the appearance changes in one or more different regions signal emotion A and there is no codeable movement signalling another emotion, the facial expression is coded as an instance of emotion A. If the facial regions encode appearance changes of more than one emotion, a blend is scored. The term blend is operationally defined as the presence of appearance changes of two emotions simultaneously or within the same second. For the purposes of the present study we distinguished between positive, negative and positive/negative blends. Positive blends were defined as the cooccurrence of the components of two different positive emotions (example: joy/interest blend). Negative blends consisted of the components of two different negative emotions (example: disgust/anger). Positive/negative blends had components of both a positive and negative emotion (example: a sadness/joy blend).

Certain adjustments in the Max system were made to accommodate its use with adults. These were mainly in the code-to-emotion-signal translations and are theoretically justified: (1) We determined that a new code (code 67) should be added for compressed lips, not seen in infants. Compressed lips, following Darwin (1872), is considered a component of anger/determination in adults. Darwin referred to the tubular protrusion of both lips as a "pout of anger." It is our observation that this mouth movement involves a tense, tight movement, unlike the softer pursed-lip configuration (code 65) connotative of interest in infants. In adults the tight lip 67 code is accompanied by a direct gaze of the eyes. (2) The 53 code in infants is part of the fear expression. In adults it can be confused with a narrow 54. Although the squarish component of the 54 is all but obscured by the tense retraction of the lips under anger induction and therefore resembles the 53, one can distinguish the two by noting the degree of tension in the mouth (tenser under anger induction with teeth usually quite visible). As a second check after coding note the eyes. Theoretically, a 53 mouth will be accompanied by 31 eyes, whereas a 54 will not. (3) In infants the 24 code participates in the interest expression, but according to Darwin, in adults it can also be caused by something distressing, disagreeable or unpleasant. Instances of 24 were therefore referred to simply as the knit brow. (4) The cooccurrence of a 61 mouth with upturned corners appeared to represent the sneer or sardonic smile described by Darwin, and therefore was scored as part of the contempt expression. (5) As the 20 and 30 codes can participate in both the surprise and interest expressions, we scored them separately as indices of the interest/surprise signal. (6) The 20-0 code is referred to by Malatesta & Haviland (1982) as the brow-flash signal whose status as an emotion signal is as yet undetermined. We include it here as a signal of interest/emphasis. A summary of codes used in the present study to identify the various emotions is given below.

Affect Component Codes

Anger: 25, 54, 55, 33 (if accompanied by another anger code), 53 (if not accompanied by a 31), 67 (unless accompanied by a 36 or 75), 68 (if accompanied by other signs of anger).

Interest: 68 (if accompanied by other signs of interest such as eyes cast upward), 33 (only if it cooccurs with a 68)

Interest/surprise: 20, 30.

Brow-flash: 20-0.

Surprise: 50.

Joy: 52.

Contempt: 21, 39, 61, 42 (if accompanied by another contempt code).

Fear: 31, 53 (only if accompanied by a 31).

Shame/shyness: 36.

Sadness: 23, 56.

Disgust: 59B, 33 (only if with a 59B or 42), 42 (if it occurs alone).

Knit/brow: 24 (if it occurs alone). May be a signal of interest or anger.

33: Indeterminate (if it occurs alone).

75: May be shame or sadness signal or caused by extraneous factor such as preparing to use the rating materials; not counted as an affect when alone.

Blinks: Number of eyeblinks were also coded because rate of blinking is thought to indicate degree of distress or apprehensiveness.

Results and Discussion

Evaluation of task engagement and self-consciousness. As indicated earlier, any assessment of age-related differences in facial expressiveness must take into account whether or not the emotion-eliciting conditions were effective in actually inducing emotion, and equally so across age groups. Examination of subjects' mean ratings of emotion intensity indicated that although blends of emotion were common, the highest ratings occurred in the emotion category specific to the induction condition. That is, more self-reported sadness was generated under the sad induction condition than any other emotion, and similarly so for the other two conditions. A multivariate analysis of variance with the intensity ratings under the three induction conditions as the dependent variables, and age as the independent variable, was nonsignificant, as were univariate analyses for each condition. Thus any age-related differences in expressivity are unlikely to be due to differential intensity of induced emotion.

Subjects experienced little self-consciousness during the task, as indexed by their self-reports. The average rating was 2.86 (based on a scale of 1 to 10), and analysis of variance revealed no significant age differences.

Facial Expression Data

General observations. For anyone who has studied and coded the emotion expressions of infants, coding adult faces provides an interesting contrast. Although adult facial expression changes can be rapid in onset and offset, as is the case of infant expressions, adults show another pattern *not* usually observed in infants, namely a slow gathering of tension in the facial muscles over a period of time. (A good cinematic example of this phenomenon exists in the facial changes shown by Liv Ullmann in an opening close-up scene in *Richard's Things,* where she shows almost the full gamut of human emotions in the space of about a minute through subtle fluid shifts in the distribution of tension in the various facial muscles; with such subtle changes it is extremely difficult to tell where one emotion expression leaves off and another begins). Thus certain emotion expression changes can be so slight and gradual that they elude capture by "objective" coding systems that are geared to perceptible movement changes.

Despite the above, many facial movements *were* codeable and provided interesting clues concerning the function of certain emotion signals in adults. For example, the slightly lowered knit brow (24; see Figure 14.1a) occurred rarely under the fear induction condition (2.2 percent of the time), with moderate frequency under anger (5.5 percent of the time) and most frequently under sadness (9.6 percent of the time). It is our hypothesis that the 24 knit brow under conditions of anger induction functions as an attenuated 25 (sharply lowered brow, see Figure 14.lb), and, under conditions of sadness, as an inhibitor of 23 (the obliquely raised brow, Figure 14.lc). The 24 in anger can function to reduce the density of sensory feedback and hence the intensity of anger feeling. In sadness the 24 can inhibit reactivation of sadness feeling by changing the pattern of sensory feedback, for the 24 (medial part of eyebrows drawn together and slightly lowered) is anatomically antagonistic to the 23 (medial part of eyebrows drawn together and raised), which is the brow component of the innate expression of sadness. As a signal, the 24 may serve to inform observers of the subject's emotional and motivational involvement without inducing

Figure 14.1a Knit Brow Expression

Figure 14.1b Anger Brows

Figure 14.1c Distress (Sadness) Brows

contagion of negative emotion in the other person, as contagion would be reduced by the relative ambiguity of the signal.

Both the self-regulatory and signal functions of the 24 in adult anger and sadness situations are thought to be functions of developmental and socialization processes, because Max assumes that in infants the 24 is one of the innate signals of the positive affect of interest. This assumption is supported by at least two empirical studies of young infants (Langsdorf, Izard, Rayias, & Hembree, 1983; Oster, 1978). The findings of these studies of infants along with the present findings suggest that the 24 that originally signalled interest can in the adult also signal (or at least accompany) attenuated and controlled sadness or anger. The relative ambiguity of this signal in sadness and anger situations may lead to it being decoded as nonspecific emotional concern and involvement. The end result of this particular aspect of the socialization of the innate emotion expressions is quite consistent with the functions of the general process of socialization — increasing self-regulatory powers and attenuating disonant or agonistic social signalling.

Another interesting finding was that of the three negative affect induction conditions, the fear condition elicitied the highest rate of smiles and positive blends (10.6 percent of the time), sadness the least (.8 percent), and anger (5.9 percent) in between. The higher incidence of smile and smile blends under the fear/anxiety condition is perhaps not surprising given the role that smiling and laughter is said to have in tension reduction and/or as a possible homologue to the primate fear grimace.

Finally, the brow flash (20-0) occurred about equally under all three induction conditions, suggesting that it serves as a general conversational marker rather than as a component related to a specific emotion.

Descriptive statistics. Because of the relative infrequency of most types of discrete facial behaviors and their (as yet) unknown frequency distributions, the data in this section are reported in the form of descriptive rather than inferential statistics.

Features of adult expressive behavior. Adults are said to be less facially expressive than children. However, our data indicate that both younger and older adults are still quite expressive. Overall, young subjects spent 62.2 percent of their peak episode time showing some kind of nonneutral facial expressive behavior. The corresponding figures for the middle-aged and older subjects are 68.2 percent and 63.3 percent. Under emotion induction conditions then, adults (at least adult women) are more expressive than not. However, it is the nature of this expressiveness that is particularly interesting. As predicted by the literature, masking, blending, and fragmenting are typical features of adult expressive behavior. Table 14.1 displays the incidence of these behaviors.

Masking. For the purpose of this study, "masking" was operationally defined as the occurrence of smiles and positive blends (smile blends) as they occurred during negative induction conditions and when subject emotion ratings indicated virtually no happy feelings. As indicated in Table 14.1, middle-aged and older subjects showed about twice as much masking as younger subjects.

Emotion blends. Our data indicate that the use of emotion blends is common in adults (Table 14.1). About 29 percent of all expressions consisted of some kind of blend: 9 percent are positive/negative blends, 16.8 percent are negative, and 2.8 percent are positive. Thus, under negative affect induction conditions blends constitute almost a third of all of the emotional expressions and these are mainly negative blends. When the data are broken down by age groups we find that it is the middle-aged and older groups (versus the youngest group) that are the most likely to use blends. As indicated in Table 14.1, the oldest subjects show more positive blends and less negative blends than their younger and middle-aged counterparts, and both older and middle-aged individuals use more positive/negative blends than the youngest group.

TABLE 14.1 Incidence of Masking,* Emotion Blends, and Partial Expressions,*** by Age Group**

	Age Group		
	Young	*Middle Aged*	*Older*
Masking	7 (3.9%)	23 (7.1%)	18 (8.0%)
Emotional blends			
Negative	21 (18.8%)	36 (17.5%)	20 (14.3%)
Positive	1 (0.9%)	5 (2.4%)	7 (5.0%)
Negative/Positive	5 (4.5%)	23 (11.2%)	15 (0.6%)
Total blends	27 (24.2%)	64 (31.1%)	42 (29.9%)
Partial expressions			
1 Component	22 (59.5%)	54 (70.0%)	41 (76.0%)
2 Components	12 (32.5%)	23 (30.0%)	12 (22.0%)
3 Components	3 (8.0%)	0 (0.0%)	1 (2.0%)

*Masking: Number of seconds (and percentage of total time) spent showing smiles and smile blends.
**Emotion blends: Number of second (and percentage of total time) spent showing the various blend types.
***Partial expressions: Number of seconds (and percentage of total time) spent showing one-, two-, or three-component expressions (summed over anger, contempt, disgust, sadness, and shame expressions).

Fragmented partial facial expressions. In order to assess the degree of age-related fragmentation of emotion expressions we computed the incidence of the differential use of one, two, or three components in the encoding of the emotion expressions of anger, contempt, disgust, sadness, and shame (for this analysis the 75 was considered part of the shame expression). The expressions of interest/emphasis, surprise, joy, and knit brow were not part of the analysis because these emotions and expressions were encoded by only one component under the present system. The expressions of interest/surprise and fear were not included because of the negligible occurrence of the 20s unaccompanied by 30s in the case of interest/surprise, and negligible instances of 31s in the case of fear. In tallying up the number of components used in expressions, only "pure" (versus blended) expressions were examined because blends, by definition, are a unique kind of fragmentation for which age differences have already been examined. Table 14.1 displays the differential use of one-, two-, and three-component expressions by the three age groups. As indicated, the youngest group used more full (three component) expressions than the middle-aged and older groups. They also used more two component expressions than both older groups. Finally, the middle-aged and older groups used more one component expressions than the youngest group. These data suggest that the growth in the use of miniaturized or fragmented expressions observed in childhood (Zivin, 1982) may continue in adulthood, with individuals in the second half of the life span making greater use of miniaturized expressions than younger adults.

Adult expressions: Signal or noise? The present study indicated that adult women are relatively facially expressive under emotion induction conditions. However, the content of this expressiveness appears to be somewhat ambiguous. About one-third of their expressions are blends, and about two-thirds of the remaining "pure" expressions consist of miniaturized one-component expressions. In other cases, expressions are masks that substitute the expression of one emotion for another. In passing we also note the informal observation that the middle-aged and, to a greater extent, older subjects often seemed to have structural changes in their faces giving the impression of particular permanent affect states. For example, three subjects appeared to have had structurally "contemptuous" faces, two structurally "surprised" faces, and two "sad" faces, to mention the clearest and most striking examples. The "background affect" contributed by these physical characteristics conceivably serves as additional background noise for observer detection of emotion state.

To confirm the impression that the emotions of these adults should be relatively difficult for untrained observers to judge if restricted to the nonverbal signals, we looked at the preliminary data gathered in a decoding task. Using an edited stimulus tape consisting of randomized film segments of the peak episodes (identical to those used for the Max coding), 30 naive adult judges rated the dominant emotional state for each of 90 film segments (30 encoders × three affect induction conditions). Tapes were played without sound.

Preliminary analysis indicates that decoders did indeed find the task difficult and made a great number of errors of attribution. However, the results are in accord with what one might anticipate on the basis of knowledge of the actual (Max-coded) signals the encoders were emitting. The fear expression, as well as blink rates (thought to index anxiety) did not differentiate the three induction conditions; similarly, inspection of the distribution of emotion attributions by naive decoders when judging subjects under the fear induction condition indicated that the fear condition could not be decoded above chance. Decoders were somewhat more successful at guessing the anger and sadness conditions (and there were more Max-coded expressions of anger and sadness) although there was still a preponderance of errors.

The high percentage of errors is readily attributable to the encoders' use of blends, fragmented expressions, and masking, as discussed earlier. In an effort to determine what signals contributed to decoder *accuracy* in the cases where decoders were relatively accurate, we grouped the encoders into high and low anger expressors and high and low sadness expressors, using a median split based on decoders' accuracy scores for the two induction conditions. We then examined the high and low expressors' differential patterns of facial behavior as indexed by the Max coding. It is within these differential patterns that we begin to discern just which particular signals allow observers to make correct inferences about emotion state, as discussed below.

Nonverbal cues indicative of adult anger. High anger expressors were found to spend over twice as much time showing facial components associated with anger, contempt, and disgust (the "hostile triad") as low expressors. On the average they spent 27.8 percent of their induction episode time showing theoretically relevant components (versus 12.6 percent for the low expressors), with the preponderance of signals consisting of three anger mouth expressions (54, 55, 67), the slightly lowered 24 knit brow, the raised brow of contempt (21), and the contempt lip (61). In terms of the most frequently used expressions, it is the 24 brow, compressed lips, and tense rounded anger mouth (55) that typify adult expressions that are decoded as angry. When the data were grouped by age of encoder, certain developmental trends were suggested. Table 14.2 displays the percentage of time spent showing the various component signals by age group. As indicated, the middle-aged and older group spent more time using components associated with anger than did the youngest group, the oldest group used more contempt components than did the two younger groups, and the youngest and middle groups used more 24s than did the oldest group.

Nonverbal cues indicative of adult sadness. High sadness expressors spent an average of 26.55 percent of their time displaying facial and head and gaze components theoretically corresponding to sadness and the closely related shame/shyness, as well as the slightly lowered 24 brow, while the low expressors spent only 9.86 percent of their time using these components. The three most common components, in order of frequency of use, were the lowered head, gaze downward and askance, and the slightly lowered 24 brow. This ranking was true of both high and low expressors. An inspection of these data by age group (collapsed over high and low groups), indicates possible developmental trends. Table 14.2 displays the percentage of time spent showing the components most associated with accurate decoding, by age group. As

TABLE 14.2 Percentage of Time Spent Showing Various Expression Components by Young, Middle-Aged, and Older Subjects During Anger and Sadness Induction Conditions

	Anger Induction Episode															
	*Anger Components**					*Contempt Components**				*Digust Components**			*Anger/ Contempt/ Disgust*		*No Expressive*	*All Other*
Age Group	*25*	*54*	*55*	*64*	*Subtotal*	*21*	*39*	*61*	*Subtotal*	*42*	*59B*	*Subtotal*	*Total*	*24s*	*Movement*	*Components*
Young	0.0	0.0	1.3	3.3	(4.6)	2.0	2.0	1.3	(5.3)	1.3	0.0	(1.3)	(11.2)	6.5	33.3	49.0
Middle	2.4	0.7	3.8	1.4	(8.3)	0.3	0.0	2.1	(2.4)	0.6	2.4	(3.0)	(13.7)	6.9	40.2	39.2
Old	0.0	0.4	3.8	4.3	(8.5)	3.0	4.3	1.7	(9.0)	0.4	0.4	(0.8)	(18.3)	0.4	33.3	47.9

	Sadness Induction Episode								
	Sadness Components			*Shame/Shyness Components*				*No Expressive*	*All Other*
Age Group	*56*	*23*	*Subtotal*	*36*	*75*	*Subtotal*	*24s*	*Movement*	*Components*
Young	5.0	0.0	(5.0)	13.3	1.7	(15.0)	23.3	41.0	15.7
Middle	5.6	0.51	(6.1)	10.3	12.8	(23.1)	1.0	47.0	22.8
Old	0.0	0.0	(0.00)	1.1	10.8	(11.8)	0.0	45.1	43.0

*Some components not shown due to very low frequency.

indicated, the youngest age group relied primarily upon the slightly lowered 24 brow and gaze downward and askance (36) under the sadness induction condition, the middle relied upon lowered head and askance gaze, and the oldest almost exclusively used the lowered head.

In summary, the youngest age group communicated both sadness and anger largely through the use of the lowered brow, the middle-aged subjects restricted the use of this signal primarily to the sadness condition, and the older subjects tended not to use it. Older subjects tended to use more anger-related signals than did the other groups under the anger condition and these were largely attenuated forms of anger (the 55 and 67 mouth) and contempt expressions, which can be seen as muted forms of anger. Sadness is communicated rarely by facial expression in the older subjects, who instead used the lowered head.

Discrepancies between Max coding and judgments of naive decoders. Despite the fact that older subjects spent proportionately more of their time showing components associated with the hostile triad relative to the young and middle-aged subjects, they received the least number of anger attributions. Also, despite the fact that older subjects used practically no sad facial cues, they received a high number of sad attributions, equal in number to the middle-aged group and more so than the youngest group. These results taken together with the data on signal noise (large percentage of blend, masking, and fragmenting behavior) suggest that low anger attribution and high sad attribution may be due to age stereotyping or the contribution of background affect and the sag of striate musculature that comes with age.

Summary and Conclusion

This study found that adults are surprisingly expressive under emotion induction conditions with little age-related difference in *sheer amount of expressiveness.* It also demonstrated that adult emotion expressions are characterized by masking, blending, and fragmentation. There is some evidence that these expressive patterns contribute to low decoder accuracy. Several age differences in type of expressivity utilized by the different age groups were noted, and although the results clearly need to be replicated in a larger and more heterogeneous sample, the findings are in accord with developmental theory and our own speculations about affective development over the life span. The theory we are working on proposes that adults learn to attentuate and transform their emotion signals to serve certain social and personal purposes, including the avoidance of social contagion of affect, maintainence of privacy, regulation of arousal, and reduction of energy expenditure. To the extent that these needs may increase with increasing age, the pattern of greater reliance on these expression strategies with age, as suggested by the present data, is not so surprising. However, while such affect-concealing and affect-reducing strategies may serve certain regulatory purposes quite adequately, there may be some less desirable side effects. Masking, blending, and fragmenting of expression contributes not only to the privacy of one's feelings but also to erroneous attributions by observers. That these practices are seen more often in older people suggests that they may be at risk for distortion of meaning in interpersonal contexts. However, there may be, of course, compensatory changes in other signalling systems that would offset any loss of meaning incurred by distortions in facial signals, say in vocal or verbal channels. Future research aimed at assessment of multichannel communication may serve to clarify the picture.

References

Darwin, C. (1872). *The expression of the emotions in man and animals.* New York: Appleton-Century-Crofts.

de Beauvoir, S. (1972). *The coming of age* (trans. Patrick O'Brian). New York: Putnam.

Demos, V. Facial expressions of infants and toddlers. In T. Field & A. Fogel (Eds.), *Emotion and early interaction.* Hillsdale, NJ: Lawrence Erlbaum.

Ekman, P., Friesen, W. V., & Ellsworth, P. C. (1982). Methodological decisions. In P. Ekman (Ed.) *Emotion in the human face.* New York: Cambridge University Press.

Exline, R. V., Paredes, A., Gottheil, E. G., & Winkelmayer, R. (1979). Gaze patterns of normals and schizophrenics retelling happy, sad, and angry experiences. In C. E. Izard (Ed.), *Emotions in personality and psychopathology.* New York: Plenum.

Izard, C. E. (1977). *Human emotions.* New York: Plenum.

Izard, C. E. (1971). *The face of emotion.* New York: Appleton-Century-Crofts.

Langsdorf, P., Izard, C., Rayias, M., & Hembree, E. (1983). Interest expression, visual fixation, and heart rate changes in 2- to 8-month-old infants. *Developmental Psychology, 19* (3), 375-386.

Lanzetta, J. T. & Kleck, R. E. (1970). Encoding and decoding of nonverbal affect in humans. *Journal of Personality and Social Psychology, 16,* 12-19.

Malatesta, C. Z. (1981). Affective development over the lifespan: Involution or growth? *Merrill-Palmer Quarterly, 27,* 145-173.

Malatesta, C. Z. & Haviland, J. M. (1982). Learning display rules: The socialization of emotion expression in infancy. *Child Development, 53,* 991-1003.

Oster, H. (1978). Facial expression and affect development. In M. Lewis & L. Rosenblum (Eds.), *The development of affect.* New York: Plenum.

Saarni, C. (1982). Social and affective functions of nonverbal behavior: Developmental concerns. In R. Feldman (Ed.), *Development of nonverbal communications in children.* New York: Springer-Verlag.

Schopenhauer, A. (1890). *Counsels and maxims* (trans. T. Bailey Saunders). London: Swon Sonnerschein & Co.

Tomkins, S. (1962). *Affect, imagery, consciousness: Vol. I, The positive affects.* New York: Springer.

Zivin, G. (1982). Watching the sands shift: Conceptualizing development of nonverbal mastery. In R. S. Feldman (Ed.), *The development of nonverbal communication in children.* New York: Springer-Verlag.

Zuckerman, M., Hall, J. A., DeFrank, R. S., & Rosenthal, R. (1976). Encoding and decoding of spontaneous and posed facial expressions. *Journal of Personality and Social Psychology, 34,* 966-977.

VI

COGNITION AND EMOTION

The two chapters in this section deal explicitly with the interaction between cognitive and affective processes in development. In the first chapter Stewart and Healy advance the thesis that the quality of affective experience for children, on the one hand, and adults, on the other, cannot be the same, owing to the progressive elaboration of cognitive structures and personality developments that occur with age. They argue that each successive experience with the sequence of emotional reactions to life events is colored by recall of past affects, memories, experiences, and perceptions associated with earlier transitions and that this mingling of present and past experience must make each new transitional experience qualitatively different. They propose that the "adult self" that results from the interaction of cognitive development and affective experiences mediates the qualitative difference between adult and child processing of affective experience, as illustrated by autobiographical material from the life of Leonard Woolf.

The second chapter by Roodin, Rybash, and Hoyer attends to the interaction of affect and cognition in moral development. They argue that there is additional moral development beyond childhood and adolescence, development that is informed by the impact of self-involving life events that are affectively meaningful. These authors propose a constructivist framework for adult morality that assumes qualitatively different forms of morality in adulthood versus childhood; further they propose that development of adult morality is influenced by contact with a variety of affectively involving, personally meaningful events. Life events are said to produce dialectical conflict, personal caring and responsibility, and an understanding of personal relativism. Thus moral dilemmas in adult life demand both analytic (cognitive) and affective involvement in the fully functioning adult. The task of adult morality is to integrate the two dimensions of affect and cognition in the resolution of real-life moral problems.

15

Processing Affective Responses to Life Experiences

The Development of the Adult Self

ABIGAIL J. STEWART
JOSEPH M. HEALY, Jr.

During the past seven years we have been exploring commonalities between adults' and children's affective responses to life changes. While we believe we have demonstrated that the sequence of emotional stances provoked by life transitions and the associated specific affective concerns are the same in children and adults, we do not believe that the actual "felt" emotional experience is the same for children and adults. Generally, adults have experienced many more significant life changes than children and, consequently, have negotiated the sequence of emotional stances many more times. No doubt each successive experience of the stances is colored by recall of past affects, memories, experiences, and perceptions associated with earlier transitions. This mingling of the sequelae of past transitions with the present affective experience must make each new transitional experience qualitatively different. Moreover, as adults use sophisticated modes of reasoning as they think about their new situation and experience of it, they subsequently experience something different from what they experienced, for example, as a child entering school for the first time.

In this chapter we hope to explore the qualitative *differences* between adults' and children's affective responses to life changes. We will begin by summarizing what we have learned about the shared base of affective experience; we will turn then to a brief review of the distinguishing features of adult thought. We will propose that the "adult self" that results from the interaction of cognitive developments and affective experience over time is a central mediator of the qualitative differences between adult and child processing of affective experience. We will explore the probable consequences of this adult self by analyzing autobiographical writings of Leonard Woolf, and will conclude with some suggestions about useful methods for studying adult inner experience.

Commonalities in Adults' and Children's Affective Responses

Different kinds of transitions (e.g., social role, psychological conversions, life events) share a common impact on individuals' lives. They all involve large-scale modifications of the individual's daily life, making them extremely salient and important to the person, and make demands on the individual for new behavioral and internal responses to the changed environment (Stewart, 1982).

Studies of a variety of life transitions have documented a pattern of similarities in children's and adults' emotional responses to major life changes. These studies include the transitions of children entering school (Wapner, Kaplan, & Cohen, 1973), students entering college (Madison, 1969), adults getting married (Rapoport, 1964) or having their first child (Oakley, 1980), and both childern and adults experiencing parental separation and divorce (Wallerstein & Kelly, 1980). The pattern of emotional responses to major life transitions described in these studies is similar for both children and adults in terms of the specific emotions experienced (e.g., loss and sadness, followed by anxiety, hostility, and eventually a complex affective equilibrium).

Using a measure of emotional responses to the external environment, we have been testing the hypothesis that this sequence of emotional responses recurs in response to any major transition experience throughout life (Stewart, 1982; Stewart, Sokol, Healy, Chester, & Weinstock-Savoy, 1982). These responses are coded as reflecting an initial period of *receptivity,* which combines a certain passivity with hopes for increased gratification and nurturance and fears of disorientation, helplessness, and loss. Then, as the individual begins to adapt to the new environment in a limited way, there is uncertainty, hesitation, and feelings of inadequacy *(autonomy).* Gradually, the individual becomes more confident in manipulating the new environment *(assertion)* and bold enough to express hostility and anger. Finally, a new *integration* is achieved with complex affect, including ambivalence and a realistic recognition of the limits and constraints of the new environment and the individual's place in it.

A series of combined cross-sectional and longitudinal studies of children and adults experiencing major transitions has provided substantial support for the theory. The transitions studied included young children entering kindergarten, students making the later school transitions to junior high and high school, freshmen entering college, and adults marrying and having their first child. Individuals who had just negotiated a transition evidenced concern in fantasy with the issues of the developmentally "earlier" emotional stances, while comparison groups of adults and children who had experienced the same transitions a year or two before had progressed to the more advanced emotional stances (Stewart et al., 1982). Moreover, follow-up data obtained from the same samples described above demonstrated progression through the sequence of emotional stances within the same people over time (Healy & Stewart, in press; Stewart, 1981, 1983).

Thus, the overwhelming evidence supports a conception of emotional stances in response to life changes that occur in *both* children and adults experiencing several school and family role transitions. In order to begin to *differentiate* children's experience of the emotional stances from adults' experience of them we must examine those cognitive and personality developments that mark the passsage from childhood to adulthood.

Differentiating Child and Adult Thought

The primary distinctions between childhood and adult thought processes lie in what are most often referred to as the cognitive achievements associated with formal operations. Three main trends are most relevant: increasing differentiation and complexity of thought, the growth of abstract reasoning, and the resulting process of integration. The increased differentiation in understanding of the interpersonal, intellectual, and physical world of adolescents and adults has been documented by researchers interested in general processes of cognitive development as well as those concerned with more specific issues, like person perceptions and self-concept. The individual develops a clearer distinction between self and others (e.g., Damon & Hart, 1982), including increasingly sophisticated conceptions of other people (Livesley & Bromley, 1973; Peevers & Secord, 1973), social roles and social systems (Selman, 1980), the nature of interpersonal relationships, and the commitments and responsibilities attached to them (see e.g., Selman, 1980; and a helpful review by Chandler, 1977). Further, reality is differentiated from hypothetical alternatives as the adolescent becomes capable of thought about possibilities he or she has never before observed or considered (Inhelder & Piaget, 1958). Thus, adolescents and adults are capable of constructing conceptions of themselves and of what their lives might be like in the future or under different circumstances, unconstrained by the limits of their present situation. Finally, adolescents and adults develop a more complex sense of self (Bernstein, 1980), differentiating aspects of their lives, the roles they play, and the components of their personalities (e.g., Damon & Hart, 1982; Elkind, 1974; Cooney & Selman, 1978).

A second significant achievement of mature thought is the development of abstract reasoning (Chandler, 1977; Inhelder & Piaget, 1958; Werner, 1961). With the increased complexity of thought and the sheer volume of discriminations fostered by differentiation, abstract reasoning is an extremely useful tool for providing conceptual organization to a rapidly expanding body of knowledge. The formal operational individual is capable of organizing the increased complexity of his or her experience by extracting rules and developing hierarchically organized conceptual frameworks in order to logically group similar ideas and experiences. Thus, the organization of experience is based on higher order concepts removed from the concrete or behavioral details of each situation. Further, abstract reasoning promotes the acquisition of sophisticated inferential concepts such as friendship, justice, trust, and loyalty that enable the person to cluster large numbers of behaviors pertaining to social relationships.

The development of abstract reasoning is the crucial prerequisite for the third cognitive process of concern to us: integration. As mentioned briefly above, abstraction promotes an integrated cognitive framework to counterbalance an endless proliferation of distinctions and discriminations. The complexity of experience is structured by the establishment of unifying rules and concepts for categorizing events, experiences, and behavior (Inhelder & Piaget, 1958). Of course children use rules and concepts too, but adults' structuring ideas are more abstract, encompass a broader range of elements, and even can be used to think about the process of thinking itself. In fact, the integrative process is turned inward, facilitating a unified sense of self, including an integration of past with present experiences, and a heightened awareness of internal processes in general.

In summary, adult thought is distinguishable from childhood thought by its increased differentiation, capacity for abstraction, and integration. Consequently, adults are capable of experiencing their environment and their selves as simultaneously more complex and unified. Moreover, the integrative cognitive processes point to an emerging sense of self that synthesizes both past and present experience, establishing the basis for both continuity and change in the self over time.

The cognitive differences between children and adults have direct implications for children's and adults' experience of major life transitions. The nature of the transition as construed by the individual depends upon the level of cognitive development. For example, children and adults experiencing social role transitions will construe the new interpersonal relationships on the basis of different conceptions of social relationships and will respond to them slightly differently as a result. However, while it is a worthwhile endeavor to chart the *direct* effects of various stages of cognitive development and their attendant abilities on the understanding of (and subsequent emotional adaptation to) transitions, that is not the purpose of this chapter. Instead we propose to explore how the integration of complex self understanding, abstract concepts, and affective experience in a central personality structure allows adults to *process affective experience* in ways children cannot.

Developmental researchers have demonstrated the importance of the initial differentiation of self from others for emotional development in infancy and early childhood (Spitz *et al.,* 1970; Sroufe, 1979). Further, prominent personality theorists have emphasized the self as a center for major personality development during the adult years (e.g., Jung, 1931/1960; Erikson, 1950/1963, 1968). Finally, theorists such as James (1892, 1910), Lifton (1976), and more recently, Blasi (1983) suggest a conception of self that has received very little empirical attention but which is generally accepted on intuitive grounds: the subjective processing self that we know to be present at one level of awareness or another at almost all times. We may plausibly expect that major cognitive developments will have consequences for this subjective processing self. With the attainment of formal operations, past and current experiences can be more fully integrated, establishing a sense of both continuity and change over the life span. As a result, the difference in the sheer number of life changes experienced by children and adults becomes especially important for formal operational individuals who, by virtue of their integrative capacity, may simultaneously process new affective experiences, and past memories, knowledge, and feelings associated with previous transitions, while reprocessing old affective experiences that are reevoked by their similarity to the current transition. We believe that this simultaneous processing and reprocessing of experiences creates and in turn transforms the adult self.

The Adult Self

Very little empirical research exists that attempts to describe developmental change in this proactive, processing self, although a few theoretical descriptions do exist (see, e.g., Allport, 1954; Blasi, 1983; Damon & Hart, 1982; Edelstein & Noam, 1982; James, 1892, 1910; Lifton, 1976). It seems likely that shifts in this central personality structure result, at least in part, from the combined effects of the interaction of other changing structures with life experience. More specifically, we propose that the vicissitudes of the self in part reflects ever more sophisticated cognitive processsing of affective and sensory stimuli. Thus, although there may not be new sensations or new affects experienced for the first time in adulthood, nevertheless qualitatively different internal experiences may result from the processing of external stimuli with richer, more developed cognitive "tools."

This qualitative difference may be understood by considering three hallmarks of adult personality according to virtually all theorists of adult personality development (see e.g., Jung, 1931/1960; Erikson, 1950/1963, 1968; Sullivan, 1953): the capacity for intimacy, the capacity for commitment, and the productive acceptance of personal extinction. Different theoretical perspectives specify the importance of these psychological characteristics differently; but all agree that intimacy, commitment, and preparation for death are important tasks of, or stimuli for, or milestones in, adult personality development (see e.g., Gould, 1978; Levinson, 1978; Neugarten, 1964; Vaillant, 1977). Nevertheless, it is clearly not the case that intimacy, commitment, or awareness of death develop first in adulthood. Infants and children experience some kind of intimacy with those providing them with warm, safe, accepting arms and laps, as well as with those who will share in their excited, giggling games. Indeed, some of the adult understanding of intimacy — that it includes safety, comfort, and acceptance as well as sharing and fun — clearly derives directly from these early intimate relationships and experiences. But we expect that adult intimacy includes something more, or different, from child intimacy. Thus, for example, Erikson and Sullivan both stress the demand intimacy makes for full recognition of the other and self-sacrifice in the service of mutuality (see e.g., Erikson, 1950/1963, pp. 263-266). Clearly this adult form of intimacy, then, depends on the development of a number of cognitive capacities (for role and perspective-taking), as well as prior personality developments (e.g., a secure and stable sense of personal identity, which can then be exposed to the risk of loss or diffusion in relationship; see, e.g., Erikson, 1968, pp. 167-169), and personal experiences (e.g., of past intimacy in a less developed form; indeed, these past experiences may provide the positive expectation that intimacy will be worth the risk to identity that it entails).

Similarly, commitment does not emerge first in adulthood. Children and adolescents make commitments — to friends, to tasks, to causes; and some of these are intense, passionate, and long lasting. But we expect qualitative differences in the commitments, or promises, of children and adults. When a child announces an intention to take up a musical instrument or a sport, we have a different set of expectations than when an adult announces the same thing. We know that a child — even a serious, thoughtful child — is trying something out, exploring, examining. We expect that while this may be true of the adult, too, something more is also involved. First, we expect that the adult has more knowledge of what is involved in this new enterprise and therefore understands the implications of this commitment more fully. We also expect that the adult has self-knowledge of his or her own capacity to make the commitment. Finally, we expect that this new commitment is not merely exploration but also an expression — a statement about some aspects of the adult self not adequately expressed in others ways.

Finally, children (at least by the time they reach school age) and adults share an awareness of the general fact of death and knowledge that that general fact has specific implications for them. Yet we expect a difference in the psychological orientation of adults and children to their own death. We expect adults to shape their present commitments and relationships differently as a result of their awareness of their own limited life span (e.g., into generative, productive activities). And we expect adults to view their commitments and relationships differently (valuing different things) because they feel more daily the pressure of the endpoint. There probably are important individual differences in how we orient to our own deaths, but for adults more than for children some orientation to one's own death permeates life decisions and activities.

Three hallmarks of adult personality, then, can be seen not to differentiate adults and children in their presence in personality, but in their form, and perhaps, too, in their relative prominence. The adult form of all three may be understood, we think, as the result of repeated reprocessing of similar life experiences, with the reprocessing occurring at ever-more-sophisticated levels of understanding. Thus, intimate relationships, personal commitments, and an awareness of death are experienced (like the self) repeatedly throughout life, beginning very early. But each new experience is built upon the fact of past experiences, memories, and constructions of those experiences, and new capacities for understanding and construing experience. (This notion, without the stress on cognitive development, is strongly implied in Erikson's epigenetic chart, first described in 1950/1963, pp. 269-274.) This reprocessing eventually yields new, qualitatively different, forms of intimacy, commitment, and orientation to death in adulthood. In the same way, continuous experience, and experience of the self, processed in qualitatively different ways, yields qualitatively different forms of the self. There is little empirical literature defining characteristics of the active, processing self, and virtually none exploring change in it over time or in adults. Nevertheless, we can find evidence for several likely characteristics of the adult self in the literature.

Empirical Evidence for an Adult Self

If the adult self is shaped through cognitive reprocessing of repeated life experiences, then we may expect the adult self to reflect directly the increased cognitive capacities of the adult. Thus we will expect the adult self to be characterized by a high degree of differentiation, abstraction, integration, and stability. Although we are not aware of research exploring how these four characteristics together produce a qualitatively different entity, there is research suggesting that each of these characteristics does differentiate adults' and children's selves.

A number of different researchers have argued that various aspects of the self are more differentiated in adults than children. Thus, some (e.g., Bernstein, 1980; Mullener & Laird, 1971) have shown that the self-concept (one aspect of the self) of adults is more differentiated or complex than that of children. Secord and Peevers (1974) have also shown that descriptions of the self are differentiated in older subjects and report (as do Bannister & Agnew, 1976) that with increasing age children are more likely fully to differentiate the self from others and to use more and finer discriminations in doing so. Thus, with general cognitive development we find a larger number of descriptors used, which are used in a more discriminating way, to describe and define the self-concept and the self.

This increasing differentiation of the self is accompanied by an increasing capacity for abstractions about the self. Thus, for example, Secord and Peevers show development in both self and other descriptions in a shift from specific qualities or preferences ("I play on swings") to broader, more general traits ("I like to be active"). Bernstein (1980) and Montemayor and Eisen (1977) report similar findings, supporting the notion that self-description "proceeds from a concrete to an abstract mode of representation" (Montemayor & Eisen, p. 314). In a related development, older adolescents and adults are far more capable of reflecting on the self and reporting on this self-reflection (see Secord & Peevers, 1974; Broughton, 1983; Selman, 1980). Clearly, this capacity for conscious awareness of self-observation depends on both a high degree of differentiation and abstraction. Indeed, Bernstein (1980) suggests the pressure to resolve apparent paradoxes resulting from differentiation may motivate the search for more abstract self-statements.

The increasingly differentiated self, including increasingly abstract elements, could result in a highly fragmented, chaotic personality structure (and probably sometimes does). However, there is evidence that there is also an increasing integration of the self with age (see Bernstein, 1980; Hauser, 1976; and an excellent review by Damon & Hart, 1982). Both Broughton (1983) and Secord and Peevers (1974) identify an increasing sense of agency and self-direction as a crucial element in this integration. Ultimately, this unification of disparate aspects of the self confers some stability on the self. Thus the self achieves some relatively long-term equilibrium that allows it to function as a central, mediating structure for adult affective experience. Its existence in turn confers some stability on adult personality by operating to select certain experiences, attend to certain aspects of these experiences, and integrate (or leave unintegrated) certain aspects of events and responses (see Ryff, 1982; Markus, 1977). In short, the coherent, differentiated self of adulthood acts as a brake on personality change, and provides for constructed, reflected continuity. It does not, and could not, preclude change, for the equilibrium of the self can be threatened, yielding a new process of differentiation, abstraction, and integration. But if the self is integrated on a base of rich differentiation and many-layered abstractions, revolutions in the self in adulthood will probably be rare (especially if the differentiation and abstractions in turn derive from a broad base in affective experience). There is, then, evidence for special characteristics of the adult self, and a suggestion that those characteristics may limit the rate of personality change in adulthood. It is also true that those characteristics may be expected to alter the adult's stance toward and experience of affective responses to life changes.

Consequences of the Adult Self for the Experience of Life Changes

The adult self hypothesized here can be expected to have some significant consequences for adult experience of life change. We have drawn upon Leonard Woolf's thoughtful five-volume autobiography (Woolf, 1960, 1961, 1963, 1967, 1969), all composed late in his long change-filled life, to identify some specific consequences of the well-articulated, adult self for affective experiences in response to change in adulthood.

The well-defined, clearly articulated self can be expected first of all to be a source of choices about many life changes. Thus, adults choose — and are aware of their choice — to experience some changes. In Woolf's case we see this clearly when he chooses, at age 31, to marry Virginia Stephen, after returning from Ceylon:

> The next five months were the most exciting months of my life. During them "Bloomsbury" really came into existence and I fell in love with Virginia. I felt the foundations of my personal life becoming more and more unstable, crisis after crisis confronting me, so that I had at short notice to make decisions whether I should or should not turn my life upside down. There is nothing more exhilarating than having to make that kind of decision, with the (no doubt false) feeling that you are the captain of your soul, the master of your fate. (Woolf, 1963, p. 47)

This sense of agency, of command over choices, can really only characterize the decisions of adults, and is in sharp contrast to the sense of being the sometimes fascinated and excited, but nevertheless helpless, object of external forces so commonly experienced in childhood and adolescence, when changes are often externally imposed. The contrast with Woolf's description of his first days at Cambridge (when he was 19), and his recollection of all school beginnings, is sharp:

> The first day at school was to me . . . terrible and terrifying, but also exhilaratingly exciting. You suddenly found yourself in a new, strange jungle, full of unknown enemies, pitfalls, and dangers. It was the feeling of complete loneliness and isolation which made the fear and misery so acute, and the depth of feeling was intensified by the instinctive knowledge of the small boy that he must conceal the fear and misery. (1960, pp. 95-96)

Here, too, Woolf was exposed to a life change he had at least in some sense chosen, but one over which he nevertheless felt far less control.

Even events that are externally imposed, and in no sense chosen, are experienced differently by Woolf in childhood and adulthood. As a child of 11, Woolf anticipated the unwelcome death of his father:

> I remember it as the night before my father died and that somehow . . . I was aware that he was dying and that his death meant not only the disaster of his death, the loss of him, but also the complete breakup and destruction of life as I had known it. (1960, p. 84)

Here Woolf clearly apprehends that something awful and pervasive in its ramifications is about to occur. A similar feeling recurs in 1914 as he senses the approach of war. In 1939 he again anticipates the impending war, but this time there is a terrible difference:

> The psychology of September 1939 was terribly different from that of August 1914. People of my generation knew now exactly what war is — its positive horrors of death and destruction, wounds and pain and bereavement and brutality, but also its negative emptiness and desolation of personal and cosmic boredom, the feeling that one is endlessly waiting in a dirty, grey railway station waiting-room, a cosmic railway station waiting-room, with nothing to do but wait endlessly for the next catastrophe. (1969, pp. 9-10)

There is a specificity in the anticipation, an understanding of what is to come. This specificity does not in any way imply a sense of agency — merely a sense of knowledge, both of the external characteristics of the experience, and of one's own responses to those characteristics:

> It was this feeling of hopelessness and helplessness, the foreknowledge of catastrophe with the forces of history completely out of control, which made the road downhill to war and the outbreak of war so different in 1939 from what they had been twenty-five years before. (1969, p. 11)

Woolf knows his own inner responses to this foreknowledge: "Life becomes like one of those terrible nightmares in which one tries to flee from some malignant, nameless and formless horror, and one's legs refuse to work, so that one waits helpless and frozen with fear for inevitable annihilation" (1969, p. 11).

Woolf possesses similarly relevant self-knowledge when anticipating less dramatic changes. Reflecting on his passage into boarding school at age 13, Woolf reports that when he went to school, he "at once began to develop the carapace, the facade, which, if our sanity is to survive, we must learn to present to the outside and usually hostile world as a protection to the naked, tender, shivering soul" (1960, p. 71). Woolf not only developed this "carapace," but was (as he put it), "half-conscious of doing so" (1960, p. 72). The motivation for this facade is complex and hard to know, but its existence changed the quality of his stance toward life changes after his school days. Thus, when he went to Cambridge, he "trod caustiously, with circumspection." This caution, this tempering of his enthusiasm helped "to conceal the uneasiness, lack of confidence, fear, which throughout my life I have been able to repress but never escape" (1960, p. 98). Woolf later views his experience in Ceylon as teaching him the "necessity of improving the facade" (1961, p. 37), partly because of the anti-intellectual, anti-introspective bias of the social environment, partly because he was exposed to many real, physical dangers. In short, Woolf was aware that as he faced frightening new situations in life he carried with him both his "real" inner responses and his "facade" of overt responses. This complex, many-leveled awareness of both the self concealed and the self constructed is characteristic of the adult self; when it directly involves (as for Woolf) responses to anxiety-provoking situations, it inevitably complicates the affective experience in anticipating life changes.

Even more, this awareness colors the actual affective responses to the changes. At age 24, Woolf left England for Ceylon. He experienced his departure as defining a radical discontinuity in his life.

> To make a complete break with one's former life is a strange, frightening, and exhilarating experience. It has upon one, I think, the effect of a second birth. . . . But because at birth consciousness is dim and it takes a long time for us to become aware of our environment, we do not feel a sudden break, and adjustment is slow, lasting indeed a lifetime. I can remember the precise moment of my second birth. (1961, pp. 11-12)

Woolf's affective response to this second birth followed the predicted sequence: "The first impact of the new life was menacing and depressing" (1961, p. 12). Over time he showed the usual pattern of adaptation, but his responses were uniquely defined by his highly developed self-observational habit.

> If . . . one suddenly uproots oneself into a strange land and a strange life, one feels as if one were acting in a play or living in a dream. . . . For seven years, excited and yet slightly and cynically amused, I watched myself playing a part in an exciting play on a brightly coloured stage or dreaming a wonderfully vivid and exciting dream. (1961, pp. 21-22)

This marked tendency to observe himself experiencing marked his response to returning seven years later.

> The curious thing about my return to England was that . . . I felt almost exactly what I had felt seven years ago in Colombo. My life in Ceylon . . . suddenly vanished into unreality; but London and myself driving through its ugly streets did not acquire any reassuring reality. Out of the corner of my eye I seemed to observe myself once more acting a part in the same complicated play in front of a new backcloth and with different actors and a different audience. (1963, p. 16)

He again experienced the usual sequence beginning with feelings of confusion and depression, but with his characteristic "caution and reserve" (1961, p. 16) and self-observation. Thus Woolf's accounts of his adult responses to life changes suggest both some general characteristics of adult responses (self-observation, and reflection on past comparable changes) and some characteristics that may have resulted from his personal life experiences and consequent adult self (the intensified split between the real and public selves, perhaps deriving from the need to conceal fear in fear-provoking situations).

It is worth noting that although Woolf reports on a number of later life changes, he views none of them as providing the kind of transformation of either the public or the private self afforded by these changes of young adulthood. No late life changes in career, marriage, or bereavement ever seemed to precipitate the radical change in the self that Woolf was aware of in early adulthood. Instead, Woolf is conscious of a number of significant continuities in his personality.

> What genuine glimpses one does get of oneself in very early childhood seem to show that the main outlines of one's character are moulded in infancy and do not change between the ages of three and eighty-three. I am sure that my attitude to sin was the same when I lay in my pram as it is today when I sit tapping this out on the typewriter and, unless I become senile, will be the same when I lie on my deathbed. And in other ways when I can genuinely remember something of myself far off and long ago, I can recognize that self as essentially myself with the same little core of character exactly the same as exists in me today. (1960, pp. 23-23)

He regards his characteristic fatalism and "half-amused resignation," as well as his obstinacy, as well developed by the age of three (1960, pp. 23-24). His intelligence and enjoyment of work, as well as his introspection and self-observation also developed early.

> From my very early years I have had in me, I think, a streak of considerable obstinacy. I was lamentably intelligent, and, as I have said, I liked to feel the mind work; I was a born swot for I enjoyed my work. I was, of course, not fully or definitely conscious of this or of the hostility towards it in the world around me, for in childhood and youth, though one feels acutely what goes on in one's own head and in the heads of other people and their often painful interactions, owing to inexperience and diffidence one rarely fully understands or acknowledges what is going on. . . . But I learned very early, I think, to go my own way behind the shutters of my mind and to be silent about much which went on there. (1960, pp. 89-90)

He is aware of a few later developments, especially of the public facade, but by the time he marries and settles in England at 31, radical self-transformation does not appear. Woolf is sometimes conscious of this absence of change in the self.

> This terrifying experience of being a new boy is, of course, not confined to one's first days at school. It may happen to one all through life, though naturally it becomes rarer as one grows older, and it is the privilege — or perhaps infirmity — of old age that it is highly improba-

> ble that you will experience it after, say, sixty unless you have the misfortune to find yourself in prison or a modern concentration camp. (1960, p. 96)

He records, too, some concern that the stable, articulated self not only shapes and colors our experience of life, but may interfere with objective understanding. In the forward to the third volume of his autobiography he writes,

> There are other bars, permanent bars of the cage of one's life, through which one has always and will always gaze at the world. The bars of one's birth and family and ancestors, of one's school and college, of one's own secret and sinuous psychology. Has not my mind . . . for the last 82 years been pacing up and down like the panther, backwards and forwards, behind these bars and gazing through them until, so weary, I have seen, not the world or life, but only the bars.(1963, p. 13)

Thus the adult self may generally compromise our objectivity; likely consequences of the adult self for affective responses to life changes include the folowing: (1) an increased sense of agency in making adult changes; (2) a sense of foreknowledge and anticipation in facing changes, including a knowledge of the self; (3) a complex self-monitoring of emotional responses and comparison with related past experiences; (4) recurrence of personal stances and strategies for coping, which derive in part from formative early change experiences; (5) reduced likelihood of transformation of the self after early adulthood. These consequences of the adult self are reflected at least in the retrospective account of responses to change contained in Woolf's writings; they seem at least to provide reasonable hypotheses deserving further exploration.

Exploring the Characteristics of the Adult Self: A Methodological Note

In this chapter, we have drawn on Leonard Woolf's autobiography not simply because it was a convenient source of illustrations. Instead we have treated the autobiography as a valid source of data about the adult self. And we recommend the autobiographies, diaries, and letters of clearly gifted "introspectionists" as a much-needed resource for the study of phenomena so difficult to define and describe as the adult self. We believe this kind of data is seriously underused by psychologists, despite lip service to its value, at least since the writings of Gordon Allport in the thirties and forties (see, e.g., Allport, 1942). We assume that psychologists' hesitation in confronting data of this kind derives in part from uncertainty about when and how such uses are "scientific." We will not attempt a review of all the methodological issues, philosophical assumptions, and scientific values involved in that uncertainty (see Runyan, 1982, and Anderson, 1981a, 1981b, for thoughtful discussions of these issues). Instead, we will point out that to date no other data source has been presented that appears to be *equally good* (far less, better) for providing insight into the adult self.

Two interesting methods seem to us to be promising ones for studying the vicissitudes of the adult self. First, systematic comparison of the adult self as presented and understood by different thoughtful autobiographers, of the same or different ages, might yield a descriptive portrait of the characteristics of the adult self at different stages of life as perceived by verbally articulate individuals capable of introspection.

A second approach might be to explore the evolving, adult self by collecting instances in which an author describes an experience at several points in life. Thus, for example, Vera Brittain (1982) recorded her passage of an exam in Greek at college in her diary at the time:

> The fateful telegram *did* arrive today, so late in the afternoon when I ceased to expect it. But it brought the good news I hoped for, that I had passed my Greek! . . . It is pleasing to think of having accomplished in seven weeks what people have been known to fail to accomplish in as many years. Mother and Daddy were very pleased and Mother came slowly to the conclusion that I really must be clever and rather exceptional or so many people wouldn't say so! (Brittain, 1982, p. 130)

The exuberance and grandiosity of her response are made clear by contrast with her discussion of the same event in her autobiography written several years later (1933/1980, p. 112):

> The second week in December brought Responsions Greek, which I passed easily enough. The fact that this was done on six weeks' study of that lovely language, which is totally unsuited to such disrespectful treatment, testifies to the simplicity of Responsions as an examination.

Characteristically, Leonard Woolf provided some insight, in his reflections on *his* experiences at univeristy, into the energy, egoism, and hope so typical of youthful responses:

> I might any day or hour or minute turn a corner and find myself face to face with someone whom I had never met before but who would instantly become my friend for life. I might casually open a book and find that I was reading for the first time *War and Peace*. . . . I might

> wake up tomorrow morning and find that I could at last write the great poem that fluttered helplessly at the back of my mind or the great novel rumbling hopelessly in some strange depths inside me. (1960, p. 159)

As he later puts it, this is "the enthusiasm, the passion with which one sees and hears and thinks and feels when everything in the world and in other people and in oneself is fresh and new to one" (1960, p. 168). It is Woolf, too, who points out that "one of the consolations of growing old is that . . . one has learnt that even the dreariest dinner party or longest week-end does come to an end" (1963, p. 91). Woolf's ability simultaneously to write articulately about his recollection of past inner experience and reflection on it, while recording current inner experience, may be quite rare. It is for that reason an especially valuable guide to complex processes more ordinary adults might be unable to describe. It is encouraging, however, that the successive reworking of one's experience in writing — in letters, diaries, autobiographies, novels — is a commonplace to literary people. It is our belief that all adults' inner lives are characterized by the kinds of processes directly described by Woolf and indirectly reflected in Brittain's later perspective on an earlier experience. It may eventually be important to find ways to explore these processes in less literary adults. But for now the natural gift for self-expression of some writers happily provides psychologists with a rich source of data about adults' inner lives.

References

Allport, G. W. (1942). *The use of personal documents in psychological science.* New York: Social Science Research Council.

Allport, G. W. (1954). *Becoming.* New Haven, CT: Yale University Press.

Anderson, J. W. (1981a). The methodology of psychological biography. *Journal of Interdisciplinary History, 11,* 455-475.

Anderson, J. W. (1981b). Psychobiographical methodology: The case of William James. In L. Wheeler (Ed.), *Review of Personality and Social Psychology,* Vol. 2. Beverly Hills, CA: Sage.

Bannister, D., & Agnew, J. (1976). The child's construing of self. *Nebraska Symposium on Motivation* (pp. 99-126).

Bernstein, R. M. (1980). The development of the self-system during adolescence. *Journal of Genetic Psychology, 136,* 231-245.

Blasi, A. (1983). The self and cognition: the roles of the self in the acquisition of knowledge, and the role of cognition in the development of the self. In B. Lee & G. G. Noam (Eds.), *Developmental Approaches to the Self.* New York: Plenum.

Brittain, V. (1982). *Chronicle of youth: The war diary 1913-1917.* New York: William Morrow.

Brittain, V. (1980). *Testament of youth.* New York: Wideview Books. (Original work published 1933)

Broughton, J. (1983). The cognitive developmental theory of adolescent self and identity. In B. Lee & G. G. Noam (Eds.), *Developmental approaches to the self.* New York: Plenum.

Chandler, M. J. (1977). Social cognition: A selective review of current research. In W. F. Overton and J. M. Gallagher (Eds.), *Knowledge and development: Vol. 1, advances in research and theory.* New York: Plenum.

Cooney, E. W., & Selman, R. (1978). Children's use of social conceptions: Towards a dynamic model of social cognition. *New directions for child development, 1,* 23-44.

Damon, W., & Hart, D. (1982). The development of self-understanding from infancy through adolescence. *Child Development, 53,* 841-864.

Edelstein, W., & Noam, G. (1982). Regulatory structures of the self and "postformal" stages in adulthood. *Human Development, 25,* 407-422.

Elkind, D. (1974). *Children and adolescents: Interpretative essays on Jean Piaget* (2nd ed.) New York: Oxford University Press.

Erikson, E. H. (1963). *Childhood and Society.* New York: Norton. (Original work published 1950)

Erikson, E. H. (1968). *Identity: Youth and crisis.* New York: Norton.

Feffer, M. (1970). A developmental analysis of interpersonal behavior. *Psychological Review, 77,* 197-214.

Gould, R. L. (1978). *Transformations: Growth and changes in adult life.* New York: Simon & Schuster.

Hauser, S. T. (1976). Self-image complexity and identity formation in adolescence: Longitudinal studies. *Journal of Youth and Adolescence, 5,* 161-178.

Healy, J. M., Jr., & Stewart, A. J. (in press). Adaptation to life changes in adolescence. In P. Karoly & J. J. Steffen (Eds.), *Adolescent behavior disorders: Foundations and applications.* Lexington, MA: D.C. Heath.

Inhelder, B., & Piaget, J. (1958). *The growth of logical thinking from childhood to adolescence.* New York: Basic Books.

James, W. (1892). *Principles of psychology.* New York: Holt, Rinehart & Winston.

James, W. (1910). *Psychology: The briefer course.* New York: Holt, Rinehart & Winston.

Jung, C. G. (1960). The stages of life In *Collected works,* Vol. 8. Princeton, NJ: Princeton University Press. (Original work published 1931)

Levinson, D. J. (1978). *The seasons of a man's life.* New York: Knopf.

Lifton, R. J. (1976). *The life of the self.* New York: Simon & Schuster.

Livesley, W. J., & Bromley, D. B. (1973). *Person perception in childhood and adolescence.* New York: John Wiley.

Madison, P. (1969). *Personality development in college.* Reading, MA: Addison-Wesley.

Mahler, M. F., Pine, F., & Bergman, A. (1975). *The psychological birth of the human infant.* New York: Basic Books.

Markus, H. (1977). Self-schemata and processing information about the self. *Journal of Personality and Social Psychology, 35,* 63-78.

Montemayor, R., & Eisen, M. (1977). The development of self-conceptions from childhood to adolescence. *Developmental Psychology, 13,* 314-319.

Mullener, N., & Laird, J. D. (1971). Some developmental changes in the organization of self-evaluations. *Developmental Psychology, 5,* 233-236.

Neugarten, B. L. (1964). *Personality in middle and later life.* New York: Atherton.

Oakley, A. (1980). *Women confined: Towards a sociology of childbirth.* New York: Schocken.

Peevers, B. H., & Secord, P. F. (1973). Developmental changes in attribution of descriptive concepts to persons. *Journal of Personality and Social Psychology, 27,* 120-128.

Rapoport, R. (1964). The transition from engagement to marriage. *Acta Sociologica, 8,* 36-55.

Runyan, W. W. (1982). *Life histories and psychobiography.* New York: Oxford University Press.

Ryff, C. D. (1982). Self-perceived personality change in adulthood and aging. *Journal of Personality and Social Psychology, 42,* 108-115.

Secord, P., & Peevers, B. (1974). The development and attribution of person concepts. In T. Mischel (Ed.), *Understanding other persons.* Oxford: Blackwell.

Selman, R. (1980). *The growth of interpersonal understanding.* New York: Academic Press.

Spitz, R., Emde, R., & Metcalf, C. (1970). Further prototypes of ego formation: A working paper from a research project on early development. *The Psychoanalytic Study of the Child, 25,* 417-441.

Spitzer, S. P. (1978). Ontological insecurity and reflective processes. *Journal of Phenomenological Psychology, 8,* 203-217.

Sroufe, L. A. (1979). Socioemotional development. In J. Osofsky (Ed.), *Handbook of infant development.* New York: John Wiley.

Stewart, A. J. (1981, December). Women's adaptation to family role changes in early adulthood. Paper presented at the International Interdisciplinary Congress on Women, Haifa, Israel.

Stewart, A. J. (1982). The course of individual adaptation to life changes. *Journal of Personality and Social Psychology, 42,* 1100-1119.

Stewart, A. J. (1983, May). Longitudinal studies of the course of adaptation to life changes. Paper presented to the Psychology Department of Northeastern University, Boston.

Stewart, A. J., Sokol, M., Healy, J. M., Jr., Chester, N. L., & Weinstock-Savoy, D. (1982). Adaptation to life changes in children and adults: Cross-sectional studies. *Journal of Personality and Social Psychology, 43,* 1270-1281.

Sullivan, H. S. (1953). *The interpersonal theory of psychiatry.* New York: Norton.

Vaillant, G. E. (1977). *Adaptation to life.* Boston: Little, Brown.

Wallerstein, J. S., & Kelly, J. B. (1980). *Surviving the breakup: How children and parents cope with divorce.* New York: Basic Books.

Wapner, S., Kaplan, B., & Cohen, S. B. (1973). An organismic-developmental perspective for understanding transactions of men and environments. *Environment and Behavior, 5,* 225-289.

Werner, H. (1961). *Comparative psychology of mental development.* New York: Science Editions.

Woolf, Leonard (1960). *Sowing: an autobiography of the years 1880 to 1904.* New York: Harcourt Brace Jovanovich.

Woolf, Leonard. (1961). *Growing: An autobiography of the years 1904 to 1911.* New York: Harcourt Brace Jovanovich.

Woolf, Leonard. (1963). *Begining again: An autobiography of the years 1911 to 1918.* New York: Harcourt Brace Jovanovich.

Woolf, Leonard. (1967). *Downhill all the way: An autobiography of the years 1919 to 1939.* New York: Harcourt Brace Jovanovich.

Woolf, Leonard. (1969). *The journey not the arrival matters: An autobiography of the years 1939 to 1969.* New York: Harcourt Brace Jovanovich.

16

Affect in Adult Cognition

A Constructivist View of Moral Thought and Action

PAUL A. ROODIN
JOHN M. RYBASH
WILLIAM J. HOYER

Until recently, psychoanalytic, social learning, and cognitive-developmental views or models have guided the study of moral development. However, with the recent growth of interest in the study of the adult life span by developmental psychologists, a fourth view, which is active, dialectical, and constructivist, has emerged. The purpose of this chapter is to explicate this view, and to propose it as a framework for the developmental investigation of mature moral thought and action. We begin with a brief overview and critique of traditional approaches to the study of moral development.

Developmental Views of Morality

The development of the capacity to articulate emotion and affect is central to a psychoanalytic or ego-analytic conceptualization of moral development. From this perspective, it is presumed that moral maturity is a manifestation of ego maturity, and full development of the ego or "self" is usually not reached or achieved until relatively late in the life course. For example, Erikson (1964) suggested that the adolescent is capable of awareness of universal ethical principles although only the adult can consistently be ethical. Thus, cognitive awareness of ethical principles is *ideological,* and moral action is not necessarily *ethical* until the developing individual is fully committed to the consistent use of a particular set of moral principles. According to Erikson (1964), mature morality depends on establishing relations of care or generativity toward others. This generativity combines with an inclusive identity with the human species, occurring usually in middle adulthood, as illustrated by the development of Ghandi (see Erikson, 1969). Similarly, Loevinger's (1966, 1976) ego developmental theory describes a sequence of dynamic stages or milestones beginning with the coming into existence of the self through impulsiveness (e.g., actions are "good" or "bad" depending on whether one gets caught), and proceeding to stages of self-protectiveness (e.g., avoids blame; fears being caught), conformity to authority (e.g., seeks approval through conformity to external rules; disapproval leads to shame), conscientiousness (e.g., development of self-standards through self-criticism), autonomy (e.g., coping with inner conflicts and needs leads to respect for others' autonomy), and, finally, integrity (e.g., reconciles inner and outer needs and conflicts).

A second and contrasting tradition considers that moral reasoning and moral behaviors are learned through social interaction. According to Bandura (1977), for example, social learning is the process through which individuals come to acquire both morally acceptable and unacceptable behaviors. Further, morality is socially defined, and there are no "universal principles" of morality according to social learning theorists. Intraindividual developmental change as well as secular sociohistorical change in moral thought and behavior is understood in terms of such learning principles as shaping, reinforcement and punishment, modeling, identification, and imitation. Recent social learning conceptions of moral behavior and development give emphasis to chance encounters, socialization specific to life paths, and factors related to the individual's self-efficacy (e.g., Bandura, 1982a, 1982b).

By far the most extensive framework yet developed to account for the emergence of moral thought and action in children and adolescents is the cognitive-developmental view. Initially proposed by Piaget (1932), cognitive-developmental theory attempts to describe the changing nature of children's *judgments, evaluations,* and *thoughts* in terms of underlying cognitive structures. Lawrence Kohlberg (e.g., Kohlberg, 1976) is generally considered to be one of the leading proponents of the cognitive-developmental approach to moral reasoning. Initially, Kohlberg focused on developmental changes in conceptions of *justice.* That is, how do children come to understand the legitimate claims of others in complex situations? Or, how do adolescents reason about complex moral conflicts, and what methods of reasoning do they employ to evaluate and resolve inner needs and external pressures? What is fair, and (how) does the meaning of fairness change developmentally (Rawls, 1971; Rest, 1979)?

By interpreting the responses of individuals of different ages to hypothetical moral dilemmas, Kohlberg (1976) formulated a structural developmental sequence consisting of three levels (preconventional, conventional, and postconventional) and six stages (two at each level). Kohlberg's highest level of postconventional reasoning (stage 6) represents an autonomously focused, mature morality based on *universal* principles of justice. According to Kohlberg, the just principles of fairness, equality, and reciprocity comprise "what is most distinctly and fundamentally moral" (1976, p. 40). His cognitive-developmental stage sequence is illustrated below:

Preconventional moral reasoning (level 1): Stages 1 and 2. Moral reasoning at this level is based on fear of punishment and the consequences of disobedience. Additionally, individuals' rights to self-interest must be extended to others: "If I can do it then others should also be allowed the same freedoms."

Conventional moral reasoning (level 2): Stages 3 and 4. Moral judgments are generally based on social convention and a desire to appear in a good light in the eyes of others in the society. The dominant themes are preserving the "golden rule," and recognizing that social order (rules, laws) *must* prevail over individual rights at all times.

Postconventional moral reasoning (level 3): Stages 5 and 6. This most mature form of moral thinking is marked by recognition that a society provides basic rights and guarantees to people and that such contracts may be denied or superceded if basic human or individual rights are violated or threatened. For example, the social contract may be discarded if people are denied their right to live or their right to basic constitutional freedoms.

Kohlberg (1976) has argued that progression through these levels and stages follows a *universal* and *invariant* sequence. Second, levels are *hierarchically integrated* such that less mature forms of moral reasoning become integrated and actually part of the more advanced forms. Third, each level represents a unique and qualitatively different form of thinking, evaluation, and conceptualization of moral issues. These qualitative differences are the result of a total and complete *structural* reorganization of moral reasoning within the individual, and each new restructured whole results in a stable and consistent form of equilibrium (Kohlberg, 1969, 1976).

Initially, Kohlberg identified the end of adolescence as that point in development at which an individual's highest stage of moral reasoning was attained (Kohlberg, 1969). According to Kohlberg (1971), the progression through the various levels and stages of moral development to an adult form of morality is dependent on (1) logical thinking as represented by cognitive level (i.e., Piagetian formal operations); (2) social perspective-taking abilities (e.g., role-taking); and (3) self-dissatisfaction with present level of moral understanding. Note that movement through the stage sequence as well as final level of moral reasoning is not directly dependent on level of biological maturity and social experience from this perspective.

Contrary to theory, Kohlberg and Kramer (1973) obtained longitudinal data indicating that high school students who had attained postconventional levels of moral thought regressed to a preconventional level during their college years. Such a clear violation of the Piagetian stage criterions of invariance forced Kohlberg and his colleagues to undertake major revisions of his theory and its measurement and assessment procedures (Colby, 1978).

Using a revised scoring system, combined with several fundamental theory modifications, Colby, Kohlberg, Gibbs, and Lieberman (1983) reported two new and important findings. First, *regression* was no longer evident in the longitudinal data using the new scoring system. Second, Kohlberg noted that there is continued moral growth well into adulthood (i.e., the mid-thirties). To quote (Colby, Kohlberg, Gibbs, & Lieberman, 1983, p. 69):

> the early scoring systems could not discriminate properly among superficially similar moral judgments at stages 3, 4, and 5. This meant that when "true Stage 5" began to emerge in early adulthood it was not recognized as a qualitatively new form of reasoning. We can now discriminate principled reasoning from superficially similar conventional reasoning, and we no longer see Stage 5 being used in junior high school or high school. This means that there is a new stage in adulthood and that many of our subjects continued to develop in their twenties and thirties, rather than reaching a ceiling in mid-adolescence.

We now see in Kohlberg's work that moral development encompasses the major developmental eras of childhood, adolescence, and adulthood. Furthermore, it is suggested that different factors are responsible for moral growth within different portions of the life span. That is, during childhod and adolescence, moral growth is largely dependent on logical thinking, social perspective-taking, and self-dissatisfaction with current moral functioning (Kohlberg, 1976). In adulthood, however, moral growth is influenced additionally by self-involving life events that are affectively meaningful. Although there is some recognition of adulthood issues in his recent work (Kohlberg, 1973, 1981), Kohlberg's theory remains relatively incomplete with regard to the developmental explication of mature moral reasoning in adulthood.

Cognitive-developmental stage theories based on the study of children and adolescents are limited in scope, and they offer unnecessarily restrictive assumptions regarding the nature of thought and action. With the exception of a few recent papers (e.g., Alexander & Langer, 1983; Basseches, 1980; Kramer, 1983; Labouvie-Vief, 1981; Pascual-Leone, 1983; Sinnott, 1984) adulthood is treated simply as the "terminal" stage in the cognitive-developmental sequence.

By general observation it is clear that there is considerable multilinearity and pluralism at many levels of affective and cognitive functioning in adults (e.g., see Baltes & Willis, 1977; Dittmann-Kohli & Baltes, 1983; Huyck & Hoyer, 1982; Malatesta & Izard, this volume). We argue that affective-cognitive complexity is characteristic and basic to adults in the domain of moral decisions. As an example of intraindividual multilinearity, some adults may be quite mature and sophisticated in their moral judgments and evaluations in some situations, and at other times and in other situations they may exhibit earlier forms of moral reasoning along with these more advanced and mature attainments. One of the central concerns for those interested in understanding adult moral development is to identify under what conditions different forms or levels of morality coexist. One of the linkages that must be considered in this investigative process is that of affective-cognitive interaction. Affective involvement for adults appears to activate differential levels of moral judgment and reasoning (Roodin & Hoyer, 1982). We argue that adult moral reasoners display cognitive-affective complexities (i.e., advancements) that are qualitatively distinct from the forms of reasoning exhibited by children and adolescents.

Nonadult stages are marked by relatively unitary forms of moral thinking while adult morality manifests a variety of forms of moral evaluations and judgments (Roodin & Hoyer, 1982). Earlier stages generally fit the cognitive-developmental criteria of a "structured-whole," but this does not appear to be the case for adult morality. Compared to adults, it seems that children and adolescents manifest roughly the same cognitive-developmental structures in their moral thinking regardless of (1) the focus of the moral dilemma, and (2) the degree of affective involvement surrounding the moral issue or ultimate resolution of the moral dilemma (cf. Gibbs, 1977, 1979).

Conceptions of Adult Morality

Many critics have questioned the efficacy and adequcy of Kohlberg's descriptions of adult morality (e.g., Vine, 1983). In addition, there is general consensus that the cognitive-developmental stage model of morality is limited by implicit organismic assumptions (cf. Reese & Overton, 1970), its child-centeredness, its attenuated conceptualization of adult cognitive and affective development, and its overconcern with the dimension of justice relative to other dimensions of morality. Ego-analytic and social learning conceptions are also thought to be limited, but in different ways (e.g., see Kohlberg, 1976; Looft, 1973). For example, ego-analytic theories are criticized on methodological grounds (e.g., Hauser, 1976). Affect and "self" are central constructs within ego-analytic theory, but frequently there is little if any empirical documentation for the proposed constructs. In contrast, social learning theory is usually associated with sound empiricism, but such environmental accounts generally ignore the integrity of the organism as shown by behavioral consistencies across moral contexts and time (Holstein, 1972, 1976). As there are no universal (i.e., cross-cultural, transsituational) moral principles from the pure social learning view, there is no search for such consistencies in the data. Further, social learning accounts are often limited to direct behavioral measures that *may* not fully index the richness and complexity of moral thought and affect. Ego-analytic, social learning, and cognitive-developmental approaches all seem to give little attention to such factors as personal commitment, individual choice and responsibility, and the developmental significance of metaethical reflection. Before elaborating these constructivist dimensions, however, we review several other recent advances in the conceptualization of adult moral thought.

Murphy & Gilligan (1980) have provided perhaps the most detailed account of the process of transition from conventional to postconventional levels of morality — an event necessarily occuring in adulthood. Murphy and Gilligan (1980) characterized postconventional levels of adult morality as marked by heightened sensitivity to content and a commitment to relativism. The notion of commitment to relativism is also found in the earlier work of Perry (1968) who argued that adult moral perspectives were rarely bounded by Kohlbergian commitments to absolute principles of justice and fairness. Perry (1968) noted that moral maturity is evidenced by a heightened concern for the ethical/existential domain and by a concern for the relativistic context in which moral values and principles exist. Following Perry, Murphy and Gilligan suggested that mature forms of moral reasoning are heightened by "experiences of moral conflict and choice [which] seem to point to special obligations and responsibility for consequences that can be anticipated and understood only within a more contextual frame of reference" (Murphy & Gilligan, 1980, p. 81). Similarly, White, Flately, and Janson (1982) observed that it is inaccurate to characterize adult moral reasoning in terms of absolute and context-invariant moral principles. Adult moral reasoning is relativistic, and adults seem to be increasingly open to the contextual properties of moral dilemmas as a function of age.

Murphy and Gilligan suggested that adult moral reasoning consists of the capacity to consider a behavior from multiple frameworks and multiple perspectives. Thus, behaviors "can be both good and bad, moral and immoral, depending upon the framework within which they are evaluated" (Murphy & Gilligan, 1980, p. 79). The developing individual's growing awareness of the contextual relativism of knowledge becomes part of the individual's identity and part of his or her level of moral reasoning.

Gibbs (1977, 1979) has also provided an account of the development of adult morality. Gibbs has accepted the first two levels in Kohlberg's theory as representative of the process of moral development typical of children and adolescents, but offers a unique conception of adult morality. For Gibbs the moral developmental accomplishments of children and adolescents represent the *Standard Phase,* which is composed of preconventional and conventional levels of moral reasoning. This Standard Phase has the characteristics of a true developmental stage (e.g., hierarchical arrangement, structural wholes), but adult moral reasoning does not appear to display stage-like characteristics. According to Gibbs adult moral reasoning, referred to as the *Existential Phase,* is marked by the capacity for metaethical reflection. The hallmark of the Existential Phase is a level of discourse and abstract reasoning that indicates the presence of an articulated self-theory of morality. This "theory-defining" level of discourse and reasoning bears little or no relationship to earlier moral function as represented by the Standard Phase (Gibbs & Widaman, 1982).

Gibb's view of adult moral reasoning is contextualistic in that it "allows for the complexity of reciprocal interactions between the organism and its many contexts" (cf. Fitzgerald, 1981, p. 5). The Existential Phase has as preconditions, the acquisition of formal operational skills, and the capacity to explore and engage in metaethical reflection. Metaethical reflection is expressed in such concerns as the search for understanding of the human condition, for finding one's place in the universe, and for the very meaning and purpose of individual lives and collective humanity. One can see that Gibbs's conception of metaethical reflection was influenced by Erich Fromm's (1941, 1947, 1955, 1973) theory that the natural equilibrium between the human organism and its ecology becomes disturbed when the limitations of existence are realized. Ultimately, there is the realization of the inevitability of nonexistence or death.

The search for understanding arises out of a broadening awareness along the dimensions of Fromm's basic core needs of (1) relatedness, (2) transcedence, (3) rootedness, (4) identity, and (5) meaning. Satisfactory answers to purpose-of-life questions become important as adults come to realize the limits of their existence. According to Gibbs even everyday, conventional actions and decisions demand greater degrees of moral responsibility, personal choice, and personal commitment with aging. As core needs become increasingly significant within the Existential Phase, the developing person seeks new and better methods of coping. It appears that the social and cognitive matrix of life experiences is sufficiently demanding in adulthood to require individuals to confront the five basic core needs in a meaningful way. Although Gibbs's theoretical emphasis is placed on the developmental advances realized by adults who cope successfully (i.e., affirmative coping), continued development of sociomoral maturity may not emerge among those adults for whom the conflicts and challenges of life are either unsuccessfully resolved or defensively ignored (i.e., abortive coping).

Gilligan (1977, 1982) has developed still another view of adult morality. She strongly criticized the dilemmas employed by Kohlberg because they focused primary concern on the emergence of the concept of justice or fairness. Women find Kohlberg's dilemmas to be particularly irrelevant to their experiences, overly hypothetical and abstract, and devoid of salient personal, historical, and affective contextual information regarding the main characters' personalities. The evaluation of justice in an affective vacuum was more difficult, and less interesting (or motivating) for women than for men; and justice-based conceptions of morality are likely to suggest a less advanced level of moral reasoning for women than for men. Specifically, men's concepts of justice centered primarily on equity, fairness, and abstract principles, whereas women's concepts of justice involved caring, compassion, and tolerance for others. Thus the transition to principled moral reasoning is not the same for men and women, and men and women are required to interpret and integrate different moral conflicts (Gilligan, 1977). Yet, the fully functioning, mature adult (man or woman) shows a sensitivity to and capacity to deal with both dimensions: Justice as equity and justice as personal caring.

Although anyone may reach a full understanding of mature morality, men and women are usually required to *integrate* different aspects of their personal lives to attain maturity. The general argument is that one must effectively integrate a developmental history to attain moral maturity, and developmental histories differ across individuals because of the circumstances of socialization. According to Gilligan (1977), for example, mature women have successfully learned to relinquish self-criticism deriving from the irrational belief that they can care for all persons equally. Further, the attainment of a postconventional level of morality among adult women is advanced by the personal experience and emotional recognition that inequitable relationships breed violence.

Men as well as women need to integrate both rights and responsibilities as a condition for attaining moral maturity. This integration is attained through *experience*. That is, principles derived from direct action and personal responsibility come to compensate for passively acquired, abstract moral principles. For illustration, development toward postconventional morality among men as well as women comes with an affective recognition that there are limits to a system of justice that does not show sensitivity to inequities in human rights (Gilligan, 1977).

Alternative Conceptions of Adult Morality: Core Issues

The core concerns of Gibbs (1977), Gilligan (1977), and Gilligan and Murphy (1980) are summarized in Table 16.1. One of the concerns in common among these theorists is that adult morality represents a system that is "born out of" and is designed to "make sense of" the events that occur within the lives of individuals. Thus, we see hints of a constructivist approach among these writers in that there is a recognition of the influence of affectively toned, personally significant life events as antecedents to mature morality. Personally significant life events are characterized by genuine affect, concern, and caring for others as well as a sense of interpersonal recognition and responsibility. According to these writers it is the feelings associated with meaningful life events that produce moral maturity — a type of maturity that is different from the abstract principles of fairness/justice derived from verbal interrogations under affectively neutral conditions. That is, by coping with real events we find ourselves interpreting life's contradictions — we may both love and hate someone, and experiences may be at once both good and bad. Thus, there are contradictory emotions, thoughts, and beliefs, which the mature moral reasoner comes to discover and accept.

Another common concern among these writers is the view that adult morality involves the understanding of contextual relativism. Adult moral reasoners come to realize that universal, invariant principles of

TABLE 16.1 Alternative Approaches to Adult Morality: Core Concerns

	Core Concerns	
Theorists	*Why are life events important for the development of adult morality?*	*What is the nature of contextual relativism?*
Murphy and Gilligan	Life events present the individual with experiences that contain contradictory thoughts as well as contradictory emotions. Life events present the individual with problems that cannot be solved solely by pure logic.	Once the individual understands the limits of formal logic, he or she begins to realize that (1) no one set of moral principles can resolve all moral conflicts; (2) all knowledge, including moral knowledge, is contextually based; (3) there is a need to commit one's self to a set of moral principles with the realization that these principles may need to be modified and/or transcended due to the unique parameters of new situations.
Gibbs	Life events present the individual with the opportunity to come to grips with a core set of existential needs that "define" and "give meaning" to our human existence.	The nature of adult morality is existential rather than structural. Therefore adults must commit themselves to a set of moral principles that they believe will preserve their contextually based understanding of what represents the full orchestra of basic human needs.
Gilligan	Life events present the individual with moral problems in which the major protagonists have "real" rather than "skeletal" lives. The individuals involved in real-life dilemmas have rich past histories as well as immediate concerns that are brought to bear on current moral conflicts.	The individual comes to realize that logically derived moral principles that focus on justice and fairness must be modified and transcended due to the "real" concerns of the "real people" involved in "real-life" moral dilemmas. The individual must learn to temper principles of justice with the need to care for others while at the same time remain responsible to him- or herself.

morality exist only in the abstract, philosophical sense. Developing adults are continually observing changes in their own moral principles as well as within- and cross-generational changes in the principles and values of others. Moral principles show change over time as persons mature, and as social contexts change; however, this change is not arbitrary, nor only the reflection of current social mores. Rather, change reflects individually chosen decisions in response to real human needs, basic inequities, and growing awareness of breadth and depth of self. This common concern is also consistent with a constructivist interpretation of moral development.

Third, adult morality is only nominally advanced by formal operational thinking skills. Although this level of cognition might help one to utilize the metareflective awareness of postadolescence, formal operational thought is not viewed as directly responsible for sociomoral maturity by these writers (see also Kramer, 1983; Labouvie-Vief, 1982).

A Framework for Adult Morality

It is assumed that adult morality is associated with different forms of thought, reasoning, and metaethical reflection than the forms characteristic of earlier developmental periods. Further, it is assumed that the development of an adult morality is influenced by contact with a variety of affectively involving, personally meaningful life events. These events are credited with promoting moral development, in part, by producing dialectical conflict, personal caring and responsibility, and an understanding of personal relativism. We now propose an emergent framework that describes adult morality and its development.

(1) Mature morality is an organized system that both defines moral concerns and helps to resolve real-life moral problems.
(2) Moral dilemmas have both analytic (cognitive) and affective (emotional) parameters. One task of adult morality is to integrate the cognitive and affective dimensions (rather than establish the primacy of one over the other).
(3) The limits of pure reason in the resolution of moral contradictions is recognized.
(4) Moral principles are in part relative and contextual.
(5) Intraindividual moral development (as well as societal mores) is dynamic across time.
(6) The moral system is part of a larger evolving self system that is capable of metaethical reflection, personal commitment, and integration of conflicting moral systems.

Our view of adult morality is based in part on the assumption of a postformal stage of cognitive development (Commons, 1984; Edelstein & Noam, 1982; Gilligan & Murphy, 1979; Labouvie-Vief, 1980). Although formal operations are important, perhaps essential to the transition from conventional to postconventional levels, in our view formal operational thought is not sufficient for the attainment of postconventional morality. Moreover, formal thought has a number of attributes that may even *restrict* sociomoral thought, as follows: (1) It favors the hypothetical over the real and allows for the contemplation of hypothetical contradictions rather than the acceptance of reality consisting of factually based contradictions; (2) it is more useful for close-system problem solving than for open-system problem finding (cf. Arlin, 1975; Basseches, 1984); (3) analysis is given more emphasis than is integration and synthesis (i.e., events are perceived as having separable cognitive and affective aspects); and (4) pure logic is viewed as the primary means of solving problems (i.e., cognition has primacy over affect).

Note Gilligan and Murphy's (1979, p. 86) concern with the primacy of cognition issue:

> in the course of human development . . . adolescents discover that the categories of their reason cannot encompass the facts of their experience. This is the time in cognitive development that Inhelder and Piaget . . . describe as the "return to reality," the shift from a metaphysical to an empirical truth that charts the "path from adolescence to the true beginnings of adulthood." . . . Then the contradictory pulls of logic and affect, and the difficulty of their integration, call into question the equation of reason with logic, giving rise to a conflict that can be the occasion for further development.

Although formal thought probably has little direct impact on adult moral development, it is our position that the attainment of postformal forms of thinking provides the foundation for mature morality (for discussions of postformal thought see Commons, 1984; Kramer, 1983). Kramer (1983), for example, in her discussion of the general characteristics of postformal thought seems to have described indirectly several of the key features of adult morality as proposed by Murphy and Gilligan (1980), and Gilligan and Murphy (1979). First, Kramer (1983) suggested that postformal thinkers display an understanding of the nonabsolute, relative nature of knowledge. All knowledge, moral knowledge included, is viewed as temporarily true rather than universally fixed. Therefore, adult conceptions of morality seems to reflect a "movement through forms" (see Basseches, 1980) such that adults tend to (1) recognize new contexts for their moral principles, and (2) construct new principles as contexts change and extant principles become outmoded.

Second, postformal thinkers accept contradiction as a basic aspect of physical and social reality. That is, a *behavior* may be viewed as both moral and immoral, *morality* may be understood as having its basis in both justice and care, and *experience* may be simultaneously perceived as both affective and cognitive.

Third, postformal thinkers possess the ability to synthesize contradictory experiences into a coherent, inclusive whole. According to Basseches (1980) the concept of wholeness implies that knowledge cannot be thought of as consisting of several "parts" that exist separate from a "whole." Instead, the whole gives meaning to its parts. Moreover, the parts of a whole may be regarded as being *constituted* (i.e., created) by their relationship to the whole. Following Basseches (1980), we suggest that affect and cognition have a constitutive relationship with regard to adult moral schemata. It is the structural characteristics of adult morality that give rise to the thoughts and feelings that accompany moral problems in living. If affect and cognition are constituted by their relationship to morality it becomes difficult to view them as existing independent of or a priori to some form of adult morality. Therefore, the question of which is more important becomes trivial when affect, cognition, and morality are viewed from a constructivist framework.

Self-Development and Adult Morality

The developmental tasks of adulthood seem to demand moral choices, moral actions, and personal commitments that serve to heighten metaethical reflection about the social order and the self. Adulthood is a period for the major restructuring of a number of psychological domains, not only the moral realm. To quote Labouvie-Vief (1982, p. 181),

> the primary mode of action shifts from reactivity to proactivity. Thus the individual, having so to speak exhausted the structure provided from without, shifts his or her predominant mode to within in an effort to create new structure with the aid of his or her own resources.

In our view adult moral development is related to this transition from external to internal developmental structure. Similarly, our proposed model of adult morality is based on the structural, recursive, and constructivist qualities that are highlighted in recent conceptions of postformal thought (e.g., Basseches, 1980, 1984; Commons, 1984; Kramer, 1983; Labouvie-Vief, 1982) and of self-development (e.g., Brim, 1968, 1976; Broughton, 1978; Kegan, 1982; Kegan, Naom, & Rogers, 1982).

With regard to the relationship between self-development and adult morality, some writers have characterized adult morality as the capacity to make self-consistent, self-justifiable decisions. Every moral decision can be questioned, critiqued, and justified from at least two positions; mature reasoners accept such relativism because they have developed a sufficiently articulated self-system of values, beliefs, thoughts, and emotions. Broughton (1978), for example, has suggested that the emerging self in adulthood is characterized by new capacities for critical self-appraisal, self-construction, and self-reflection.

It can be argued that a fully developed self-system gives consistency to moral thought and action. Erikson (1964) observed that the adolescent is cognitively capable of universal ethical principles, but only the adult can be consistently ethical in thought and action. The cognitive awareness of ethical principles is *ideological,* and insufficient for consistent moral action because the "self" may not as yet be fully committed to their use. According to Erikson (1964) adult morality depends on establishing relations of care or generativity toward others. This generativity combines with a more inclusive identity with the human species in adulthood or middle age, as in the case of Ghandi (see Erikson, 1969).

The self in adulthood is often an overlooked system in the study of morality. We suggest that a self-constructed moral system or schema becomes increasingly articulated during the adult years, and that thought and action in adulthood comes more under the control of the individual's self-constructed moral system with age-related experience. From a dialectical-constructivist framework it is suggested that the hallmark of adult morality is the capacity to recognize, resolve, integrate, and synthesize tensions such as justice versus caring, and affect versus cognition.

Self as Coper

Several writers have noted the relationship between the emerging self, life experiences, and advances in moral maturity (Bielby & Papalia, 1975; Gibbs, 1977, 1979). Bielby and Papalia (1975) found that moral judgments were at their highest average level in middle age, and that middle-aged adults were better able than other adults to reflect on moral solutions and to see things from another person's perspective. Middle-aged adults referred to life experiences (e.g., responses to illness, conflicts with children) as having influenced their moral reasoning. Recall that for Gibbs (1977, 1979), adult sociomoral maturity is the outgrowth of affirmatively coping with critical life experiences. Existential moral reasoning is attributed to both personal experience and metaethical reflection in Gibbs's theory.

In a recent study of Gibbs's theory (Lonky, Kaus, & Roodin, in press), adult women (mean age = 38.7 years) were questioned using an Existential Coping Interview that assessed Fromm's five basic core needs (discussed earlier). The individual's mode of coping (affirmative versus abortive) with the experience of personal loss was assessed and related to level of moral reasoning. The results supported Gibbs's theory; postconventional reasoners dealt with their experience of loss and the corresponding core needs aroused through this life event in a predominantly affirmative fashion, whereas conventional reasoners were abortive in response to the same loss experience. In addition, affirmative copers displayed a "constructive" balance between cognitive and affective orientations to the loss experience and to themselves as persons.

These results were replicated and extended to both men and women in three age groups (20-23 years, 35-54 years, and 55-78 years) by Lonky, Kaus, and Roodin (in press), and a clear relationship between affirmative coping in response to loss and advances in moral reasoning was found for all age groups. Coping style (affirmative versus abortive) to personal loss accounted for 48 percent of the variance in moral reasoning level, independent of age and education. Interestingly, both affirmative and abortive copers experienced the loss as similarly intense, disruptive, and traumatic. Mode of coping was found to be related to the personality dimension "openness to experience" (cf. Costa & McCrae, 1978) such that affirmative copers tended to have high scores on the openness to experience dimension (e.g., seeking out and resolving novel, challenging experiences; active exploration and participation in the world; showing a broad range of interests). Openness to experience was found to be highly related to levels of moral reasoning across all age groups (partial r = .58, independent of age). Similar findings regarding the relationship between openness to experience and moral level among adults have been reported by Rybash (1982).

Finally, Kaus, Lenhart, Roodin, and Lonky (1982) explored the interaction between moral reasoning and mode of coping by examining the potential resources for coping suggested by Folkman, Schaefer, and Lazarus (1979) as follows: health, cognitive problem-solving skills, social networks, material resources, and beliefs. Consistent with Lazarus (1980), Kaus and her colleagues found that adults with higher levels of moral reasoning (e.g., those with metaethical reflection and self-awareness) used a variety of available coping resources and were more successful in coping with the loss event than were others. These basic results were replicated and extended by Lonky, Kaus, and Roodin (1984) using different methods of assessing mode of coping and potential resources for coping.

Self as Definer

The individual's moral system serves to define the affective and cognitive significance of life events. Rybash, Roodin, and Hoyer (1982), for instance, have found that the self-reported moral dilemmas experienced by older adults are rarely focused on abstract principles of equity and justice. Most of the older adults in the sample (mean age = 70.1 years) had moral concerns characteristic of a social-conventional level. Their moral dilemmas centered on problems with close family members such as (1) whether to give or take advice, (2) living arrangements and care giving, and (3) problems related to providing or accepting financial support. Interestingly, some of the subjects in this study reported complete freedom from social-conventional and other moral concerns as illustrated by the following self-report of a 73-year-old man:

> At this point in time I feel there are no moral decisions I have to make. I have reached a point in my life where I have peace of mind, and am

content with my life. I'm in good health and live each day not worrying about having to make moral decisions. There were times when I was younger that I had to make moral decisions, but now all I have to decide about is where I want to go, or what I want to do. You come to this point in your life, and I feel everyone about the same age as me feels the same.

Thus, for some older adults the environment seems to present a set of social-conventional problems, and for others there seems to be a far more independent, internal, and autonomous level of morality. There are wide individual differences in moral reasoning in older adult samples, and part of the variability may be related to the role of affect in reasoning. It may be that the "very old" (see Neugarten's old-old versus young-old distinction, 1977 and 1978) choose to invest less affect in moral situations than adults in middle age or late adulthood. Kuhlen (1964) observed a reduction in drive level and a decrease in ego involvement with aging. Havighurst, Neugarten, and Tobin (1968) also noted that there is less "ego energy" available to deal with conflict situations, especially as they involve emotions.

TABLE 16.2 Approaches to the Study of Adult Moral Development: A Comparative Overview

Critical Dimensions for Comparison	*Cognitive-Developmental Approach*	*Constructive Framework*
World view	Organismic	Contextual
Direction of moral growth	Unidirectional: Moral growth represents the self-construction of universal moral principles.	Multidirectional: Moral growth may take several different pathways dependent on (1) the sociohistorical and ontogenetic contexts from which morality is "constructed," and (2) the situational contexts to which morality is "applied."
Cognitive abilities underlying adult morality	Formal operational thought	Postformal thought (e.g., dialectic thinking)
Relationship between cognition and affect	Moral reasoning is viewed as "rational thinking" that may be clouded and/or impaired by emotion. Therefore, cognition takes precedence over emotion.	Moral reasoning represents the recognition and integration of cognition and emotion. Therefore, neither cognition nor emotion takes precedence over the other.
	Affect and cognition are viewed as interactive forces that exist "prior to" and "independent of morality."	Affect and cognition are viewed as interactive forces that are constituted by their relationship with morality.

Conclusions

In this chapter, we have argued that Kohlberg's and other traditional viewpoints regarding the nature of adult morality rest upon a limited conception of adult cognition. Adult cognition, we have suggested, is best understood within the context of postformal operations. We have attempted to describe the nature of the relationship between adult morality, adult cognition, and affect.

We have suggested that personally significant life events serve to give rise to observed forms of adult morality. Coming to terms with the events of one's life allows the adult "self" to (1) recognize the dialectic interplay between cognition and affect, justice and care, and right and wrong; and (2) construct a set of abstract moral principles that are firmly grounded in reality. We have portrayed the self-construction of such principles as the basis for mature thought and action.

References

Alexander, C., & Langer, E. (Eds.). (in press). *Beyond formal operations: Alternative endpoints to human development.*

Arlin, P. K. (1975). Cognitive development in adulthood: A fifth stage? *Developmental Psychology, 11,* 602-606.

Baltes, P. B., & Willis, S. L. (1977). Towards psychological theories of aging and development. In J. E. Birren & K. W. Schaie (Eds.), *Handbook of the psychology of aging.* New York: Van Nostrand Reinhold.

Bandura, A. (1977). *Social learning theory.* Englewood Cliffs, NJ: Prentice-Hall.

Bandura, A. (1982a). Self-efficacy in human agency. *American Psychologist, 37,* 122-147.

Bandura, A. (1982b). The psychology of chance encounters and life paths. *American Psychologist, 37,* 747-755.

Basseches, M. (1980). Dialectical schemata: A framework for the empirical study of dialectical thinking. *Human Development, 23,* 400-421.

Basseches, M. (1984). *Dialectical thinking.* Norwood, NJ: Ablex.

Bielby, D., & Papalia, D. E. (1975). Moral development and perceptual role taking egocentrism: Their development and interrelationships across the life-span. *International journal of aging and human development, 6,* 293-308.

Brim, O. G., Jr. (1968). Adult socialization. In J. A. Clausen (Ed.), *Socialization and society.* Boston: Little, Brown.

Brim, O. G., Jr. (1976). Life-span development of the theoryof oneself: Implications for child development. In H. W. Reese (Ed.), *Advances in child development and behavior* (Vol. 11). New York: Academic Press.

Broughton, J. (1978). Development of concepts of self, mind, reality, and knowledge. In W. Daman (Ed.), *New directions for child development, 1,* 75-100.

Colby, A. (1978). Evolution of moral-developmental theory. In W. Damon (Ed.), *New directions for child development,* Vol. 2, (pp. 89-104). San Francisco: Jossey-Bass.

Colby, A., Kohlberg, L., Gibbs, J., & Lieberman, M. A. (1983). Longitudinal study of moral development. *Monographs of the Society for Research in Child Development, 48,* 91, Serial no. 200.

Commons, M. (Ed.). (1984). *Beyond formal operations.* New York: Praeger.

Costa, P. T., & McCrae, R. R. (1978). Objective personality assessment. In M. Storandt, I. C. Siegler, & M. F. Elias (Eds.), *The clinical psychology of aging.* New York: Plenum.

Dittmann-Kohli, F. & Baltes, P. B. (in press). Toward a neofunctionalist conception of adult intellectual development: Wisdom as a prototypical case of intellectual growth. In C. Alexander & E. Langer (Eds.), *Beyond formal operations: Alternative endpoints to human development.*

Edelstein, W., & Noam, G. (1982). Regulatory structures of the self and "post formal" stages in adulthood. *Human Development, 25,* 407-422.

Erikson, E. H. (1964). *Insight and responsibility.* New York: Norton.

Erikson, E. H. (1969). *Ghandi's truth on the origins of militant nonviolence.* New York: Norton.

Fitzgerald, J. M. (1981). Implicit psychology and development. In *Newsletter of the Society for the Advancement of Social Psychology,* 7 (5), pp. 2, 21-22.

Folkman, S., Schaefer, C., & Lazarus, R. S. (1979). Cognitive processes as mediators of stress and coping. In V. Hamilton & D. W. Warburton (Eds.), *Human stress and cognition.* New York: John Wiley.

Fromm, E. (1941). *The sane society.* New York: Holt, Rinehart, & Winston.

Fromm, E. (1947). *Man for himself: An inquiry into the psychology of ethics.* Holt, Rinehart, & Winston.

Fromm, E. (1955). *Escape from freedom.* New York: Holt, Rinehart, & Winston.

Fromm, E. (1973). *The anatomy of human destructiveness.* New York: Holt, Rinehart, & Winston.

Gibbs, J. .C (1977). Kohlberg's stages of moral judgment: A constructive critique. *Harvard Educational Review, 47,* 42-61.

Gibbs, J. C. (1979). Kohlberg's moral stage theory: A Piagetian revision. *Human Development, 22,* 89-112.

Gibbs, J. C., Widaman, K. E. (1982). Social intelligence: Measuring the development of sociomoral reflection. Englewood Cliffs, NJ: Prentice-Hall.

Gilligan, C. (1977). In a different voice: Women's conceptions of the self and of morality. *Harvard Educational Review, 47,* 481-517.

Gilligan, C. (1982). *In a different voice.* Cambridge, MA: Harvard University Press.

Gilligan, C., & Murphy, J. M. (1979). Development from adolescence to adulthood: The philosopher and the dilemma of the fact. In W. Damon (Ed.), *New directions for child development,* (Vol. 5, pp. 85-100). San Francisco: Jossey-Bass.

Hauser, S. T. (1976). Loevinger's model and measure of ego development: A critical review. *Psychological Bulletin, 83,* 928-955.

Havighurst, R. J., Neugarten, B. L., & Tobin, S. S. (1968). Disengagement and patterns of aging. In B. L. Neugarten (Ed.), *Middle age and aging (pp. 161-172.* Chicago: University of Chicago Press.

Holstein, C. B. (1972). The relation of children's moral judgment level to that of their parents and to communication patterns in the family. In R. D. Smart & M. S. Smart (Eds.), *Readings in child development and relatioships.* New York: Macmillan.

Holstein, C. B. (1976). Irreversible, stepwise sequence in development of moral judgment: Longitudinal Study of males and females. *Child Development, 47,* 51-61.

Huyck, M. H., & Hoyer, W. J. (1982). *Adult development and aging.* Belmont, CA: Wadsworth.

Kaus, C.R., Lenhart, R.E., Roodin, P.A., & Lonky, E. (1982, August). *Coping in adulthood: Moral reasoning and cognitive resources.* Paper presented at the American Psychological Association Meetings, Washington, DC.

Kegan, R. (1982). *The evolving self.* Cambridge, Massachusetts: Harvard University Press.

Kegan, R., Noam, G.G., & Rogers, L. (1982). The psycho-logic of emotion: A neo-Piagetian view. In D. Cicchetti & P. Hesse (Eds.), *New directions for child development: Emotional development (pp. 105-128).* San Francisco: Jossey Bass.

Kohlberg, L. (1969). Stage and sequence: The cognitive developmental approach to socialization. In D.A. Goslin (Ed.), *Handbook of socialization theory and research.* Chicago: Rand-McNally.

Kohlberg, L. (1971). Form is to ought: How to commit the naturalistic fallacy and get away with it in the study of moral development. In L. Kohlberg (Ed.), *Cognitive developmental epistemology.* New York: Academic Press.

Kohlberg, L. (1973). Continuities and discontinuities in childhood and adult moral development revisited. In *Collected papers on moral development and moral education.* Moral Education Research Foundation, Harvard University, Cambridge, Massachusetts.

Kohlberg, L. (1976). Moral stages and moralization: The cognitive-developmental approach. In T. Lickona (Ed.), *Moral development and behavior: Theory, research, and social issues.* New York: Holt, Rinehart, & Winston.

Kohlberg, L., & Kramer, R. (1973). Continuities in childhood and adult moral development revisited. In P.B. Baltes & K.W. Schaie (Eds.), *Life-span developmental psychology: Personality and socialization.* New York: Academic Press.

Kohlberg, L. (1981). *Essays on moral development. Volume 1: The philosophy of moral development.* New York: Harper & Row.

Kramer, D. (1983). Post-formal operations? A need for further conceptualization. *Human Development, 26,* 91-105.

Kuhlen, R.G. (1964). Developmental changes in motivation during the adult years. In J.E. Birren (Ed.), *Relations of development and aging, (pp. 209-246).* Springfield, IL: Charles C. Thomas.

Labouvie-Vief, G. (1980). Beyond formal operations: The uses and limits of pure logic in life-span development. *Human Development, 23,* 141-161.

Labouvie-Vief, G. (1981). Proactive and reactive aspects of constructivism: Growth and aging in life-span perspective. In R.M. Lerner & N.A. Busch-Rossnagel (Eds.), *Individuals as producers of their development.* New York: Academic Press.

Labouvie-Vief, G. (1982). Dynamic development and mature autonomy. *Human Development, 25,* 161-181.

Lazarus, R.S. (1980). The stress and coping paradigm. In L.A. Bond & J.C. Rosen (Eds.), *Competence and coping during adulthood.* Hanover, New Hampshire: University of New England Press.

Loevinger, J. (1966). The meaning and measurement of ego development. *American Psychologist, 21,* 195-206.

Loevinger, J. (1976). *Ego development: Conceptions and theories.* San Francisco: Jossey-Bass.

Lonky, E., Kaus, C.R., & Roodin, P.A. (in press). Life experience and mode of coping: Relationship to moral judgment in adulthood. *Developmental Psychology.*

Looft, W.R. (1973). Socialization and personality throughout the life span: An examination of contemporary psychological approaches. In P.B. Baltes & K.W. Schaie (Eds.), *Life-span developmental psychology: Personality and socialization.* New York: Academic Press.

Murphy, J. M., & Gilligan, C. (1980). Moral development in late adolescence and adulthood: A critique and reconstruction of Kohlberg's theory. *Human Development, 23,* 77-104.

Neugarten, B. L. (1977). Personality and aging. In J. E. Birren & K. W. Schaie (Eds.), *Handbook of the psychology of aging.* New York: Van Nostrand Reinhold.

Neugarten, B. L. (1978). The wise of the young-old. In R. Gross, B. Gross, & S. Seidman (Eds.), *The new old: Struggling for a decent aging.* Garden City, Doubleday.

Pascual-Leone, J. (1983). Growing into human maturity: Towards a metasubjective theory of adulthood stages. In P. B. Baltes & O. G. Brim (Eds.), *Life-span development and behavior* (Vol. 5). New York: Academic Press.

Perry, W. B. (1968). *Forms of intellectual and ethical development in the college years: A scheme.* New York: Holt, Rinehart, & Winston.

Piaget, J. (1962). *The moral judgment of the child.* (1st edition, 1932) New York: Collier.

Rawls, J. (1971). *A theory of justice.* Cambridge, Massachusetts: Harvard University Press.

Reese, H. W., & Overton, W. F. (1970). Models of development and theories of development. In L. R. Goulet & P. B. Baltes (Eds.), *Life-span developmental psychology: Theory and research.* New York: Academic Press.

Rest, J. (1979). *Development in judging moral issues.* Minneapolis: University of Minnesota Press.

Riegel, K. F. (1973). Dialectic operations: The final period of cognitive development. *Human Development, 16,* 346-370.

Roodin, P. A., & Hoyer, W. J. (1982, August). *A framework for studying moral issues in later adulthood.* Paper presented at the American Psychological Association Meetings, Washington, DC.

Rybash, J. M. (1982). *Moral development during adulthood: The contributing influences of formal operations and openness to experience.* Unpublished doctoral dissertation, Syracuse University, Syracuse, New York.

Rybash, J. M., Roodin, P. A., & Hoyer, W. J. (1983). Expression of moral thought in late adulthood. *The Gerontologist, 23,* 254-260.

Sinnott, J. D. (1984). Postformal reasoning: The relativistic stage. In M. Commons (Ed.), *Beyond formal operations.* New York: Praeger.

Vine, I. (1983). The nature of moral commitments. In H. Weinreich-Haster & D. Locke (Eds.), *Morality in the making.* New York: John Wiley.

White, C. B., Flately, D., & Janson, P. (1982, August). *Moral reasoning in adulthood: Increasing consistency or contextual relativism?* Paper presented at the American Psychologicl Asociation Meetings, Washington, DC.

VII

KEEPING CULTURE IN PERSPECTIVE

In the closing chapter by Sommers we are reminded that differential patterns of emotional response are forged not only within the family (see Halberstadt, this volume), but also within the larger context of culture. As Izard, Ekman, Tomkins, and others have repeatedly stressed, although there are certain pancultural features to the emotions in their elicitation and expression, the universal features are frequently overridden (through masking, dissimulation, repression) as a means of permitting adaptation to particular sociocultural niches. Sommers's research on the emotional preferences and attitudes of American, Greek, Chinese, and West Indian adults toward different classes of emotion, illustrates just how differently ethnic heritage impacts on the emotional sector of life experience. In the context of discussion of the differential pattern of respones, she raises some important questions concerning emotion and the course of adult development in diverse cultures.

17

Adults Evaluating Their Emotions

A Cross-Cultural Perspective

SHULA SOMMERS

Psychological accounts of adult development have tended to neglect two important areas of relevant concern. The discussion has largely ignored specific affect-related issues and at the same time it has failed to give proper consideration to cross-cultural dimensions. The present article seeks to attend to both these factors by dealing with similarities and differences across cultures in emotional preferences, attitudes, and in modes of evaluating specific emotions. The question of differential evaluation of the emotions has been given a central position in the present research because it provides a means of identifying and highlighting points of contact between cultural values and emotional responses. The research reported in the chapter focuses on a particular stage of the life cycle, young adulthood, and is thus to be viewed as preliminary in the exploration of adult emotionality in the context of culture. In the final section of the chapter suggestions are offered for extending the present approach to the study of the individual's affective orientation at different phases of development.

Emotion and Culture

Cross-cultural studies of the emotions have mainly been concerned with their outward expression (e.g., Ekman, Friesen, & Ellsworth, 1972; Izard, 1971). Researchers studying culturally diverse groups have tended to focus on facial expression and the recognition of emotions. (see Izard, 1980). A number of studies (e.g., Izard, 1971; Boucher & Carlson, 1980) have yielded evidence in favor of the universality of certain emotion expressions, but there have also been some findings indicating cultural variability in emotional display (e.g., Ekman & Friesen, 1975). It has been suggested (Ekman, 1977; Izard, 1980) that cultures differ in their "display rules," the cultural norms and conventions regulating affective expression.

More recently, however, there has been a growing body of anthropological studies indicating that the outward expression of emotion may not be all that is culturally variable. Cultures seem also to differ in their way of experiencing, perceiving, and evaluating various emotions. Of special relevance to the cross-cultural perspective is the work of Hallowell (1967), Geertz (1973), Levy (1982), and Rosaldo (1980) whose analyses of culture as a "system of meaning," a "world view," or an ideology, emphasize the role of cultural variables in molding the individual's basic orientation to self and environment. From this perspective human groups seem to differ largely in using different "lenses" or interpretive frameworks. It has been suggested that individuals interpret experiences in accordance with local cultural schemata, in terms of values and beliefs that have prominence in the cultural ideology.

What are the implications of the above accounts for the analysis of emotions and culture? The implications may become apparent if we consider these accounts from a cognitive perspective on affect (e.g., Arnold, 1970; Averill, 1980; de Rivera, 1977; Lazarus, Averill & Opton, 1970; Leeper, 1970; Lyons, 1980; Mandler, 1975; Sommers, 1981), a perspective that insists that emotions involve cognitive evaluations or appraisals. Appraisal-related emotions (e.g., appraising a situation as frustrating, a person as worthy of admiration and repsect, or an act as a betrayal) might well involve culturally grounded concepts (Solomon, 1978) which, in turn, may be viewed as mechanisms linking culture and emotional experiences.

The possibility that the emotional life of diverse cultural groups may differ in some important respects also emerges from ethnographic descriptions of Myers (1979), Rosaldo (1980), and Lutz (1982) of the emotionality of some non-Western communities. In addition, cultural differences in attitudes towards various emotions were reported by Izard

(1971). Finally Solomon (1978), in discussing the reported rarity of anger among the Utku Eskimos, brings into focus the relations between affective experiences and cultural "world views." Solomon (1978) argues that the Utku ideology with its strong emphasis on stoical acceptance, even resignation, with its valuing of "equanimity under trying circumstances" (p. 192) might act as a deterrent of anger — an emotion not considered useful by the Utku. In sharp contrast to this cultural affective orientation one may consider the Ilongot of the Philippines described by Rosaldo (1980). The Ilongot consider "passion" and "knowledge" to be of equal importance for a complete and satisfactory life. An emotion like anger tends to be viewed by the Ilongot as a necessary, even desirable, experience and at the same time as potentially dangerous.

Focus of the Present Study

The foregoing studies stimulated the present investigation in which young adults of culturally diverse groups were compared for their respective ways of perceiving and evaluating emotions. The study focused on such questions as, Which emotions are emphasized by different cultures and treated as constructive experiences, and conversely, which emotions are depicted as dangerous and destructive and thus ought to be avoided? Different cultural groups were compared in affective preferences, in attitudes to the experience and expression of various emotions, and in their evaluations of a wide range of emotions. The exploration of these questions also drew on H. Geertz's (1974) thesis that suggests that the range and quality of emotional experience is potentially the same in all cutlures, but that different cultures select and reinforce different emotions from the spectrum of human emotions.

Method

Subjects

Subjects were of four diverse cultural groups. There were 60 Americans, 21 Greeks, 20 Chinese, and 20 West Indians. There were both males and females balanced in number in each sample. The subjects were of student age, all enrolled in universities in the United States. Except for the U.S. sample, subjects in all other samples had spent less than three years away from their country of origin at testing time. Subjects included in these cultural samples were also selected on the basis of a pretest screening conducted to assess the subject's familiarity with the English emotion words. This was done by means of an emotion words list constructed for the purpose of the study. To be selected subjects were required to show familiarity with all the emotion words contained in the list.

Materials and Interviewing Procedure

A sample of emotion words was selected from the emotion terms listed by Davitz (1969), de Rivera (1977) and Izard (1972). The list included 45 emotion words (e.g., love, liking, joy, pride, anger, irritation, frustration); both positive and negative emotions at various levels of intensity were well represented. To ensure representation of a wide range of adult emotions, the sampling of emotion terms was done in accordance with the procedure devised by de Rivera (1977, and this volume). The list was used as a basis of the interview.

The interview. Each subject was interviewed individually by the investigator. Upon arrival at the laboratory the subject was presented with the emotion words list. He or she was asked to carefully review the list that was presented as containing words people commonly use in describing feelings. The subject was also instructed to make use of the list during the interview as responses to each question required the subject to select emotion terms from the list, with no further verbal elaboration. For example, in responding to the question, Which emotions do you most like to experience? the subject was required to select from the emotion words list those terms that appropriately characterize his or her most preferred emotional experiences. Subjects were further told that there were no right or wrong answers. The investigator added that answers to the questions might include one, two or ten or more emotions, and that the responses to the different questions might vary considerably in terms of number of affects selected by the subject. The six interview questions were then presented in the following order:

(1) Which emotions do you most like to experience?
(2) The experience of which emotions makes you feel uncomfortable?
(3) Which emotions do you dread having?
(4) Which emotions do you prefer to "keep in," to hide, rather than show?
(5) In your view, which emotions are most useful and constructive to experience?
(6) In your view, which emotions should be avoided as most dangerous and destructive?

Results

Responses to each question were analyzed separately. First, the response distribution for each question was tabulated revealing the number of subjects in each of the four cultural samples who referred to each of the listed emotions. Only those emotions selected by at least 25 percent of the subjects of one cultural sample are included in the tables or are dealt with in the chi-square analyses. As some of the cultural samples were fairly modest in size, sex was not considered as a variable in these analyses. Tables 17.1-17.6 report the percentages of subjects in each cultural group selecting the various emotions in their responses to the interview questions.

Which emotions do you most like to experience?

As can be seen in Table 17.1, the majority of subjects in all cultural groups viewed love, happiness, and joy as the most preferred emotional experiences. Among the Americans there was also a strong tendency to favor enthusiasm. Chi-square analyses revealed that the Americans differed significantly from the Chinese in referring more often to enthusiasm as a desirable experience ($X^2[1] = 6.3$, $p < .05$). In the account of the West Indians, pride was one of the most prominent emotions. Compared with the Americans and the Chinese, significantly more West Indians tended to favor the experience of pride ($X^2s > 12.2$, $ps < .001$). It should also be noted that the Greeks and the Chinese tended to favor respect. Both of these cultural samples referred to respect significantly more often than did the American sample ($X^2s > 9.3$, $ps < .01$).

The experience of which emotions makes you feel uncomfortble?

The cultural groups were in a good deal of agreement in responding to this question. An examination of the data (see Table 17.2) reveals that depression, guilt, frustration, fear, embarrassment, shame, and discouragement tended to be viewed as the most uncomfortable and unpleasant experiences. Note, however, that the cultures differed in the extent to which they emphasized different emotions. Guilt was the modal category for both the Greek and the Chinese samples, and depression was the modal category for the Americans. For the West Indians anger was the modal category. Analyses involving anger revealed that the West Indians differed significantly from the Greeks ($X^2 > 4.4$, p. $< .05$), a group in which comparatively very few subjects considered anger as aversive. The suggestion that the Greeks do not tend to view anger with discomfort also emerges from Izard's (1971) research findings. Neither do the Greeks seem to treat feelings of

TABLE 17.1 Response Distribution for Question One (in percentages): Which emotions do you most like to experience?

	Americans (N = 60)	*Greeks (N = 21)*	*West Indians (N = 20)*	*Chinese (N = 20)*
Love	85	71	95	65
Happiness	73	71	75	65
Joy	48	52	60	55
Pride	30	47	75	20
Respect	15	48	35	60
Enthusiasm	47	28	35	15
Hope	23	33	30	25
Serenity	40	33	20	15

TABLE 17.2 Response Distribution for Question Two (in percentages): The experience of which emotions makes you feel uncomfortable?

	Americans (N = 60)	*Greeks (N = 21)*	*West Indians (N = 20)*	*Chinese (N = 20)*
Depression	62	33	35	30
Guilt	57	52	30	50
Frustration	50	33	35	30
Fear	35	38	45	30
Embarrassment	37	43	25	40
Shame	28	48	30	35
Discouragement	27	38	40	20
Jealousy	57	38	40	20
Anger	38	19	50	20
Anxiety	40	38	15	10
Upset	11	19	15	35
Loneliness	40	14	15	30
Envy	25	24	20	10

loneliness with aversion. When compared with the Americans, significantly fewer Greeks (and West Indians) were found to refer to loneliness in their account of the most uncomfortable emotional experiences ($X^2s > 6.1$, $ps < .05$).

Which emotions do you dread having?

Subjects' responses to this question are summarized in Table 17.3. No single emotion emerged as the most dreaded emotion across all cultures. Hate, fear, terror, discouragement, and loneliness were viewed

TABLE 17.3 Response Distribution for Question Three (in percentages): Which emotions do you dread having?

	Americans (N = 60)	*Greeks (N = 21)*	*West Indians (N = 20)*	*Chinese (N = 20)*
Hate	40	33	50	10
Guilt	22	43	50	15
Fear	15	28	30	25
Loneliness	33	19	35	30
Discouragement	25	33	40	15
Jealousy	38	24	35	10
Terror	30	38	25	10
Rage	32	9	30	10
Anger	10	0	25	0

by a large number of subjects in three cultural groups as emotions to be dreaded. As can be seen, the West Indian was the only cultural group that had a substantial number of subjects reporting that they dreaded anger. It should be noted that the Chinese differed noticeably from other cultural groups in that they selected fewer emotions with substantial frequency as emotions to be dreaded. Only two emotions, fear and loneliness, were selected by about a quarter of the Chinese sample as emotions to be dreaded.

Which emotions do you prefer to "keep in," to hide, rather than show?

A fairly large number of subjects in all cultural groups expressed a strong preference for concealing jealousy (see Table 17.4). Comparisons involving other emotions revealed, however, some significant differences among the cultures. The Americans were distinguished from all other cultural groups in expressing more often the preference for hiding anger ($X^2_s > 5.2$, $ps < .05$). It is of interest to note that although the West Indians had depicted the experiences of anger so negatively in their responses to previous questions, relatively few of them revealed a preference for preventing the expression of anger. Emerging from this is the suggestion that the attitudes toward the experience of an emotion may not coincide with the attitudes toward its expression. An emotion might be viewed as utterly unpleasant in terms of its experiential qualities, but as relatively unproblematic in its expressionistic features. Conversely, a pleasantly felt emotion might be viewed as problematic in terms of the consequences of its outward expression. In this connection it is worth discussing the findings concerning the emotion of love.

As shown in Table 17.4, a very large percentage of the Chinese and the West Indian samples expressed a preference for concealing love.

TABLE 17.4 Response Distribution for Question Four (in percentages): Which emotions do you prefer to "keep in," to hide, rather than show?

	Americans (N = 60)	*Greeks (N = 21)*	*West Indians (N = 20)*	*Chinese (N = 20)*
Positive affect				
Love	12	5	50	70
Negative affect				
Jealousy	48	43	50	35
Guilt	38	33	20	30
Anger	55	9	25	20
Fear	42	28	25	10
Discouragement	12	33	30	30
Terror	10	38	25	10

This contrasted sharply with the responses of the Americans and the Greeks, groups in which very few subjects indicated that they prefer to hide love ($X^2_s > 10.6$, $ps < .01$). It should be recalled that the groups' responses to previous questions did not reveal substantial cultural variability in attitudes toward love. Thus, we should note that despite the significant cutural differences in attitudes toward the expression of love, this emotion was prominent in the reported affective preferences of all cultural groups.

In your view, which emotions are most useful and constructive to experience?

Responses to this question are summarized in Table 17.5. Looking first at the results involving the positive emotions, it is apparent that there was considerable cross-cultural agreement in evaluating this class of affect. Love, happiness, compassion, respect, joy, pride, and hope tended to be viewed by all cultural groups as the most constructive emotions. All the same, there were noticeable cultural differences in the extent to which they emphasized the various emotions. The Chinese were found to place less emphasis on love ($X^2_s > 7.1$, $p < .05$). Among the Americans there was a fairly strong tendency to value enthusiasm, an emotion frequently mentioned by this group in responses to the first question. The Americans were found to be significantly more likely to value enthusiasm in comparison with the West Indian and the Chinese samples ($X^2_s > 6.0$, $ps < .05$). In the account of the West Indians pride emerged, once again, as a prominent emotion. Compared with the Greeks and the Chinese significantly more West Indians considered

TABLE 17.5 Response Distribution for Question Five (in percentages): Which emotions are most useful and constructive to experience?

	Americans (N = 60)	*Greeks (N = 21)*	*West Indians (N = 20)*	*Chinese (N = 20)*
Positive affects				
Love	92	80	85	45
Happiness	62	48	60	50
Compassion	53	48	30	55
Respect	53	80	60	60
Joy	43	43	35	55
Pride	48	33	65	25
Hope	47	62	30	40
Enthusiasm	52	28	20	10
Negative affects				
Anger	53	33	0	60
Fear	17	5	15	45
Sadness	32	9	10	15
Jealousy	0	0	0	43
Discouragement	5	9	0	30

pride to be beneficial ($X^2s > 3.9$, $ps < .05$). Likewise, the Greeks placed a characteristic emphasis on respect. This emotion was viewed as constructive by significantly more Greeks than Americans ($X^2 = 5.0$, $p < .05$).

Examining now the cultural groups' evaluations of the negative emotions, we find (see Table 17.5) that anger was treated by most cultural groups as a useful emotion. The West Indians formed an exception; none of the subjects in this cultural group evaluated anger positively. Another point of interest concerns the responses of the Chinese, a group that tended to consider comparatively more negative emotions as useful experiences. In addition to anger, a substantial number of the Chinese subjects viewed jealousy, fear and discouragement as emotions having utility. As can be seen, the Chinese response forms its sharpest contrast with the responses of the West Indians and the Greeks.

In your view, which emotions ought to be avoided as most dangerous and destructive?

As shown in Table 17.6 all cultural groups tended to cast hate, terror, and rage as the most destructive emotions. Except for the Chinese, all cultural samples tended to evaluate jealousy and envy as emotions that ought to be avoided. The responses of the Chinese reveal that this

TABLE 17.6 Response Distribution for Question Six (in percentages): Which emotions should be avoided as most dangerous and destructive?

	Americans (N = 60)	*Greeks (N = 21)*	*West Indians (N = 20)*	*Chinese (N = 20)*
Hate	77	77	65	50
Terror	43	66	50	35
Rage	60	66	50	35
Jealousy	62	55	50	20
Envy	32	71	40	15
Discouragement	32	24	35	30
Guilt	30	38	40	50
Despair	16	43	15	10
Anger	20	10	30	10

cultural group had comparatively fewer subjects referring to the negative emotions as emotions to be avoided. Especially in the case of jealousy there were significantly fewer Chinese treating this emotion so negatively (X^2s > 6.6, ps $< .05$). The finding that the Chinese were less likely to cast the negative emotions as dangerous and destructive is obviously consistent with the responses of this cultural group to previous questions. An attitude of relatively greater acceptance of the negative emotions might be reflected in this set of findings.

Discussion

The results reported here need to be interpreted with caution in view of several methodological points that require clarification. First, it should be recalled that the reported analyses are based on data obtained in the United States, and it therefore can be questioned whether the Greek, Chinese, and West Indian samples accurately represent the populations of their respective countries. In an attempt to deal with the problem of acculturation, participation in the present study was restricted to subjects who had been away from their native country for a relatively short time. Future research seeking to elaborate upon the present findings might attempt to study populations other than college students and preferably these studies should be carried out in the countries of origin. It is also advisable to use alternative methods of assessing orientations to the emotions.

Another methodological question — one that arises frequently in cross-cultural research — concerns choice of language for testing. Given that previous researchers (e.g., Werner & Campbell, 1970) have expressed doubts as to whether translation across languages can be accomplished satisfactorily, there may be some methodological advantages in using one language system, as was the case in the present study.

A further examination of the procedure is, however, needed. Then, too, there are questions with regard to the meaning of various emotion words for different people. It is not clear whether the subjects of the present research had the same thoughts about different emotion words. Consider, for example, the term "love." What is the primary referent of love for college students? When presented with this term do college students tend to think only of romantic love, or do different subjects tend to think of different types of love? Future studies should address issues such as these.[1]

Leaving temporarily aside some of the above qualifications and considerations, I will now turn to a discussion of some of the more striking cross-cultural similarities and differences in ways of viewing and in evaluating emotional experiences uncovered in the present study.

Cross-Cultural Similarities

Several positive emotions emerged as prominent in the accounts of the four cultural groups. Love, happiness, and joy tended to be viewed as the most *desirable* experiences. It should be mentioned that Izard's (1971) findings have yielded a similar suggestion regarding the high favorableness of joy across different cutlures. Love, happiness, and joy also emerged in the present study as emotions that are highly *valued* across cultures. These emotions, along with compasssion, respect, pride, and hope, were evaluated by the various cultural groups as the most useful and constructive experiences.

The emotions evaluated most negatively were hate, terror, and rage. These emotions were perceived across cultures as the most dangerous and destructive, experiences that ought to be avoided. In view of the perceived negative character of hate, rage, and terror, it is not surprising that most cultural groups tended to dread the experience of these emotions. The findings obtained by Izard (1971) similarly suggest that fear and terror tend to be viewed in many cultures as emotions that could have devastating effects on the person. Jealousy was identified in the present study as an emotion that tends to be viewed as problematic in terms of its expressionistic features. All cultural groups reported a strong preference for concealing this emotion. Finally, there was considerable cross-cultural similarity in the perceived unpleasantness of various negative affective experiences. Guilt, frustration, fear, shame, and embarrassment were among the emotions that tended to be viewed as aversive.

Cross-Cultural Differences

Some of the cultural differences observed in the present research involve emphasis on different emotions. The Americans placed a special emphasis on enthusiasm, and the Greeks were found to refer more often than the Amercians to the experience of respect. As for the West Indians, they were distinguished from other cultural groups in giving pride special prominence. Obviously the present findings cannot explain why the cultural groups differed in their emphasis on various emotions. Some of these differences may become more meaningful if viewed against the background of the different cultural milieux.

Consider, for example, the prominence of respect in the reports of the Greek subjects. This finding may be better understood if viewed in close connection with the traditional strong emphasis the Greeks have tended to place on "in-group" relations (e.g., Triandis, Vassiliou, & Nassiakou, 1968; Vassiliou & Vassiliou, 1973). A cultural system in which the in-group is a key social institution might emphasize the value of respect, an emotion that may allow for smooth functioning of the in-group. The account of respect given by the Greek subjects in the present research could reflect a dominant theme in the Greek cultural ideology. Clearly, these are suggestions that need to be tested in future research. Other studies might attempt to examine more closely how different cultural groups view the emotions that receive differential emphasis in their accounts. For example, it is well worth examining the concerns of pride shared by the West Indians. And further, there is a need to ask how do these concerns compare with pride-related issues in other cultures. Such an investigation could yield useful suggestions regarding values emphasized in different cultural environments that may encourage or discourage the experience of various emotions.

The present findings also indicate that cultures differ in their attitudes toward the spontaneous expression of some emotions. Americans were distinguished from ther other cultural groups in expressing a strong preference for concealing anger or inhibiting its expression. This finding should not be interpreted as suggesting that Americans view anger as a worthless experience. It should be recalled that in their responses to question five Americans tended to depict anger as beneficial, a finding that is consistent with Averill's (1978) and Izard's (1971) research results. It is only the *expression* of anger that seems to be negatively sanctioned by Americans. Perhaps Americans fear that an open expression of anger may lead to a negative outcome in the person's relations with others. These results make it apparent that the study of the individual's affective orientation requires the use of a variety of emotion dimensions — for example, dimensions pertaining to *emotional experience* and *emotional expression* as well as those related to the *perceived value of an emotion*. Approaching the problem of how the emotions are viewed cross-culturally from these different angles might highlight more complexities in adults' orientations to the experience and expression of emotions.

Some extraordinary cultural differences in attitudes toward love also emerged from the present study. The Chinese and the West Indians differed significantly from other groups in reporting a strong preference for concealing love. Some of these cultural differences may not be difficult to understand given other kinds of information about the different cultures. Consider, in this connection, the Chinese conceptions of human bonding and their traditional marriage ideology (see Croll, 1981). The expressed tendency on the part of the Chinese subjects to curb their feelings of love makes sense given the long history of arranged marriages in China. Interestingly, Croll (1981) has observed that despite the newly recommended "freedom of marriage" in contemporary China, there still exists a strong tendency to play down the expression of love. This may be because the changing marriage ideology does not seem to be accompanied by a significant change in attitudes toward romantic love. Typical Chinese sayings such as "Compared with revolutionary work, marriage and love is really a small matter" (see Croll, 1981, p. 56) indicate that although romantic love is currently recognized in China as a basis for marriage, its role in human life is still perceived as secondary. This suggestion is reflected in some aspects of the present data. It should be recalled that fewer Chinese, as compared with other cultural groups, considered love to be one of the most useful emotions. In order to understand the Chinese conception of love we should also note that this cultural group did not signifcantly differ from the other groups in the perceived favorableness of love. Like other cultural groups the Chinese seem to view love as a desirable experience. Yet they may view this emotion as of comparatively less social usefulness.

The evaluations of the negative emotions were also found to be culturally variable. As we have seen, the cultural samples differed considerably in referring to the negative affects in response to the question; Which emotions are most useful and constructive to experience? In comparison to the other groups, the Chinese were found to consider more negative emotions as having utility. Among them were fear, jealousy, and discouragement, emotions denied usefulness by other cultural groups. It is important to bear in mind that the Chinese were similar to the other cultural groups in viewing jealousy, fear, and discouragement as unpleasant experiences. Yet despite their unpleasantness, these emotions tended to be evaluated as constructive by the Chinese sample.

These results converge in some respects with recent findings, in both the fields of psychology and anthropology, on ways of viewing negative affects in relation to positive affects. Thus, on the basis of recent anthropological studies, Lutz (1982) has argued that there may be major differences among cultures in criteria used in evaluating emotions. In some cultures the positively evaluated emotions are those that feel pleasant, whereas in other cultures dimensions other than the pleasantness or unpleasantness of the feeling state seem to be used in evaluating the positive and negative character of an emotion. Ethnographic accounts strongly suggest (see Lutz, 1982) that in some cultures emotions are evaluated for their social usefulness, and that this criterion overrides considerations of pleasantness/unpleasantness.

The U.S. sample, when compared with the Chinese sample, was found to consider fewer negative emotions as beneficial. In another investigation of college students attitudes toward the positive and negative emotions, Sommers (1984) found that Americans tend to make a sharp distinction between these classes of affects. It seems that Americans mainly value the pleasantly felt emotions, those commonly considered as positive, and devalue the negative emotions. Other studies may seek to identify predominant themes in contemporary American ideology as well as cultural "feeling rules" (Hochschild, 1979) that may be related to the ways of evaluating positive and negative affects in the United States.

Future cross-cultural research might seek to study more closely the Chinese affective orientation. The Chinese subjects' evaluation of the negative emotions and their reaction to love seem to suggest that this cultural group does not view affective experiences as being sharply divided by the positive-versus-negative distinction that seems so prevalent in the United States. It may prove useful to study the Chinese reaction to various emotions in close association with values and beliefs that are dominant in the Chinese world view. What aspects of the Chinese cultural system might render the negative emotions more acceptable in the eyes of young adults of this culture? is a question worthy of pursuit. At present there are no empirical studies to cast light on this issue. More attention has heretofore been given to the study of affective disorders in China (e.g., Kleinman, 1980) than to the study of emotional reactions in the general population. The difficulties presented to Western social scientists seeking to study the Chinese culture have been recently discussed by Metzger (1977) who has argued that many facets of this culture have thus far been misinterpreted. Despite these difficulties it is well worth embarking on a careful study of the Chinese treatment of emotions as part of a series of studies on the affective orientations of adults in different cultures.

Implications: Emotion, Culture, and Adult Development

Although there appear to be some commonalities across cultures in ways of viewing the emotions, the present research strongly suggests that young adults of culturally diverse groups may possess different affective orientations. The interpretation of the data given above stressed possible links between modes of evaluating emotions and dominant cultural values, and it highlighted some values that might help to explain differential affective response. It is perhaps through the study of cultural variations with an emphasis on certain emotions and their associated values that we could enhance our understanding of cultural influences on the individual's emotional life. Also, it might prove useful to study the individual's emotional range (de Rivera, this volume; Sommers, 1981) in different cultures. If it were demonstrated that there are variations in the range of the culturally accepted emotions, we would want to learn more about the nature of the cultural ideologies and values that encourage the experience and expression of different ranges of emotions.

From both the developmental and cultural perspectives it would be illuminating to follow the present line of inquiry with older and aged adults. A number of questions emerge: Do the differences in affective orientations observed in the present study persist throughout the life span or do these differences tend to diminish or perhaps even disappear alogether with increasing age? In other words, are there some age trends independent of culture or do cultural pressures have an impact in all stages of life? With regard to specific emotions, Are certain emotions and the attitudes toward them more worthy of study with older adults because of their assumed prevalence in this group? Feelings of loneliness may be one such emotion. It should be recalled that the present study uncovered some cultural differences in young adults' attitudes toward loneliness. Compared with the Greeks and West Indians, Americans were more likely to view loneliness with discomfort. Do such cultural variations in viewing loneliness become sharper with increasing age or does the fear of loneliness become more widespread in later stages of life, affecting older people even in societies that strongly emphasize filial respect and responsibility? The need to devote attention to questions such as these has recently become apparent in view of a growing literature suggesting marked differences in the mode of functioning of the elderly in different cultures. The works, for example, of Guttman (1974) and Kerns (1980) reveal that the kind of "disengagement" considered to be a characteristic part of aging in the United States (Cumming & Henry, 1961) may not be present in other cultures.

Other literature relevant to the question of cultural variations in the life cycle leads one to expect differences in emotional orientation and in emotionality throughout the adult years and not only in early and late adulthood. Thus, it has been suggested (e.g., Benedict, 1938; Clark, 1967; Forner & Kertzer, 1978) that societies vary considerably in their manner of structuring adult development. More specifically, it appears that cultures define the role of the adult at various ages levels in different ways, imposing different transitional requirements on the individual as he or she progresses through the life cylce. While some societies stress continuities across the life span, other emphasize sharp discontinuites in the emotional lives of maturing persons. The Ilongot of the Philippines is one such culture that expects dramatic transitions from one age level to another. In describing the emotional change that accompanies adult development, Rosaldo (1980) alludes to a chronological cycle of the emotions in the Ilongot society: Bachelor youth is expected to be passionately angry, even vengeful, in contrast to the mature adult on whom there are cultural demands to respond with less anger but with a set of emotions considered more appropriate for that age.

Interestingly, there are some indications that in the American cultural milieu there may similarly be a change in the prominence of anger in later life. A longitudinal study of women conducted by Malatesta and Culver (this volume) reveals that with increasing age there was a significant decline in anger themes. Reflecting back upon the results of the present study regarding American young adults' evaluation of anger, one is prompted to wonder whether their belief that anger has utility persists in later life. Is the suggested decline accompanied by a revised evaluation of anger? Along similar lines, one is led to ask how anger tends to be perceived among the elderly West Indians. Recall that the present findings revealed a highly negative view of anger among young West Indians. Does this attitude remain constant or is there a different patterning in the assessment of anger across the life cycle in this culture? Also of relevance to the question of anger, culture, and age, are the findings of Malatesta and Izard (this volume) suggesting that among American women there is with increasing age a stronger tendency to mask anger. It should be kept in mind that the present research identified a strong preference for hiding anger among American young adults (see Table 17.4). Taken together, these studies suggest that in the United States there may be strong cultural norms against the overt expression of anger across all age groups. The observed trend toward a greater masking of anger over time need not be taken to imply that in the United States there are different norms regulating affective expression for young and older adults. Rather, it seems reasonable to suggest that older adults might have acquired a greater ability to accommodate their expression of emotion to prevalent cultural norms. In light of the foregoing studies it is becoming more apparent that we need to identify the emotional changes in adulthood that are required by particular cultures as well as those changes that may be independent of cultural demands. Aside from anger, emotions such as love and pride, identified by the present research as receiving differential emphasis cross-culturally, need to be the focus of research assessing age-related differences across cultures in responsiveness to various emotions.

Another noteworthy implication of the present research stems from the findings revealing cultural variations in emphasis on positive versus negative emotions. It would be illuminating to study the extent to which older adults accept and emphasize emotions from the two classes of affect. Note that the suggestion made earlier that in some societies there may be a move away from anger in later years does not imply that older people tend to avoid a wide range of the so-called negative emotions. We need to learn more about the relative prominence and perceived value of different types of emotions in later life across cultures. It might be especially worthwhile to examine a sample of older Chinese in view of the results of the present research that reveal an attitude of relatively strong acceptance of the negative emotions among Chinese young adults. Research along these lines could shed some light on a topic of considerable importance — that is, cultural factors influencing life satisfaction. An emphasis on positive affective experiences and a corresponding deemphasis of negative emotions has been discerned as a strategy for enhancing one's subjective sense of well-being in the American environment (see Felton & Shaver, this volume). It would be interesting to see whether this strategy is applicable in other cultures.

What other consequences might there be of a cultural accentuation of the positive pole of the affective spectrum? Would a strong emphasis on positive affective experiences render the experience of some negative emotions especially stressful? Here it is worth noting that in the present research Americans reported relatively more discomfort about depression than other cultural groups (see Table 17.2). Recall also that our American subjects placed a high value on enthusiasm, viewing it as one of the most desirable experiences. A culture that especially values the excitement/enthusiasm dimension of experience might well experience depression as highly aversive, its affective qualities being rendered more negative by perceived contrast with the highly valued affect of enthusiasm. The suggested link between a high valuation of enthusiasm and the discomfort associated with felt depression has obvious implications for late life experiences that require attention. Does the valuation of enthusiasm remain consistently high across the life cycle in the United States? If so, what are the consequences for older people in this country who might be especially prone to the experience of depression? Does this population find the experience of depression more aversive than older people in other cultures that do not place such a high value on enthusiasm? These are but a few of the questions that are open to investigators seeking to examine adult emotions in the context of culture.

Note

1. Those interested in cross-cultural comparisons of the connotative meanings of emotion words should consider the research methodology and the "atlas of affective meanings" developed by Osgood, May, and Miron (1975).

References

Arnold, M. B. (1970). Perennial problems in the field of emotion. In M. B. Arnold (Ed.), *Feelings and emotions: The Loyola Symposium.* New York: Academic Press.

Averill, J. R. (1980). A constructivist view of emotion. In R. Plutchik & H. Kellerman (Eds.), *Theories of emotion.* New York: Academic Press.

Averill, J. R. (1978). Anger. In H. Howe & R. Dienstbien (Eds.), *Nebraska Symposium on motivation.* Lincoln: University of Nebraska Press.

Benedict. R. (1938). Continuities and discontinuities in cultural conditioning. *Psychiatry, 1,* 161-167.

Boucher, J. D. & Carlson, G. E. (1980). Recognition of facial expressions in three cultures. *Journal of Cross-Cultural Psychology, 11,* 58-70.

Clark, M. M. (1967). The anthropology of aging, a new area for studies of culture and personality. *The Gerontologist, 7,* 55-64.

Croll, E. (1981). *The politics of marriage in comtemporary China.* Cambridge: Cambridge University Press.

Cumming, E. & Henry, W. E. (1961). *Growing old: The process of disengagement.* New York: Basic Books.

Davitz, J. R. (1969). *The language of emotions.* New York: Academic Press.

de Rivera, J. (1977). *A structural theory of the emotions.* New York: International Universities Press.

Ekman, P. (1977). Biological and cultural contributions to body and facial movement. In G. Blacking (Ed.), *The anthropology of the body.* London: Academic Press.

Ekman, P., & Friesen, W. V. (1975). *Unmasking the face.* Englewood Cliffs. NJ: Prentice-Hall.

Ekman, P. Friesen, W. V., & Ellsworth, P. (1972). *Emotion in the human face.* New York: Pergamon.
Forner, A., & Kertzer, J. (1978). Transitions over the life course: lessons from age-set societies. *American Journal of Sociology, 83,* 1081-1104.
Geertz, C. (1973). *The interpretation of cultures.* New York: Basic Books.
Geertz, H. (1974). The vocabulary of emotions. In R. A. Levine (Ed.), *Culture and personality.* Chicago: Aldine.
Gutman, D. L. (1974). Alternatives to disengagement: The old men of the Highland Druze. In R. A. Levine (Ed.), *Culture and personality.* Chicago: Aldine.
Hallowell, A. I. (1967). *Culture and experience.* New York: Schocken Books.
Hochschild, A. (1979). Emotion work, feeling rules and social structure. *American Journal of Sociology, 75,* 551-575.
Izard, C. E. (1971). *The face of emotion.* New York: Appleton-Century-Crofts.
Izard, C. E. (1972). *Patterns of emotions: an new analysis of anxiety and depression.* New York: Academic Press.
Izard, C. E. (1980). Cross-cultural perspectives on emotion and emotion communication. In H. C. Triandis & W. Lonner (Eds.), *Handbook of cross-cultural Psychology,* Vol. 3, Boston: Allyn & Bacon.
Kerns, V. (1980). Aging and mutual support relations among the Black Carib. In C. L. Fry (Ed.), *Aging in culture and society.* New York: Praeger.
Kleinman, A. (1980). *Patients and healers in the context of culture.* Berkeley: University of California Press.
Lazarus, R. S., Averill, J. R. & Opton, E. M. (1970). Toward a cognitive theory of emotion. In M. B. Arnold (Ed.), *Feelings and emotions: The Loyola Symposium.* New York: Academic Press.
Leeper, R. W. (1970). The motivational and perceptual properties of emotions as indicating their fundamental character and role. In M. B. Arnold (Ed.), *Feelings and Emotions: The Loyola Symposium.* New York: Academic Press.
Levy, R. I. (1982). On the nature and functions fo the emotins: An anthropological perspective. *Social Science Information, 21,* 511-528.
Lutz, C. (1982). The domain of emotion words on Ifaluk. *American Ethnologist, 9,* 113-129.
Lyons, W. (1980). *Emotion.* Cambridge: Cambridge University Press.
Mander, G. (1975). *Mind and emotion.* New York: John Wiley.
Metzger, T. A. (1977). *Escape from predicament.* New York: Columbia University Press.
Myers, F. (1979). Emotion and self: A theory of personhood and political order among Pintupi Aborigines. *Ethos, 7,* 343-370.
Osgood, C. E., May, W. H., & Miron, M. S. (1975). *Cross-cultural universals of affective meaning.* Urbana: University of Illinois Press.
Rosaldo, M. Z. (1980). *Knowledge and Passion: Ilongot notions of self and social life.* Cambridge: Cambridge University Press.
Solomon, R. C. (1978). Emotion and anthropology: The logic of emotional world views. *Inquiry, 21,* 181-199.
Sommers, S. (1981). Emotionality Reconsidered: The role of cognition in emotional responsiveness. *Journal of Personality and Social Psychology, 41,* 553-561.
Sommers, S. (1984). Reported emotions and conventions of emotionality among college students. *Journal of Personality and Social Psychology, 46,* 207-215.
Triandis, H. C., Vassiliou, V., & Nassiakou, M. (1968). Three cross-cultural studies of subjective culture. *Journal of Personality and Social Psychology, 4,* part 2, 1-42.

Vassiliou, V., & Vassiliou, G. (1973). The implicative meaning of the Greek concept of Philotimo. *Journal of cross-cultural Psychology, 4,* 326-341.

Werner, W. & Campbell, D. (1970). Translating, working through interpreters and the problem of decentering. In R. Naroll & R. Cohen (Eds.), *A Handbook of Method in Cutlural Anthropology.* New York: Columbia University Press.

ABOUT THE AUTHORS

JAMES R. AVERILL is Professor of Psychology at the University of Massachusetts, Amherst. He received his B.A. in psychology and philosophy from San Jose State College and his Ph.D. in physiological psychology from the University of California, Los Angeles. He also studied at the Düsseldorf Medical Academy and the University of Bonn, Germany, while on a Fulbright Fellowship. Before coming to the University of Massachusetts in 1971, Averill worked as a research psychologist at the University of California, Berkeley. In addition to numerous articles published in professional journals, Dr. Averill is editor of *Patterns of Psychological Thought* (1976), a survey of the historical and philosophical foundations of psychology, and is author of *Anger and Aggression: An Essay on Emotion* (1982).

ANDREW M. BOXER is a doctoral student in the Department of Behavioral Sciences (The Committee on Human Development), University of Chicago, and an NIMH predoctoral fellow in the program on Clinical Research Training in Adolescence. His research interests include the study of the perception of their own adolescence among parents of adolescents, and the relationship of parental perceptions to adolescent personality development.

BERTRAM J. COHLER is William Rainey Harper Professor of Social Sciences in the College, the University of Chicago. He is also Professor in the Departments of Behavioral Science (the Committee on Human Development), Education, and Psychiatry. He received his Ph.D from Harvard University in 1967. His current research concerns the changing significance of social relationships across the course of life. He is presently Director of the university's research training program on adulthood and aging.

RANDOLPH R. CORNELIUS is Assistant Professor of Psychology at Vassar College. His research interests center around the study of emotions in their social context. For the past four years he has devoted much of his attention to the study of weeping. As an antidote, he recently began a study of love, with a focus on the interpersonal aspects of the phenomenon. He is also currently involved in research investigating the relatioships between children's cognitive and affective development.

PAUL T. COSTA, Jr., is Chief of the Section on Stress and Coping in the National Institute on Aging's Gerontology Research Center, and Assistant Professor of Behavioral Biology, Department of Psychiatry and Behavioral Science, Johns Hopkins School of Medicine. He has published articles on the structure and stability of personality and its influence on perceived health, wellbeing, and cognition, and on many aspects of the aging process. He has served in both the Gerontological Society and the Adult Development and Aging Division of the APA, and is currently Editor for Biobehavioral and Social Sciences for *Experimental Aging Research.*

L. CLAYTON CULVER received a Master of Science in psychology from the University of New Orleans in 1981. He is currently pursuing a Ph.D. in psychology at the New School for Social Research. His major research interest is in the cognitive processes of schizophrenia.

JOSEPH DE RIVERA served in the Naval Medical Service Corps and taught at Dartmouth College and New York University before coming to Clark University, where he currently is a Professor in the Department of Psychology. He is the author of *The Psychological Dimension of Foreign Policy,* and *A Structural Theory of the Emotions,* and the editor of *Field Theory as Human Science,* and *Conceptual Encounter: A Method for the Exploration of Human Experience.* He is currently developing a program of research to investigate the relation of emotion to action and to the development of public policy.

BARBARA J. FELTON, Associate Professor in Community Psychology at New York University, has done research on environmental factors in late-life adjustment, including studies of the role of the larger social context in defining the meaning of social relationships. Most recently, she has been investigating the impact of coping responses on older people's adjustment to chronic illness.

MARJORIE GELFOND is an Assistant Professor of Psychology at the County College of Morris in Randolph, New Jersey. She is presently completing her doctoral work in the Department of Environmental Psychology at the City University of New York. Related to the theme of this chapter, the subject of her dissertation is "Agoraphobia and Environmental Meaning." Her primary research interests are stress and psychopathology in women. In addition to having a background in clinical work, Professor Gelfond has chaired and served on a number of hospital boards that address community mental health needs.

AMY G. HALBERSTADT is an Assistant Professor at Vassar College in Poughkeepsie, New York. She received her Ph.D. at the Johns Hopkins University. Her primary research interests are nonverbal communication, interpersonal behavior and skill, and the development of emotional expression and reasoning.

ROBERT O. HANSSON is Associate Professor of Psychology at the University of Tulsa. A University of Washington Ph.D., Hansson's theoretical interests involve aging and adult development, and the implications of these processes for stress and adjustment. Recent work has focused on factors affecting the ability of older adults to cope successfully with widowhood, sensory loss, environmental stress, and unemployment.

JOSEPH M. HEALY, Jr., is a doctoral candidate in the Personality Program in the Psychology Department at Boston University. His major research interest is the study of the process of emotional adaptation to life transitions and its effect on cognitive performance.

ROBERT HOGAN, is McFarlin Professor and Chair of the Psychology Department at the University of Tulsa. He completed his Ph.D. at the University of California, Berkeley. Currently, Hogan serves as Editor of the *Journal of Personality and Social Psychology* (Personality Processes and Individual Differences section). His theoretical interests include the structure and determinants of personality, moral development, and interpersonal competence. He is author of *Personality Theory: The Personological Tradition,* and presented his *Socioanalytic Theory of Personality* at the 1981 Nebraska Symposium on Motivation.

WILLIAM J. HOYER received his B.S. degree from Rutgers University in 1967. He completed his M.A. and Ph.D. degrees from West Virginia University in 1968 and 1972, respectively. Hoyer's major research interests involve the study of cognitive changes in adulthood from a developmental perspective. He is the coauthor of *Adult Development and Aging* (published by Wadsworth) and the author of numerous articles and chapters in the area of cognitive aging. Currently, Hoyer is Professor of Psychology at Syracuse University, New York.

CARROLL E. IZARD is Unidel Professor of Psychology, University of Delaware. He received his Ph.D. from Syracuse University in 1952. Most of his career has been devoted to the development and validation of differential emotions theory. For the past several years this theory has guided his research on emotions in early development and the development of depression during childhood.

WARREN H. JONES is Associate Professor of Psychology at the University of Tulsa, having received his Ph.D. from Oklahoma State University. He is Associate Editor of the *Journal of Personality and Social Psychology* (Personality Processes and Individual Differences section). Jones's theoretical interests center on the nature of personal relationships, relational competence, and loneliness. Coauthor of *Anomolistic Psychology,* he is also a contributor to *Loneliness: A Sourcebook of Current Theory, Research and Therapy.*

M. POWELL LAWTON has been Director of Behavioral Research at the Philadelphia Geriatric Center for the past 20 years, as well as an Adjunct Professor of Human Development at the Pennsylvania State University and a Research Scientist at Norristown State Hospital. His docorate was in clinical psychology from Columbia University. He has done research in the environmental psychology of later life, assessment of the aged, the psychological wellbeing of older people, and evaluative studies of programs for the aged and for the mentally ill. He is the author of *Environment and Aging,* and coeditor of *The Psychology of Adult Development and Aging.*

CAROL ZANDER MALATESTA is a member of the Graduate Faculty of the New School for Social Research and is Director of the Developmental Communications Laboratory. She received her Ph.D. in developmental psychology (1980) from Rutgers University. As a lifespan developmentalist her research ranges from studies of infant emotion communication to adult development and aging. Her most recent work concerns the socialization of emotion.

DAN P. McADAMS is Assistant Professor of Psychology at Loyola University of Chicago. His research interests include human motivation, identity in adulthood, intimacy and attachment, and personality assessment. He is currently writing a book entitled *Power, Intimacy, and the Life Story: Personological Inquiries into Identity.*

ROBERT R. McCRAE, Research Psychologist in the Section on Stress and Coping in the National Institute on Aging's Gerontology Research Center, received his undergraduate degree from Michigan State University and his Ph.D. from Boston University. His research interests include dimensional models of personality, mechanisms of coping and defense, and the influence of personality on the life course. With Paul T. Costa, Jr., he is the author of *Emerging Lives, Enduring Dispositions* (in press).

PAUL A. ROODIN received his A.B. degree from Boston University in psychology in 1965. He completed his M.S. and Ph.D. degrees at Purdue University in 1969. Roodin's major research interests life in the areas of general cognitive development, eidetic imagery, and moral judgment. He is the author of numerous publications in developmental psychology and the recent coauthor of a basic text in child psychology (published by D. Van Nostrand). He serves as Consulting Editory for *Perceptual and Motor Skills* and also for *Child Development.* Currently Dr. Roodin is a Professor in the Department of Psychology at the State University of New York, Oswego.

JOHN M. RYBASH received his B.S. degree in 1970 in psychology from State University of New York, College at Oswego. He completed his M.S. degree from the same institution in 1973. His Ph.D. was completed in 1982 at Syracuse University in the Department of Psychology. Rybash's major research interests are in the domain of cognitive development from the Piagetian perspective, and moral development and reasoning across the life span. He is a frequent contributor to developmental psychology journls and has presented papers at both regional and national conferences in psychology. Currently Dr. Rybash is an Associate Professor in the Department of Human Services and Psychology at Mohawk Valley Community College, Utica, New York.

PHILLIP SHAVER, Associate Professor and Head of Graduate Studies in Personality and Social Psychology at the University of Denver, is coauthor of *Measures of Social Psychological Attitudes* (Michigan) and of the recently published *In Search of Intimacy* (Delacorte). He is editor of the *Review of Personality and Social Psychology.*

SHULA SOMMERS is an Assistant Professor of Psychology at the University of Massachusetts, Boston. Her research is mainly concerned with adult emotionality and its cognitive correlates, conventions of emotionality across cultures, and the relationship between emotions and values.

ABIGAIL J. STEWART is an Associate Professor in the Psychology Department at Boston University. While on leave from Boston University, she served as Director of the Henry A. Murray Research Center of Radcliffe College (1978-1980). Her major research interest is the study of change, both at the individual and social level.